THE QUIET BATTLE

THE QUIET BATTLE

Writings on the Theory and Practice of Non-violent Resistance

Edited with an Introduction and Afterword by
MULFORD Q. SIBLEY

Chicago

QUADRANGLE BOOKS
1963

First published 1963 by Quadrangle Books, Inc.,

180 North Wacker Drive, Chicago 6,

and as a Doubleday Anchor Original

Grateful acknowledgment is made to the following for permission to reprint material in this book:

to the Columbia University Press for sections of *Anti-Dictator,* by Etienne de La Boétie, translated by Harry Kurz, published 1942.

to the Navajivan Trust for portions of *Satyagraha in South Africa,* by M. K. Gandhi.

to The Christian Century Foundation, copyright holder, for "Is Coercion Ever Justifiable" by Kirby Page and "What Is Violence?" by George A. Coe.

to Appleton-Century-Crofts for extracts from *Non-violent Coercion,* by C. M. Case, published 1923.

to E. P. Dutton & Company, Inc., and Routledge & Kegan Paul, Ltd., for passages from *The Conquest of Violence,* by Barthélemy de Ligt, translated by Honor Tracy, Copyright 1937 by Bart. de Ligt.

to Richard B. Gregg, Fellowship Publications, James Clarke & Co., Ltd., and the Navajivan Trust for excerpts from *The Power of Non-Violence,* by Richard B. Gregg, Copyright 1934, 1959 by Richard B. Gregg.

to the Shoe String Press, Inc., for extracts from *Communism and the General Strike,* by Wilfred H. Crook, Copyright 1960 by the Shoe String Press, Inc.

to *Peace News* for "New Way in Norway," by A. K. Jameson, "Tyranny Could Not Quell Them," by Gene Sharp, and extracts from the *Peace News Supplement* of October 20, 1960.

to Mrs. Arthur Griffith, copyright holder, for sections of *The Resurrection of Hungary: A Parallel for Ireland,* by Arthur Griffith, published in 1919.

to Holt, Rinehart & Winston, Inc., and Weidenfeld & Nicolson, Ltd., for the excerpt from *Vorkuta,* by Joseph Scholmer, translated from the German by Robert Kee. Copyright 1954, © 1955 by Holt, Rinehart & Winston, Inc.

to Harold Ober Associates, Inc., and Mrs. Sundari K. Shridharani, for selections from *War Without Violence,* by Krishnalal Shridharani, Copyright © 1939 by Harcourt, Brace & World, Inc.

to Yale University Press and Jonathan Cape, Ltd., for the selection from *Passive Resistance in South Africa,* by Leo Kuper, Copyright 1957 by Yale University Press.

to C. Eric Lincoln and *The Reporter* for "The Strategy of a Sit-In," by C. Eric Lincoln, Copyright 1962 by The Reporter Magazine Company.

to the New York *Times* and Martin Luther King, Jr., for "The Time for Freedom Has Come," by Martin Luther King, Jr., reprinted from the New York *Times Magazine,* Copyright by the New York *Times.*

to the Committee for Non-violent Action and Neil Haworth for "Civil Disobedience at Newport News," by Neil Haworth.

to the War Resisters League and Jessie Wallace Hughan for "Pacifism and Invasion," by Jessie Wallace Hughan.

to Pendle Hill, Wallingford, Pennsylvania, and Cecil E. Hinshaw for "Non-violent Resistance: A Nation's Way to Peace," by Cecil E. Hinshaw, Pendle Hill Pamphlet No. 88.

CONTENTS

viii CONTENTS

THE QUIET BATTLE

INTRODUCTION

This book is about the problem of struggling against injustice without the use of violence.

In our day—as perhaps in most epochs—the major issues of injustice are two: the danger of military invasion, and economic and social exploitation within nations. How can we prevent military invasion or, if it occurs, overcome it? How can we undermine exploitative economic and social systems?

With respect to military invasion, the traditional answer has been that we must threaten and ultimately use counter-violence. For the most part, nations have assumed an almost complete identity between "military defense" and defense. Today when we think of defense of the United States, we automatically begin to consider military postures and cannot conceive of a nation being defended except by military means.

Domestically, too, the answer to exploitation and social injustice has frequently been violence and often civil war. The great revolutions of modern times were efforts through use of violent force to correct domestic injustice, whether it took an economic or a social form. This was true of the French Revolution and, more recently, of the Russian and Chinese revolutions; today violence in the cause of revolution is ubiquitous.

Despite the fact, however, that we have so frequently turned to violence as a method of resisting military invasion and correcting social injustice, we have also had in our tradition a strong emphasis on the values of non-violent conduct. Whether in religious ethics or in secularist morals, we have held up the ideal of non-violent action. We have attempted to establish political institutions which would minimize violence, and democracy has often been held to be the political form which most nearly prevents resort to violence. Our everyday life, moreover, is mostly free of overt violence, whatever the psychiatrists may say about the potential violence within us.

Thus there has been a conflict between, on the one hand, our actions in using violence to resist invasion and correct injustice and, on the other, our repudiation of violence in our statements of ethical principle and ordinary life. We have sought to justify this violation of our professed beliefs by saying that certain evils can be opposed effectively, if reluctantly, only through war or violent revolution (both democrats and totalitarians will defend certain wars and violent revolutions, although they may not agree on those which deserve support). Every war is held to be defensive: no modern nation will ever say that it is waging an aggressive war. And the violence used in revolutions by those who oppose injustice is always said to be a last resort: the ruling classes, it is usually argued, have left the revolutionists no other alternative (Americans defend the violent overthrow of British rule in the eighteenth century just as Russians argue that violence was essential to overthrow the Czars).

In this book, the major argument is that there *is* an alternative to violence, both for purposes of external defense and in correcting social injustice. We do not have to be divided psychologically, so to speak, between our theoretical repudiation of violence, on the one hand, and our actual resort to violence in war and social struggle, on the other. Nor do we have to acquiesce in the covert violence of many governments and social systems because we fear that action on our part might lead to violence. We can, so the major argument goes on, both keep our ethical ideal relatively uncorrupted and at the same time overcome invaders and correct social injustice. In fact, we can in the long run accomplish these objectives *better* through non-violence than through violence, even against "totalitarian" systems. Violence, the argument maintains, makes more difficult the defense of a community and the achievement of social justice. Not only can the United States be defended non-violently against the Soviet Union, but it can be defended *better* without military force than with military force. Not only can American Negroes and South African Zulus gain equality through non-violent power, but the utilization of violence for such ends constitutes a hindrance.

Thus the advocates of non-violence seek to bridge the gap between our professed beliefs and our frequent resort to violence. In trying to work out techniques and strategies of non-violent power, they endeavor to show us how we can keep our integrity as human beings both with respect to means and in relation to ends; we do not need to threaten to destroy millions of human beings through H-bombs in order to defend a nation. In fact, we cannot really defend any nation through such means—at least in modern times. Non-violent defense of some kind is an imperative if we are to survive as civilized human beings. We must eliminate the old identification of national defense with military defense and discover means of defense that will no longer rely on the military. To attempt to defend a nation by military means under modern conditions is to run the risk of throwing out the baby with the bath; or, to change the figure, to produce roast pig by burning down one's house.

But what is this method of non-violent action and defense? What are its foundations in thought? Has it ever been tried? If it has been tried, has it been successful? If so, to what degree? If not, why not? These are some of the questions for which this book attempts to provide, if not answers, at least materials on the basis of which answers may be developed.

The book is divided into three parts, each of which is preceded by a brief introduction outlining the major questions with which the part is concerned. Within each part are a number of readings, with an introductory statement attached to each.

In the first part—FOUNDATIONS OF NON-VIOLENCE AND NON-VIOLENT RESISTANCE—some of the theoretical problems of non-violent action are explored and an effort is made to deal with questions that are often asked about it. Reference is made, too, to the religious and ethical tradition upon which many doctrines of non-violence have been built.

In PART II—NON-VIOLENT POWER WITHOUT EXPRESS PRINCIPLE—the readings present case studies of situations in which men have resorted to collective non-violent power without having any elaborate philosophy to guide them; often they acted in this way simply because the instruments of violence were not available.

PART III—NON-VIOLENT POWER WITH EXPRESS PRINCIPLE—gives instances of social struggle or examples of societies consciously motivated by some version of the philosophy of non-violence. It concludes by asking how a large nation-state might act were it to be converted to the ideas of non-violence and non-violent resistance.

In "Concluding Reflections," we present a brief recapitulation and suggest some of the problems with which a doctrine of non-violence and a strategy of non-violent resistance must always be concerned.

PART I

FOUNDATIONS OF NON-VIOLENCE AND NON-VIOLENT RESISTANCE

The term "non-violence" in itself is ambiguous and has, in fact, several different shadings of meaning. In general, of course, it implies an attitude of repugnance to the use of violence—a repugnance that is very widespread. More specifically, however, the term indicates bodies of belief or theory which assert that even if one party to a conflict utilizes violence, the other should respond non-violently. In other words, violent action does not justify retaliation in terms of violence. This conclusion is reached either on religious grounds (some kind of a commitment to the proposition that violence is always wrong in itself) or on what might be called grounds of utility (it doesn't work, particularly in the long run), or on a combination of the two.

Distinctions are often made, too, between the personal ethic of non-violence and its political significance. Thus certain groups—like the Mennonites—think of it as a personal religious commitment and, in fact, argue that it cannot be a strategic instrument of politics. Groups of this kind passively obey the State so long as it does not require them to perform positive acts that run counter to their non-violent professions. Taxes may be paid, but there can be no active participation in office and no entering of the army—both of which are regarded as participations in violence. Non-violence of this kind is sometimes called "non-resistance"—although the terms used vary.[1] "Resistance" is anathema, reminding one as it does of war.

Non-violence in a political sense is usually associated with the term "non-violent resistance"—the deliberate use of collective non-violent techniques (the strike, boycott, fast, civil disobedience, and so on) as devices either for changing the attitude of the opponent or for compelling him without violence to reach some kind of compromise or resolution of the conflict. Sometimes non-violent resistance is called "non-violent coercion," for there would seem to be something approaching what we usually call coercion in such acts of resistance.

But this broad differentiation between non-resistance and non-violent resistance is not always clear in the writings of those who deal with the theory of non-violence. Gandhi in a reading in this Part seems to make little distinction between the

[1] On the Mennonite position see, for example, Guy F. Hershberger, *War, Peace, and Nonresistance* (Scottdale, Pennsylvania: Herald Press, 1944).

two, unless one identifies "passive resistance" (in his sense) with "non-violent resistance" and "non-resistance" with Satyagraha—and this identification does not seem to be warranted. Many writers would think of the early Christian attitudes (note the excerpt from Origen—Reading 1) as "non-resistance," yet Gandhi seems to think they resemble Satyagraha—or soul force —which he certainly used politically.

The problem of defining violence itself is not an easy one and is dealt with in several of the readings presented here (Coe, Page, Gandhi, for example). Some would seem to identify it with the use of any physical force (Gandhi), while others would not draw the line between physical and non-physical force (Coe, Page). Most writers would, however, agree that war is a species of violence; and no doubt there would also be widespread agreement on the nature of other acts as well. But this is still a problem for the doctrine of non-violence.

More positively, the readings in Part I seek to deal with the ways in which opponents in a struggle can be influenced by actions that repudiate what might generally be regarded as violence. In opposing exploitation, social injustice, or invasion, several of the readings suggest that the opponent can indeed undergo a change of attitude, which will be brought about by his awareness of the voluntary suffering undergone by the exponents of non-violence or by his increasing consciousness of his own irrationality. But there is also the argument that even though the opponent's attitudes are not fundamentally changed, non-violent resistance can win away his supporters, thus undermining his power to wield violence, or at least make his position so inconvenient that he is willing to compromise or make concessions. In any given instance, perhaps, there may be elements that evoke a change in the basic attitude of the opponent as well as appeal to his self-interest. All exponents of non-violence are agreed that if its followers are dedicated and adhere to their creed, the probability of reaching a satisfactory agreement with the opponent is much greater than it would have been had violence been used. The religious advocates of non-violence would probably say that this is because the means are intrinsically "right"; because they are "right" they lead to "good" results. Those who emphasize the utilitarian approach might contend that on the basis of experience (whether in treatment of criminals, invasion, or resistance to injustice, as with Gregg in Reading 8) it simply "works" better than violent approaches.

In the theory of non-violence, particularly as expressed in the doctrine of non-violent resistance, it is emphasized that structures of power (governments, social organizations) always depend upon the voluntary co-operation of great numbers of individuals even when the structures seem to rely on physical force. The chief wielders of power, in other words, must have the assistance and co-operation of hundreds or even thousands of persons for the administration of physical force. The task of those who oppose a structure having physical force at its command is, therefore, to persuade hundreds of men to refuse any longer to co-operate with the tyrant or other administrator of violence. (Godwin, Shelley, and de La Boétie, among others, emphasize this theme.) The question then becomes: How does one induce police administrators, soldiers, clerks, heads of departments, and others to desert the tyrant? Exponents of non-violent power believe this task is hindered by resort to counter-violence; for threat of violence simply leads followers of the tyrant to support him the more for the sake of their own defense. Non-violent organized opposition, on the other hand, by confronting the wielder of violent power with an unexpected kind of opposition, takes him off guard and, by appealing to the sympathies of his followers, deprives him of his instruments. This analysis of the nature of power leads many exponents of non-violence to conclude that if the devotees of non-violence are well-organized and disciplined and willing to suffer, they can always have an important effect in checking social injustice and in frustrating possible gains of military invasion. This notion is particularly emphasized in the reading by Gregg.

An important idea in the theory of political non-violence is that under modern circumstances, non-violence affords the only real possibility of checking tyranny. Where constitutional forms of government are preserved, non-violence takes the form of ordinary political activities, votes, and discussion which nip the tyranny in the bud. Where constitutional forms have declined and ordinary democratic methods are no longer available, non-violence assumes the guise of non-violent resistance. Even where constitutional forms are preserved, minorities may be exploited and forced to resort to non-violent resistance for the sake of both justice and self-protection. In either case, non-violent resistance is a particularly vital weapon today because the instruments of violence (tanks, H-bombs, missiles, and so on) have become so expensive that rebel groups simply cannot afford them. Moreover, weapons are now so destructive that any resort to violence, whether in international relations or in internal social conflict, almost always promises greater loss—whoever is the victor—than gain (if one reckons gain and loss socially and includes both material and non-material factors).

The readings in this Part, in sum, lay the groundwork for thinking about specific instances of non-violent resistance. These instances will be developed in the subsequent two Parts.

1. ANCIENT RELIGIOUS STATEMENTS

Ancient religious writings contain many statements which have frequently inspired thinkers about non-violent power. Mohandas Gandhi felt that parts of the Hindu scriptures (the *Bhagavad-Gita* and the *Upanishads,* for example) sustained his doctrine of soul force. Similar claims have been made for parts of the Buddhist scriptures.

Here we present brief extracts from ancient Taoist and Jewish scriptures and well-known passages from the New Testament. We also include selections from the early Christian apologist Origen and an excerpt from the trial transcript of a third-century Christian who refused military service on religious grounds.

Lao-tzu (sixth century B.C.), author of the *Tao Tê Ching,* from which our first section is taken, was the founder of the world outlook, or religion, known as Taoism and had a considerable influence on Chinese culture. In the extracts presented here[1] he places his emphasis on love, moderation, and a non-violent way of life. Somewhat paradoxically—at least to ordinary ways of looking at things—he thinks that the person (whether private individual or ruler) who is most loving, humble, and harmless is in the long run most powerful. Lao-tzu obviously exalts the ethic of non-retaliation.

Among the ancient Jews, there was a belief that Yahweh, or the Lord, was more powerful in protecting the Israelites than chariots and horsemen; that doing justice was in the long run more efficacious in preventing injurious conflict than reliance on the repressive military force of the State. Among the great prophets—the two Isaiahs, Jeremiah, Amos, Hosea, Zechariah —utopian visions of a world in which men regulated their affairs in accordance with the instructions of the Lord were not uncommon. While these visions are subject to varying interpretations, some see in the later prophets (men like Jeremiah and

[1] Translation by James Legge in *Sacred Books of the East* (Oxford University Press, 1891), Vols. 39 and 40.

the second Isaiah) anticipations of the general ethic of non-violence and even of specific notions of non-violent resistance. Thus Jeremiah advised the residents of Judah not to resist the Babylonians by military force and was looked upon by most of the political leaders of Judah as unpatriotic. And much later on, the Jewish sect of the Essenes, or at least some communities of the sect, apparently repudiated violence on principle and developed an ethic of non-violence. There is some speculation that Jesus may have been influenced by the Essenes. Our passages from the Old Testament are taken from the prophecy of the first Isaiah (who flourished in the eighth century B.C.) and from Zechariah (who lived in the sixth century B.C.).

In the selections from the New Testament, Jesus develops the ethic of non-retaliation and love of enemies and commands one of his followers to put up the sword with which he has just cut off the ear of the high priest's servant. Then occur the well-known words: "All they that take the sword shall perish with the sword" (Matthew 26:52). This statement has often been taken as a text by those who point to the long-run futility of all violence: to reply to violence with counter-violence simply perpetuates a cycle of violence from which mankind can never be liberated. Paul's statement in Romans 12:17–21 continues this theme.

The early Christians, and particularly their intellectual leaders, were very much troubled by the problem of violence and war. According to one of the leading scholars of the subject, Adolf von Harnack, they probably refused to enter the army— or left military service on conversion—until relatively late. We do not definitely hear of Christians in the army until the reign of Marcus Aurelius (A.D. 161–80). When they did join the army, it was against the advice of such early Christian writers as Tertullian, Clement of Alexandria, Cyprian, and the renowned scholar Origen (A.D. 185–254). Service in war meant killing fellow human beings and perhaps executing convicted criminals, another form of deliberate killing. Moreover, one had to take an oath of unqualified allegiance to the emperor and thus deny the supreme authority of Christ.[2]

Our reading from Origen illustrates the way in which many early Christians undoubtedly reasoned. The selection is taken

[2] For a thorough discussion of the early Christian rejection of war and violence, see Cecil John Cadoux, *The Early Church and the World* (New York: Scribner, 1925).

from Origen's famous treatise, *Contra Celsum*,[3] in which he answers charges against Christianity brought by the pagan writer Celsus. One of Celsus's most serious allegations was that Christians refused to join the imperial armies. Origen in effect admits that this is true: Christians cannot enter the armies of the emperor because loyalty to Jesus forbids them to participate in war. But this does not mean that Christians cannot help the emperor, he continues; for by refusing to participate in violence and attempting to convert others (including the barbarians) to this view, they eliminate violent opposition to the emperor and thus remove his excuse for using violence.

Although most early Christian martyrs went to their deaths for refusing to participate in what they regarded as the cult of emperor worship, some were killed by the State for their adamant stand against military service. This was true even after most Christians had begun to abandon their early opposition to military violence. Thus in A.D. 295, Maximilianus was ordered to enter the army under a law that made him liable for service as the son of a soldier. The transcript of his hearing before the Roman proconsul has been preserved and our reading ends with an excerpt from it.[4]

From the TAO TE CHING

The partial becomes complete; the crooked, straight; the empty, full; the worn out, new. He whose desires are few gets them; he whose desires are many goes astray.

Therefore the sage holds in his embrace the one thing of humility, and manifests it to all the world. He is free from self-display, and therefore he shines; from self-assertion, and therefore he is distinguished; from self-boasting, and therefore his merit is acknowledged; from self-complacency, and therefore he acquires superiority. It is because he is thus free from striving that therefore no one in the world is able to strive with him.

* * * * *

If any one should wish to get the kingdom for himself, and to effect this by what he does, I see that he will not succeed.

[3] Translation by Rev. Frederick Crombie in Rev. Alexander Roberts and James Donaldson, editors, *Ante-Nicene Christian Library,* (Edinburgh: T. and T. Clark, 1872), Vol. XXIII.

[4] From the original Latin transcript of the hearing reprinted in Adolf von Harnack, *Militia Christi: Die Christliche Religion und der Soldatenstand in den ersten drei Jahrhunderten* (Tübingen: Verlag von J. C. B. Mohr [Paul Siebeck], 1905), pp. 114–17.

The kingdom is a spiritlike thing, and cannot be got by active doing. He who would win it destroys it; he who would hold it in his grasp loses it.

*   *   *   *   *

He who would assist a lord of men in harmony with the Tao will not assert his mastery in the kingdom by force of arms. Such a course is sure to meet with its proper return.

Wherever a host is stationed, briars and thorns spring up. In the sequence of great armies there are sure to be bad years.

*   *   *   *   *

Passages from THE OLD TESTAMENT

Woe to them that go down to Egypt for help; and stay on horses and trust in chariots, because they are many; and in horsemen, because they are very strong; but they look not unto the Holy One of Israel, neither seek the Lord!

Yet he also is wise and will bring evil, and will not call back his words: but will arise against the house of the evildoers, and against the help of them that work iniquity.

Now the Egyptians are men, and not God; and their horses flesh, and not spirit. When the Lord shall stretch out his hand, both he that helpeth shall fall, and he that is holpen shall fall down, and they shall all fail together. (Isaiah 31:1–3)

*   *   *   *   *

And the angel that talked with me came again, and waked me, as a man that is wakened out of his sleep.

And said unto me, What seest thou? And I said, I have looked, and behold a candlestick all of gold, with a bowl upon the top of it, and his seven lamps thereon, and seven pipes to the seven lamps, which are upon the top thereof:

And two olive trees by it, one upon the right side of the bowl, and the other upon the left side thereof.

So I answered and spake to the angel that talked with me, saying, What are these, my lord?

Then the angel that talked with me answered and said unto me, Knowest thou not what these be? And I said, No, my lord.

Then he answered and spake unto me, saying, This is the word of the Lord unto Zerubbabel, saying, Not by might, nor by power, but by my spirit, saith the Lord of hosts. (Zechariah 4:1–6)

Passages from THE NEW TESTAMENT

Blessed are the peacemakers, for they shall be called the children of God.

*   *   *   *   *

. . . I say unto you, That except your righteousness shall exceed the righteousness of the scribes and Pharisees, ye shall in no case enter into the kingdom of heaven.

Ye have heard that it was said by them of old time, Thou shalt not kill; and whosoever shall kill shall be in danger of the judgment:

But I say unto you, That whosoever is angry with his brother without a cause shall be in danger of the judgment. . . .

* * * * *

Ye have heard that it hath been said, An eye for an eye, and a tooth for a tooth:

But I say unto you, That ye resist not evil: but whosoever shall smite thee on thy right cheek, turn to him the other also.

And if any man will sue thee at the law, and take away thy coat, let him have thy cloak also.

And whosoever shall compel thee to go a mile, go with him twain.

Give to him that asketh thee, and from him that would borrow of thee turn not thou away.

Ye have heard that it hath been said, Thou shalt love thy neighbour, and hate thine enemy.

But I say unto you, Love your enemies, bless them that curse you, do good to them that hate you, and pray for them which despitefully use you, and persecute you:

That ye may be the children of your Father which is in heaven: for he maketh his sun to rise on the evil and on the good, and sendeth rain on the just and on the unjust.

For if ye love them which love you, what reward have ye? do not even the publicans the same?

And if ye salute your brethren only, what do ye more than others? do not even the publicans so?

Be ye therefore perfect, even as your Father which is in heaven is perfect. (Matthew 5:9, 20–22, 38–48)

* * * * *

. . . Then came they, and laid hands on Jesus, and took him.

And, behold, one of them which were with Jesus stretched out his hand, and drew his sword, and struck a servant of the high priest's, and smote off his ear.

Then said Jesus unto him, Put up again thy sword into his place; for all they that take the sword shall perish with the sword. (Matthew 26:50–52)

* * * * *

Recompense to no man evil for evil. Provide things honest in the sight of all men.

If it be possible, as much as lieth in you, live peaceably with all men.

Dearly beloved, avenge not yourselves, but rather give place unto wrath: for it is written, Vengeance is mine; I will repay, saith the Lord.

Therefore if thine enemy hunger, feed him; if he thirst, give him drink; for in so doing thou shalt heap coals of fire on his head.

Be not overcome of evil, but overcome evil with good. (Romans 12:17–21)

ORIGEN AGAINST VIOLENCE

. . . To those who inquire of us whence we come, or who is our founder, we reply that we are come, agreeably to the counsels of Jesus, to "cut down our hostile and insolent 'wordy' swords into ploughshares, and to convert into pruning-hooks the spears formerly employed in war." For we no longer take up "sword against nation," nor do we "learn war any more," having become children of peace, for the sake of Jesus, who is our leader, instead of those whom our fathers followed, among whom we were "strangers to the covenant," and having received a law, for which we give thanks to Him that rescued us from the error of our ways. . . .

* * * * *

Celsus goes on to say: "We must not disobey the ancient writer, who said long ago, 'Let one be king, whom the son of crafty Saturn appointed' "; and adds: "If you set aside this maxim, you will deservedly suffer for it at the hands of the king. For if all were to do the same as you, there would be nothing to prevent his being left to utter solitude and desertion, and the affairs of the earth would fall into the hands of the wildest and most lawless barbarians; and then there would no longer remain among men any of the glory of your religion or of the true wisdom." . . . If, in the words of Celsus, "they do as I do," then it is evident that even the barbarians, when they yield obedience to the word of God, will become most obedient to the law, and most humane. . . .

* * * * *

But if all the Romans, according to the supposition of Celsus, embrace the Christian faith, they will, when they pray, overcome their enemies; or rather, they will not war at all, being guarded by that divine power which promised to save five entire cities for the sake of fifty just persons. For men of God are assuredly the salt of the earth: they preserve the order of the world; and society is held together as long as the salt is uncorrupted. . . .

* * * * *

In the next place, Celsus urges us "to help the king with all our might, and to labour with him in the maintenance of justice, to fight for him; and if he requires it, to fight under him, or lead an army along with him." To this our answer is that we do, when occasion requires, give help to kings . . . To those enemies of our faith who require us to bear arms for the commonwealth, and to slay men, we can reply: "As we by our prayers vanquish all demons who stir up war, and lead to the violation of oaths, and disturb the peace, we in this way are much more helpful to the kings than those who go into the field to fight for them. . . . And none fight better for the king than we do. We do not indeed fight under him, although he require it; but we fight on his behalf, forming a special army . . . by offering our prayers to God.

THE TRIAL OF MAXIMILIANUS

The Proconsul Dion said: "What are you called?"

Maximilianus answered: "But why do you want to know my name? I dare not fight, since I am a Christian."

The Proconsul Dion said: "Measure him."

But on being measured Maximilianus answered: "I cannot fight, I cannot do evil; I am a Christian."

The Proconsul Dion said: "Measure him."

And after he had been measured, the attendant read out: "He is five feet ten."

Dion said to the official: "Sign him up."

And Maximilianus cried out: "I won't; I cannot be a soldier."

Dion said: "Get into the war-service or it will cost you your life."

Maximilianus answered: "I do no war-service. . . . I do no war-service to this age, but I do war-service for my God."

* * * * *

Dion to Maximilianus: "Serve and accept the badge" [the leaden badge with the Emperor's effigy on it and worn by all soldiers].

Maximilianus answered: "I do not accept the badge; for I have the badge of Christ my God.

* * * * *

. . . I will accept no badge from this age. . . . I am a Christian and can wear no trumpery bit of lead around my neck, now that I already bear the saving sign of my Lord Jesus Christ. . . ."

2. Etienne de La Boétie:
VOLUNTARY SERVITUDE

In 1548, a French youth of eighteen wrote an essay which has become a classic in the literature of non-violence. The young man was Etienne de La Boétie and the treatise was called *Discours de la servitude volontaire* or *Discourse on Voluntary Servitude*. The following reading is an excerpt from the *Discourse*.

La Boétie was born at Sarlat in the Dordogne on November 1, 1530, and was graduated from the University of Toulouse law school in 1553. Throughout his boyhood and youth he was fond of Greek and Roman classics and particularly of the literature that treated of tyranny and its causes. The writing of his famous essay was apparently his way of acknowledging his debt to the classics, for it abounds in allusions to events in ancient history and in references to the authors of antiquity.

On graduating from law school, he became a judge and was noted for his efforts to reconcile Protestants with Catholics in the religious struggles which were beginning to darken the horizon. When Michel de L'Hôpital, the Chancellor of France, issued a charter in 1562 granting certain freedoms to Protestants, the young judge approved heartily; for although he remained a devout Roman Catholic down to the day of his early death in 1563, he was distressed by the wars of religion, which had begun in 1560 and were to continue with some interruptions until the Edict of Nantes in 1598. La Boétie was apparently a young man of unusual charm and kindness and throughout his brief life tried in every way possible both to oppose violence and to resist tyranny.

In his essay he points out that basically men create their own tyrants—whether domestic or foreign—by giving obedience to them, usually from hopes of personal gain. Once this obedience is undercut, tyranny will collapse; for the tyrant always needs instruments and if he cannot find them he can no longer rule. Tyranny reposes on "voluntary servitude."

Our reading is taken from Harry Kurz's translation of the *Discours de la servitude volontaire,* published as *Anti-Dictator* (Columbia University Press, 1942).

. . . I should like merely to understand how it happens that so many men, so many villages, so many cities, so many nations, sometimes suffer under a single tyrant who has no other power than the power they give him; who is able to harm them only to the extent to which they have the willingness to bear with him; who could do them absolutely no injury unless they preferred to put up with him rather than contradict him. Surely a striking situation!

*   *   *   *   *

. . . Who could believe reports of what goes on every day among the inhabitants of some countries, who could really believe that one man alone may mistreat a hundred thousand and deprive them of their liberty? Who would credit such a report if he merely heard it, without being present to witness the event? Obviously there is no need of fighting to overcome this single tyrant, for he is automatically defeated if the country refuses consent to its own enslavement: it is not necessary to deprive him of anything, but simply to give him nothing; there is no need that the country make an effort to do anything for itself provided it does nothing against itself. It is therefore the inhabitants themselves who permit, or, rather, bring about, their own subjection, since by ceasing to submit they would put an end to their servitude. A people enslaves itself, cuts its own throat, when, having a choice between being vassals and being free men, it deserts its liberties and takes on the yoke, gives consent to its own misery, or, rather, apparently welcomes it. If it cost the people anything to recover its freedom, I should not urge action to this end, although there is nothing a human should hold more dear than the restoration of his own natural right, to change himself from a beast of burden back to a man, so to speak. I do not demand of him so much boldness; let him prefer the doubtful security of living wretchedly to the uncertain hope of living as he pleases. . . .

Everyone knows that the fire from a little spark will increase and blaze ever higher as long as it finds wood to burn; yet without being quenched by water, but merely by finding no more fuel to feed on, it consumes itself, dies down, and is no longer in flame. Similarly, the more tyrants pillage, the more they crave, the more they ruin and destroy; the more one yields to them, and obeys them, by that much do they become mightier and more formidable, the readier to annihilate and destroy. But if not one thing is yielded to them, if, without any violence they are simply not obeyed, they become naked and undone and as nothing, just as, when the root receives no nourishment, the branch withers and dies.

* * * * *

. . . It is not the troops on horseback, it is not the companies afoot, it is not arms that defend the tyrant. This does not seem credible on first thought, but it is nevertheless true that there are only four or five who maintain the dictator, four or five who keep the country in bondage to him. Five or six have always had access to his ear, and have either gone to him of their own accord, or else have been summoned by him, to be accomplices in his cruelties, companions in his pleasures, panders to his lusts, and sharers in his plunders. These six manage their chief so successfully that he comes to be held accountable not only for his own misdeeds but even for theirs. The six have six hundred who profit under them, and with the six hundred they do what they have accomplished with their tyrant. The six hundred maintain under them six thousand, whom they promote in rank, upon whom they confer the government of provinces or the direction of finances, in order that they may serve as instruments of avarice and cruelty, executing orders at the proper time and working such havoc all around that they could not last except under the shadow of the six hundred, nor be exempt from law and punishment except through their influence.

* * * * *

3. William Godwin and Percy B. Shelley:
FREEDOM AND NON-VIOLENCE

Like Etienne de La Boétie, the great eighteenth-century political philosopher William Godwin (1756–1836) held that if
men are subject to tyranny it is because the great mass agree
to be tyrannically ruled. In his monumental *An Enquiry Concerning Political Justice* (1793), from which our reading is
taken, Godwin asserted that the best way to effect a revolution
in any political system—whether it was imposed by foreigners
or was of native origin—was to change through persuasion the
opinion on which all government is founded. He went on to
discuss the corruption of ends that results from using violence
as a means to freedom and to point out the futility of both war
and tyrannicide. Never denying that reliance on truth and
reason called for sacrifices, Godwin advanced cogent reasons
why such sacrifices would not be vain.

Percy Bysshe Shelley (1792–1822), the eminent early
nineteenth-century poet, thoroughly agreed. Shelley was Godwin's son-in-law, and some have maintained that parts of his
work are simply Godwin's prose transformed into poetry. This
is particularly true of his *The Masque of Anarchy*, sections of
which are reprinted as the second portion of this reading.
Shelley wrote *The Masque* after reading about the Peterloo
Massacre, an incident in 1819 when British troops fired on
and killed peaceful demonstrators protesting their economic
lot during the depression following the Napoleonic wars. The
government headed by the Duke of Wellington met requests
for a redress of grievances only with hostility and violence,
and Shelley saw an occasion for celebrating the theory and
practice of Godwinian non-violence as the weapons most appropriate for those who would enlarge personal freedom and
protect national autonomy.

William Godwin: OF GOVERNMENT, VIOLENCE, AND TRUTH

There is no such disparity among the human race as to enable one man to hold several other men in subjection, except

so far as they are willing to be subject. All government is founded in opinion. Men at present live under any particular form, because they conceive it their interest to do so. One part indeed of a community or empire may be held in subjection by force; but this cannot be the personal force of their despot; it must be the force of another part of the community, who are of opinion that it is their interest to support his authority. Destroy this opinion, and the fabric which is built upon it falls to the ground. (Bk. II, Ch. IV)

*   *   *   *   *

To return to the enquiry respecting the mode of effecting revolutions. If no question can be more important, there is fortunately no question perhaps that admits of a more complete and satisfactory general answer. The revolutions of states, which a philanthropist would desire to witness, or in which he would willingly co-operate, consist principally in a change of sentiments and dispositions in the members of those states. The true instruments for changing the opinions of men are argument and persuasion. The best security for an advantageous issue is free and unrestricted discussion. In that field truth must always prove the successful champion. If then we would improve the social institutions of mankind, we must write, we must argue, we must converse. To this business there is no close; in this pursuit there should be no pause. Every method should be employed—not so much positively to allure the attention of mankind, or persuasively to invite them to the adoption of our opinions—as to remove every restraint upon thought, and to throw open the temple of science and the field of enquiry to all the world.

Those instruments will always be regarded by the discerning mind as suspicious, which may be employed with equal prospect of success on both sides of every question. This consideration should make us look with aversion upon all resources of violence. When we descend into the listed field, we of course desert the vantage ground of truth, and commit the decision to uncertainty and caprice. The phalanx of reason is invulnerable; it advances with deliberate and determined pace; and nothing is able to resist it. But when we lay down our arguments, and take up our swords, the case is altered. Amidst the barbarous pomp of war and the clamorous din of civil brawls, who can tell whether the event shall be prosperous or miserable? (Bk. IV, Ch. II)

*   *   *   *   *

Because individuals were liable to error, and suffered their apprehensions of justice to be perverted by a bias in favour of themselves, government was instituted. Because nations were susceptible of a similar weakness, and could find no sufficient umpire to whom to appeal, war was introduced. Men were induced deliberately to seek each other's lives, and to adjudge the controversies between them, not according to the dictates of reason and justice, but as either should prove most successful in devastation and murder. This was no doubt in the first instance the extremity of exasperation and rage. But it has since been converted into a trade. One part of the nation pays another part to murder and be murdered in their stead; and the most trivial causes, a supposed insult or a sally of youthful ambition, have sufficed to deluge provinces with blood.

We can have no adequate idea of this evil, unless we visit, at least in imagination, a field of battle. Here men deliberately destroy each other by thousands without any resentment against or even knowledge of each other. The plain is strewed with death in all its various forms. Anguish and wounds display the diversified modes in which they can torment the human frame. Towns are burned, ships are blown up in the air while the mangled limbs descend on every side, the fields are laid desolate, the wives of the inhabitants exposed to brutal insult, and their children driven forth to hunger and nakedness. It would be despicable to mention, along with these scenes of horror, and the total subversion of all ideas of moral justice they must occasion in the auditors and spectators, the immense treasures which are wrung in the form of taxes from those inhabitants whose residence is at a distance from the scene. (Bk. V, Ch. XVI)

Percy B. Shelley: CALM AND RESOLUTE

*   *   *   *   *

Let a vast assembly be,
And with great solemnity
Declare with measured words that ye
Are, as God has made ye, free—

Be your strong and simple words
Keen to wound as sharpened swords,
And wide as targes let them be,
With their shade to cover ye.

Let the tyrants pour around
With a quick and startling sound,
Like the loosening of a sea,
Troops of armed emblazonry.

Let the charged artillery drive
Till the dead air seems alive

With the clash of clanging wheels,
And the tramp of horses' heels.

Let the fixèd bayonet
Gleam with sharp desire to wet
Its bright point in English blood
Looking keen as one for food.

Let the horsemen's scymitars
Wheel and flash, like sphereless stars
Thirsting to eclipse their burning
In a sea of death and mourning.

Stand ye calm and resolute,
Like a forest close and mute,
With folded arms and looks which are
Weapons of unvanquisht war,

And let Panic, who outspeeds
The career of armèd steeds
Pass, a disregarded shade
Thro' your phalanx undismayed.

*   *   *   *   *

On those who first should violate
Such sacred heralds in their state
Rest the blood that must ensue,
And it will not rest on you.

And if then the tyrants dare
Let them ride among you there,
Slash, and stab, and maim, and hew,—
What they like, that let them do.

With folded arms and steady eyes,
And little fear, and less surprise
Look upon them as they slay
Till their rage has died away.

Then they will return with shame
To the place from which they came,
And the blood thus shed will speak
In hot blushes on their cheek.

*   *   *   *   *

Rise like Lions after slumber
In unvanquishable number—
Shake your chains to earth like dew
Which in sleep had fallen on you—
Ye are many—they are few.

4. Henry D. Thoreau: CIVIL DISOBEDIENCE AND NON-VIOLENT RESISTANCE

In anarchist or near-anarchist thought, there is an important strain that supports the notion of non-violent resistance both to social injustice and to the State which anarchists hope will eventually disappear. Most anarchists associate violence with the State and with politics; and while some, like Bakunin in the nineteenth century, have thought of violence as a means for eliminating the State and with it organized violence, many modern anarchists have doubted whether violence could be used effectively. Those who, on the whole, reject violence as means argue in part on what might be called utilitarian grounds and in part from religious considerations. A good example of the religious anarchist view of non-violence will be found in the doctrines of Leo Tolstoy (1828–1910), who during the latter part of his life came increasingly to believe that the Sermon on the Mount constituted a kind of command to offer non-violent resistance to the State and to war. The undermining of institutions (like law, the State, and war) which he thought of as rooted in violence to human personality would be the result of men's collective and non-violent disobedience to orders of the State.

During the nineteenth century, one of the great classics of non-violent civil disobedience was written by Henry David Thoreau (1817–62). In his *Civil Disobedience,* published in 1849, he protested against the institutions of slavery and of war and particularly attacked the war with Mexico. If only enough men would offer non-violent non-co-operation, he argued in the extract printed here, the institution of slavery would crumble. Men are too attached to the State and too little concerned with the right. They are afraid to go to jail for a cause. Yet until they are willing to do so in considerable numbers, the State will continue to have its willing instruments for wars and institutions like slavery.

The essay has had an enormous influence among those seeking to work out theories of non-violence. Gandhi read it with great interest and profit, as did Tolstoy; and leaders of the current American Sit-In movement for racial integration are familiar with Thoreau.

I heartily accept the motto, "That government is best which governs least"; and I should like to see it acted up to more rapidly and systematically. Carried out, it finally amounts to this, which also I believe—"That government is best which governs not at all"; and when men are prepared for it, that will be the kind of government which they will have. Government is at best but an expedient; but most governments are usually, and all governments are sometimes, inexpedient. The objections which have been brought against a standing army, and they are many and weighty, and deserve to prevail, may also at last be brought against a standing government. The standing army is only an arm of the standing government. The government itself, which is only the mode which the people have chosen to execute their will, is equally liable to be abused and perverted before the people can act through it. Witness the present Mexican war, the work of comparatively few individuals using the standing government as their tool; for, in the outset, the people would not have consented to this measure.

This American government—what is it but a tradition, though a recent one, endeavoring to transmit itself unimpaired to posterity, but each instant losing some of its integrity? It has not the vitality and force of a single living man; for a single man can bend it to his will. It is a sort of wooden gun to the people themselves. But it is not the less necessary for this; for the people must have some complicated machinery or other, and hear its din, to satisfy that idea of government which they have. Governments show thus how successfully men can be imposed on, even impose on themselves, for their own advantage. It is excellent, we must all allow. Yet this government never of itself furthered any enterprise, but by the alacrity with which it got out of its way. *It* does not keep the country free. *It* does not settle the West. *It* does not educate. The character inherent in the American people has done all that has been accomplished; and it would have done somewhat more, if the government had not sometimes got in its way.

*   *   *   *   *

But, to speak practically and as a citizen, unlike those who call themselves no-government men, I ask for, not at once no government, but at once a better government. Let every man make known what kind of government would command his respect, and that will be one step toward obtaining it.

After all, the practical reason why, when the power is once in the hands of the people, a majority are permitted, and for a long period continue, to rule is not because they are most likely to be in the right, nor because this seems fairest to the minority, but because they are physically the strongest. But a government in which the majority rule in all cases cannot be based on justice, even as far as men understand it. Can there not be a government in which majorities do not virtually decide right and wrong, but conscience?—in which majorities decide only those questions to which the rule of expediency is applicable? Must the citizen ever for a moment, or in the least degree, resign his conscience to the legislator? Why has every man a conscience, then? I think that we should be men first, and subjects afterward. It is not desirable to cultivate a respect for the law, so much as for the right. The only obligation which I have a right to assume is to do at any time what I think right. It is truly enough said that a corporation has no conscience; but a corporation of conscientious men is a corporation *with* a conscience. Law never made men a whit more just; and, by means of their respect for it, even the well-disposed are daily made the agents of injustice. A common and natural result of an undue respect for law is, that you may see a file of soldiers, colonel, captain, corporal, privates, powder-monkeys, and all, marching in admirable order over hill and dale to the wars, against their wills, ay, against their common sense and consciences, which makes it very steep marching indeed, and produces a palpitation of the heart. They have no doubt that it is a damnable business in which they are concerned; they are all peaceably inclined. Now, what are they? Men at all? or small movable forts and magazines, at the service of some unscrupulous man in power?

*   *   *   *   *

The mass of men serve the state thus, not as men mainly, but as machines, with their bodies. They are the standing army, and the militia, jailers, constables, *posse comitatus,* etc. In most cases there is no free exercise whatever of the judgment or of the moral sense; and wooden men can perhaps be manufactured that will serve the purpose as well. Such command no more respect than men of straw or a lump of dirt. They have the same sort of worth only as horses and dogs. Yet such as these even are commonly esteemed good citizens. Others—as most legislators, politicians, lawyers, ministers, and office-holders—serve the state chiefly with their heads; and, as they rarely make any moral distinctions, they are as likely to serve the devil, without *intending* it, as God. A very few—as heroes, patriots, martyrs, reformers in the great sense, and *men*—serve the state with their consciences also, and so necessarily resist it for the most part; and they are commonly treated as enemies by it. . . .

How does it become a man to behave toward this American government to-day? I answer, that he cannot without disgrace be associated with it. I cannot for an instant recognize that political organization as my government which is the slave's government also.

All men recognize the right of revolution; that is, the right to refuse allegiance to, and to resist, the government, when its tyranny or its inefficiency are great and unendurable. But almost all say that such is not the case now. But such was the case, they think, in the Revolution of '75. If one were to tell me that this was a bad government because it taxed certain foreign commodities brought to its ports, it is most probable that I should not make an ado about it, for I can do without them. All machines have their friction; and possibly this does enough good to counterbalance the evil. At any rate, it is a great evil to make a stir about it. But when the friction comes to have its machine, and oppression and robbery are organized, I say, let us not have such a machine any longer. In other words, when a sixth of the population of a nation which has undertaken to be the refuge of liberty are slaves, and a whole country is unjustly overrun and conquered by a foreign army, and subjected to military law, I think that it is not too soon for honest men to rebel and revolutionize. What makes this duty the more urgent is the fact that the country so overrun is not our own, but ours is the invading army. . . .

Unjust laws exist: shall we be content to obey them or shall we endeavor to amend them, and obey them until we have succeeded, or shall we transgress them at once? Men generally, under such a government as this, think that they ought to wait until they have persuaded the majority to alter them. They think that, if they should resist, the remedy would be worse than the evil. But it is the fault of the government itself that the remedy *is* worse than the evil. *It* makes it worse. . .

*   *   *   *   *

I meet this American government, or its representative, the State government, directly, and face to face, once a year—no more—in the person of its tax-gatherer; this is the only mode in which a man situated as I am necessarily meets it; and it then says distinctly, Recognize me; and the simplest, the most effectual, and, in the present posture of affairs, the indispensablest mode of treating with it on this head, of expressing your little satisfaction with and love for it, is to deny it then. My civil neighbor, the tax-gatherer, is the very man I have to deal with —for it is, after all, with men and not with parchment that I quarrel—and he has voluntarily chosen to be an agent of the government. How shall he ever know well what he is and does as an officer of the government, or as a man, until he is obliged to consider whether he shall treat me, his neighbor, for whom he has respect, as a neighbor and well-disposed man, or as a maniac and disturber of the peace, and see if he can get over his obstruction to his neighborliness without a ruder and more impetuous thought or speech corresponding with his action? I know this well, that if one thousand, if one hundred, if ten men whom I could name—if then *honest* men only—ay, if one HONEST man, in this State of Massachusetts, *ceasing to hold slaves,* were actually to withdraw from this copartnership, and be locked up in the county jail therefor, it would be the abolition of slavery in America.

* * * * *

Under a government which imprisons any unjustly, the true place for a just man is also a prison. . . .

* * * * *

5. Mohandas K. Gandhi: THE ORIGINS OF SATYAGRAHA DOCTRINE

Mohandas K. Gandhi (1869–1948) has been, of course, the greatest exponent of the theory and practice of non-violence in the twentieth century. Trained as a lawyer, he spent the early part of his career in South Africa, where he first came to his basic convictions about non-violent struggle. Later—at the time of World War I—he returned to India, where he became a leader of the Congress movement for Indian independence. The independence movement came to be dominated by Gandhi's idea of non-violent struggle; for while many of his followers—including Pandit Nehru—did not regard non-violence as a matter of principle, most of them respected Gandhi so much and were so conscious of the hopelessness of violent techniques in the struggle against British rule that they practiced non-violence on expediential grounds. Eventually (1947) India won its political independence; and although there is still a dispute as to precisely what factors were most important in leading Great Britain to give up the Indian Empire, there can be little doubt that the non-violent campaigns led by Gandhi from 1920–21 onward played a very important role.

Elsewhere we analyze some of the specific techniques used by the Gandhi movement in India (see Reading 18, p. 236). Here, however, we are concerned with the origins of Gandhi's general idea of Satyagraha (truth or soul force) during his early campaigns in South Africa and the influence of certain parts of the Hindu scriptures, by the New Testament (particularly the Sermon on the Mount), the writings of Leo Tolstoy, and Thoreau's *Civil Disobedience*.

In the passage printed here, Gandhi tells us of the circumstances that led him to evolve the idea of Satyagraha and of the conditions under which it was first applied. The South African Government's passing of a discriminatory Registration Ordinance (the so-called Black Act) required all Indians to register and to undergo certain indignities. Some members of the Indian community, which was neither previously consulted nor allowed to vote, were on the point of advocating violent resistance, but Gandhi's leadership eventually prevailed. He describes how a substantial part of the community became Satyagrahis, or non-violent fighters, how their techniques, in conjunction with other events, led to the government's agreement to repeal the ordinance under certain conditions, and ends with an account of his famous conference with General Jan Smuts, the Prime Minister.

Gandhi explains why an intense commitment to truth counts more than numbers in non-violent struggles and attempts to distinguish between Satyagraha, the instrument of those who are "strong in soul," and passive resistance, which he thinks of as the weapon of weak men, without arms but equally without conviction. He discusses Christ as an example of the Satyagrahi, and the effectiveness of voluntary suffering.

Through his conception runs the notion that physical force is the equivalent of brute force, ethically wrong and to be eschewed in social and political struggles. The reader may question the truth of this. Is all physical force under all circumstances more evil than what Gandhi calls "soul force"? Whether it is the Satyagrahi's intention or not, the effect of the use of soul force is often to injure the opponent's interests, as the methods used in South Africa increased the difficulties of the police and the boycott of foreign cloth in India deprived thousands of English workers of employment. Can *any* social struggle be carried on without some injury, however mild, to the opponent? A strike injures the employer and the public; the fast of a Gandhi causes severe emotional hardship to his friends and supporters. A boycott hurts tradesmen and manufacturers, and civil disobedience might result in the disruption of transportation and communications, thus causing real difficulties for many people.

The critic, while asking Gandhi these questions, will not necessarily deny considerable validity to the conception of Satyagraha. Some types of social struggle undoubtedly cause less injury to the opponent than others—particularly less irreparable injury. Perhaps the line should be drawn between those forms of struggle likely to lead to irreparable injury and those that may result only in secondary or relatively minor inconveniences. In his *Christian Pacifism Re-examined* (1939), C. J. Cadoux develops a thesis of this kind, making a distinction between the use of "injurious" and "non-injurious" force. Some kinds of physical force (restraining an impetuous child, for example) are relatively non-injurious while certain types of non-physical pressure (a general strike of hospital employees, for instance) might be close to the extreme of injurious force.

The extract printed here is taken from Gandhi's *Satyagraha in South Africa* (Stanford, California: Academic Reprints, 1954), pp. 97–115, with certain omissions.

THE REWARD OF GENTLENESS—THE BLACK ACT

Before dealing with this Ordinance in detail, it would be well to dispose of an important event in a few words. As I was the author of the Satyagraha movement, it is necessary to enable the reader fully to understand some events of my life. The Zulu 'rebellion' broke out in Natal just while attempts were thus being made to impose further disabilities upon Indians in the Transvaal. I doubted then and doubt even now if the outbreak could be described as a rebellion, but it has always been thus described in Natal. Now as in the Boar War, many European residents of Natal joined the army as volunteers. As I too was considered a resident of Natal, I thought I must do my bit in the war. With the community's permission, therefore, I made an offer to the Government to raise a Stretcher-bearer Corps for service with the troops. The offer was accepted. I therefore broke up my Johannesburg home and sent my family to Phoenix in Natal where my co-workers had settled and from where *Indian Opinion* was published. I did not close the office as I knew I would not be away for long.

I joined the army with a small corps of twenty or twenty-five men. Most of the provinces of India were represented even on this small body of men. I have always been thankful to God for the work which then fell to our lot. We found that the wounded Zulus would have been left uncared for, unless we had attended to them. No European would help to dress their wounds.

*   *   *   *   *

The Corps was disbanded in a month. Its work was mentioned in despatches. Each member of the Corps was awarded the medal especially struck for the occasion. The Governor wrote a letter of thanks.

*   *   *   *   *

While I was working with the Corps, two ideas which had long been floating in my mind became firmly fixed. First an aspirant after a life exclusively devoted to service must lead a life of celibacy. Secondly, he must accept poverty as a constant companion through life. He may not take up any occupation which would prevent him or make him shrink from undertaking the lowliest of duties or largest risks.

Letters and telegrams, asking me to proceed to the Transvaal at once, had poured in, even while I was serving with the Corps. On return from the war, therefore, I just met the friends at Phoenix and at once reached Johannesburg. There I read the draft Ordinance referred to above. I took the Transvaal Government Gazette Extraordinary of August 22, 1906 in which the Ordinance was published home from the office. I went up a hill near the house in the company of a friend and began to translate the draft Ordinance into Gujarati for *Indian Opinion*. I shuddered as I read the sections of the Ordinance one after another. I saw nothing in it except hatred of Indians. It seemed to me that if the Ordinance was passed and the Indians meekly accepted it, that would spell absolute ruin for the Indians in South Africa. I clearly saw that this was a question of life and death for them. I further saw that even in the case of memorials and representations proving fruitless, the community must not sit with folded hands. Better die than submit to such a law. But how were we to die? What should we dare and do so that there would be nothing before us except a choice of victory or death? An impenetrable wall was before me, as it were, and I could not see my way through it. I must acquaint the reader with the details of the proposed measure, which shocked me so violently. Here is a brief summary of it.

Every Indian, man, woman or child of eight years or upwards, entitled to reside in the Transvaal, must register his or her name with the Registrar of Asiatics and take out a certificate of registration.

The applicants for registration must surrender their old permits to the Registrar, and state in their applications their name, residence, caste, age, etc. The Registrar was to note down important marks of identification upon the applicant's person, and take his finger and thumb impressions. Every Indian who failed thus to apply for registration before a certain date was to forfeit his right of residence in the Transvaal. Failure to apply would be held to be an offence in law for which the defaulter could be fined, sent to prison or even deported within the discretion of the court. Parents must apply on behalf of their minor children and bring them to the Registrar in order to give their finger impressions, etc. In case of parents failing to discharge this responsibility laid upon them, the minor on attaining the age of sixteen years must discharge it himself, and if he defaulted, he made himself liable to the same punishments as could be awarded to his parents. The certificate of registration issued to an applicant must be produced before any police officer whenever and wherever he may be required to do so. Failure thus to produce the certificate would be held to be an offence for which the defaulter could be fined or sent to prison. Even a person walking on public thoroughfares could be required to produce his certificate. Police officers could enter private houses in order to inspect certificates. Indians entering the Transvaal from some place outside it must produce their certificates before the inspector on duty. Certificates must be produced on demand in courts which the holder attended on business, and in revenue offices which issued to him a trading or bicycle licence. That is to say, if an Indian wanted any Government office to do for him something within its competence, the officer could ask to see his certificate or to supply such particulars or means of identification as may be prescribed by regulation. . . .

I have never known legislation of this nature being directed against free men in any part of the world. I know that indentured Indians in Natal are subject to a drastic system of passes, but these poor fellows can hardly be classed as free men. However even the laws to which they are subject are mild in comparison to the Ordinance outlined above and the penalties they impose are a mere fleabite when compared with the penalties laid down in the Ordinance. A trader with assets running into *lakhs* could be deported and thus faced with utter ruin in virtue of the Ordinance. And the patient reader will see later on how persons were even deported for breaking some of its provisions. There are some drastic laws directed against criminal tribes in India, with which this Ordinance can be easily compared and will be found not to suffer by the comparison. The giving of finger prints required by the Ordinance, was quite a novelty in South Africa. . . . Again, the registration of women and children under sixteen was proposed for the first time by this Ordinance.

The next day there was held a small meeting of the leading Indians to whom I explained the Ordinance word by word. It shocked them as it had shocked me. . . . All present realized the seriousness of the situation and resolved to hold a public meeting at which a number of resolutions must be proposed and passed. A Jewish theatre was hired for the purpose.

THE ADVENT OF SATYAGRAHA

The meeting was duly held on September 11, 1906. It was attended by delegates from various places in the Transvaal. But I must confess that even I myself had not then understood all the implications of the resolutions I had helped to frame; nor had I gauged all the possible conclusions to which they might lead. The old Empire Theatre was packed from floor to ceiling. I could read in every face the expectation of something strange to be done or to happen. Mr. Abdul Gani, Chairman of the Transvaal British Indian Association, presided. He was one of the oldest Indian residents of the Transvaal, and partner and manager of the Johannesburg branch of the well-known firm of Mamad Kasam Kamrudin. The most important among the resolutions passed by the meeting was the famous Fourth Resolution, by which the Indians solemnly determined not to submit to the Ordinance in the event of its becoming law in the teeth of their opposition and to suffer all the penalties attaching to such non-submission.

I fully explained this resolution to the meeting and received a patient hearing. The business of the meeting was conducted in Hindi or Gujarati; it was impossible therefore that any one present should not follow the proceedings. For the Tamils and Telugus who did not know Hindi there were Tamil and Telugu speakers who fully explained everything in their respective languages. The resolution was duly proposed, seconded and supported by several speakers. . . .

* * * * *

. . . The meeting heard me word by word in perfect quiet. Other leaders too spoke. All dwelt upon their own responsibility and the responsibility of the audience. The President rose. He too made the situation clear, and at last all present, standing with upraised hands, took an oath with God as witness not to submit to the Ordinance if it became law. . . . The community's enthusiasm knew no bounds. The very next day there was some accident in the theatre in consequence of which it was wholly destroyed by fire. On the third day friends brought me the news of the fire and congratulated the community upon the good omen, which signified to them that the Ordinance would meet the same fate as the theatre. I have never been influenced by such so-called signs and therefore did not attach any weight to the coincidence. I have taken note of it here only as a demonstration of the community's courage and faith. . . .

The workers did not let the grass grow under their feet after this great meeting. Meetings were held everywhere and pledges of resistance were taken in every place. The principal topic of discussion in *Indian Opinion* now was the Black Ordinance.

At the other end, steps were taken in order to meet the Local Government. A deputation waited upon Mr. Duncan, the Colonial Secretary, and told him among other things about the pledges. Sheth Haji Habib, who was a member of the deputation, said, 'I cannot possibly restrain myself if any officer comes and proceeds to take my wife's finger prints. I will kill him there and then and die myself.' The Minister stared at the

Sheth's face for a while and said, 'Government is reconsidering the advisability of making the Ordinance applicable to women, and I can assure you at once that the clauses relating to women will be deleted. Government have understood your feeling in the matter and desire to respect it. But as for the other provisions, I am sorry to inform you that Government is and will remain adamant. General Botha wants you to agree to this legislation after due deliberation. Government deem it to be essential to the existence of the Europeans. They will certainly consider any suggestions about details which you may make consistently with the objects of the Ordinance, and my advice to the deputation is that your interest lies in agreeing to the legislation and proposing changes only as regards the details.' I am leaving out here the particulars of the discussion with the Minister, as all those arguments have already been dealt with. The arguments were just the same, there was only a difference in phraseology as they were set forth before the Minister. The deputation withdrew, after informing him that his advice notwithstanding, acquiescence in the proposed legislation was out of the question, and after thanking Government for its intention of exempting women from its provisions.

*   *   *   *   *

None of us knew what name to give to our movement. I then used the term 'passive resistance' in describing it. I did not quite understand the implications of 'passive resistance' as I called it. I only knew that some new principle had come into being. As the struggle advanced, the phrase 'passive resistance' gave rise to confusion and it appeared shameful to permit this great struggle to be known only by an English name. Again, that foreign phrase could hardly pass as current coin among the community. A small prize was therefore announced in *Indian Opinion* to be awarded to the reader who invented the best designation for our struggle. We thus received a number of suggestions. The meaning of the struggle had been then fully discussed in *Indian Opinion* and the competitors for the prize had fairly sufficient material to serve as a basis for their exploration. Shri Maganlal Gandhi was one of the competitors and he suggested the word 'Sadagraha,' meaning 'firmness in a good cause.' I liked the word, but it did not fully represent the whole idea I wished it to connote. I therefore corrected it to 'Satyagraha.' Truth (*Satya*) implies love, and firmness (*agraha*) engenders and therefore serves as a synonym for force. I thus began to call the Indian movement 'Satyagraha,' that is to say, the Force which is born of Truth and Love or non-violence, and gave up the use of the phrase 'passive resistance,' in connection with it, so much so that even in English writing we often avoided it and used instead the word 'Satyagraha' itself or some other equivalent English phrase.

*   *   *   *   *

SATYAGRAHA V. PASSIVE RESISTANCE

As the movement advanced Englishmen too began to watch it with interest. Although the English newspapers in the Transvaal generally wrote in support of the Europeans and of the Black Act, they willingly published contributions from well-known Indians. They also published Indian representations to Government in full or at least a summary of these, sometimes sent their reporters to important meetings of the Indians, and when such was not the case, made room for the brief reports we sent them.

These amenities were of course very useful to the community, but by and by some leading Europeans came to take interest in the movement as it progressed. One of these was Mr. Hosken, one of the magnates of Johannesburg. He had always been free from colour prejudice but his interest in the Indian question deepened after the starting of Satyagraha. The Europeans of Germiston, which is something like a suburb of Johannesburg, expressed a desire to hear me. A meeting was held, and introducing me and the movement I stood for to the audience, Mr. Hosken observed. 'The Transvaal Indians have had recourse to passive resistance when all other means of securing redress proved to be of no avail. They do not enjoy the franchise. Numerically, they are only a few. They are weak and have no arms. Therefore they have taken to passive resistance which is a weapon of the weak.' These observations took me by surprise, and the speech which I was going to make took an altogether different complexion in consequence. In contradicting Mr. Hosken, I defined our passive resistance as 'soul force.' I saw at this meeting that a use of the phrase 'passive resistance' was apt to give rise to terrible misunderstanding. I will try to distinguish between passive resistance and soul force by amplifying the argument which I made before that meeting so as to make things clearer.

I have no idea when the phrase 'passive resistance' was first used in English and by whom. But among the English people, whenever a small minority did not approve of some obnoxious piece of legislation, instead of rising in rebellion they took the passive or milder step of not submitting to the law and inviting the penalties of such non-submission upon their heads. When the British Parliament passed the Education Act some years ago, the Non-conformists offered passive resistance under the leadership of Dr. Clifford. The great movement of the

English women for the vote was also known as passive resistance. It was in view of these two cases that Mr. Hosken described passive resistance as a weapon of the weak or the vote-
less. Dr. Clifford and his friends had the vote, but as they were
in a minority in the Parliament, they could not prevent the
passage of the Education Act. That is to say, they were weak
in numbers. Not that they were averse to the use of arms for
the attainment of their aims, but they had no hope of succeeding by force of arms. And in a well-regulated state, recourse to
arms every now and then in order to secure popular rights
would defeat its own purpose. Again some of the Non-conformists would generally object to taking up arms even if it
was a practical proposition. The suffragist movement did not
eschew the use of physical force. Some suffragists fired buildings and even assaulted men. I do not think they ever intended
to kill any one. But they did intend to thrash people when an
opportunity occurred, and even thus to make things hot for
them.

But brute force had absolutely no place in the Indian movement in any circumstance, and the reader will see, as we proceed, that no matter how badly they suffered, the Satyagrahis
never used physical force, and that too although there were
occasions when they were in a position to use it effectively.
Again, although the Indians had no franchise and were weak,
these considerations had nothing to do with the organization of
Satyagraha. This is not to say, that the Indians would have
taken to Satyagraha even if they had possessed arms or the
franchise.

*   *   *   *   *

We are only concerned to note the distinction between passive resistance and Satyagraha, and we have seen that there is
a great and fundamental difference between the two. If without understanding this, those who call themselves either passive resisters or Satyagrahis believe both to be one and the
same thing, there would be injustice to both leading to unto-
ward consequences. The result of our using the phrase 'passive
resistance' in South Africa was, not that people admired us
by ascribing to us the bravery and the self-sacrifice of the suffragists but we were mistaken to be a danger to person and
property which the suffragists were, and even a generous
friend like Mr. Hosken imagined us to be weak. The power of
suggestion is such, that a man at last becomes what he believes
himself to be. If we continued to believe ourselves and let
others believe, that we are weak and helpless and therefore
offer passive resistance, our resistance would never make us
strong, and at the earliest opportunity we would give up passive resistance as a weapon of the weak. On the other hand if

we are Satyagrahis and offer Satyagraha believing ourselves to be strong, two clear consequences result from it. Fostering the idea of strength, we grow stronger and stronger every day. With the increase in our strength, our Satyagraha too becomes more effective and we would never be casting about for an opportunity to give it up. Again, while there is no scope for love in passive resistance, on the other hand not only has hatred no place in Satyagraha but is a positive breach of its ruling principle. While in passive resistance there is a scope for the use of arms when a suitable occasion arrives, in Satyagraha physical force is forbidden even in the most favourable circumstances. Passive resistance is often looked upon as a preparation for the use of force while Satyagraha can never be utilized as such. Passive resistance may be offered side by side with the use of arms. Satyagraha and brute force, being each a negation of the other, can never go together. Satyagraha may be offered to one's nearest and dearest; passive resistance can never be offered to them unless of course they have ceased to be dear and become an object of hatred to us. In passive resistance there is always present an idea of harassing the other party and there is a simultaneous readiness to undergo any hardships entailed upon us by such activity; while in Satyagraha there is not the remotest idea of injuring the opponent. Satyagraha postulates the conquest of the adversary by suffering in one's own person.

These are the distinctions between the two forces. But I do not wish to suggest that the merits, or if you like, the defects of passive resistance thus enumerated are to be seen in every movement which passes by that name. But it can be shown that these defects have been noticed in many cases of passive resistance. Jesus Christ indeed has been acclaimed as the prince of passive resisters but I submit in that case passive resistance must mean Satyagraha and Satyagraha alone. There are not many cases in history of passive resistance in that sense. One of these is that of the Doukhobors of Russia cited by Tolstoy. The phrase 'passive resistance' was not employed to denote the patient suffering of oppression by thousands of devout Christians in the early days of Christianity. I would therefore class them as Satyagrahis. And if their conduct be described as passive resistance, passive resistance becomes synonymous with Satyagraha. It has been my object in the present chapter to show that Satyagraha is essentially different from what people generally mean in English by the phrase 'passive resistance.'

*   *   *   *   *

THE FIRST SATYAGRAHI PRISONER

When the Asiatic Department found, that notwithstanding all their exertions, they could not get more than 500 Indians to register, they decided to arrest some one. In Germiston there lived many Indians, one of whom was Pandit Rama Sundara. . . . He became the cynosure of all eyes as if he were a great man put upon his trial. Government need not have taken, but it did take, special measures for the preservation of peace. In the Court, too, Rama Sundara was accorded due respect as no ordinary prisoner but a representative of his community. Eager Indian spectators filled the Court-room. Rama Sundara was sentenced to a month's simple imprisonment, and kept in a separate cell in the European ward in Johannesburg gaol. . . . There was no trace of depression, but on the other hand there was exultation and rejoicing. Hundreds were ready to go to jail. The officers of the Asiatic Department were disappointed in their hope of a bumper crop of registrants. . . . The month was soon over. Rama Sundara was released and was taken in a procession to the place where a meeting had been arranged. Vigorous speeches were made. Rama Sundara was smothered with garlands of flowers. . . .

But Rama Sundara turned out to be false coin. There was no escape from the month's imprisonment, as his arrest came as a surprise. In jail he had enjoyed luxuries to which he had been a stranger outside. Still accustomed as he was to licence, and addicted as he was to bad habits, the loneliness and the restraints of jail life were too much for him. In spite of all the attention showered upon him by the jail authorities as well as by the community, jail appeared irksome to him and he bade a final good-bye to the Transvaal and to the movement. There are cunning men in every community and in every movement and so there were in ours. These knew Rama Sundara through and through, but from an idea that even he might become an instrument of the community's providence, they never let me know his secret history until his bubble had finally burst.

*   *   *   *   *

I have thus detailed the whole history of Rama Sundara not in order to expose his faults, but to point a moral. The leaders of every clean movement are bound to see that they admit only clean fighters to it. But all their caution notwithstanding, undesirable elements cannot be kept out. And yet if the leaders are fearless and true, the entry of undesirable persons into the movement without their knowing them to be so does not ultimately harm the cause. When Rama Sundara was found out, he became a man of straw. The community forgot him, but the movement gathered fresh strength even through him. Imprisonment suffered by him for the cause stood to our credit, the enthusiasm created by his trial came to stay, and profiting by his example, weaklings slipped away out of the movement of their own accord.

* * * * *

'INDIAN OPINION'

I propose to acquaint the reader with all the weapons, internal as well as external, employed in the Satyagraha struggle and now therefore proceed to introduce to him *Indian Opinion,* a weekly journal which is published in South Africa to this very day. . . . It was formerly published in English, Gujarati, Hindi and Tamil. But the Hindi and Tamil sections were eventually discontinued, as the burden they imposed upon us seemed to be excessive, we could not find Tamil and Hindi writers willing to settle upon the farm and could not exercise a check upon them. The paper was thus being published in English and Gujarati when the Satyagraha struggle commenced. . . . Through the medium of this paper we could very well disseminate the news of the week among the community. The English section kept those Indians informed about the movement who did not know Gujarati, and for Englishmen in India, England and South Africa, *Indian Opinion* served the purpose of a weekly newsletter. . . .

As the community was transformed in course of and as a result of the struggle, so was *Indian Opinion.* In the beginning we used to accept advertisements for it, and also execute job work in the printing press. I observed that some of our best men had to be spared for this kind of work. If we did receive advertisements for publication, there was constant difficulty in deciding which to accept and which to refuse. Again one would be inclined to refuse an objectionable advertisement, and yet be constrained to accept it, say because the advertiser was a leading member of the community and might take it ill if his advertisement was rejected. . . . Moreover, the view commended itself, that if the paper was conducted not because it yielded profit but purely with a view to service, the service should not be imposed upon the community by force but should be rendered only if the community wished. And the clearest proof of such wish would be forthcoming if they became subscribers in sufficiently large numbers to make the paper self-supporting. Finally it seemed that it was in every way better for all concerned that we should approach the generality of the community and explain to them the duty of keeping their newspaper going rather than set about to induce a few traders to place their advertisements with us in the name of service. On all these grounds we stopped advertisements in the paper with the gratifying result that those who were at first engrossed in the advertisement department could now devote their labours to improving the paper.

*   *   *   *   *

Just as we stopped advertisements in the paper, we ceased to take job work in the press, and for nearly the same reasons. Compositors had now some time to spare, which was utilized in the publication of books. As here too there was no intention of reaping profits and as the books were printed only to help the struggle forward, they commanded good sales. Thus both the paper and the press made their contribution to the struggle, and as Satyagraha gradually took root in the community, there was clearly visible a corresponding moral amelioration of the paper as well as of the press from the standpoint of Satyagraha.

A SERIES OF ARRESTS

*   *   *   *   *

The workers had realized at the very outset that secrecy had no place in a movement, where one could do no wrong, where there was no scope for duplicity or cunning, and where strength constituted the single guarantee of victory. The very interest of the community demanded, that if the disease of weakness was to be eradicated, it must be first properly diagnosed and given due publicity. When the officers [of Government] saw that this was the policy of *Indian Opinion,* the paper became for them a faithful mirror of the current history of the Indian community. They thus came to think the strength of the movement could not by any means be broken so long as certain leaders were at large. Some of the leading men were consequently served with a notice in Christmas week of 1907 to appear before the Magistrate. It must be admitted that this was an act of courtesy on the part of the officers concerned. They could have arrested the leaders by a warrant if they had chosen to do so. Instead of this they issued notices and this, besides being evidence of their courtesy, also betrayed their confidence that the leaders were willing and prepared to be arrested. Those who had thus been warned appeared before the Court on the date specified, Saturday, December 28, 1907, to show cause why, having failed to apply for registration as required by law, they should not be ordered to leave the Transvaal within a given period.

*   *   *   *   *

The Magistrate conducted each case separately, and ordered all the accused to leave the Transvaal within forty-eight hours in some cases and seven or fourteen days in others.

The time limit expired on January 10, 1908 and the same day we were called upon to attend court for sentence.

None of us had to offer any defence. All were to plead guilty to the charge of disobeying the order to leave the Transvaal within the stated period, issued by the Magistrate on failure to satisfy him that they were lawful holders of certificates of registration.

I asked leave to make a short statement, and on its being granted, I said I thought there should be a distinction made between my case and those that were to follow. I had just heard from Pretoria that my compatriots there had been sentenced to three months' imprisonment with hard labour, and had been fined a heavy amount, in lieu of payment of which they would receive a further period of three months' hard labour. If these men had committed an offence, I had committed a greater offence and I therefore asked the Magistrate to impose upon me the heaviest penalty. The Magistrate, however, did not agree to my request and sentenced me to two months' simple imprisonment. I had some slight feeling of awkwardness due to the fact that I was standing as an accused in the very Court where I had often appeared as counsel. But I well remember that I considered the former role as far more honourable than the latter, and did not feel the slightest hesitation in entering the prisoner's box.

In the Court there were hundreds of Indians as well as brother members of the Bar in front of me. On the sentence being pronounced I was at once removed in custody and was then quite alone.

* * * * *

In jail I was asked to put off my own private clothing. I knew that convicts were made naked in jail. We had all decided as Satyagrahis voluntarily to obey all jail regulations so long as they were not inconsistent with our self-respect or with our religious convictions. The clothes which were given to me to wear were very dirty. I did not like putting them on at all. It was not without pain that I reconciled myself to them from an idea that I must put up with some dirt. . . .

* * * * *

From the second or third day Satyagrahi prisoners began to arrive in large numbers. They had all courted arrest and were most of them hawkers. In South Africa every hawker, Black or White, has to take out a licence, always to carry it with him and show it to the police when asked to do so.

Nearly every day some policeman would ask to see the licences and arrest those who had none to show. The community had resolved to fill up the jail after our arrests. In this
the hawkers took the lead. It was easy for them to be arrested. They only had to refuse to show their licences and that
was enough to ensure their arrest. In this way the number of
Satyagrahi prisoners swelled to more than a hundred in one
week. And as a few were sure to arrive every day, we received the daily budget of news without a newspaper. When
Satyagrahis began to be arrested in large numbers, they were
sentenced to imprisonment with hard labour . . .

*   *   *   *   *

THE FIRST SETTLEMENT

We had thus been in jail for a fortnight, when fresh ar-
rivals brought the news that there were going on some negotiations about a compromise with the Government. . . .

*   *   *   *   *

The substance of the proposed settlement was that the Indians should register voluntarily, and not under any law; that
the details to be entered in the new certificates of registration should be settled by Government in consultation with the
Indian community, and, that if the majority of the Indians
underwent voluntary registration, Government should repeal
the Black Act, and take steps with a view to legalize the voluntary registration. The draft did not make quite clear the condition which required Government to repeal the Black Act. I
therefore suggested a change calculated to place this beyond
all doubt from my own standpoint.

Mr. Cartwright [the negotiator] did not like even this little
addition and said, 'General Smuts considers this draft to be
final. I have approved of it myself, and I can assure you that
if you all undergo re-registration, the Black Act is bound to
be repealed.'

I replied, 'Whether or not there is a settlement, we shall always be grateful to you for your kindness and help. I should
not like to suggest a single unnecessary alteration in the draft.
I do not object to such language as would uphold the prestige
of Government. But where I myself am doubtful about the
meaning, I must certainly suggest a change of language, and
if there is to be a settlement after all, both the parties must
have the right to alter the draft. General Smuts need not confront us with an ultimatum, saying that these terms are final.
He has already aimed one pistol in the shape of the Black

Act at the Indians. What can he hope to gain by aiming a second?'

Mr. Cartwright had nothing to say against this argument, and he promised to place my suggestion for the change before General Smuts.

I consulted my fellow-prisoners. They too did not like the language, but agreed to the settlement if General Smuts would accept the draft with my amendment. New-comers to jail had brought a message from the leaders outside, that I should accept any suitable compromise without waiting for their consent. I got Messrs Leuing Quinn and Thambi Naidoo to sign the draft along with myself and handed it to Mr. Cartwright.

The second or third day, on January 30, 1908, Mr. Vernon, the Superintendent of Police, Johannesburg, took me to Pretoria to meet General Smuts, with whom I had a good deal of talk. He told me what had passed between him and Mr. Cartwright. He congratulated me on the Indian community having remained firm even after my imprisonment, and said, 'I could never entertain a dislike for your people. You know I too am a barrister. I had some Indian fellow students in my time. But I must do my duty. The Europeans want this law, and you will agree with me, that these are mostly not Boers, but Englishmen. I accept the alteration you have suggested in the draft. I have consulted General Botha also, and I assure you that I will repeal the Asiatic Act as soon as most of you have undergone voluntary registration. When the bill legalizing such registration is drafted, I will send you a copy for your criticism. I do not wish there should be any recurrence of the trouble, and I wish to respect the feelings of your people.'

So saying General Smuts rose. I asked him, 'Where am I to go?' . . .

* * * * *

The General laughed and said, 'You are free this very moment.' . . . There was now only one more train for Johannesburg, and I was able to catch it.

6. George Coe and Kirby Page: VIOLENCE, NON-VIOLENCE, AND THE USES OF COERCION

Such notions as "violence" and "non-violence" are used in different ways, depending partly on the school of thought employing them. Is violence to be equated with physical force? Is non-violence to be identified with refusal to use physical force? Or should the distinction between "violence" and "non-violence" cut across the difference between physical and non-physical force? Under what circumstances is the use of physical force legitimate and when is it illegitimate? What meaning can be ascribed to such conceptions as "spiritual" or "intellectual" violence?

These are a few of the questions which have troubled those who have thought about the utilization of violence in human affairs. Most would agree that war is an example of violence; but beyond this there are disagreements of many kinds. The problem of violence and non-violence is, of course, closely connected with that of coercion. Some believe that, theoretically, no form of coercion is ever justifiable, while others maintain that coercion of various types is inseparable from life itself and that the main problem is to differentiate between "harmful" (violent) coercion and "constructive" or "harmless" (non-violent) coercion.

It is to questions of this kind that the two readings that follow address themselves. In general they endeavor to distinguish between morally legitimate (non-violent) types of coercion and those that can be termed illegitimate (violent). In the first reading, George A. Coe points out some of the difficulties involved in the use of such terms as "violence" and "non-violence" and attempts to redefine the distinction between them, rejecting the idea that all use of physical force is to be repudiated. In the second, Kirby Page, writing within the context of Christian ethics, asks whether, and under what circumstances, coercion is ever justifiable.

Both readings are excerpted from *The World Tomorrow,* the Coe selection from Vol. 15, October 19, 1932, pp. 378–80 and the Page statement from Vol. 15, June 1932, pp. 173–75. *The World Tomorrow* was a leading pacifist and radical American publication of the twenties and thirties. It was active in the critical analysis of militarism and social injustice and included among its contributors men like Norman Thomas, the Socialist leader. Both Coe and Page were frequent contributors. Page, a Christian minister, was the author of a long volume, *National Defense* (New York: Farrar, 1931), which embodied a vigorous attack on military methods of national defense. Throughout their writings both Coe and Page sought to deal with ethical problems not only in the abstract but also in terms of the concrete dilemmas men faced in their social and political struggles.

George A. Coe: *WHAT IS VIOLENCE?*

The decision of Mr. Gandhi to starve himself as a means of bringing his fellow Indians and the British to their senses thrusts into the light an obscurity in the current antithesis between violence and non-violence as methods of social change. Killing a human being surely is the employment of what is ordinarily meant by violence. That this human being is oneself rather than another does not alter the nature of the act as far as violence, in the ordinary sense, is concerned. Rather, the deliberate selection of a particular person for this fate accentuates the question how such an act can be included in a policy of non-violence. I do not mean to intimate that the Mahatma has departed a hair's breadth from his announced principles, but rather that his principles themselves are ambiguous. There is, of course, an enormously important difference between his line of conduct and that of the violent among his countrymen, but the nature of this difference has not been made clear.

We of the West who favor drastic social reconstruction but shrink from forcible coercion have likewise failed to define the boundaries of our intended conduct. If anyone has even attempted to define the violence from which we shrink, I have not been fortunate enough to learn of the fact. Moral judgments have been plentiful, but the object judged, the *fact-element* in the judgment, is shadowy.

The usual assumption appears to be that one passes over from non-violence to violence if, in addition to mental influences, one employs unwelcome mechanical means and measures, especially such means as cannot be reversed by the one towards whom they are directed. Here fall such acts as destroying or maiming a human body, or putting it under physical restraint; taking away the means of life, such as food, or the instruments of voluntary activity, implements for the production of goods and for the communication of ideas. Threats of such action likewise are accounted violent; indeed, putting one in terror of physical harm is recognized by the common law as one mode of assault.

Some persons would include under the head of violence not only the taking away of the means of life and action, but also preventing men from securing these means, as by an embargo. But here a gap in the concept of violence begins to appear. For mere non-intercourse, mere refusal to buy and sell, can produce hunger and death just as surely as an embargo by means of warships. Shall we, then, include such non-inter-course, which is mechanical passivity rather than mechanical action, under the category of violent conduct? I do not see how the answer, if violence is an ethically significant con-cept, can be anything other than affirmative. For certainly, given the present interdependence of men, we can weaken, distort, and destroy the bodies of our fellows by merely doing nothing. We can gain the ends of overt violence either by em-ploying mechanical forces or by declining to employ them.

It appears, therefore, that the ethical distinction that we have in mind is not happily expressed by the terms "violent" and "non-violent." This will be the more evident if we ask ourselves how even non-violent mental influences operate. For communication between persons is a psycho-physical affair; we know of no bodiless, non-mechanical social relation what-ever. When you speak to me, you start mechanical processes in the air, in my ears, and in my brain—processes from which I have no means of escape if I am in your presence. Hence it is that a spoken word can smite as truly as a fist. Public opin-ion can restrain me physically as effectively as prison bars. A few whispers in a community can start a run upon a bank. A prejudice passed on from parents to children can disinherit a whole race economically and socially.

Yet the current antithesis between violent and non-violent, unclear though it be, points towards an ethical distinction, a real difference in conduct, that is immeasurably great. This difference, as our discussion should help us to see, concerns altogether our relations to one another as persons, not at all the contrast between mental and physical forces. The really basic demand of the non-violents is that we recognize ultimate worth in every person without exception, even in our worst enemies. Here is the reason for recoiling from the use of physical compulsion: it seems to place ultimate reliance upon what is non-spiritual, non-ethical; it lends itself too readily to selfishness and self-will; it sets person against person, and thus tends to multiply the original evil.

This reasoning is sound as far as it goes, but its sufficiency as a guide for conduct depends upon a fact-element in experience, namely, the conditions that promote or hinder the realization of ourselves as persons. These conditions cannot be ascertained *a priori*, and they are not included in the concept of the value of persons. In our conduct we have to do with cause-and-effect relations within the order of nature; specifically, relations within a psycho-physical complex. Empirical research has shown that we develop as persons through reciprocity with one another as well as through manipulation of things. But these two factors do not stand upon the same level. Without reciprocity, development is impossible, no matter how much opportunity or freedom one has in the mechanical sphere. He who oppresses his fellows depresses his own self. Respect for his personality, therefore, cannot be effectively exercised by permitting him to persist in his conduct. Indeed, there is plenty of evidence that some children and some adults "come to themselves" only through encountering an ultimatum that thwarts their desires.

Nor is this the whole of the matter. Since the value of persons is our basic consideration, we have to do with a triadic relationship. We have to guard and promote personality not only in the oppressor and in ourselves as would-be deliverers, but also in the whole of a given society. Injustice, when it is habitual, rooted, and from its own point of view successful, becomes conventional, an accepted thing, and a force in the informal education that every society bestows upon the young. Such a social atmosphere is full of disease-germs of the spirit. Witness the ethical stupefying of our young people, and the ethical paralysis of the present generation of adults, because of daily contacts with greed that is allowed to have its own way. Is it not clear that by abstaining from the use of force to stop injustice we might abandon to an evil fate both the personality of the oppressor and the personalities of the rising generation? Irresistible mechanical action against stubborn men is the only way, under some conditions, to demonstrate complete respect for persons.

The test of all proposals to employ compulsion, and likewise of every refusal to employ it, is this: Is the proposed act or inaction likely to increase, in the long run, the reciprocity through which personality thrives and in which society has its being? Will the growth of children into distinct, varied, self-determining men and women be protected and furthered? Will the coöperative mastery and use of natural resources increase? Will these resources be devoted more than now to the development and use of the worthwhile capacities of men?

By this test all governmental compulsions are to be judged. From the confused point of view that we have been considering, taxation might be construed as violence. Indeed, the cry of "confiscation" attends almost any endeavor to increase taxes. But the ethical question is, Does this tax provide opportunity for the life, growth, happiness and fellowship of the persons who are affected by it? This, and this only, determines the ethical limits of the taxing power. Similarly, the police power in all its phases, and the participation of government in production and distribution, are to be weighed, not in the scales of abstract and pre-determined rights, but by noting the level of personal life and fellowship that they produce in the long run. Any use of force that raises this level is justified. To deny this would imply either that we subordinate persons to things, or else that some persons are mere means while others are ends.

The practical problem that hides within the antithesis, "non-violence versus violence," can be solved therefore only by a pragmatic and scientific inquiry into the question, What use of force does, as a matter of fact, protect life, further health and growth, increase mutuality, and enrich enjoyments? The great illusion that befogs the world concerns this matter of fact. Men expect from force what it does not accomplish, at the same time that they refuse to employ force where it would be socially constructive. The demonstrable folly of war is that it expends enormous and irreplaceable resources of every sort without attaining the idealistic ends that it sets before itself. To become a pacifist, one need only be realistic. The non-pacifists are the visionaries; they are the "impracticable idealists"! Similarly, the faults of our dreadful penal system and the lack of system center, as Warden Lawes has shown in his remarkable book on Sing Sing, constitute a persistent illusion concerning the effectiveness of force.

Concerning all class rule two things can be said: It maintains itself ultimately, whatever its legal form, by reliance upon force rather than consent, and it does not and cannot provide the conditions for maximum personal growth whether of the privileged few or of the many. The fact that special privilege warps the personalities of its beneficiaries has an important bearing upon the method of getting rid of this sort of social incubus. These ailing personalities cannot cure themselves; they have neither the insight nor the grit to do it; "it is easier for a camel to pass through the eye of a needle." Their privileges must be removed by surgery; there is no other way. This implies on the part of men of good will an implacable determination to enforce laws that are good, to make and enforce needed new laws, to apply economic pressure, to destroy the social standing of oppressors and parasites, to circumvent their designs to employ armed force, and in general to exhaust them by unremitting aggressive action on all sides.

This policy relies fundamentally upon wit rather than upon might, upon developing and organizing and toning up the wit of increasing masses of men. At strategic points it may require the forcible disarming of the armed. If the food supply of the world should be concentrated in the hands of a few while the many hunger, no ethical reason could be alleged why the masses should not take forcible possession of the means for their life and for the health and growth of their children. And if a defender of special privilege should interpose his body between hungry children and available food, his body should be gotten out of the way. It should be gotten out of the way by the method that gives greatest promise of releasing his mind from its prison, but in any case the children should be fed.

This is dangerous doctrine, undoubtedly; but all policies with respect to special privilege are dangerous. They are dangerous, all of them, for one and the same reason—our proneness to forget that the ultimate victory must lie in a positive increase of fellowship among enriched personalities. Absolute pacifists and non-resisters do not escape this danger. To the degree that they are unready to apply a pragmatic test to the use of force, alleging that they are unwilling to invade the sacredness of the oppressor's personality, they are in danger of ignoring the sacredness of child-personalities that at the moment are being stunted and distorted by agencies that could in some cases be checked by a judicious show of determined force.

* * * * *

The sum of the matter is that, as long as violence and nonviolence are conceived in physical or mechanical terms, the distinction between them carries no ethical meaning whatever; that ethical meaning is reached for the first time when we fix attention upon the growth of immature persons and the possible integration of mature ones into a rich and varied voluntary fellowship; that the use of force, psychical and mechanical, is unavoidable, whatever our plans and purposes; that force is one essential to fellowship, and that failure to use it aggressively for social ends implicates us in other people's aggressive use of it for anti-social ends; that the ethically justified scope of force is not restricted to what is commanded or permitted by law; that the test for all employment of force is its observed effect in opportunities and incentives for growth of persons and for fellowship and coöperation; and that, finally, the danger that is in this doctrine is inherent in personal life as such—it is a risk that the Creator took when he made man.

Kirby Page: IS COERCION EVER JUSTIFIABLE?

This generation threatens to destroy its own choicest values by the reckless use of violence. Greed creates fear, and fear resorts to violence. If life consists chiefly in grabbing for self, family, nation or race; and if competition and strife are encouraged and stimulated on every level; and if man's genius is prostituted to the search for annihilating weapons; and if the units of combat become more titanic in size and power; then the doom of our civilization is imminent. The futility and menace of ruthlessness are everywhere evident. Hanging and electrocution cannot hold back the crime wave; military and naval preparedness cannot afford security, and only accentuates the danger; suppression of civil liberties and resort to intimidation and brutality cannot preserve property rights and safeguard human values in industry. Urgently and desperately, this generation needs an effective alternative for violence.

Jesus' experience of God and his attitude toward men offer an inestimable contribution to modern society. To the degree that men live every day as good members of God's Home, greed and violence disappear. Does this mean, then, that Tolstoy was right in maintaining that every use of force and coercion is contrary to the spirit of Jesus and therefore immoral? That all depends upon whether or not coercion is necessarily a violation of the family spirit. If the answer is in the affirmative, the only consistent philosophy for a follower of Jesus is that of anarchism, and the only logical procedure that of withdrawal from all responsibility for and participation in organized society.

But the evidence does not drive us to such a conclusion. It is possible that coercion may be administered in such a way as to prove restraining and redemptive. Wherever in a home there is immaturity, lack of self-control, and anti-social stimuli, coercion may be necessary in order to safeguard the other members of the family, and to prevent remorse for irreparable wrongdoing. To say that restraint administered in love and with the welfare of all concerned vividly in mind is immoral, is to reduce society to anarchy and chaos.

*   *   *   *   *

Unless effective non-violent means of coercion can be devised and utilized, the victims of injustice will, in blindness and desperation, take up weapons of violence. In our kind of world, to rely upon anarchy and inaction is to turn the reins over to violence.

*   *   *   *   *

If the family circle is to be extended beyond blood relatives and made to embrace men of all classes and races, effective social organization must be created and maintained by mutual goodwill, supported in emergencies and abnormal instances by ethical and effective restraints. Here we are confronted with one of the most urgent problems of our day. How can society restrain criminals, and restore them to right relations with their fellows, without vengeance in the form of a noose or an electric chair? How can the workers utilize the strike and other forms of economic coercion, and at the same time avoid hatred and violence? How can Mahatma Gandhi exert sufficient pressure through non-violent non-coöperation to secure freedom for India, without stimulating hatred and resorting to violence?

* * * * *

Our difficulty comes, of course, in deciding where ethical coercion ends and unethical violence begins. The only person who is able to escape from this dilemma is the complete anarchist who repudiates every form of restraint and compulsion—and such a man has no solution to offer for the imminently menacing problems of the hour. All other persons are obliged to draw the line somewhere, and orderly progress depends upon the intellectual keenness and ethical sensitiveness with which the situation is confronted.

None of the three possible ways of dealing with social injustice can entirely prevent or remove human suffering. Resistance by violence tends to increase and intensify suffering; inaction or failure to exert effective restraint perpetuates the misery of the victims of crime or exploitation; non-violent coercion likewise often results in suffering. We are driven, therefore, to the conclusion that, in an imperfect and developing world, suffering is inescapable. The policy of wisdom is to use that method which involves a minimum of suffering and which offers a maximum of redemption.

No method of dealing with crime can entirely eliminate suffering. Ruthlessness and capital punishment, on the one hand, and ineffective restraint, on the other, produce terrible havoc. The imprisonment of a criminal likewise causes suffering to his family and to the man himself. If, however, during the period of separation from society, redemptive processes—physical, educational, moral and spiritual—are brought to bear upon the evildoer, the result may be deliverance from anti-social tendencies or habits, and the restoration of the individual to his family and to society.

Failure to restrain greed and exploitation produces much misery, as does also resort to violent class warfare. The industrial strike likewise may and frequently does cause intense suffering, both to the public and to the strikers. But a non-violent strike may enable the exploited workers to gain more justice and fuller liberation from degradation. In spite of the fact that workers are often goaded to the point of desperation by misery, oppression, and the violent tactics used by employers, violence on their part seems ineffective and unethical. Likewise a strike that results in direct and inescapable starvation seems indefensible.

Imperialist powers are blinded by tradition, prestige and self-interest, and vainly imagine that it is for the good of humanity that they should perpetuate their rule and continue to bear "the white man's burden." Their assumption of superiority and the contemptuous way in which they often treat the "natives" is humiliating and degrading. Sensitive Indians, for example, are at the breaking point, and regard continued British domination as intolerable. Violent revolution is the historic method of handling such an inflammable situation. Mahatma Gandhi's campaign of non-violent non-coöperation is undoubtedly causing much suffering, both in England and in India. It is to be observed, however, that the additional unemployed in British textile areas are not starving, but constitute an extra burden upon the unemployment fund. To the extent that the people of India will follow Gandhi in refraining from hatred and violence, on the one hand, and refusing all coöperation with the British Government, on the other, they will be able to exert effective non-violent pressure upon Great Britain. The strike and the non-violent boycott seem to be more ethical than acquiescence in an evil situation or the use of violence.

*   *   *   *   *

7. C. M. Case: THE SOCIAL SIGNIFICANCE OF NON-VIOLENT CONDUCT

The present reading is significant in that it is the effort of a professional sociologist to analyze the problems and place of non-violent conduct in human life. The author points out that besides those human activities in which one co-operates, there are others in which submission or resistance to others appear to be the only alternatives. And we can resist either by repelling the aggression which we impute to others or by attempting to change the activities of others in order to advance our own principles. The writer then discusses the methods whereby we can resist or attempt to change conduct, giving much attention to persuasion and non-violent coercion.

One of his most important observations is that campaigns of non-violent coercion, while potentially very effective in the struggle for justice, are not infrequently frustrated either through discouragement or because discipline is insufficient to prevent an outbreak of violence.

He emphasizes that the "political" method, through democratic procedures, normally offers the best way to promote orderly social change. Discussion, conciliation, legislative activity, and voting can be used to develop a public will for justice. Yet such devices depend in the end on an enlightened electorate, which may be slow in developing. Meanwhile, some method of social struggle must be discovered which will have the capacity to dramatize injustice, arouse the sluggish electorate, and correct imbalances of power. The means of non-violent coercion, correctly used, would seem to fulfill this need.

The author of the reading, Clarence Marsh Case, was born in 1874. He was educated at Earlham College and was awarded the Ph.D. by the University of Wisconsin. In the early part of his career he was pastor of a Friends (Quaker) Meeting and later on taught history and sociology at William Penn College (Oskaloosa, Iowa), the State University of Iowa, and the University of Southern California. He wrote several books. Our reading is taken from Chapter XXI of his *Non-*

violent Coercion (New York: Century, 1923), probably his best-known work.

There are obviously two or three possible types of response to the activities of other persons as they impinge upon one's own interests. Aside from those in which one actively coöperates, or maintains an attitude of indifferent neutrality, there arise countless situations in which the choice lies between submission and resistance. The last named is the domain of conduct with which we are here concerned, and it also in turn presents two aspects. The first is the case where the subject resists or repels the aggressions of others; the second is that where he seeks to modify the conduct of others for the purpose of promoting his own ideals. While this often tends to merge into some form of coercion, such is not necessarily the case; since for one who resists or seeks actively to control the conduct of others there are three, and if our analysis is correct, only three, methods of procedure. These are persuasion, non-violent coercion, and violence.

Persuasion is that form of social action which proceeds by means of *convincing* others of the rightness or expediency of a given course of conduct. It may rely upon *argumentation,* which is the recognized procedure to which the name is commonly applied; or it may seek to convince by *suffering.* Persuasion through suffering presents two types. The first is that so abundantly illustrated in passive resistance of the older, orthodox type. Perhaps nothing has stood out more prominently in our account of the great passive resistants than their stress upon capacity and willingness to suffer. This suffering may be passively endured at the hands of others or self-inflicted, as in the modern instances known as the "hunger-strike." In either case the method is to produce in the mind of the one appealed to, i.e., the subject, a change of mental attitude without the use of coercion. In persuasion of the ordinary type he is convinced by a series of ideas or chain of reasoning. In persuasion by suffering it is done through the sight of distress which a word or simple act of desistance or consent on his own part would avert. When the suffering is self-inflicted for the express purpose of producing such a dilemma in the mind of the subject, as in the hunger-strike, this form of persuasion partakes of the nature of non-violent coercion, as explained below. But in the typical situation, where the suffering, while not self-originated, is passively endured, the subject is persuaded and swerved from his course by a rush of admiration, gratitude, compassion, remorse, or other powerful emotion, while sometimes his hostile and threatening attitude is suddenly changed into one of active benevolence. All this has been concretely illustrated and fully explained in our earlier chapters, and the purpose here is simply to bring it under its proper category as essentially a form of persuasion. In a recent sociological treatise the psychology of such situations is clearly formulated as follows: "A significant feature of sentiments and attitudes is inner tension and consequent tendency to mutation. Love changes into hate, or dislike is transformed into affection, or humility is replaced by self-assertion. This mutability is explained by the fact . . . that the sentiment-attitude is a complex of wishes and desires organized around a person or object. In this complex one motive—love, for example—is for a moment the dominant component. In this case components which tend to excite repulsion, hostility, and disgust are for the moment suppressed. With a change in the situation . . . these suppressed components are released and, gaining control, convert the system into the opposite sentiment, as hate."[1]

In the situation under discussion here, wherein the aggressor and passive resistant confront each other, the mental movement is in the opposite direction, i.e., from hate to love; but it will be readily perceived that the process described is the same.

In meeting the opposition of hostile social forces the typical passive resistant has always shown himself strong to *suffer.* Therein are seen his "tokens of power," which have helped the laws of crowd psychology to work oftentimes in his favor. The courage and spectacular sufferings of the unresisting martyr impress tremendously the imagination of the crowd, producing "a startling image that fills and besets the mind."[2] In studying the religious persecutions of earlier passive resistants, the further fact must not be overlooked that the infliction of punishment and martyrdom is made a *public* affair by the persecuting authorities, in the very nature of the case. For they not only seek to impress the public mind but even depend upon the multitude to make the affair a success, although the people sometimes play a disappointing part from the point of view of the party of bigotry. Allard shows[3] how it was the practice during the early Christian persecutions to make of the occasion "a spectacle and fête." The crowd gathered around the scene of torture, he finds, were "not only spectators, they were almost actors: the crowd filled then a rôle analogous to that of the chorus in the ancient tragedy; it was heard loudly expressing its sentiments: many times even, as if unconsciously, it fell to it to distinguish the various moral aspects of

[1] R. E. Park and E. W. Burgess, *Introduction to the Science of Sociology,* University of Chicago Press, 1921, p. 442.

[2] Gustave Le Bon, *The Crowd* (New York: Macmillan), p. 58.

[3] In his *Dix Leçons sur le Martyre,* pp. 332–33.

the drama which was being played before it."[4] A sort of social dialectic is thus set in motion by these "men of ardent conviction" who have always exercised the power to sway the multitude.[5] The spectacle of such suffering for a cause may lead even the persecutor to reëxamine his own dogmas, if for no other purpose than to revel in their correctness. But reëxamination admits new light, this modifies his view, and often the conquered becomes in the end the conqueror; for so effective is this social *indirection* of the passive resistant in forming public opinion that eventually persuasion may become the wiser policy on the part of government.

As a result of his striking devotion to principle, and his peculiarities, the image of the peace sectarian, as the symbol of a certain moral and social integrity, becomes impressed upon the public mind, figures in literature, art, and even in advertising,[6] and is of value to all concerned. It protects its bearers by capitalizing the past history of the sect for integrity and good will, and it inspires, through imitation, the same qualities in others. Thus, in the end, persecution, as "a shortcut to uniformity,"[7] goes down in defeat before the roundabout moral and social indirection of passive resistance.

It should be understood, however, that this applies only to those few instances where a passively suffering individual or group causes, by such means, an assailant to desist from his purpose, or advances an unpopular social policy toward final acceptance by society. It is to the process operating in such situations only that the term persuasion through suffering is herein applied.

The forms of non-violent coercion described in the later chapters of this book constitute the purest, most typical examples of *indirect* action in the field of social behavior. They are the strike, the boycott, and non-coöperation, which lastnamed is an extension of both the preceding to non-economic relations. One and the same principle underlies all these various manifestations, and that is a strategic recognition of the fundamental and indispensable importance of *coöperation* in every form and phase of associated life. More vital even than this is its recognition that this coöperation is necessarily more or less *voluntary* in every social situation and process, not excepting the grossest forms of exploitation, oppression, and tyranny. In the last analysis the victims always gild their

---

[4] Allard, op. cit., pp. 332–33.

[5] Le Bon, op. cit., p. 114.

[6] For example, the various commercial labels exploiting the picturesque images of the Shaker, Puritan, and Quaker.

[7] Cf. E. A. Ross, *Social Psychology* (New York: Macmillan, 1908), Chap. XVII.

own chains, even where they do not help to forge them. No people on earth ever yet had the dignity and self-control to refrain from gaping at the triumphal processions of its conquerors, or to refuse to validate the master's aggressions by accepting at his own valuation the titles and honors bestowed by his hand. . . .

* * * * *

The strike, as every one knows, cuts off the employer-workman relation, while the boycott suspends the contact of buyer and seller. In all such situations the subject against whom pressure is being directed is presented a pair of real alternatives, provided the strike (or boycott) is correctly conceived and opportunely carried out. To take a concrete instance, the employer is given the choice between ceasing to purchase raw materials from non-union sources or to suffer the interruption of the productive operations brought about by the withdrawal of his labor supply. Neither of these alternatives appeals to his desires or his judgment, yet he is compelled by the situation to choose between them. In the example assumed no act or threat of physical force or violence is used against him, on the one hand, nor is he persuaded of the excellence of either alternative, on the other. He is utterly opposed to the idea of ceasing to purchase his materials in the accustomed place, but he looks upon the disruption of his productive operations as scarcely a lesser evil. Whichever he accepts of the alternatives, he remains unconvinced, either by the assent of his judgment to facts and reasons given in argument, or by a reversal of his emotional state, his sentiment-attitude,[8] through the contemplation of suffering passively endured. He is coerced, non-violently coerced it is true, but coerced nevertheless.

For many persons, perhaps to most, the word "coercion" has an ominous and odious sound; and this is especially true of those who might otherwise feel a special interest in non-violent procedure apart from coercion. In fact, we have noticed in earlier pages the argument of those who condemn the *strike* in itself, no matter how just or peaceable, for the simple reason that it is a form of coercion. Moreover, even among those who do not lay so much stress upon distinctly pacific and conciliatory conduct, there is a tendency to think of all coercion as necessarily involving the application of physical force. Such is not the correct interpretation, even in the common usage recorded in the dictionary. Thus Webster speaks of coercion as "the application to another of such force, *either physical or moral*, as to induce or constrain him to do against his will something that he would not otherwise have done."[9] This in

[8] Cf. Park and Burgess, op. cit., pp. 451–90.
[9] Italics mine.

itself disposes of the notion that the justification of coercion carries with it the indorsement of injurious physical force, but other authority, both lay and clerical, is easy to find. Thus De Maeztu contends: "Coercion . . . is bad when it is used for evil purposes, as . . . to punish thought, to put difficulties in the way of the production of wealth, and to impede the development of human values, either cultural or vital. Coercion is a good thing, on the other hand, when it sacrifices individual apathy on the altar of national defence or the progress of thought, hygiene, morality, or national wealth."[10] A clerical writer likewise maintains that that aspect of a strike which consists in "the enforcing of certain demands is by its very nature morally indifferent."[11]

It is beyond dispute that the most righteous means can be used for the wickedest ends, and evil methods are oftentimes practised that good may come. Nevertheless, there is an intrinsic quality about *methods,* apart from the motives and objects of those who use them, and it renders them unequally desirable in themselves. Accordingly it is here maintained that some methods, notably violence, i.e., the use of physical force in private hands for personal ends, are essentially and incurably evil. On the other hand, persuasion is essentially good, or at worst non-injurious, in itself. Government, in the political sense, is a combination of both the preceding, and tends toward good or bad according to the relative emphasis placed upon persuasion or violence. Non-violent coercion presents a less simple problem, since it combines the inherent excellence of non-violence with the more questionable element of coercion, so that it, more than any of the other methods named, is good or bad according to the object sought and the spirit in which it is pursued. This makes it of first importance to understand clearly the essential spirit of passive, or non-violent, resistance.

Willingness to suffer is inseparable from all passive resistance of the purest type; and a measure of the same fortitude and self-control must be at their command who would successfully wield the related methods of non-violent coercion. It is eminently right that this should be so, for thus only can the interests of society be secured. True non-violent coercion is, and ought to be, a two-edged sword. In other words, it causes,

[10] *Authority, Liberty, and Function, in the Light of the War,* by Ramiro De Maeztu (London and New York: 1916), p. 113.

[11] *The Morality of the Strike,* by the Rev. Donald Alexander McLean, M.A., S.T.L. (New York: Kenedy, 1921), p. 44. This work relies mainly on the papal letters on social questions and other Roman Catholic authorities; it contains an introduction by the Rev. John A. Ryan, D.D.

and it is well that it should cause, inconvenience and suffering to those who wield it, as well as to those against whom it is invoked. In this it is exactly contrary to violent methods; for a principal reason accounting for the appalling growth of terrorism in modern times is the unfortunate fact that the development of firearms and high explosives carries no automatic check and penalty for all who use them, as in the case before us. As for the methods of non-violent coercion, particularly the strike and the boycott, the public usually stands more or less in position to determine which way the blow shall fall, that is, which party to the controversy shall suffer the greater loss. It is well that this should be so, for it is not in the interest of the general good that any group of men should exert irresponsible power. So it constitutes a saving virtue of these methods that in the strike or boycott in their pure form, the voluntary moral, financial, and social coöperation of the public is required for success. When violence or intimidation is resorted to on either side, it constitutes a confession of weakness in the party using it, suggesting a lack of confidence in the ability of one's cause to command the necessary support, or a greater willingness to inflict than to endure pain and loss. For these reasons, we hold that there is a most vital, salutary, and socially necessary connection between the open, truthful, self-denying spirit of passive resistance and the *constructive* use of non-violent coercion in any of its forms. This fairness and willingness to face the consequences are characteristic of passive resistance, whether its opponent be private parties or the state itself.[12]

The unflinching willingness of the passive resistant to bear his just punishment for refusing to obey the commands of the law has been frequently alluded to in earlier chapters. It is safe to say that no true non-violent resistant ever entered into a combination to evade the consequences of civil disobedience, as in certain *clubs for fine paying* reported in an English legal journal.[13] For, as the commentator on this phenomenon points out, "the object of the infliction of fines is to deter per-

[12] The position taken by the principal actor in the now famous Debs Case was distinctly that of a true passive, i.e., non-violent and moral resistance. "I had my own views in regard to the war, and I knew in advance that an expression of what was in my heart would invite a prison sentence under the Espionage Law. I took my stand in accordance with the dictates of my conscience, and was prepared to accept the consequences without complaint." Eugene V. Debs, in *The Century Magazine,* July 1922.

[13] "Clubs for Fine Paying," in *The Justice of the Peace, and County, Borough, Poor Law Union, and Parish Law Recorder,* London, Vol. LXXXIV, No. 8, February 21, 1920.

sons from breaches of the law which would render them liable to such punishment, so that it necessarily follows that when an offender has no longer to suffer the punishment, because the fine need not be paid by him, the object of the law in decreeing the punishment is frustrated." Such agreements are therefore held by jurists to partake of the nature of a conspiracy to defeat the ends of justice. But we have yet to hear of an instance where non-violent resistants have shown the least disposition toward such a purpose.

The truth is that passive resistance and non-violent coercion are methods of social behavior that possess in theory the most extraordinary claims upon the consideration of all men and women who are actuated by a zeal for truth and social justice, unmixed with the spirit of hatred and reprisal. Indeed, it does not seem too much to affirm that here lies at hand, so far as its *theoretical* merits are concerned, the most just and powerful weapon conceivable in human affairs. If resolutely applied, in a spirit of unswerving fairness, by populations or classes able to control themselves and to pay the price in suffering, non-coöperation seems capable of destroying every last program of tyranny and exploitation in the world. But, while the abstract truth of this can hardly be denied, it is valid largely in theory alone. In actual practice the strike, the boycott, non-coöperation, and every other program of non-violence is dogged by two mortal enemies, to either one or the other of which it is almost sure to fall a prey. That is to say it either ebbs away through discouragement and apathy, or flares forth into self-destructive violence. And the longer the struggle the more sure is its defeat through the one or the other of these betrayals. In short, non-violent coercion demands a stronger self-control, a more enduring solidarity of purpose, a greater capacity for passive suffering, a higher ethical development, than most human beings have thus far attained. It is capable of great achievements at favorable moments, but its victories must be swift, its campaigns not too long drawn out, and its field of operations more or less restricted. In the strike and the boycott, and all other applications of this principle, an unusually heavy draft is made upon human emotions and sentiments, whether of resentment, moral indignation, group-loyalty, class-consciousness, or devotion to a cause, all of which require a nervous tension greater than that required for the ordinary conduct of life. Non-violence, therefore, whether it takes the form of *persuasion* or *coercion*, seems *too idealistic and exacting to accomplish* the every-day work of the world. Yet both these methods are of greatest value when kept within the bounds set by the emotional limitations of human nature.

In connection with this tendency to rapid exhaustion on the part of mental exaltation, another practical merit of the *po-*

litical method appears. It avoids the overstrain on feeling by combining the advantages of intermittency and permanence. In the periodical excitement of the political campaign, the processes of argumentation and persuasion have free play, and emotional tension rises, with safety, to great heights. This, once registered at the polls, permits the feelings to relax, because they have thereby become more or less permanently embodied as the public will expressed in law or legal procedure, which endure by their own momentum until contrary forces accumulate in sufficient volume for their modification or repeal. Thus the purpose of an hour of high feeling, when expressed through the semi-rational processes of political procedure, may be counted on to operate long after the ebbing away of the emotions that attended its origin.

Because of these facts, among others, it may truly be said that the liberties of a people consist largely in its institutions, or at least in its accumulated culture. Of course no stupid and ignoble population could permanently maintain a high and free institutional life. Mr. Herbert Spencer was most finely right when he said that "there is no political alchemy by which you can get golden conduct out of leaden instincts."[14] Nevertheless, a rich social heritage will carry a people a long way, not only because of initial momentum but also because such structures constitute social forces in themselves. While it is not true in the long run, yet, for the time being, the culture, and particularly the political institutions, of a people may be better than those who created it. This is because it embodies in permanent form the experiences of the better moments of the social life. In fact, many of the permanent treasures of liberty, which seem to endure with the uncreated and impersonal stability of Gibraltar, were really the slogans of some particular, local place and hour. For example, the struggle of the American colonials against Great Britain, was . . . the protest of a very limited, commercially motived class at first, and it was directed against specific measures of trade which it sought merely to have repealed. Even after it was widened both in scope and purpose the struggle was for a long time very much in the nature of a political family quarrel. Yet in the course of events it was said that "taxation without representation is tyranny," and this has been enshrined in American tradition as a universal principle of freedom which moves on a level above the accidents of time and place. So will it be found with the earlier principles, i.e., "bills of rights," upon which this one rested in part; and so will it be found with all that have followed it. Struck off from the fire of conflict, and for parti-

[14] *Social Statics and The Man vs. the State,* essay on "The Coming Slavery."

san purposes, in an hour of high feeling, they embody truths and ideals that come to possess an eternal and universal signifi-cance, and are so accepted during the more placid times that succeed their stormy origin. Then, suddenly and unexpectedly, as in England and America under the shadow of the World War, they rise up to hamper and plague those who never sus-pected that their allegiance to those "sacred and immutable principles of freedom" was a mere lip-service. In such a situa-tion, if those bending all their energies to meet an actual crisis in the world of action can hear this voice of the nation's calmer and better reflections and permit it to rule even the passionate purposes of the moment, the traditions and institu-tions will act as a balance-wheel, and its liberties will be pre-served. We repeat, then, that in this systematic blending of the feeling and the remembering aspects of the social experience, this combination of partisan persuasion and impersonal coer-cion, lies the strongest claim of the political method.

It is plain that, if persuasion and non-violent coercion must fall short of realizing the largest hopes of aroused and eager social crusaders, it is still more clearly demonstrated that *the methods of violence offer infinitely less of permanent good*. But in the processes of democratic and progressive govern-ment, the excellencies of all of these, as has been shown, are blended, along with some of their evils which it may be en-tirely possible to eliminate. Therefore, in so far as the cause of the masses of disinherited men makes lasting headway, we cannot but believe that it will turn of necessity toward the state as the one supreme adjuster of all conflicting interests, and as the only agency wherein the social gains of to-day may be permanently funded for the needs of to-morrow.

* * * * *

In magnifying the state as the supreme agency of social self-direction we are in no sense concerned with the advocacy of any abstract theory of sovereignty, or the exaltation of politi-cal authority for its own sake. "Sovereignty," as Professor Giddings forcibly phrases it, "is never under any circumstances the absolute power to compel obedience babbled of in political metaphysics. It is finite and conditioned."[15]

* * * * *

In holding to this non-occult and thoroughly utilitarian view of the state and politics, the present argument is not impaired by the new conception of political authority advanced by plu-

[15] F. H. Giddings, *Studies in the Theory of Human Society* (New York: Macmillan, 1922), p. 276.

ralistic thinkers.[16] Social reconstruction through the agency of the truly democratic state offers the one method which does not lure men to grasp more than they can hope to hold; consequently, if they reject political methods in the outset they will inevitably return to them in the end. . . . When a nation has once reached the stage of constitutional liberty and adult suffrage no short cut to social amelioration, through the exercise of physical force in any form whatsoever, can thenceforth be looked for; since beyond the point where real political freedom is reached the road of social progress lies straight, though long perhaps, through moral territory controlled by the state and the appropriate political procedure. Professor Small puts it well when he says: "The modern state is both a political organization and an economic system, but it is much more. The State is a microcosm of the whole human process. The State is the coöperation of the citizens for the furtherance of all the interests of which they are conscious."[17]

Yet it must be confessed that, while we argue in theory for social progress by political methods, we witness too often in practice merely a political gesture; while the dynamic economic and social forces, after more or less of disappointment and delay, continue their immemorial way of cutting directly across lots to the destined goal, but always at the expense of enormous suffering, disorder, and waste. One need not, however, embrace Mr. Herbert Spencer's gospel of social despair,[18] but must at least admit that the ultimate and complete success of the legislative and political method will have to wait upon the social and political enlightenment of the voters, and that methods of non-violent coercion seem capable of really constructive social usefulness in the meantime, if used in that open, truth-asserting spirit of fair play and long-suffering fortitude which we have seen to be the hall-mark of non-violent resistance. Perhaps it is only through a working partnership of such seemingly incongruous forms of behavior as non-violence and coercion that the problems of social collision can be permanently solved. For the solution must be twofold in character, avoiding the devastating furies of violence and terrorism on the one hand, and the stagnant and deadening unanimity sought by insipid sentimentalism upon the other.

* * * * *

[16] *Authority in the Modern State,* by Harold J. Laski (Yale University Press, 1919); *The New State,* by Mary Parker Follett (New York: Longmans, 1920).

[17] *General Sociology,* by Albion W. Small (University of Chicago Press, 1905), p. 226.

[18] Op. cit., particularly the essays on "The Sins of Legislators" and "The Limits of State Duty."

To *social coercion,* therefore, the last words are devoted at the end of this investigation. As used in this study it stands between private coercion on the one hand and public, i.e., governmental or political, coercion on the other. It is called *social* because its enforcing sanctions are neither in the personal use of force nor the appeal to formally constituted political authority . . . but to the concerted manipulation of the ordinary social relations of daily life.

*   *   *   *   *

8. Richard Gregg:
NON-VIOLENCE, THE STATE, AND WAR

Richard Gregg is one of the great twentieth-century formu-
lators of the theory of non-violent resistance. In this reading
he analyzes two of its fundamental themes: the relation of
non-violence to political institutions and the possibilities of
non-violent resistance as an effective substitute for war.

His discussion ranges over such complex questions as the
commitment to truth and frankness in diplomatic relations
(where we are reminded of William Godwin), foreign wars
as a symptom of violent discord within a State, theories of
non-violence in relation to crime, punishment and treatment
of the mentally ill, and the nature of the protests of those often
regarded as deviants.

Most of these issues require little preliminary comment.
However, brief observations on mental illness, police work,
crime, and the role of law may help underline Gregg's points.

Psychiatrists and sociologists in recent years have come to
stress the role of the "self-fulfilling prophecy" in relations
among individuals and groups.[1] Others, that is to say, tend
often to act with reference to us according to the "image" we
have of them. If we treat them as mere beasts, they will tend
to become like beasts, even though originally they may have
had little of the beastly about them. Thus if we expect mental
patients to be violent and treat them as if violence were inevitable, they are likely to measure up to our expectations.
On the other hand, if we create an atmosphere in which we
assume their non-violence, they will respond accordingly. The
director of a mental hospital ward experimented several years
ago exactly along these lines. Over a period of about ten
months, he sought deliberately to create the expectation among
both staff and patients that the latter would be self-controlled.

[1] For a sociological discussion see Robert K. Merton, *Social Theory and Social Structure* (Chicago: The Free Press of Glencoe,
1957).

Of some one thousand patients admitted, not a single one had to be restrained physically.[2]

The principle of the self-fulfilling prophecy is probably also involved (at least in part) in unarmed police work. Many Americans seem to hold that a policeman without arms is not really a policeman. Our Western movie thrillers appear to strengthen this belief. Yet perhaps the most successful police system in the world has for the most part deliberately rejected arms, despite the fact that when it was established London criminals were notoriously violent. The most effective police work is preventive and not repressive. We might well ask ourselves how this discussion relates to the much-discussed problem of a world police.

As for the prison system and its severe restraints, the writer was once told by the warden of a leading state penitentiary that an adequate probation system would enable him to discharge "about 90 per cent" of his one thousand prisoners.

The image of law typically held by many has been that law is a command of the government and gains its authority thereby. Associated with this view has been the idea that law is chiefly sanctioned by what some have called the State's "monopoly of violence." Many thinkers have challenged positions of this kind, relating their criticisms to natural law, to "consensual," and to pluralist schools of thought.[3]

In the second division of the reading, Gregg maintains that non-violent resistance evokes the same virtues called forth by war, while avoiding the viciousness inseparably connected with it. Moreover, non-violence is far more effective than war in attaining just goals.

Born in 1885, Gregg trained to be a lawyer. While acting as arbitrator in labor disputes he became acquainted with Gandhi's life and thought. His own experiences in social conflict corroborated all that Gandhi had said about the futility and cost of violence. In *The Power of Non-Violence* (origi-

[2] See Harry A. Willmer, "Toward a Definition of the Therapeutic Community," *American Journal of Psychiatry* (1958), Vol. 114, pp. 824–34.

[3] For discussions of some basic problems of legal thought, see Fritz Berolzheimer, *The World's Legal Philosophies*, tr. by Rachel S. Jastrow (New York: Macmillan, 1912); Léon Duguit, *Law in the Modern State,* tr. by Frida and Harold Laski (New York: Viking Press, 1919); and Morris R. Cohen, *Law and the Social Order* (New York: Harcourt, 1933).

nally published, 1934; second revised edition Nyack, New York: Fellowship Publications, 1959), he explored the social, ethical, and psychological foundations of non-violence. The section reprinted here is from Chapters VII and VIII of that work.

NON-VIOLENCE AND THE STATE

Non-violent resistance is the key to the problem of liberty in the modern State. That seems like a large claim until we begin to reflect upon the part which force and compulsion play in all the relationships in which the State takes part.

All observers recognise that compulsion, intimidation and violence have been and still are a very large and perhaps predominating element in the State, and especially in political government.[4] If anyone felt inclined to dispute the scholars on this point, let him examine the figures showing that the expenditures for past and future wars form a very high percentage of the total expenditures of the governments of the majority of nations. To this he should add the State expenditures for prisons, the administration of criminal law and a certain part of the administration of civil law. The State has many fine elements, but they perhaps do not counterbalance the large part played by force and compulsion.

This condition of affairs is due not to a particular ruling class, as the Communists would have us believe, but to an inner psychological attitude which prevails through all groups and classes in the so-called "civilised" world. The Marxians say that political forms and methods are determined entirely by economic forces. We would say that both political and economic processes, at least in relation to violence and coercion, are due to still deeper psychological factors. The amount of coercion and violence in the State is a reflection or resultant of a similar tendency and attitude in all our life and activities, both individual and associative.

The non-violent resister believes that a large part of the activities of the State are founded upon a mistake, namely, the idea that fear is the strongest and best sanction for group action and association. He believes that fear is divisive and therefore cannot be the foundation for permanent unity and

[4] See Randolph Bourne, "The State," in *Untimely Papers* (New York: Viking Press, 1919); L. P. Jacks, "The Insane Root: War and the State," *Atlantic Monthly,* January 1917; Reinhold Niebuhr, *Moral Man and Immoral Society* (New York: Scribner, 1932); Sigmund Freud, *Reflections on War and Death* (New York: Moffat Yard, 1918); and various writings of John Dewey, Admiral A. T. Mahan, Leo Tolstoy, and Thorstein Veblen.

strength. He believes that in the family and in education it has now been realised that fear is not a sound basis for action. There we find substituted the more positive and growth-stimulating forces of intellectual curiosity, wonder, love and co-operation. The non-violent resister looks forward to a time when a similar realisation will come in regard to the larger associations of States. He believes that non-violent resistance will probably be an important means in reaching this realisation.

The principles of non-violent resistance can be applied to diplomacy as well as war, for the two are closely allied. Compared with war, non-violent resistance is a safer and more effective instrument of policy. By its use the entire military and naval expenses of all nations can be eliminated.

In so far as diplomacy has been characterised by secrecy and deceit, the principle of truth involved in non-violent resistance will bring about reform. Secrecy and deceit are signs of fear, but non-violent resistance proceeds upon the basis of control and eventual elimination of fear. It insists on truth and openness in all dealings. Gandhi's practice is a living embodiment of this principle.

Non-violent resistance can be used internationally, with or without economic boycott as circumstances require. Causes that some people think cannot be submitted to arbitration may be handled by such means. Mere nonresistance will not do. There must be constructive resistance. The Indian Non-Co-operative Movement in 1922 gave an example which was promising.

*   *   *   *   *

Attempts to improve international relations absorb the time, energy and money of many people. While I admire the devotion shown, most of it seems to me to be wasted because it deals with symptoms instead of the root of the trouble. It is like putting poultices on a cancer. War is an institution, and institutions are external expressions of previous inner attitudes and ways of thinking.[5] To try merely to alter the institution is like

[5] The great Indian philosopher, Aurobindo Ghose (1872–1950), writes: "So long as war does not become psychologically impossible, it will remain, or, if banished, for a while, return. . . . Only when man has developed not merely a fellow-feeling with all men, but a dominant sense of unity and commonalty, only when he is aware of them not merely as brothers—that is a fragile bond—but in a large universal consciousness, can the phenomenon of war, with whatever weapons, pass out of his life without the possibility of return." *War and Self-determination* (Calcutta: S. Ghose, 1922).

This opinion is in substance echoed by Bertrand Russell: "The supposed economic causes of war, except in the case of certain

locking the stable door after the horse is stolen. Even the Mosaic commandment "Thou shalt not kill" begins psychologically at the wrong end of the problem.

* * * * *

World courts, leagues of nations, peace pacts and peace congresses do little toward improving the inner attitudes or psychological dispositions and habits of mind. Too many peacemakers work only on externals, and disregard deepseated inconsistencies and forces working for war in many parts of the economic, social, educational and organised religious systems. To say this is not to oppose their effort, but only to wish that it might be more efficient.

Inasmuch as peacemakers need to be especially sensitive to the truth, it seems desirable to present here two criticisms of their activity, for them to ponder. One was well phrased by Niebuhr:

". . . The implication is that England and America are the only two really solvent nations in the Western World, and that, since they have what they want and need, it is to their interest to preach peace. The hungry nations will meanwhile fail to react to this moral idealism. They will shrewdly and cynically observe that it is always the tendency of those who have to extol the virtue of peace and order and to place those who have not at a moral disadvantage.

"It is quite impossible for the strong to be redemptive in their relation to the weak if they are not willing to share the weakness of the weak, or at least to equalise in some degree the disproportion of advantages."[6]

[Trotsky] said that "a responsible function is allotted to pacifism in the economy of warfare."[7] By this he refers to the

capitalistic enterprises, are in the nature of a rationalization; people wish to fight, and they therefore persuade themselves that it is to their interest to do so. The important question, then, is the psychological one—"Why do people wish to fight?" And this leads on from war to a host of other questions concerning impulses to cruelty and oppression in general. These questions in their turn involve a study of the origins of the malevolent passions, and thence of psychoanalysis and the theory of education. . . .

"The basis of international anarchy is man's proneness to fear and hatred. This is also the basis of economic disputes; for the love of power, which is at their root, is generally an embodiment of fear." "What I Believe," *The Forum* (New York), September 1929.

[6] Reinhold Niebuhr, "A Critique of Pacifism," *Atlantic Monthly*, May 1927, reprinted in Reinhold Niebuhr, *Love and Justice*, ed. by D. B. Robertson (Philadelphia: Westminster Press, 1957).

[7] Leon Trotsky, "Democracy, Pacifism and Imperialism," in N.

pacifists who go around talking about "our sacred duty to do all in our power to preserve the nation from the horrors of war," yet always carefully adding, "If war should come, we will all support the government, of course." Trotsky proceeds [in incisive criticism]:

" 'To do everything in our power against the war,' means to afford the voice of popular indignation an outlet in the form of harmless demonstration, after having previously given the government a guarantee that it will meet with no serious opposition, in the case of war, from the pacifist faction."

* * * * *

It is easy to see how that type of pacifism helps to rally the entire country to the support of militarists at the time they most need it. They are glad to let such pacifists throw a gentle moral glow over affairs before war and then fill themselves and the masses with moral fervour in support of war as soon as it comes.

International peace requires the development of a world community.[8] The mood of mutual tolerance, respect and good will needed for the establishment and operation of such a community will best be created, in social practice, by the use of non-violent resistance for the righting of existing wrongs.

One weakness of most peace proposals is that they all expect the action to be taken by governments or large organisations, or at least someone other than the proponent. The advantage of non-violent resistance is that it begins at home and can and needs to be practised in all the small private relations between people as a preparation for and accompaniment of its use on a large scale. Nobody can dodge the responsibility for its success. The poorest and most insignificant can practise it as finely, successfully and usefully as prime ministers, presidents, financiers, labour leaders or other powerful persons. Through non-violent resistance we can reach an active, reasoned belief in peace which is capable of continuous practice in all grades of life and all sorts of conflict, so as to educate everyone into a conviction that it gives better results, more efficiently, than violence.

* * * * *

Lenin and L. Trotsky, *The Proletarian Revolution in Russia,* ed. by L. Fraina (New York: The Communist Press, 1918), p. 196 f.

[8] Salvador de Madariaga, *Disarmament* (New York: Coward-McCann, 1929), pp. 42, 45, 48, 56, 61, 198. But this need not mean a super-State with supremely powerful armed forces. As soon as one nation organizes itself for non-violent resistance and wins an international struggle by those tactics, there will be imitators, and our present international relationships will change completely.

The causes of disagreement and conflict between nations are legion, and need not be discussed here. Yet there is one group of causes so very important at present that it may not be out of place to consider it briefly. This is the economic and political relationship between nations of the temperate zone and those of the tropics, together with the international jealousies resulting therefrom between nations of the former group. . . . Modern industrialism and much commerce are inherently exploitative and violent in spirit. . . . A large amount of self-dependence for the essential necessities of national life is the economic basis of national self-respect, mutual international self-respect and a preventative of economic parasitism. Beyond and above that, let trade proceed as merrily as it can, but with a minimum of exploitation.

* * * * *

Let us now consider the internal relationships of the State.

The upholders of the State sometimes assert that non-violent resistance to the State or to a specific law is not only unlawful but promotive of anarchy. But democracy is a valid form of government and social order, and democracy is founded on the consent of the governed. The theory of democracy does not assert that that consent or refusal must or can be evidenced only by marks on pieces of paper, the ballot. Refusal of consent may be democratically evidenced by action, by non-violent resistance together with willingness to go to jail for violation of the law. This form of resistance, together with suffering the penalty, is a mode of persuasion, an appeal to the moral sensitiveness of the governors and the people. Persuasion is also a part of the democratic process.

The group within each state toward which the state uses compulsory force most constantly is that of the criminals. It is therefore interesting to find that the attitude and methods of non-violent resistance are the conclusions toward which all the experience of penology and the investigations of psychiatrists, criminologists and social reformers are steadily tending.[9]

If there is ever any reform after forceful punishment or imprisonment, it is not caused by the force or even the suffering. The change depends upon the reaction of the suffering person, and cannot take place unless there is stimulus to some latent or potential goodness in the criminal. Intelligent kindness is a

[9] See Curtis Bok, *Star Wormwood* (New York: Knopf, 1959); Alfred Hassler, *Diary of a Self-made Convict* (Nyack, New York: Fellowship, 1958); Giles Playfair and Derrick Sington, *The Offenders* (New York: Simon & Schuster, 1957); Arthur Koestler, *Reflections on Hanging* (New York: Macmillan, 1957); G. M. Sykes, *The Society of Captives* (Princeton University Press, 1958).

far more effective stimulus than any force can be. If force were the true cause of rehabilitation, its efficacy would increase with repetition. But all experience shows that a repetition of force merely hardens the prisoner and stimulates a desire for revenge.

Violence and severe punishment have proved unavailing for thousands of years. The facts compel us to admit that cruel punishment is not only ineffective but is injurious to prison wardens and guards and to society as well as to the criminal. Also we now know that society is itself responsible for many of the conditions that create criminals. Non-violent, loving, curative methods are the only ones that work or can possibly work. This means careful psychiatric examinations and psychiatric treatment; remedial diet;[10] medical care if need be; training in a useful craft or occupation; wise general education, good food, good quarters; decent, kindly, respectful treatment; many sorts of stimuli and opportunities for normal expression and living; wise probation; good juvenile and delinquent courts. The criminal courts should have only the function of deciding whether or not the crime has been committed and the accessory facts. They should have no power of punishment. Thereafter the case should be handled by physicians, psychiatrists, psychologists, social workers, teachers, and employment agencies. The object should be not to make good prisoners but to make criminals into good citizens.

* * * * *

When really sound treatment is given the criminals and when society steps forward in its own reform, the prison population will greatly decrease. Even the feebleminded and insane are capable of great improvement by proper treatment.

* * * * *

Carefully worked-out information codified into rules and made a subject of intelligent instruction would be of immense assistance to prisons, houses of correction, reform schools, hospitals, mental hospitals, private nurses, policemen and physicians. But before these can be put into effect, a majority of citizens must give up their belief in and desire for punishment and revenge and the idea that the threat of violent punishment is an effective deterrent to crime.

* * * * *

Violent defense against thieves and burglars arises out of our ideas about property and the true nature of the self. Most

[10] See Henry A. Cotton, *The Defective, Delinquent and Insane,* in Dr. Cotton's 1953 report as Medical Director and Director of Research of the New Jersey State Hospital.

killings by thieves and other criminals are not strictly "in cold blood," but out of fear that the victim will somehow harm the criminal. If the threatened victim is wholly unafraid, friendly, kind, generous and imaginative, there is relatively small chance of his receiving physical injury.[11]

Such considerations indicate that it will be eventually possible and practicable to forego violent defense of property. It is a part of the duty of non-violent resisters to help bring about such a state of affairs. It will be for mankind as a whole a slow process, but there is no reason why the progress should not be steady and sometimes, and in some places, rapid.

It is interesting to realize that non-violent resistance can be used both by the state and the prisoners. If the state considers itself the injured party and the criminal the attacker, it can offer him non-violent reformatory treatment. If the criminal is mentally competent and feels that really he is the victim of an unjust social system and brutal wardens and police, he too may offer non-violent resistance and do his share toward prison reform. . . .

In some instances where innocent men have been sentenced to long imprisonments and even death, there has been much severe criticism directed against the governors, judges and other officials involved. This seems to me a waste of energy based on a misconception of the real forces at work. The fault does not lie with the men in office. The real causes are psychological and spiritual, and it is these and this institutionalized form that must be resisted and transformed. Governments are the external results of inner concepts and attitudes. They are the institutionalized forms of our habitual inner attitudes and ideas. Each one of us is partly responsible. The re-education must be directed primarily at this foundation, though, of course, it should find expression in all situations and relationships.

The police system also needs constant modification in the direction of less violence. Certain police functions are necessary in any complex modern society—such as directing traffic in city streets, providing information for strangers, helping to settle altercations without violence, helping lost children, directing large crowds, providing a disciplined orderly nucleus of leaders and helpers in times of public disaster such as fires, floods, earthquakes, severe storms, epidemics of disease, etc. Even after the advantages of non-violence become widely recognized, there will still be people whose habits of violence persist, whose self-control is poor, or who will still occasionally

---

[11] See Allan A. Hunter, *Courage in Both Hands* (New York: Fellowship, 1951) and *Three Trumpets Sound* (New York: Association Press, 1939).

hope to gain their ends by violence. For a generation or two after such recognition, it may be necessary to permit the police to use a greatly restricted amount of physical compulsion in certain cases where physical violence has already been used or overtly threatened by some other person. Long experience in England indicates that under such circumstances probably no firearms, sticks or brutality would be needed. . . .

AN EFFECTIVE SUBSTITUTE FOR WAR

Despite the horrors, futilities and destructiveness of war, there are nevertheless certain virtues and truths associated with it which humanity cannot afford to lose. In any discussion of new ways of settling conflicts, these military virtues cannot safely be disregarded.

Before the First World War, the romance and glamor of war was an undoubted fact, especially for those who never had taken part in war. The two world wars have destroyed all the glamor. Yet there is in all hearts a desire to live a significant life, to serve a great idea and sacrifice oneself for a noble cause, to feel the thrill of spiritual unity with one's fellows and to act in accordance therewith. We all wish for strenuous action and the exercise of courage and fortitude, to be carried away by the enthusiasm of daring. We all love to undergo a common discipline and hardship for the sake of a fine ideal; to be in good effective order; to be strong, generous and self-reliant; to be physically fit, with body, mind and soul harmoniously working together for a great purpose, thus becoming a channel of immense energies. Under such conditions, the whole personality is alert, conscious, unified and living profoundly, richly and exaltedly. Then one can be truly and gloriously happy. Martial music suggests many of these elements and their consequent exhilaration and exaltation.

Probably war and conflict seem to promise such results partly because our ordinary life of alleged peace is so often dull, trivial, monotonous and devoid of fine purpose. It is so full of frustration, resentments, balked disposition, hidden violence, oppression, pettiness and meanness; so insipid, fragmentary, full of cross-purposes and evil.

"Such a hopeless snarl, Anything to be relieved of such a mess!" So cries the heart. Yet what a risk, to wrench ourselves from established life.

One reason why we take such deep delight in risk attending the search for this release is that such adventures may turn possibilities into accomplished facts. They are modes of creation, of "free activity of the soul," as Clausewitz says. Hence, after men have long been chained to an industrial routine, feeling themselves helpless cogs in a vast machine, the call of an immeasurable risk cannot easily be resisted. But war is attractive not merely for its orderly action and sense of unity for a great purpose; it also has solid elements of truth and virtue.

The most outstanding virtue of violence is that of courage. But violence is not the only occasion for test or proof of courage.

Another virtue is energy. All the deep emotions, especially fear and anger, are generators of tremendous energy. To be a channel of immense energy gives one a thrill and a satisfaction that can never be forgotten. Fear, anger and hatred are doubtless evil, but the energy that they arouse is, by itself, good; for as William Blake said, energy is divine.

Furthermore, the sincerity of many fighters and warriors is admirable. They live and work, sacrifice and die for their vision of the truth, even though they may be too inarticulate to express it in words. . . .

Another virtue of the militarists which deserves our admiration is discipline. Discipline establishes and maintains effective habits, creates solidarity and reliability, promotes self-respect and elicits respect from others.

The militarist is right when he says that conflict is an inevitable part of life. This world is inherently diverse and changing, and since human beings differ so much in the values they hold, in environment, inheritance, intelligence, tolerance and unselfishness, and are so bound by tradition and habit, the adjustments involved in change and growth necessarily result in conflicts. No strong or sensible person would want to abolish growth or change or the positive achievements that often issue from struggle. Struggle is a part of the very meaning of life.

These, then, seem to be the important virtues of the violent fighter: enterprise, courage, strenuous action, and endurance; sincerity, devotion and a sense of unity with one's own kind; order, training and discipline. His truth that conflict is inevitable is another element of his strength.

All these virtues and truths of war are given full scope and exercise in the non-violent method of settling great disputes. If any nation or group adopts mass non-violent resistance, no moral losses will result.

Walter Lippmann, in an excellent article on "The Political Equivalent of War," quotes from William James' essay, "The Moral Equivalent of War,"[12] and continues:

[12] In William James, *Memories and Studies* (New York: Longmans, 1911). An abridgement of the essay is more conveniently available in *Living Ideas in America*, ed. by Henry Steele Commager, (New York: Harper, 1951).

"It is not sufficient to propose an equivalent for the military virtues. It is even more important to work out an equivalent for the military methods and objectives. For the institution of war is not merely an expression of the military spirit. It is not a mere release of certain subjective impulses clamoring for expression. It is also—and, I think, primarily—one of the ways by which great human decisions are made. If that is true, then the abolition of war depends primarily upon inventing and organizing other ways of deciding those issues which hitherto have been decided by war. . . .

"Any real program of peace must rest on the premise that there will be causes of dispute as long as we can foresee, and that those disputes have to be decided, and that a way of deciding them must be found which is not war."[13]

"A way of deciding them which is not war." Is that way non-violent resistance? Closer examination shows that it satisfies Lippmann's requirements. Non-violent resistance not only utilizes the military virtues; it uses also on a moral plane many of the military methods and principles; it employs many of the same psychological processes; and it even retains some of the military objectives, with moral modifications. Military men know much about human nature, but non-violent resisters know still more. If war has been in the past a practical method of making great human decisions, of settling great disputes, this new method will be still more effective for such a purpose.

The very principles of military strategy operate in this new mode of struggle.

Clausewitz's principles of war have been summarized by a British writer as follows:

"Retaining the initiative, using the defensive as the decisive form of action, concentration of force at the decisive point, the determination of that point, the superiority of the moral factor to purely material resources, the proper relation between attack and defense, and the will to victory.[14]

Other authorities state them somewhat differently, Foch, for instance, laying more stress on the offensive.

We have seen that the non-violent resister begins an entirely new line of conduct. He seizes and maintains the moral initiative. He uses the principle of surprise most effectively. Clause-

[13] Walter Lippmann, "The Political Equivalent of War," in the *Atlantic Monthly,* August 1928, p. 181 f.
[14] A. A. Walser, "Air Power," in *The Nineteenth Century and After* (London), April 1923, p. 598.

witz said: "surprise plays a much greater part in strategy than in tactics; it is the most powerful element of victory,"[15] and a long line of military authorities agree.

The surprise of non-violent resistance is effective partly because it is startling and partly because the opponent is so bound by his violent habits that he is ill-prepared to utilize the new tactics himself. He is like a wrestler using European methods pitted against a Japanese using jiu-jitsu. The surprise of non-violent resistance, unlike that of war, is not due to deceit or stratagem but simply to its novelty and daring.

* * * * *

. . . Non-violent resistance is not directed against the *energy* of the opponent's desires but merely against their immediate direction, form or method. It seeks to discover for him a new and wiser channel for his energy.

This does not mean reducing the conflict to a tame debating society. Although sometimes a safe and easy issue of the conflict may be found, the non-violent resister may feel assured of a fair probability that he will sooner or later have to suffer hardships and perhaps wounds, imprisonment and even death. If the struggle is against a powerful group, a corporation, a government or an established system of socio-economic beliefs, and is prolonged, the resisters may have to suffer a great deal. "War is hell," and in a long struggle soldiers and police may abandon all restraints. We assume that the peaceful resister is really in earnest, really believes in his cause, is ready to sacrifice for it, and is no more a coward than any soldier is. He must take risks. This is a real adventure, no parlor make-believe for pretenders or boasters.

But psychologically, non-violent resistance differs in one respect from war. The object is not to make the opponent believe that he is crushed, but to persuade him to realize that he can attain practical security, or whatever else his ultimate desire may be, by easier and surer means than he saw formerly. The effort is furthermore to help him work out such new means, not rigidly or on any *a priori* plan, but flexibly in accordance with the deepest growing truth of the entire situation in all its bearings. Non-violence does not destroy the opponent's courage, but merely alters his belief that his will and desire must be satisfied only in *his* way. Thus he is led to see the situation in a broader, more fundamental and far-sighted way, so as to work out a solution which will more nearly satisfy both parties in the light of a new set of conditions.

[15] Karl von Clausewitz, *On War,* tr. by Col J. J. Graham (New York: Dutton, 1914), Vol. 3, p. 210. See also B. H. Liddell Hart, *The Real War, 1914–1918* (Boston: Little, 1930), p. 446.

Does the non-violent resister "concentrate his force at the decisive point," and is he active in "the determination of that point"? He certainly is. He decides, with Marshal Saxe, that "the secret of victory lies in the hearts of human beings"—that is, that it is a matter of psychology. Therefore he concentrates upon the psychological forces in the situation, and deals with them as efficiently and powerfully as he possibly can. And in so far as concentration means bringing strength to bear against weakness, he does that also, for in this moral or psychological field he is far stronger and better prepared than his opponent.

*   *   *   *   *

"The proper relation between attack and defense" has been very searchingly considered by the peaceful resister. He knows that the best relation of all between these two energies is not one of opposition but of resolution, integration and sublimation. He thus enables both sides to win, and conquers both his own possible short-sightedness of aim and that of his enemy at the same time. The result is not a triumphant victor on the one side and a despondent, repressed vanquished on the other. Both sides are happy in the joint victory of their better selves and the common defeat of their mistakes.

Does the peaceful resister have the "will to conquer" which Foch calls "the first condition of victory"?[16] He surely does. Indeed, he must have an indomitable will to victory in order to endure the suffering put upon him. . . .

There are other principles of strategy which also find parallels here—such principles as the economy of forces, the importance of information, mobility, endurance, etc.—but we need not discuss all of these. The similarities to the principles of military strategy are clear.

But the similarities between war and non-violent resistance are not merely an interesting set of analogies. This entire chapter up to this point answers two doubts: namely, whether this method of struggle is not utterly foreign and new and suited only to Oriental peoples, and therefore whether it could be adopted by people with the modern Western attitude of mind. The facts that the military virtues are used and needed in this new form of struggle, and that the principles of military strategy apply here too, show that if we adopt this new mode of settling conflicts we will not be entirely reversing our previous experience, nor abandoning whatever true principles and val-

[16] Marshal Foch, *Principles of War* (New York: H. K. Fly, 1918), p. 316.

ues the human race may have garnered from its age-long experience of war.

*　*　*　*　*

In cases where Asians and Africans have tried to relieve themselves of the economic and military pressure of European domination, they have complained that the West cannot understand any language but that of force. If that is true, it means that the West will be utterly unprepared and helpless in the face of well-disciplined, thoroughly organized and wisely led non-violent resistance, especially if it is accompanied by an equally thorough temporary non-vindictive economic boycott. The strategic principle of surprise would operate most dramatically and effectively. . . . But I am inclined to think that the West will come to understand the new language fairly soon, once it is shown to be strong language. Already there is a partial understanding of the new language, and considerable worry to boot. The grant of freedom to Ghana by the British government is one instance of this.

If, in some future conflict, both sides should use non-violent resistance, that side would win which most deeply understood and was best disciplined and prepared in this new method. That would be the side which achieved the most self-purification, which attained the most social truth and showed the finest love. It would thereby attain the greater inner unity and strength, the greater respect from its opponents and the public.

In summary, we see that non-violent resistance resembles war in these eight ways: (1) It has a psychological and moral aim and effect. (2) It is a discipline of a parallel emotion and instinct. (3) It operates against the morale of the opponents. (4) It is similar in principles of strategy. (5) It is a method of settling great disputes and conflicts. (6) It requires courage, dynamic energy, capacity to endure fatigue and suffering, self-sacrifice, self-control, chivalry, action. (7) It is positive and powerful. (8) It affords an opportunity of service for a large idea, and for glory.

It does not avoid hardships, suffering, wounds or even death. In using it men and women may still risk their lives and fortunes and sacrifice all. Nevertheless, the possibilities of casualties and death are greatly reduced under it, and they are all suffered voluntarily and not imposed by the non-violent resisters.

In the Indian struggle for independence, though I know of no accurate statistics, hundreds of thousands of Indians went to jail, probably not more than five hundred received permanent physical injuries, and probably not over eight thousand were killed immediately or died later from wounds. No British, I believe, were killed or wounded. Considering the importance and size of the conflict and the many years it lasted, these numbers are much smaller than they would have been if the Indians had used violence toward the British.

* * * * *

Considering the completeness of its effects, non-violent resistance is as quick and probably quicker than war. It is a weapon that can be used equally well by small or large nations or groups, by the economically weak and by the apparently strong, and even by individuals. It compels both sides and neutrals to seek the truth, whereas war blinds both sides and neutrals to the truth.

As we have already seen and will show further, non-violent resistance certainly produces less ill-effects, if any, than war does, and this decrease of ill-effects applies to the users of non-violence, to the opposing side, and to society and the world at large.

It is interesting to note that in early 1958 there was published a book by a British naval officer (not a pacifist), Commander Sir Stephen King-Hall, in which he argues that non-violent resistance is now the best and only possible successful mode of defense of Great Britain against armed attack. He argues the points in detail and cogently: "We must," he says, "ask ourselves this question: 'If the contribution of violence (*i.e.*, military operations) to the settlement of differences of opinion or conflicts (*werre*) between sovereign states has evolved to such intensity that it is totally destructive, has not violence outlived its usefulness in disputes between large states?' It looks to me as if this is the truth. Bearing in mind that in major disputes violence has become equated with nuclear energy violence, I am forced to consider what possibilities are open to us if we exclude violence from our defense plans on the grounds that violence has become our master instead of our slave."[17] Many other keen thinkers all through the West agree that nuclear weapons have destroyed the effectiveness of war as a means to settle large disputes between nations.

May we not then fairly describe non-violent resistance as an effective substitute for war?

It is realistic in that it does not eliminate or attempt to eliminate possibilities of conflict and differences of interest, and includes *all* factors in the situation—both material and imponderable, physical and psychological.

* * * * *

[17] *Defense in the Nuclear Age* (London: Gollancz), p. 110.

PART II

NON-VIOLENT POWER
WITHOUT EXPRESS PRINCIPLE

In Part I, we were concerned primarily with conceptions of violence, non-violence, and non-violent struggle.

The readings in Part II center primarily on instances of non-violent resistance largely unguided by previously thought-out doctrines. In considerable degree, that is to say, the readings in this Part provide case studies in what might be called non-violent resistance for want of other methods. It has often been observed that when groups or nations are unarmed and yet feel that they are suffering injustice of some kind they turn to non-violent struggle. They may have no exponent of a philosophy of non-violence to provide standards and no previously disciplined groups of resisters. Yet the sense of injustice is so strong and the awareness of military helplessness so great that they almost instinctively adopt many of the strategies and tactics that theorists of non-violence have worked out.

The first selection in this Part is a review by Barthélemy de Ligt of the effectiveness of non-violent struggle in general. In his survey, he includes illustrations both of "spontaneous" non-violent struggle (as in our Part II) and of what might be termed principled non-violence (our Part III). De Ligt was himself firmly convinced that, at least under modern circumstances, non-violent resistance was the only form of group struggle that gave promise of resolving conflicts and preserving the contestants' legitimate claims.

The other readings in Part II serve to illustrate the wide variety of circumstances under which some form of more or less spontaneous non-violent struggle has been used. Reading 10 suggests that it was responsible for one of the greatest political changes in the history of the ancient Roman Republic. Reading 11 tells of the non-violent demonstration of the Jews against the armed might of Rome in the days of the Emperor Caligula. Reading 12 summarizes a few significant general strikes: although most of them were only partially "successful" (depending, of course, on how one defines that term), all of them were important episodes in our experience with non-violent non-co-operation.

The nineteenth century was an age of wars for liberation and of violent revolutions for freedom. In a day when ordinary citizens could still afford roughly the same kinds of arms as those often used by the government, appeals to the barricades were frequent. But there was one struggle for national autonomy, according to Arthur Griffith, which was carried on in considerable degree by non-violent resistance. Hungary became an equal partner with Austria in the "Dual Monarchy" established in 1867; and this result was brought about in great measure through the leadership of Francis Deák, who insisted that non-violent tactics were the only ones that would work under the circumstances. Reading 13 is Griffith's perhaps overly dramatized account of the Hungarian struggle.

The overriding question about non-violent struggle usually asked in our day is: "Can it be used against totalitarian regimes?" This is the issue to which Readings 14 and 15 address themselves. The answer they provide is not a conclusive one; but Norwegian resistance against the German occupation during World War II and the dramatic strike in the Soviet Union's Vorkuta camp must certainly be given serious consideration in any judgment about the future of non-violent resistance. In neither instance, it should be emphasized, were the participants familiar with the general idea of non-violent resistance; nor were they prepared through previous training for its rigors and demands.

In examining instances where non-violent resistance played a large role, we should never forget that it was not the only factor in the whole situation. Beyond the immediate context affected by non-violent strategies were always wider historical trends and contingencies militating for or against the objectives of the struggle. Like violent conflict, non-violent struggle is conditioned by the larger environment within which it occurs, so that it is often difficult to say what element or elements play the major part in effecting the ultimate result. Thus Roman imperial politics, as well as Jewish non-violent resistance, helped shape the outcome under Caligula; and international events strongly conditioned the result in nineteenth-century Hungary and 1953 Vorkuta. Under some circumstances, non-violent struggle would appear to be doomed to ineffectiveness, even with careful preparation. Under other conditions, and even with little preparation, it might give promise of considerable success.

Although most of the readings in this part offer examples of more or less unprincipled non-violent resistance, we should not make the dichotomy between expedient and principled non-violence too sharp. Almost every act of collective non-violence involves at least a minimal preparation; and while the scheme of thought of which this planning is the expression may not be highly developed, there is often an embryonic framework. Thus in several of the general strikes, we find resistance guided by rather elaborate codes of discipline which were themselves based on something akin to a partially developed theory of non-violent action. Perhaps we might say that in Part II the use of non-violent resistance *implies* a theory of non-violent struggle; whereas the illustrations in Part III exemplify an *explicit* doctrine.

9. Barthélemy de Ligt: THE EFFECTIVENESS OF NON-VIOLENT STRUGGLE

Many of those who have written about non-violent struggle have been impressed by the fact that under modern circumstances the utilization of violence for purposes of fundamental social change is usually self-defeating. Today all the advantages of modern weapons rest with the State, and therefore, whatever the moral issues may be, many thinkers have concluded that it is nearly impossible to use violence effectively against those wielding public authority.

But there remains the question whether non-violent struggle can be effective. To show that violent attacks on inequitable governments can hardly be successful under twentieth-century conditions does not in itself demonstrate that non-violent strategies will yield better results. The author of our next selection, however, believes they will, particularly when one considers the disproportion in the price, in terms of suffering and degradation, paid for gain.

Barthélemy de Ligt was a great Dutch anarchist theorist who devoted a large part of his life to the study of violence and non-violence in human affairs. He wrote this general survey of the possibilities of non-violent struggle from the viewpoint of an agnostic revolutionary who had reached the conclusion, on strictly utilitarian grounds, that in neither war nor social struggle could violence be an effective instrument for human liberation.

De Ligt compares violent and non-violent struggles in terms of the span of time necessary, the chances for success, and the toll taken in human suffering, and examines the efficacy of such methods as the general strike and non-payment of taxes. He discusses the tradition of non-violence in Western revolutionary thought and its relation to the prevention of war, the reform of the social order, and the treatment of criminals, bringing together strands of thought from such diverse sources as John Ruskin, Gandhi, William Morris, Georges Sorel, and the Irish Land League.

The essay is excerpted from de Ligt's *The Conquest of Violence: an Essay on War and Revolution,* published in Honor Tracy's English translation by E. P. Dutton & Co., New York, 1938. De Ligt is also the author of *La Paix creatrice,* an important study in which he examined the problems of non-violent power and peace in various cultures and epochs in history.

How much more noble non-violent methods of struggle are than the violent! And how much more effective, when they are well prepared.

In the Transvaal, a country which in spite of the justice of its cause, the religious fanaticism of its people, its famous marksmen and a favourable position was unable to hold out against the brutality of British imperialism—in the Transvaal at the beginning of the century there lived a group of Hindu immigrés, subject to harsh and special laws, which shackled them socially and economically and were profoundly offensive to their dignity as human beings.

Indian coolies were employed in the mines of Natal and elsewhere in South Africa, and they were tied to their work by five-year contracts. As a rule, they were very industrious. A great number of Indians, once their contracts had expired, stayed behind in the country to set up as small peasants or tradesmen. At the beginning of this century, there were 12,500 in the Transvaal. The white people, although they themselves had formerly penetrated into the country by violence, soon began to look on these peaceable rivals as undesirable intruders.

In 1906 these Indians were placed on the same footing as criminals: every one of them had to report regularly to the police and have his finger-prints taken. On the advice of their fellow countryman, Gandhi, a Hindu lawyer at Pretoria, some thousands of them decided to ignore the new regulation and to bear the penalties incurred by this infraction in a dignified manner. Meanwhile they continued to look on those who were treating them with mistrust and cruelty as their fellow men and only appealed to their human feelings. They did not wish to overcome by violence, but by *satyagraha,* or sacrifice and moral force, according to the methods of civil disobedience.

The Government met this entirely non-violent rebellion with severe imprisonments. The non-violent combatants were even threatened economically. But enthusiasm was high and solidarity great, the more so as the whole movement was based on the ancient Hindu tradition of *ahimsa,* the religious belief in non-violence.

Gandhi, who had already been in prison, went to London in 1910 to make a personal appeal to the British Government. But they would not yield. In 1912, all marriages according to Hindu law were declared illegal, with the result that all offspring of these marriages were considered to be illegitimate and therefore unable to inherit. Further, an extraordinary tax was imposed on every Indian living in Africa. Up till then, the struggle had been carried on only by the small bourgeoisie—peasants and tradesmen. Now Gandhi called on the Indian workers as well, on the coolies working in the mines. Indian women made demonstrations in the mining districts and urged their countrymen everywhere to stop work until the wicked measures of the British Government were done away with. And so it was that the strike was added to the non-co-operation. The Government was on the verge of relaxing and promised to do away with the poll-tax, but the Hindus wanted this to be done immediately and further demanded full recognition of their rights. They organized a great demonstration which spread all over the Transvaal.

Large detachments of police were mobilized. Gandhi was arrested. But his non-violent army went on its way without a leader. Once more, Gandhi was released but when he rejoined his comrades he found that large numbers of the demonstrators were being seized upon, packed into trains and sent back to their own country.

But they had attained their object: public opinion was shaken. Gandhi had just been sent to prison for the third time, for a period of fifteen months, when the Government finally gave in. In 1913, the poll-tax was abolished, the validity of Hindu marriages was recognized and the Indian immigrants obtained the same rights as the other South African citizens. The one-time Boer general, Smuts, who had declared in 1906 that he would never abolish the special laws had to acknowledge himself morally defeated.

One thing is indisputable, and that is, that if this little handful of men had offered armed resistance to the violence of the British, they would have been crushed, and more fearfully than ever the Boers were—for these had been more numerous, better equipped and much more favourably placed from the strategic point of view, than the Hindu immigrants.

And besides, such an attitude was no novelty for the Indians. For example, when the British Government had introduced an extremely unjust tax in 1912, the population of Benares retaliated by practising non-co-operation and paralysed the life of the community, by simply refusing to work for their rulers. The natives obeyed the leaders they had chosen under a free discipline. The British Government had to give way and the tax was abolished.

The Indians have often used similar methods in their struggle against native tyranny. In 1830, in the State of Mysore, the entire population refused to work in the fields or to pay their taxes, leaving their villages and retiring to the forests as a protest against the intolerable exploitation of a native despot. Nowhere—as the official report of the British Government stated—was there any disorder. None resorted to arms. "The natives understand very well the use of such measures to defend themselves against the abuse of authority. The method most in use, and that which gives the best results, is complete non-co-operation in all that concerns the Government, the administration and public life generally."

How much more effective non-violence is than violence as a means of carrying on a struggle, especially when it is against heavily armed powers, is shown by what happened at the beginning of the century in Bengal. There again, under the leadership of Aurobindo Ghose, sprang up an energetic non-co-operation movement to combat the scandalous measures of the British Government. They ignored the entire administration systematically, by ceasing to co-operate with the Government in any department whatever. At the same time, they boycotted all British goods. Tagore, by his passionate songs, inspired his countrymen to sacrifice possessions and life itself for the liberation of their country. They built up stakes and burnt everything English on them: woven materials and other merchandise. Ghose wished his people to be so independent that they could supply their material and spiritual needs without paying tribute to a foreigner.

As the British Government refused to give way, the Bengalese turned against the British régime as such. Ghose called on his compatriots not only to ignore official authority but also, and above all, to help themselves in order that they might thereby demonstrate their fitness for political and economic independence: they were to fight against bad hygienic conditions, found schools everywhere, establish a network of roads, develop agriculture, etc. But the masses had become impatient, let themselves be carried away by fanatical leaders and fell back on violence. The British Government asked nothing better. They seized the opportunity of pitilessly crushing this movement, which had begun so well.

So it was not surprising if, in 1917, the peasants of Champaran resorted once more to non-violent weapons. They were forced by law to plant indigo on three-twentieths of their land and subjected to all kinds of oppressive measures on the part of the planters. Gandhi, who had returned to India, set about examining the situation of the peasants. Much disturbed, the planters demanded of the authorities that Gandhi should be expelled from the country. They did actually order Gandhi to leave the district at once. To which Gandhi replied that he had come on purpose, from a sense of duty, that he had done nothing but state certain facts perfectly calmly and that he would remain in the district to finish his task, being at the same time ready to undergo the punishment incurred by his dis-obedience. Without letting themselves be intimidated, he and his friends continued their campaign. But thenceforward, po-lice officials were present and took notes of all that went on. Gandhi and his collaborators organized their work in such a way that in case the leader was imprisoned or banished, two of them were able to carry on the inquiry, and if these were imprisoned in turn, two others would replace them and so on.

Gandhi was called before the court. He confessed he was guilty in the eyes of the law and declared that there was a con-flict of duty in him. Should he obey the law, or his own con-science and serve the truly humane purpose for which he had come to the country? It was left to the British administration to assume the responsibility of eventually turning him out. The authorities deferred judgment and before it was pronounced the Lieutenant-Governor gave orders that Gandhi should be set free to pursue his inquiry. The Governor, having himself had a discussion with Gandhi, set up a Governmental Commission of Inquiry, of which Gandhi was a member. This Commission was not long in recognizing that the law about indigo and the exactions of the planters were unjust. The law in question was abolished and the peasants had gained their cause without any violence whatever having been used.

*   *   *   *   *

We saw again in 1924, how the Untouchables of the Vykom village, in the Travancore State in South India, carried on, under the guidance of Gandhi and his friends, a struggle against the Brahmans, who for reasons of caste had forbidden them the entry of a certain raised route which was of great importance for trade. At that time, Gandhi was lying ill a hundred kilometres from the above-mentioned village. But the leaders of the movement came to get his advice on their plan of campaign, and kept in touch with him by letter and wire. These leaders, accompanied by some of the Untouch-ables, proceeded along the forbidden way towards the Brah-man quarters. They were cruelly beaten by their enemies: one of them was grievously wounded, but refrained from offering any violence in return. A number of them were then arrested by the police for having incited the Untouchables to break the law. They were sentenced to penalties which went up to one year in prison. But immediately, and from all parts of the country, volunteers surged towards the forbidden road to take their place. The Government made no further arrests and enjoined on the police that they were to prevent any of the "re-formers" from crossing the road. Then, at the instigation of Gandhi, the "reformers" placed themselves before the police cordon in the attitude of prayer. In six-hour shifts, they kept up this singular struggle for months, in order to soften the hearts of the Brahmans. More than once these non-violent combatants found themselves plunged up to their necks in water after a downpour, while the police maintained their cordon in boats above the water. At such times the Untouchables would relieve each other every three hours.

This action, seemingly so naïve, had nevertheless the effect of making this vexed question discussed through the whole of India. At last, in the autumn of 1925, after six months' strug-gle, the Brahmans gave way, perceiving that they could not hold out against such moral force. And the Untouchables were allowed to use the road, to pass the temple and to cross the Brahman quarters. This was the first of a whole series of re-forms with regard to the caste system.

And finally in 1928, the peasants of Bardoli Taluca, in the Bombay province, numbering 90,000, opposed by non-violent methods an agrarian tax which was swallowing up as much as 60 per cent. of their revenues. The Government ignored all protests. Under the direction of Vallabbhai Patel and the in-spiration of Gandhi, the peasants refused to pay their taxes although State representatives confiscated their goods and sold their lands. Insults, threats, even terrorization on the part of the Government did nothing but strengthen the moral com-bativity of the peasants who went on to a complete boycott of everything of an official nature. The local newspapers could speak of nothing but this enterprise, and sympathy was aroused throughout India. The matter was not only debated in the British administration in India, but even in the London Parliament. After six months of non-violent struggle, the un-just taxes were abolished.

* * * * *

In 1921, India gave, under Gandhi's guidance, its first great example of national civil disobedience. We know the character of such an undertaking: a social group, a class, a people, acts in many circumstances as if the Government did not exist and ignores it systematically in the whole of economic and social life. The schools stand empty, the laws are not carried out, taxes do not come in, etc. Above all, obedience is refused to certain decrees or laws the abolition of which is the primary aim. Very often, such a full-stop or check in the life of the community is accompanied by strikes as well as by a refusal to sell or buy those goods the sale of which is a profit to the en-emy. In India, for instance, it is salt, alcohol and English woven materials. And so, joined to non-co-operation, we have the boycott, a method of struggle which is of the greatest efficacy, as China has been showing for 3,000 years past. Drawing their inspiration from age-old religious and moral conceptions, the Indian non-co-operators bear even the most cruel attacks of police and army, and the punishments laid down for breaking the law, with resignation, prepared as they are to suffer endlessly for the triumph of their cause. One can persecute them, ill-treat them, throw them into prison, they only hold the faster to the moral and spiritual forces by which they are ruled, rising above the base violence their enemies use, although they still appeal to them as their fellow men.

Even more remarkable than the abstention from any kind of violence in the unarmed combatants is the absence of all fear before the aggressor and the absence of all hatred against the enemy. Even they go so far as to show profound confidence in the better feelings of those against whom they are struggling.

The world knows for the best part how much of moral and spiritual force was shown by the awakened India in this struggle, and how, in the course of non-violent demonstrations and picketings before the shops, alcohol booths, etc., men and women—women especially—the young and the old, vied with each other in heroism. The British Empire had to give way: India won its first great victory. This country, which did not possess a single military means of defence, would never have won such a victory by non-pacific methods over the hyper-modern violence of the adversary.

"However, the Indians are still far from being free!"

But why do they always judge non-violent methods of fighting in a different way from the homicidal methods? Even in war the first victory is seldom the decisive one. A struggle, whether violent or otherwise, as a rule goes on for years. It is made up of luck and ill-luck, of victories and defeats, and only in the more favoured cases does it end in a decisive victory for one side or the other.

In spite of some temporary successes, how remote a hope of success the Netherlands seemed to have, in their War of Independence against Spain in the sixteenth century. It took them eighty years (1568–1648) to achieve their goal, and success was very far from being complete even then, since they had to give up the whole southern part of the land. The Indian struggle for independence will certainly take less time.[1]

*   *   *   *   *

[1] Indian political independence was finally achieved in 1947. —Ed.

"But, you will object, Gandhi is a Hindu. He follows a religious tradition that is hundreds of years old. He is a saint, an ascetic. How does such an example affect us? In India, non-violence is a traditional form of religion, while our Christianity is impregnated with violence through and through."

We can reply that other Indians, who do not reject violence in principle and follow utterly different religious and moral traditions from those of Gandhi, have been so impressed by the efficacy of his fighting methods that they have adopted them. As is known, the British Army of Occupation in India recruits chiefly from among the Sikhs. These people, whose religion goes so far as to forbid them to lay down their sabres, had a serious quarrel with the Government during the period 1922 to 1924 on the subject of the control of certain properties belonging to some temples. Unable to solve the matter by violence, they decided to try direct, non-violent action. Proud and immovable, the sword at their side but their arms crossed, they put up with the most brutal behaviour on the part of the British police and Army without offering the slightest physical resistance, until they had obtained what they wanted.

This shows that non-violent methods of struggle are not bound up with the person of Gandhi in particular, nor with any special form of religion. This is shown still more clearly by what happened with the Pathans, in Northern India. These tribes are well-known for their passion for revenge. Very touchy, intolerant of the slightest offence, the Pathans were accustomed to respond immediately with violence. That is, until 1930, when Abdul Ghaffar Khan, a Mahometan leader of the Puritan Revolution, the "Khudai Khitmatgars" or Servants of God, and therefore outside the ancient Hindu tradition of non-violence, managed to convince them of the efficacy of unarmed resistance. From that day on, the British Government tried in vain to shatter the collective action of the "Red Shirts." This movement, which in April 1930 had 500 members, had 40,000 three months later and, towards the end of the year, 300,000.[2] Persecutions, imprisonments, executions without trial, so far have not shaken their courage.

In August 1934, several leaders were set free after two years of prison, among others Abdul Ghaffar Khan himself, the "Gandhi of the frontier provinces," though he was not allowed to go back to the Punjab or the north-west district. In December 1934, the papers announced that Abdul Ghaffar Khan, "that fine man and true, beloved of millions" had again been sentenced to two years imprisonment, on account of a speech he made at Bombay, where he remarked that the part

[2] Jawaharlal Nehru, *India and the World* (London: Allen & Unwin, 1936), p. 76.

played by the British police was not to protect the Indian population but to persecute them and make false charges against them. He had further stated that in the northern provinces, some Hindu soldiers had refused to fire on a quiet and unarmed crowd, and that some British troops had then opened fire, killing more than 200 people in a few minutes.

*   *   *   *   *

In the middle of the last century, the French revolutionary Anselm Bellegarrigue, as a consequence of his social and political experiences in the United States and in France, lost all confidence both in the Governments whose very nature is violence and in revolutions from the moment they allow themselves to be involved in bloodshed: in one case as in the other, everything rests in the final analysis on oppression and murder, and once caught in this trap there is no way of getting out. The barricades, in his view, are usually raised by those who wish to rule against those who are ruling. Let us do away with all forms of Government and govern ourselves in reasonable fashion, and henceforward all barricades will be superfluous for ever.

"In the end," Bellegarrigue goes on, "there are no tyrants, only slaves." The Socialist movement has only arisen from the profound thirst of humanity for freedom. The exercise of power, even in the name of Socialism, can only kill it. A people is always too much governed.

That is why Bellegarrigue spread the idea of a *refusal of assistance,* which is identified with the principle of non-co-operation and civil disobedience. He developed a whole "theory of calm" which opens up possibilities of overcoming even the most powerful régime "by abstention and inertia." Everything must succumb to the power of Abstention: social privileges, unjust taxes, spy systems, military hierarchies, must all give way before it, when the masses withdraw their support from the régime of violence and concentrate on their own moral force.

*   *   *   *   *

So the non-violent methods of struggle are not bound then either to a particular religion or to a special race or people. European and American lovers of freedom discover its worth just as much as Hindu mystics, rebellious Negroes and warlike Sikhs. Besides, the general strike, practised as much by English, Russian and Scandinavian Socialists as by French, Italian, Spanish and South American anarchists and syndicalists, and regarded since the beginning of the century as a typically proletarian means of struggle, is in itself a way of action foreign to the traditional violent methods. . . .

*   *   *   *   *

The revolutionary syndicalist Sorel, a well-known atheist, whose doctrine is anything but a plea for non-violence, has clearly defined the difference between "Bourgeois force" and "Proletarian violence" (we should say: bourgeois violence and proletarian strength). Sorel sees in the general strike a sublimation of war, a method of fighting which is fundamentally in keeping with the dignity of the proletariat. To fight against the terror of the bourgeoisie, which rears its system on the ruin of its enemies and whose political inquisition claims more victims than the old Holy Inquisition ever did, there is no need for the proletariat to institute a counter-terror. It must, also, oppose all wars of conquest, a crime typical of bourgeois rapacity. The proletariat has a very different task to perform than aping the bourgeois fighting methods, a thing which Sorel reproaches Marx for having too easily forgotten: "Too often, he follows inspirations which belong to the past: in his writings, he even includes a good deal of old rubbish."[3]

That Western egoist Max Stirner, a well-known atheist who in no way adhered to the school of absolute non-violence did nevertheless recognize that the greatest power the workers had lay in the possibility of their withdrawing their working-power from the bourgeoisie and feudal powers. The State only rests, according to him, on the enslavement of labour. The instant labour frees itself, the State is lost. That is why he, too, urges the necessity of general strikes.[4]

And in many popular meetings in the West they recited this verse of Herwegh:

> Mann der Arbeit aufgewacht
> Und erkenne deine Macht!
> Alle Räder stehen still
> Wenn dein starker Arm es will.[5]

The German libertarian, John Henry Mackay, of Scottish origin, a supporter of extreme individualism, based on egoism, also regarded passive resistance as the only means the masses had to defend themselves effectively against aggressive violence.[6]

Mackay was deeply influenced by Benjamin Tucker, who, while he admitted the right of each man to defend himself by violence, had come by way of purely utilitarian considerations

[3] Georges Sorel, *Réflexions sur la Violence* (1908), p. 266.
[4] Stirner, *Der Einziger und sein Eigentum* (1845), p. 148.
[5] Working Man, awake!
   Learn your own power,
   All the wheels are still
   If your strong arm so wishes it.
[6] See his novel, *The Anarchists*.

to the conclusion that passive resistance was the best means of defence for the oppressed masses. He considers it to be the only way of breaking both the political bureaucracy and the military discipline. Violent revolt is usually crushed very easily by the brutality of the Government. But there is no army capable of overcoming peaceable men who do not run out on the streets but who, for instance, simply abstain from voting at the elections and refuse to do their military service or to pay their taxes.

First of all, Tucker examined the method of non-payment of rents and taxes on the occasion of the fight of the Irish Land League for Home Rule, a league founded by Michael Davitt in 1879 which was a sort of agrarian movement for secession. Henry George describes in *Irish Land Questions* (1881) how the Irish Catholic peasants refused to pay their rent to the landlords, who usually were very rich Englishmen. While one section of the movement, led by C. S. Parnell, went in for the lowering of the rents and the creation of small Irish properties, the other members of the League, under the direction of Davitt, insisted that the land should go to the people. The Government mobilized 15,000 military police and 40,000 soldiers, but the Irish Land League got the upper hand in the country by boycotting the peasants and tradesmen who had taken sides with the Government. Doubtless, there would have been a certain amount of violence in this, for the Irish people have never been educated for unarmed struggle, but in principle and in practice, the methods used were far above the usual level of the masses in revolt. The British Government took extraordinary measures to imprison all who seemed to it "suspect." But each offensive act of the police or the army was met by the population with a strong passive resistance. Just like the Indians later on under Gandhi, the Irish were ready at this period to let themselves be imprisoned *en masse* and to replace their imprisoned countrymen in the struggle and in communal life.

*   *   *   *   *

In an article entitled "Passive Resistance," Tucker had described the Irish Land League as one of the most instructive movements in the whole of history: although it was wrecked by the unscrupulous politics of Parnell, followed blindly as he was by the over-simple masses, the collective resistance of the Irish peasantry went far enough to show that the British Government is helpless when confronted with such an enterprise: had it continued, by now there would not have been one single landed property in Ireland.

As regards taxes, Tucker thinks that in America it is easier and more effective to refuse State taxes than ground-rents.

For this reason, he encourages all countries placed in similar circumstances collectively to resist taxes. "If one-fifth of the people were to resist taxation, it would cost more to collect their taxes, or try to collect them, than the other four-fifths would consent to pay into the treasury . . . 'Passive resistance,' said Ferdinand Lassalle, 'is the resistance which does not resist.' Never was there a greater mistake. It is the only resistance which in these days of military discipline resists with any result. There is not a tyrant in the civilized world to-day who would not rather do anything in his power to precipitate a bloody revolution rather than see himself confronted by any large fraction of his subjects determined not to obey." For nothing is easier for modern Governments than to crush revolutionary violence. "Neither the ballot nor the bayonet is to play any great part in the coming struggle; passive resistance is the instrument by which the revolutionary force is destined to secure in the last great conflict the people's rights forever."[7]

We must admit that the Irish have always shown a marked taste for violence. So that, during several centuries they have fought against the hard domination of the British with the most brutal and even treacherous methods. But, being unable to attain their ends in this way, towards 1880 they tried to practise a boycott, though in a sufficiently violent manner. The very word "boycott" is of Irish origin, although it describes a fighting method which, as we have already said, has been in use for thousands of years in China, and of which the efficacy has been proved many times by the United States, England and Japan.

We have already seen how Gandhi himself admits that he owes a great many of his ideas to Tolstoy. If we do not linger much here over the ideas of the great Russian relating to non-violent direct action, both individual and collective, and the international influence which they have had, it is because we assume they are already well-known to the reader. What is not generally known, is that the great general strike to happen in Russia, in 1905, the only one of the three which was truly successful, was absolutely peaceable and of the sort Tolstoy had been urging for years.

"Workmen, clerks, professional men, even Government employees and dvorniks (janitors converted into spies and informers) simply dropped their tools, briefs, documents, and what not, and refused to carry on the activities of industrial and political life. The result, on the Government's side, was panic. A constitution was granted; a whole series of reforms —on paper—followed.

[7] B. R. Tucker, *Individual Liberty* (New York: Vanguard Press, 1926), pp. 78, 244–47.

"The second strike was called when the circumstances were unfavourable, and the causes distinctly doubtful in the opinion of the majority of the Government's enemies. It failed, and the consequent bitterness and apprehension led to a third strike, with an appeal to arms at Moscow. That appeal was most unfortunate. . . .

"Of course, human nature is human nature, and it were both idle and unfair to blame the distracted and exasperated Russian radicals for the turn events have taken. . . . Still, the fact remains that, had the policy of strictly passive resistance been continued, and had not the strike and boycott weapon been too recklessly used, the cause of freedom and progress in Russia would to-day rejoice in much brighter prospects."

That is the conclusion reached by Tucker with regard to the events in St Petersburg in 1905–6, set down in his American paper "Liberty"[8] where he developed, à propos of the non-violent methods of struggle of the working-classes, exactly the same point of view as that upheld by Tom Mooney, during the hearings of the Tom Mooney *habeas corpus* proceedings, closed finally in San Francisco on August 18, 1936: "Violence is the weapon used by the employers. . . . Violence wins no strike . . . only education and organization."[9]

* * * * *

. . . John Ruskin, without believing in non-violence on principle—indeed, this anarchistically inclined spirit sometimes showed an imperialist nationalism in its most extreme form[10] —stressed the responsibility which exists with regard to all work to be done and advocated the refusal of all work which is harmful. During the Franco-Prussian war, while English industry was reaping huge profits from munition making, Ruskin urged the British workers not to take part in this shameful business, nor to do any work which was unworthy of men.

"The first reason for all wars, and for the necessity of national defences, is that the majority of persons, high and low, in all European nations, are Thieves, and, in their hearts, greedy of their neighbours' goods, land and fame. But beside being Thieves, they are also fools. . . . And the guilty Thieves of Europe, the real sources of all deadly war in it, are the Capitalists. . . . The Real war in Europe is between these and the workman, such as these have made him.

8 Tucker, op. cit., pp. 79–80.
9 Tom Mooney Molders' Defence Committee, Press Service, August 26, 1936.
10 See Bertrand Russell, *Freedom versus Organization, 1814– 1914* (New York: Norton, 1934), p. 461.

"You are to do good work, whether you live or die. It may be that you will have to die;—well, men have died for their country often, yet doing her no good; be ready to die for her in doing her assured good: her, and all other countries with her. Mind your own business with absolute heart and soul; but see that it is a good business first. That it is corn and sweet peas you are producing,—not gunpowder and arsenic. And be sure of this, literally: you must simply die rather than make any destroying mechanism or compound.

"There is no physical crime, at this day, so far beyond pardon,—so without parallel in its untempted guilt, as the making of war-machinery, and invention of mischievous substance. Two nations may go mad, and fight like harlots—God have mercy on them;—you, who hand them carving-knives off the table, for leave to pick up a dropped sixpence, what mercy is there for you?"

So John Ruskin wrote in July 1871, in his VIIth Letter to the Workmen and Labourers of Great Britain.

By a happy chance, a Dutch translation of these words fell beneath the eye of the author of this book while he was still adolescent, and they have been an inspiration to him throughout his whole life.

Ruskin was one of the rare Europeans who are against all forms of vengeance and retribution (an eye for an eye). Although he did not reject certain kinds of punishment, he pleaded for non-retaliation, just as Gandhi did. In the same letter to the British Workers as we have just quoted, Ruskin wisely charges them never to take revenge for injuries.[11]

In his book *Time and Tide* (1867), a series of twenty-five letters to the Sunderland workers, Ruskin deals in the last two with the task of the soldier and urges the transformation of military warfare into social and cultural works: "Our whole system of work must be based on the nobleness of soldiership."[12] . . .

That gifted workman, William Morris, poet and thinker at once, deeply influenced by Karl Marx and Pyotr Kropotkin, condemned all horizontal violence, whether foreign wars or colonial, and accepted only the social war, the class struggle. . . .

Morris also establishes a clear distinction between useful work and useless toil. In his essay *Useful Work versus Useless Toil* he attacks the conception generally adopted by the ruling class that work is useful in itself, especially for the exploited class, as a vulgar lie. For there is work which is useful and also work which is both useless and harmful. "The first has hope in

[11] John Ruskin, *Fors Clavigera*, II, pp. 15–20.
[12] Ruskin, *Time and Tide*, Letter XXV.

it, the other has not. It is manly to do the one kind of work and manly also to refuse to do the other";[13] the first has a creative and emancipating significance, the second is only the shameful work of a slave. As for war work, Morris declares in his essay *How We Live and How We Might Live:* "I won't submit to be dressed up in red and marched off to shoot at my French, German or Arab friend, in a quarrel that I don't understand: I will rebel sooner than do that."[14]

Morris was one of those who, in England, held that "British Socialism is not a purely materialistic criticism of economic theory, but behind it there is a basis of ethical criticism and theory."[15]

This view was also held by Bruce Glasier and Keir Hardie, the founder of the Independent Labour Party, which, during the World War, upheld internationalism above the mêlée, together with the Russian, Italian and American Socialist Party. The essentials of their conception may be summed up in this one word: humanism.

*   *   *   *   *

In the same way, the I.L.P. at the International Socialist Congress at Copenhagen (1910) proposed an amendment to the resolution concerning the fight against war, demanding extra-Parliamentary action, especially general strikes, in industries that supply war material, as one of the methods of preventing war; and Keir Hardie declared that the point of view of labour had not only to be anti-war but anti-military, because militarism and freedom could not exist side by side. Keir Hardie did not expect that the workers were at present ready to strike against war; but they never would be ready to do so unless we helped to educate them by pointing out to them their duty.[16] "The Nation that has the courage to be the first to throw away its arms will win for itself one of the greatest names in history," he declared.

*   *   *   *   *

In Holland, it was the late Dr. Clara Meijer-Wichmann, an eminent sociologist of German origin, who, inspired by Marx, Hegel, Tolstoy, Sorel and the French syndicalists of the beginning of the century, developed in particular the thesis of a

[13] William Morris, *Stories in Prose, Stories in Verse, Shorter Poems, Lectures and Essays,* Centenary Edition, ed. by G. D. H. Cole (New York: Random House, 1934), p. 604.

[14] Ibid., p. 581.

[15] John Bruce Glasier, *William Morris* (New York: Longmans, 1921), p. vii.

[16] W. Stewart, *J. Keir Hardie* (London: Cassell, 1921), pp. 298–302.

compelling harmony between the goal to be reached and the means to be used in the revolutionary study. The maxim that the end justifies the means can only be allowed in one sense, according to her, a sacred goal demands sacred means. Since Socialism coincides perfectly with humanity—the human feeling in men—its methods must never be at variance with, nor offend against, this humanity. For this reason, revolution ought to bring to the human race the noblest of moral qualities, that of solidarity. A real revolutionary can never be an enemy to his enemies nor a criminal to criminals, the more so as criminals are in the first place victims of society. The revolution demands not only the renunciation of all violence in regard to nations and classes, but also to individuals. Complete anti-militarism transforms itself in this way into a new individual and social education which, combining with modern psychological knowledge and psychotherapy at last renders the barracks as unnecessary as the prisons.

It was by no mere chance that in Holland Clara Meijer-Wichmann took the initiative in creating a Committee of Action against the traditional ideas on crime and punishment. She was not only the head of the Judicial Department in the Statistics Bureau at the Hague, but she was also married to Jo Meijer, one of the bravest of conscientious objectors who himself had to undergo terms of imprisonment.

The question of the treatment of the victims of common law presented itself in Holland in the same way as in England. There, too, the imprisonment of a large number of advanced men and women, who had refused to take any part in the War, faced these anti-War believers with one of the most burning questions of the day: the fate of criminals—especially as they themselves had experienced it. In England it was notably A. Fenner Brockway who, after undergoing severe punishments during the World War, simply because he remained faithful to International Socialism, became the champion of this cause.[17]

In Holland, it was Clara Meijer-Wichmann again who declared that in the history of civilization, criminal law is one of the branches which has stayed centuries behind compared with the advancement and transformation of the others. While modern psychologists and pedagogues have recognized the inefficacy and the injustice of all kinds of retaliation and intimidation, justice is still a kind of social vengeance whose aim is to intimidate and to put out of harm's way. The widespread criminality that we meet with nowadays has always been a symptom of abnormal times, the degree of criminality being more or less determined by the relative order or disorder of the society in question. A great number of the degenerates who

[17] See Fenner Brockway, *A New Way with Crime* (London: Williams & Norgate, 1928).

fill the prisons come from unfavourable surroundings where alcoholism, scrofula and syphilis, flourish, that is to say, these criminals are first and foremost victims of hereditary and social blemishes, and they should be treated as victims to be rescued and succoured, and no longer be driven out from among their fellow men as scapegoats. The fight for entire revision of the treatment accorded to criminals must be supplemented by the struggle for social justice and for physical, moral and mental hygiene.[18]

And here are some remarkable conclusions reached by Henrietta Roland Holst, one of the best-known theorists of modern Socialism, after a long life of revolutionary activity. A friend of Rosa Luxembourg and Karl Liebknecht, she belonged, even before the war, to that group of neo-Marxists who worked out a new kind of tactic against modern imperialism. Madame Holst, after the experiences of the Russian revolution in 1905, became a firm believer in direct action on the part of the masses and in non-co-operation as regards national defence. During the Great War, she joined the Zimmerwald movement with Lenin, and when the Russian revolution broke out, she was extremely enthusiastic. At one time, she even maintained the view that to ensure the success of the Revolution the end justifies the means, and that, in case of failure, the revolutionary must give up even the highest demands of his conscience. This was all the more remarkable because, some years ago, Madame Roland Holst had published a long historical and sociological study on the revolutionary action of the masses, in which she had laid great stress on the importance of the moral factor in the battle for a new society.[19] And there had even been a debate, which became a classic, between Clara Meijer-Wichmann and Henrietta Roland Holst, on the subject of social revolution and violence.[20] But the way the Russian revolution went, its militarization, its bureaucratization, the violent injustices it perpetrated in the name of revolutionary justice—a whole string of these errors at last brought Madame Holst to break with Moscow.

Under the title of *Sterft gij oude vormen en gedachten*, which is a line taken from the Dutch version of the Internationale meaning "Let us raze the past to the ground," she published a pamphlet on the occasion of the defeat of the Austrian Socialists in their attack against Fascism in February 1934. In these pages after honouring the courage of the Social

[18] Meijer-Wichmann, *Misdaad, Straf en Maatschappij; Mensch en Maatschappij; Bevrijding.*

[19] Roland Holst, *Revolutionnaire Massa-Aktie.*

[20] See *Gewalt und Gewaltlosigkeit.* A Handbook of Active Pacifism, published by Franz Kobler.

Democrats, who had been defeated weapons in hand, she warns her readers against the halo of romantic heroism which had already sprung up round this tragic episode. According to Madame Holst, Austrian Socialism had fallen through using political and strategical methods which were obsolete, and through the traditional faith it put in collective violence. One thing, she says, must be noticed, which is that in modern Socialism there are two contradictory tendencies, one which is in favour of confidence in all that is human and humanitarian, the other which accepts war, dictatorship and even terror. The first, which at the beginning seemed very strong, has been more and more neglected while the second has grown at its expense. The masses in Austria, as elsewhere, had been educated with a view to a final armed struggle, beside which general strikes, non-co-operation and other forms of non-violent struggle were held to be of secondary importance. But "it is unhappily a law that the energy which one uses in one kind of fight is just so much energy lost in another . . . The Austrian workers who resorted to arms had remained enslaved by the technique of modern war. . . . Modern armaments have reduced the armed revolts of the masses to absurdity, and they are doomed simply to become a vulgar copy of the system they are attacking." . . .

In 1937, Madame Holst expressed her satisfaction over the fact that non-violent action had taken on a new form, that of the sit-down strike, of which the first example was given in October 1934 by 1,200 coal miners in the Hungarian town called Pecs. During a wage conflict, these miners refused to leave the mine and said that unless their economic conditions were improved they would starve themselves to death.[21] In 1936, millions of workers in the French industries used the same methods. "No blood was shed, and hundreds of thousands of workers thus took a step towards a higher humanity."[22] And they did this solely by their own moral strength. . . .

There is a surprising agreement between the latest conclusions of Henrietta Roland Holst and those of the Russian revolutionary J. Steinberg, one time People's Commissar for Justice, in the first Bolshevist Government. Steinberg had accepted his commission in the hope of directing the Russian Revolution towards really humane ways of battle. Against his will, he found himself dragged into terror. In his book on violence and terror in revolution, he has described how certain methods

21 See R. B. Gregg, *The Power of Non-Violence* (Philadelphia: Lippincott, 1934), pp. 15–17.
22 Henrietta Roland Holst, in *Vrienden van India*, April 20, 1937.

drag inexorably on those who use them to the point where they are completely lost and at sea, how these methods are in contradiction with the proposed aim: the revolution is bound to perish when, for purely utilitarian motives, it neglects the moral factor or acts according to the childish maxim "since the others are doing it, we can too." According to him, every kind of terror should be banished from the methods of revolutionary struggle, and violence can only be given the smallest place. A revision of the whole revolutionary tactic is called for.[23]

*   *   *   *   *

Nothing is more superficial and more false than the statement of Edouard Berth:

"Yes, war between States or war between Classes—the question is put and the dilemma insoluble: and revolutionaries are only pacifist when it comes to war between States: they consider that war between States has had its day and must give way to the Class war: a complete pacifist would be a man who denies both and supports peace international and social: but such a man could only be a Buddhist ascetic or a Christian or a Tolstoyan. A man of this sort renounces the world, withdraws into his cell or the desert, and, fundamentally, cuts himself off from life."[24] . . .

For we mean something entirely different: a revolutionary anti-militarism, a continual social struggle in which the aggressive instinct affirms itself on the highest level and which opens up the way to victories and triumphs that the working-class movement would never obtain by any kind of homicidal "class-war."

Berth's great mistake was to think of war as "the absence of peace," a conception against which Erasmus once took his stand.[25] From this point of view, Emmanuel Mounier is right in maintaining the thesis that true peace is the expansion of all human powers: "Peace, true peace, is not a feeble state in which Man gives up. Neither is it a reservoir indifferent to good and evil alike. It is strength." As de Montherlant says, "Bring about a peace which shall have the same spiritual grandeur as war. Bring to peace the war virtues." "Peace is

[23] Steinberg, *Gewalt und Terror in der Revolution; Als ich Volkskommissar war.*

[24] Berth, *Guerre des États ou Guerre des Classes,* pp. 80–81.

[25] "Upon the whole it must be said that the first and most important step towards peace is sincerely to desire it. They who once love peace in their hearts will eagerly seize every opportunity of establishing or recovering it." Erasmus, *Querela Pacis,* ed. Grieve, p. 71.

not declared, it comes from within. . . . It is on the way to this peace you will find the battalion of pacifists."[26] To the negative pacifism which would renounce the world, and even life itself—and which, by the way, has nothing in common with the revolutionary pacifism of a Tolstoy—we oppose this pacifist battle, which, using methods which are both new and truly worthy of men, creates a harmonious commonwealth over and above all frontiers.

*   *   *   *   *

[26] Mounier, *Révolution personnaliste et communautaire*, pp. 247–48.

10. Theodor Mommsen:
A REVOLUTIONARY STRIKE IN
ANCIENT ROME

One of the classic examples of non-violent revolution in ancient times was the non-violent non-co-operation of the Roman plebeians in the third century B.C. Carried out almost spontaneously, it shook the foundations of the aristocratic republic and led to substantial economic and political reforms.

Before the revolution, the plebeians suffered under rigorous laws that imprisoned them for debt and made them virtual slaves of the wealthy in certain crucial respects. Moreover, while the plebeians were expected to serve as soldiers in the army of the State and to be assiduous workers in civil life, they had little voice in the government of the Republic. Nor did they have any effective way to redress grievances through the regularly established machinery of the State. When finally they did act directly against patrician control, it was not as the result of an abstract philosophy of non-violent power but rather because they seemed to realize almost subconsciously that the withdrawal of their labor would itself precipitate a settlement.

The author of our reading, Theodor Mommsen (1817–1903), ranks as one of the greatest scholars of modern times. For a time, he was professor of Roman law at Leipzig but was dismissed from his position because he was too "liberal." In 1858, he became professor of ancient history at the University of Berlin. He was also active in politics, being a member of the Prussian Parliament from 1873 to 1882.

The reading presented here is excerpted from Mommsen's *The History of Rome,* English translation by William Purdie Dickson, new edition, revised (London: Richard Bentley and Son, 1894), Vol. I, pp. 346–50.

The distinction between rich and poor, which arose out of these relations, by no means coincided with that between the clans and the plebeians. If far the greater part of the patricians were wealthy land-holders, opulent and considerable families

were, of course, not wanting among the plebeians; and as the
senate, which even then perhaps consisted in greater part of
plebeians, had assumed the superintendence of the finances to
the exclusion even of the patrician magistrates, it was natural
that all those economic advantages, for which the political privileges of the nobility were abused, should go to the benefit of
the wealthy collectively; and the pressure fell the more heavily
upon the commons, since those who were the ablest and the
most capable of resistance were by their admission to the senate transferred from the class of the oppressed to the ranks of
the oppressors.

But this state of things prevented the political position of the
aristocracy from being permanently tenable. Had it possessed
the self-control to govern justly and to protect the middle class
—as individual consuls from its ranks endeavoured, but from
the reduced position of the magistracy were unable effectually,
to do—it might have long maintained itself in sole possession of
the offices of state. Had it been willing to admit the wealthy
and respectable plebeians to full equality of rights—possibly
by connecting the acquisition of the patriciate with admission
into the senate—both might long have governed and speculated
with impunity. But neither of the courses was adopted; the
narrowness of mind and short-sightedness, which are the
proper and inalienable privileges of all genuine patricianism,
were true to their character also in Rome, and rent the powerful commonwealth asunder in useless, aimless, and inglorious
strife.

The immediate crisis, however, proceeded not from those
who felt the disabilities of their order, but from the distress of
the farmers. The rectified annals place the political revolution
in the year 244, the social in the years 259 and 260; they certainly appear to have followed close upon each other, but the
interval was probably longer. The strict enforcement of the
law of debt—so runs the story—excited the indignation of the
farmers at large. When in the year 259 the levy was called
forth for a dangerous war, the men bound to serve refused to
obey the command. Thereupon the consul Publius Servilius
suspended for a time the application of the debtor-laws, and
gave orders to liberate the persons already imprisoned for debt
as well as prohibited further arrests; so that the farmers took
their places in the ranks and helped to secure the victory. On
their return from the field of battle the peace, which had been
achieved by their exertions, brought back their prison and their
chains: with merciless rigour the second consul, Appius Clau-
dius, enforced the debtor-laws and his colleague, to whom his
former soldiers appealed for aid, dared not offer opposition. It
seemed as if collegiate rule had been introduced not for the
protection of the people, but to facilitate breach of faith and

despotism; they endured, however, what could not be changed. But when in the following year the war was renewed, the word of the consul availed no longer. It was not till Manius Valerius was nominated dictator that the farmers submitted, partly from their awe of the higher magisterial authority, partly from their confidence in his friendly feeling to the popular cause—for the Valerii were one of the old patrician clans by whom government was esteemed a privilege and an honour, not a source of gain. The victory was again with the Roman standards; but when the victors came home and the dictator submitted his proposals of reform to the senate, they were thwarted by its obstinate opposition. The army still stood in its array, as usual, before the gates of the city. When the news arrived, the long threatening storm burst forth; the *esprit de corps* and the compact military organization carried even the timid and the indifferent along with the movement. The army abandoned its general and its encampment, and under the leadership of the commanders of the legions—the military tribunes, who were at least in great part plebeians—marched in martial order into the district of Crustumeria between the Tiber and the Anio, where it occupied a hill and threatened to establish in this most fertile part of the Roman territory a new plebeian city. This secession showed in a palpable manner even to the most obstinate of the oppressors that such a civil war must end with economic ruin to themselves; and the senate gave way. The dictator negotiated an agreement; the citizens returned within the city walls; unity was outwardly restored. The people gave Manius Valerius thenceforth the name of "the great" (*maximus*)—and called the mount beyond the Anio "the sacred mount." There was something mighty and elevating in such a revolution, undertaken by the multitude itself without definite guidance under generals whom accident supplied, and accomplished without bloodshed; and with pleasure and pride the citizens recalled its memory. Its consequences were felt for many centuries: it was the origin of the tribunate of the plebs.

*   *   *   *   *

11. Flavius Josephus:
JEWISH NON-VIOLENCE AND ROMAN
MILITARY POWER

The ancient Jewish historian Flavius Josephus (A.D. 37–95?) has left us a dramatic account of non-violent resistance among the Jews during the reign of the Roman emperor Caligula (A.D. 37–41). Although certain Jews living at that time did espouse principled doctrines of non-violent resistance, the Jewish community's behavior during the incident that Josephus relates seems to have been motivated by its helplessness in a military sense, rather than by any articulated set of beliefs and, as such, is included here instead of in Part III. (Caligula is here referred to as Caius.)

The incident had its beginnings in Caligula's determination to force the Jews to erect his statue in the Temple at Jerusalem, to which end he appointed Petronius president of Syria and dispatched him to the eastern Mediterranean. To the Jews, of course, the erection of any man's statue within the sacred portals of the Temple would have been an act of idolatry, and Josephus' account is a description of the methods by which they tried to dissuade Petronius and the emperor from their course.

Josephus' interpretation of the episode emphasizes "providential" factors. Basing his notions on an important current in the Jewish tradition, he holds that because the Jews were willing in large numbers to suffer passively rather than deliberately violate their law, God took mercy on them and protected them. Yet the reader will see that the cancellation of the order was, in the end, due as much to events in Rome as it was to the Jews' efforts, and so the story serves to illustrate one of the major difficulties we face in assessing the effectiveness of non-violent action: the influence of events in no way connected with the non-violent struggle in question, yet helping to bring about a successful outcome.

The reading is taken from Book XVIII, Chapter 8, of William Whiston's translation of Josephus' *Antiquities of the Jews*. This translation first appeared in 1737.

Hereupon Caius, taking it very heinously that he should be thus despised by the Jews alone, sent Petronius to be president of Syria, and successor in the government to Vitellius, and gave him order to make an invasion into Judea, with a great body of troops; and if they would admit of his statue willingly, to erect it in the temple of God; but if they were obstinate, to conquer them by war, and then to do it. Accordingly, Petronius took the government of Syria, and made haste to obey Caesar's epistle. He got together as great a number of auxiliaries as he possibly could, and took with him two legions of the Roman army, and came to Ptolemais, and there wintered, as intending to set about the war in the Spring. . . . But there came many ten thousands of the Jews to Petronius, to Ptolemais, to offer their petitions to him, that he would not compel them to transgress and violate the law of their forefathers; "but if," said they, "thou art entirely resolved to bring this statue, and erect it, do thou first kill us, and then do what thou hast resolved on; for while we are alive we cannot permit such things as are forbidden us to be done by the authority of our legislator, and by our forefathers' determination that such prohibitions are instances of virtue." But Petronius was angry at them, and said, "If indeed I were myself emperor, and were at liberty to follow my own inclination, and then had designed to act thus, these your words would be justly spoken to me; but now Caesar hath sent to me, I am under the necessity of being subservient to his decrees. . . ." Then the Jews replied, "Since, therefore, thou art so disposed, O Petronius! that thou wilt not disobey Caius's epistles, neither will we transgress the commands of our law. . . ."

When Petronius saw by their words that their determination was hard to be removed, and that . . . he should not be able to be subservient to Caius in the dedication of his statue, and that there must be a great deal of bloodshed, he took his friends, and the servants that were about him, and hasted to Tiberias, as wanting to know in what posture the affairs of the Jews were; and many ten thousands of the Jews met Petronius again, when he was come to Tiberias. These . . . made supplication to him, that he would by no means reduce them to such distresses, nor defile their city with the dedication of their statue. Then Petronius said to them, "Will you then make war with Caesar, without considering his great preparations for war, and your own weakness?" They replied, "We will not by any means make war with him, but still we will die before we see our laws transgressed." So they threw themselves down upon their faces, and stretched out their throats, and said they

were ready to be slain; and this they did for forty days together, and in the meantime left off the tilling of their ground,
and that while the season of the year required them to sow it.
Thus they continued firm in their resolution, and proposed to
themselves to die willingly, rather than to see the dedication
of the statue.

When matters were in this state, Aristobulus, king Agrippa's
brother, and Helcias the Great, and the other principal men of
that family with them, went in unto Petronius, and besought
him, that since he saw the resolution of the multitude, he would
not make any alteration, and thereby drive them to despair.
. . . So Petronius, partly on account of the pressing instances
which Aristobulus and the rest with him made, and because of
the great consequence of what they desired, and the earnest-
ness wherewith they made their supplication,—partly on account of the firmness of the opposition made by the Jews,
which he saw, while he thought it a horrible thing for him to be
such a slave to the madness of Caius, as to slay so many thousand men. . . . Petronius, I say, thought it much better to
send to Caius . . . that if this mad resolution continued he
[Petronius] should turn his hatred against himself, [that] it
was fit for virtuous persons even to die for the sake of such
vast multitudes of men. Accordingly, he determined to hearken
to the petitioners in this matter.

He then called the Jews together to Tiberias, who came
many ten thousands in number. . . . Said he, "I do not think it
just to have such a regard to my own safety and honour, as to
refuse to sacrifice them for your preservation, who are so
many in number, and endeavour to preserve the regard that is
due to your law. . . . I will, therefore, send to Caius, and let
him know what your resolutions are, and will assist your suit
as far as I am able, that you may not be exposed to suffer on
account of the honest designs you have proposed to yourselves;
and may God be your assistant. . . . But if Caius be irritated,
and turn the violence of his rage upon me, I will rather undergo all that danger and that affliction that may come either
on my body or my soul, than see so many of you to perish. . . ."

. . . When Petronius had said this, and had dismissed the
assembly of the Jews, he desired the principal of them to take
care of their husbandry, and to speak kindly to the people, and
encourage them to have good hope of their affairs. Thus did
he readily bring the multitude to be cheerful again. . . . He
wrote to Caius . . . to entreat him not to make so many ten
thousands of these men go distracted; whom, if he should slay
. . . he would lose the revenue they paid him, and would be
publicly cursed by them for all future ages.

*   *   *   *   *

But king Agrippa, who now lived at Rome, was more and more in the favour of Caius; and when he had once made him a supper, and was careful to exceed all others, both in expenses and in such preparations as might contribute most to his pleasure; nay, it was so far from the ability of others, that Caius himself could never equal, much less exceed it (such care had he taken beforehand to exceed all men, and particularly to make all agreeable to Caesar); hereupon Caius admired his understanding and magnificence, that he should force himself to do all to please him, even beyond such expenses as he could bear, and was desirous not to be behind Agrippa in that generosity which he exerted in order to please him. So Caius, when he had drank wine plentifully, and was merrier than ordinary, said thus during the feast, when Agrippa had drunk to him: "I knew before now how great a respect thou hast had for me, and how great kindness thou hast shown me, though with those hazards to thyself, which thou underwentest under Tiberias on that account. . . . Every thing that may contribute to thy happiness shall be at thy service, and that cheerfully, and so far as my ability will reach." And this was what Caius said to Agrippa, thinking he would ask for some large country, or the revenues of certain cities. . . . Agrippa replied, "Since thou, O my lord! declarest such is thy readiness to grant, that I am worthy of thy gifts, I will ask nothing relating to my own felicity; for what thou hast already bestowed on me has made me excel therein; but I desire somewhat which may make thee glorious for piety . . . ; for my petition is this, that thou wilt no longer think of the dedication of that statue which thou hast ordered to be set up in the Jewish temple by Petronius."

Caius, who was mightily taken with Agrippa's obliging behaviour, . . . granted him what he had requested. He also wrote thus to Petronius, commending him for his assembling his army, and then consulting him about these affairs. "If therefore," said he, "thou hast already erected my statue, let it stand; but if thou hast not yet dedicated it, do not trouble thyself further about it, but dismiss thy army, go back, and take care of those affairs which I sent thee about at first, for I have now no occasion for the erection of that statue." . . . And this was what Caius wrote to Petronius, which was before he received his letter, informing him that the Jews were very ready to revolt about the statue. . . . When therefore Caius was much displeased that any attempt should be made against his government, as he was a slave to base and vicious actions on all occasions, he wrote thus to Petronius: "Seeing thou esteemest the presents made thee by the Jews to be of greater value than

my commands, . . . I will make thee an example to the present and to all future ages, that they may not dare to contradict
the commands of their emperor."

This was the epistle which Caius wrote to Petronius; but Petronius did not receive it while Caius was alive, that ship which
carried it sailing so slow, that other letters came to Petronius
before this, by which he understood that Caius was dead; for
God would not forget the dangers Petronius had undertaken
on account of the Jews, and of his own honour. But when he
had taken Caius away, out of his indignation of what he had
so insolently attempted in assuming to himself divine worship,
both Rome and all that dominion conspired with Petronius,
especially those that were of the senatorian order, to give Caius
his due reward, because he had been unmercifully severe to
them; for he died not long after he had written to Petronius
that epistle which threatened him with death. . . . Now that
epistle which informed Petronius of Caius's death came first,
and a little afterward came that which commanded him to kill
himself with his own hands. Whereupon he rejoiced at this coincidence as to the death of Caius, and admired God's providence. . . .

12. Wilfred H. Crook:
THE GENERAL STRIKE AND NON-VIOLENT POWER

Collective withholding of labor, or the "strike," is a familiar phenomenon in industrial relations. Most strikes, however, have as their objectives only immediate economic gains for the workers who organize them. The majority, moreover, involve only one or two industries at most.

In contrast with the usual type, the general strike has been characterized as a "walk-out of the workers in the key industries and services of a particular area, local or national."[1] It is less immediately self-interested than the ordinary strike and may be employed as a technique for political as well as economic objectives. In one of his essays, the American author Jack London imagines the general strike being used to destroy what he regards as the whole exploiting capitalist system of property relations.[2] Some thinkers regard the general strike as particularly effective against regimes founded on brute force and lacking free parliamentary institutions. Others see it as a method for overcoming public inertia even in parliamentary and democratic societies.

The notion of the general strike probably has its roots in the ideas of the British Chartist movement of more than a hundred years ago. According to one of its leaders, William Benbow, there was to be a "grand national holiday" of the workers that would, through mass refusal to work, put pressure on the government for fundamental parliamentary reform. In the United States, the first general strike occurred in 1835, when workers in Philadelphia sought to gain the ten-hour day. Another notable example was the St. Louis strike of 1877, which was led by the Workingman's Party. And of course there was the famous Seattle affair of 1919.

General strikes have often been associated with violence, even though their leaders may have cautioned against the use

[1] Wilfred H. Crook, *Communism and the General Strike* (Hamden, Connecticut: the Shoe String Press, 1960), p. 6.
[2] *The Dream of Debs.* (Chicago: Kerr, 1919).

of violence as being self-defeating. In practice, of course, it is extremely difficult in any conflict to prevent all violent manifestations; and general strikes obviously occur in the context of acute conflict. Much, however, can be done to develop discipline among those who are conducting the strike, and experience would seem to show that the strikes most likely to be relatively successful are characterized by the least violence on the part of those conducting them. If strikers resort to violence, whether initially or in response to provocation, they simply provide an excuse for the government to use force against them; and once force has been employed, the original issues leading to the strike become confused or are often forgotten.

The reading below presents several examples of recent general strikes, from the Belgian strike of 1913, which sought to gain universal suffrage and the abolition of plural voting, to the "June Days" strike against the Communist government in East Germany in 1953. These are political strikes, either work stoppages to gain a defined political end, or demonstrations arising more or less spontaneously out of political discontent. In only one of them, is there an articulated and developed theory of non-violence. In several, elements of violence creep in, either because of a lack of acquaintance with the theory of non-violence and an insufficiency of determination, or because of extreme and unlooked-for provocation.

It cannot be concluded, from these examples, that the general strike is necessarily either non-violent or successful. It does seem possible, however, given proper leadership trained in the theory and practice of non-violent resistance, to reduce the element of violence to very small proportions. Much, of course, depends upon the context in which the strike is employed, the strikers' firmness and willingness to suffer, the degree of sympathy among the general public, and the nature of the goal. It has been suggested that strikes conducted for relatively simple and understandable goals are, other things being equal, most likely to achieve success.

But because many general strikes appear to have been either unsuccessful or tinged with violence is no reason for the student of non-violence to discard them. Potentially they constitute one of the most effective means for developing what C. M. Case called "non-violent coercion," even though before they can be fully effective, many more strike leaders must evolve principled theories of non-violence.

This selection is reprinted from *Communism and the General Strike,* by Wilfred H. Crook, pp. 210–19, 236–40, 265–68, 270–71, and 354–56, published in 1960 by the Shoe String Press.

(1) THE BELGIAN STRIKE OF 1913

Belgian labor thoroughly learned the lessons of the previous general strikes. The strike of 1913, while not as complete as the British one, because none of the transport workers took part, was far more impressive than that of 1902. In 1913 the strike was prepared with great care as to resources and the preservation of order; the number of trades involved was larger, and the cooperation of the Flemish workers was marked. Strict discipline held from start to finish. While its immediate political effect was not startling, it was in no wise the defeat of 1902.

A sympathetic writer on Belgium wrote of the segregation of Catholics and Socialists: "Thus in one town there will be a Catholic, a Liberal and a Socialist trade union, a Catholic, a Liberal, and a Socialist cooperative bakery, a Catholic, a Liberal and a Socialist thrift society, each catering for similar people, but each confining its attentions to members of its own political party. The separation extends to cafes, gymnasia, choral, temperance, and literary societies; indeed it cuts right through life."[3] Before the electoral campaign of 1912 there was a good deal of mutual logrolling by Liberal and Socialist candidates, with a common plank in both platforms of universal suffrage at twenty-five and abolition of the plural vote. The Walloon districts returned a large majority of Liberals and Socialists, but the rural districts continued the Catholic Party majority. The middle class, disturbed at the possibility of defeat of the government, swung to its support, to the surprise and anger of labor.

There followed a mad explosion of rage by the workers, particularly in the Walloon districts. Workers went on strike spontaneously. The Socialist leaders did not attempt to stop it immediately, but tried to play for time. The government did not hesitate to use pitiless methods of repression. The General Council of the Labor party went into the provinces to calm the people. The militants of their party brought fierce pressure to bear upon them for an instant general strike. The Council ultimately convinced the workers—for a while. When the Party

[3] B. Seebohm Rowntree, *Land and Labour; Lessons from Belgium* (London: Macmillan, 1910), as quoted in R. C. K. Ensor, *Belgium* (London: Williams & Norgate, 1915), p. 171.

Congress met it was found that 1,500 out of 1,584 delegates had been given a mandate to vote for a general strike.[4]

A special national committee was formed for "Universal Suffrage and the General Strike," which included the Labor party's General Council, the Trade Union Commission, the Federation of Cooperatives, and the national federation of crafts. Thus the National Committee symbolized all aspects of the labor movement. Its task was to prepare for the general strike, and to call it when the time appeared fitting. The Committee was to prepare for a six-week stoppage involving half a million workers. The changed emphasis on the strike this time was to be its peacefulness. When the House reassembled in November, Vandervelde, in the name of the Socialists, gave notice of revision of the franchise. Not until January, 1913, was the motion debated, and then the Prime Minister refused to consider the motion while under the threat of a general strike, even though it had not been called. Not until the resolution for revision had been defeated by ninety-nine votes to eighty-three did the National Committee decree a general strike, with the date fixed for April 14, leaving ample time for negotiation. What perilously approached a subsequent double-crossing by the government led to the calling of a special congress of the Socialist party and a determined resolve to stand by the date fixed.[5]

The structure evolved for the conduct of a long but peaceful strike consisted of four vital commissions: Propaganda, finances, food, and the evacuation of the strikers' children. The most important principle upon which the campaign was organized was centralization of propaganda, but decentralization of financial responsibility. But for this strong central control of propaganda, the "young guard" of the Socialists might easily have run away with the movement and have ended in yet another violent strike. Once the struggle started, however, the need for financial resources would be greater than any central body could meet, unless the districts had for some time raised their own local and regional funds. The idea was emphasized that the workers must not jeopardize the strike funds reserved for economic strikes. Speakers were to bring home to their audiences that without electoral justice economic justice was impossible, since all the workers' efforts for material improvement ran foul of hostile legislation. To be a success, the general strike must be both formidable and peaceful. "Formidable" implied around half a million strikers. "Peaceful" meant

[4] Emile Vandervelde, *La grève générale en Belgique* (Paris: F. Alcan, 1914), pp. 94–97.

[5] E. Mahaim, "The General Strike in Belgium," *Economics Journal,* June 1913.

the avoidance of all sabotage or attacks on the liberty to work. Before Parliament met in November, literally thousands of meetings had been held, millions of leaflets had been distributed. General strike stamps, buttons and songs were commonplace.

The Propaganda Commission appealed to Catholics and rural workers, as well as to their own group of organized labor, but the fact that the "rural vote was the plural vote" told against these efforts. The country folk who worked in the cities were more affected than the farm workers, and it was through them that the Commission was able to reach even the rural spots. Attempts to convert the industrial middle class did not get very far, though a few individual employers made donations to the fund. For small retail business a good deal of the psychology of fear was used. It was hinted that, since the workers were saving for the strike, small businesses would inevitably go bankrupt in large numbers unless they threw their efforts into the persuasion of the government to yield universal suffrage without a general strike.[6]

Space forbids any detailed description of the manner in which the Propaganda Commission proceeded to rouse interest among public employees, despite grave warnings that such employees would be immediately replaced if they deserted their posts. The hardest job before the Commission was to impress on the workers the non-violent aspect of the struggle. "A general strike of several weeks cannot remain peaceful," said one of the leaders of manual workers. Yet Vandervelde, top Socialist leader, remained convinced that such a phenomenon as a peaceful general strike was possible. He gained his assurance from the experience of the Swedish strike of 1909, forgetting that that strike was defeated. It was something smacking of genius which suggested that the younger and more militant Socialists be called upon to play the part of Labor Police, with the prime task of keeping order in the ranks.

The Commission on Finance had a huge task of raising funds for the ten months of propaganda, and for the strike period when nearly half a million strikers would have to be kept alive, only a third of whom would be members of any union. There was no plan of providing strike pay in the actual strike, but rather the feeding of the poorest by community meals for them or for their children. Further relief was planned in the scheme for sending strikers' children into the country districts or to sympathizers in other lands. These two tasks were the specific duty of the last two Commissions. They

[6] Cyrille van Overbergh, *La grève générale* (Brussels: Misch et Thron, 1913), pp. 56–57.

found it easier to get homes for the children than they did to persuade the parents to let the children go and thus ease the drain on the strike funds.[7]

Public Opinion

As the day of the general strike drew near,

> An intense and widespread uneasiness made itself felt throughout a great portion of the population, especially in the large towns and the industrial districts. Catastrophes, violence, and terrorism were predicted by some; others were sure that the strike would be a miserable failure; all, whether openly or secretly, took elaborate precautions. There was not a middle-class housewife but laid in a stock of coal and provisions, and many supplied themselves out of all proportion to the danger. In fact there was a very extraordinary panic before the event.[8]

The Catholic press and the experience of former years gave strong reason for these fears of violence. Now that the Liberals and Socialists were working together for suffrage, people began to whisper of civil war, even of the disloyalty of the troops. The Catholics, the Catholic unions, and the manufacturers were hostile to the general strike method, and the "yellow" (Catholic) unions did their utmost to increase their numbers. As these unions counted on some hundred thousand members, their influence was considerable.[9]

The state and the municipalities and most of the manufacturers gave warning to their employees that joining the strike would mean instant and permanent dismissal. Simultaneously there was a tremendous preparation of armed force. The soldiers were placed where there was not much expectation of trouble, and the *gendarmerie* in the more densely populated areas.[10] As the fateful day approached, the press began to write of the "Strike against the State," and to predict the immediate arrest of the National Committee and the seizure of all strike funds.

In contrast to all these rumors of class struggle there was growing assurance and enthusiasm among the Socialist trade unionists. Only the leaders were anxious. In spite of all care and constant exhortation, would the ranks break out into violence? At a great demonstration in Mons the evening before the strike, Vandervelde said: "Tomorrow, by hundreds of

---

[7] Ibid., pp. 104–9.
[8] Mahaim, op. cit., pp. 294–97.
[9] Vandervelde, op. cit., p. 237.
[10] Ibid., p. 234 ff.; Overbergh, op. cit., p. 148.

thousands, the workers will go on strike. You know I have not
desired you to do it. But since it cannot be avoided, let it be
peaceful and impressive. It is not Belgium that watches you,
but all of Europe."[11]

The Political Strike Runs Its Course

At its height the Belgian strike of 1913 claimed a "large
third" of the industrial workers. The railway workers did not
join the walkout, to the great disappointment of the Socialists,
but the strike was sufficiently "general" to upset the national
economy profoundly. From the start, order and discipline
were shown to a remarkable degree. Workers left the factories
in excellent order, cleaning and oiling their tools and machines
so that there would be little delay when the time came to re-
start industry. Further, this behavior showed that the strike
was not against individual employers. In Hainault, the chief
industrial province, 173,000 out of 204,000 quit work. The
total figures for the nation were not kept by the government,
which claimed that this was a political and not an economic
strike, and that therefore the strikers were not eligible for out-
of-work pay. Each side suspected the other as far as data on
the numbers on strike were concerned. Vandervelde claims
that at the peak some 450,000 were out. An anti-Socialist journal, *Le Correspondent,* carried a list of strikers daily, and
held that not more than 300,000 were out at the peak. Professor Mahaim puts the figure at 300,000 at the outset of the
strike and nearly 400,000 at the peak.[12]

Apart from the industrial area known as the Black Country,
the life of the great cities functioned as usual, and the strike
was barely visible. Yet it was felt. Stores were open, taxis and
tramways ran, but business was poor. Salesmen and businessmen stayed home, tourists followed their example, and the
workers had nothing to spend. Shipowners and business firms
diverted many ships to Rotterdam and elsewhere. At the port
of Antwerp a large number of workers quit work, but their
places were filled by country folk under pressure from their
priests.[13] The energetic action of the five hundred labor police who patrolled the docks continuously, alert to prevent violence against the "yellow unions," probably had much to do
with the fact that no disturbances occurred.[14]

[11] Overbergh, op. cit., pp. 149, 151.
[12] Ibid., p. 154; Mahaim, loc. cit.; *The Times,* London, April 21,
1913.
[13] Overbergh, op. cit., p. 176 ff.
[14] Vandervelde, op. cit., p. 246.

Great efforts were made to stop the press, even the Socialist papers (with the exception of the official strike bulletins put out by the National Committee). The first ballot of the Typographical union was against joining the strike, but four days after the strike started the vote in favor of striking was overwhelming. When this happened, the strike bulletin had to be printed in France. Six hundred Typographical union men struck in Brussels, but, barring the Liberal and Socialist papers, most of the press got through in one way or another.[15]

The Great Silence

Everyone outside the Labor party expected violence. The aspect of the great strike that most impressed the public and the foreign correspondents was the profound quiet and calm discipline with which the strike ran its course. The London *Times* correspondent kept his daily reports harping on the amazing quiet and order of the strike. At the end he could still wire: "The Government failed to believe that their opponents could control the elements for the passive coercion with which they were threatened. These opponents have demonstrated their ability."[16] True, armed forces were everywhere. The assembly of more than a few persons in front of any Catholic cooperative was forbidden. Rail stations and tracks were guarded. On the first day of the strike soldiers were present at six in the morning at all factories and workshops. The labor police were everywhere—at fetes, conferences or factory gates. Each member of the "force" carried his identity card, to be shown whenever intervention became necessary. No parades were permitted without the express sanction of the regular trade union committee.[17]

The workers themselves walked around town, looked into store windows, slept late, and went to bed early. They cultivated their gardens. They visited the local *Maison du Peuple* to read the press or hear the news from the local control committees. Many visited their parents in other towns. Others took part in organized group visits to museums and galleries, or attended labor lectures. Metal workers obtained work in France and sent back part of their earnings to the strike fund. The militants occupied themselves with running the soup kitchens, acting as strike police, distributing strike cards, or aiding the Propaganda Commission.[18]

[15] Overbergh, op. cit., p. 173.
[16] *The Times,* London, April 15, 21, 25, 1913.
[17] Overbergh, op. cit., pp. 160–66.
[18] Ibid., pp. 167–69, 182–89.

Victory or Defeat?

The general strike began on Monday, April 14. Two days later, Parliament reassembled and was immediately concerned wholly with the strike. A Liberal deputy moved a resolution in which the Prime Minister's promise of a Commission to consider municipal and provincial franchise was expanded to include the Parliamentary vote. This resolution was passed by unanimous vote, and an amending paragraph condemning the general strike method was carried by a three-to-one vote. The National Committee for the Suffrage and the General Strike proposed a resolution of immediate return to work, in view of the achievement of the Parliamentary debate and motion. This proposal was accepted after a long, and at times bitter, discussion.[19] The Masson Resolution in the Belgian Parliament did not give complete satisfaction to the strikers. It was a partial victory, the first decisive step towards a revision of the franchise. The Liberal press claimed that the Prime Minister had yielded in the strike what he had refused to yield beforehand—the consideration by the Commission of Parliamentary suffrage as well as local and provincial. "Perhaps," wrote the London *Times* reporter, "we may concede that the strike has impressed the extreme wing of the Catholic Party, and thus at any rate . . . hastened the proposed inquiry into the electoral system. . . ."[20]

Impartial Belgian observers could agree that the Labor party had enhanced its reputation and given evidence of a remarkable control over the working population, inasmuch as, from start to finish, the strike remained completely peaceable. Not, however, until the first World War had ended did the vote at twenty-one years, without the plural vote, actually become the law of the land. *Whether it was the war or the general strike,* Belgian union membership of the non-Catholic

[19] The Resolution proposed follows:

(1) That the strike had . . . proved the power and solidarity of the working class.

(2) That the strike had placed before the public in the most pressing manner the question of universal suffrage.

(3) That the strike had compelled discussion of the question in Parliament for more than a week, and had won a precise statement of intention from the Government leader as to the establishment of an electoral commission. That in view of these achievements the National Committee would propose to Congress the immediate resumption of work. Overbergh, op. cit., pp. 221–23.

[20] *The Times,* London, April 28, 1913.

type jumped from 120,000 to 600,000 between 1913 and 1919.

What of the general strike and its future, after this Belgian experience? Professor Mahaim, not a Socialist, predicted that "the temptation to repeat this kind of experiment will be very strong." It should be no surprise, therefore, to the reader to learn that in the nineteen-fifties two more Belgian political general strikes were called, one to resist the return to Belgium of King Leopold III after World War II, and the other to set lower limits to an existing law on compulsory military service.

(2) LEOPOLD III, FRIEND OF NAZIS?

Intense feeling was roused in Belgium after World War II over the issue of whether the nation should take back its king, Leopold III, who had ordered the Belgians to surrender to the Nazis, and had himself been taken prisoner within eighteen days of the German attack on Belgium. The Cabinet of Hubert Pierlot, Catholic, escaped to Britain and formed a Belgium-in-exile government in London. Large numbers of workers feared Leopold's wartime friendship with Nazis. Enthusiasts of the Belgian underground looked upon Leopold as a traitor to his country and to the veterans who had in so many cases been held in prison camps (while their king was "imprisoned" in a Nazi mansion). This opposition of the non-Catholic organized workers in Belgium was in no sense hostility to a king, as was shown when Paul Spaak, one-time Socialist Premier, wrote an open letter to Leopold III, adjuring him to abdicate and let his nineteen-year-old son, Baudouin, take his place. Spaak warned Leopold that his return to Belgium would be opposed by organized labor even to the point of a general strike.[21]

The Socialists, powerful in Brussels and Wallonia and the main industrial centers, felt that Leopold had betrayed his country by his "friendly sojourn" with notorious Nazi leaders during the Nazi occupation of Belgium. They believed him to represent in his thought the fascist philosophy (*corporatisme*), and they feared that he would rule his country as a dictator. To solve the dispute the Catholic government in office resorted to a referendum on Leopold's return. Leopold had said that he would abdicate if the referendum gave him less than 55 per cent. In fact it gave him an overall vote of 57 per cent. Catholic Flanders had given him 70 per cent of the vote, but Brussels and Wallonia only 42 per cent to 48 per cent. The Socialists contended that they had not sought the referendum; that it had been the act of Leopold and the government, but that

21 Paris *Herald Tribune*, March 22, 1950.

since it had been taken it was evident that Leopold could not possibly bring his nation to a sense of unity.[22]

Scathing comment on a "57 per cent king" was common in the labor press and Socialist speeches. The Belgian Federation of Labor, through its weekly organ *Syndicats,* declared that the return of Leopold would signify the loss of democratic liberty, and would provoke one of the worst crises through which the nation had passed. It urged the workers to vote "no," lest all their progress, gained through a half century of union struggle, be nullified by a "reactionary clique which hides behind an 'elected' king."[23] On March 17, 1950, less than a week after the referendum figures were announced, some 300,000 Belgian workers walked off their jobs. These strikes were confined to anti-Leopold provinces such as Liège, Hainault, and Charleroi. In Mons the stoppage was complete in all branches of industry, including the public utilities. Strikers paraded with banners inscribed: "We'd rather starve than be ruled by a dictator." Belgium's largest iron and steel works was shut down, as also her only armaments plant. These "spontaneous" strikes were originally intended to last only twenty-four hours. In private, labor leaders admitted that the initiative had been taken by the Socialist party's Central Action Committee.[24]

On March 20 the press recorded the resignation of the Cabinet. The protest strikes continued. It was made evident that they would be stepped up to the completeness of a general strike as a last resort. The Socialists emphasized that they were not cooperating with the Communists, who had taken no part. The Socialists feared "a clericalist Fascism à la Salazar under a 57 per cent King"—Salazar being Premier of Portugal.[25] Finally, on March 24, Belgium saw a full-fledged general strike, for twenty-four hours in industry and public utilities, and for rail traffic while the railwaymen attended mass demonstrations in Brussels, Liège, Mons, Charleroi and La Louvière. In this strike nearly half a million workers were idle in French-speaking Wallonia, the industrial heart of the country. In Brussels the "Christian Unions" (Catholic) made possible a 10 per cent service in public transport. Even that was interfered with by University students.[26] It may be of interest to add that the abdication of King Leopold III did not actually take place until July, 1951, when his son Baudouin took his place.

[22] Paris *Herald Tribune,* March 18, 1950.

[23] *Syndicats,* March 4, 11, 1950.

[24] Paris *Herald Tribune,* March 18, 1950.

[25] Paris *Herald Tribune,* March 20, 1950.

[26] Paris *Herald Tribune,* March 25, 1950; New York *Times,* March 25, 1950.

(3) STRIKE PROTEST AGAINST UNIVERSAL SERVICE

A matter of grave concern to all young male Belgians was the twenty-four month universal service requirement, in order to uphold Belgian responsibilities in connection with European Defense agreements. The other five countries and Belgium were to meet in August, 1952, to decide upon a common length of service, since some were less than twenty-four months. In the meantime, demonstrations of young military trainees and young industrial workers were taking place in protest against the twenty-four month spell.[27]

Early in August the National Committee of the Belgian Federation of Labor decreed a general strike of twenty-four hours for Saturday, August 9. For that day mass demonstrations were to be organized. The Federation of Labor pledged itself to mobilize all international union forces to achieve a common training period for all six nations involved. National defense, the Federation held, was not at issue, only the "useless, superfluous months" of training. Workers' families must "sacrifice their young men to serve the stupid policy of a supercapitalist such as Van Zeeland." At the same time the Federation took a column in its organ *Syndicats* to warn its members against attempts of the Communists to take over the general strike, prolong it and make it indefinite. Strict discipline was called for, and obedience to no other group but the Federation of Labor.[28]

The Christian (Catholic) and Liberal trade unions denounced the strike as political in purpose. The stoppage was almost complete in metalworking plants, coal mines and other industry in Southern and Southeastern Belgium, but the railways and 95 per cent of the public services functioned as usual. Despite pouring rain, large Socialist demonstrations occurred. A week later the government announced that militiamen would be sent on furlough after they had served twenty-one months. This brought the Belgian period of military training into line with that of the Netherlands, which had the next longest training period to Belgium's. To this extent, then, it could be said that the strike served its purpose.[29]

The experience of Belgian labor in its efforts to wrest the universal (single) vote for all citizens from the conservative government, at the point of the general strike weapon, led naturally enough to its further use many decades later to prevent an unpopular king from becoming a dictator, and still more

[27] New York *Times,* August 10, 1952.

[28] *Syndicats,* August 9, 1952.

[29] *Le Peuple,* August 11, 1950; New York *Times,* August 10, 14, 1952.

recently to the modification of the long twenty-four month military training stint required of all Belgian males. Only by a stretch of the meaning of the word "revolutionary" could the last three Belgian general strikes be considered anything other than *political*.

FROM THE KAPP-PUTSCH TO 1959[30]

* * * * *

There are not many nations which, like Belgium, offer a long history of the general strike used for political purposes. In most instances the strike aims involved have been complex. This is particularly true of France and Italy. . . . This was true of France's successful general strike of February 12, 1934. It was equally true of the Kapp-Putsch in Germany in 1920. . . .

(4) THE KAPP-PUTSCH

Critics may say that the general strike which defeated the reactionary effort to recapture the German government in 1920 was a counter-revolutionary rather than a political strike. The writer merely points out that the mass of the strikers did not desire their Social Democrat government overthrown by the Kapp-Putsch, and they fought to save it with this labor weapon. With this as their aim it was a *political,* rather than an economic or a revolutionary strike. This is clear, inasmuch as more than one general strike had been attempted in Germany between 1918 and 1920, to bring into power a left-wing government, by pro-Soviet leaders such as Karl Liebknecht, Rosa Luxemburg, and the Spartacists. In each case the effort had been prevented or defeated. The Spartacist strikes *were* revolutionary, whereas the strike against Kapp and his Baltic Brigades was primarily political.

The German reactionaries in politics and military life had learned little from World War I or the subsequent revolution. Their contempt for the German working class made it easy for them to look upon the workers and their Social Democratic party, signatories to the hated peace treaty, as traitors to Germany. Discredited military leaders such as Ludendorff had escaped any penalty for their deeds. Such men were kept in the background, and a fanatical patriot, Wolfgang Kapp, born in New York State from German republican stock, was used as the immediate titular leader. The senior acting military member of the group was General von Lüttwitz, who had helped suppress the Spartacists in 1918–1919.

[30] In certain parts of this section the author has drawn heavily upon his book, *The General Strike,* published in 1931 by the University of North Carolina Press, which is now out of print.

The spark that set off the military explosion was the Allies' order that the Baltic troops should be disbanded. These were units formed of the "toughest fighting material brought by severity to a high pitch of internal discipline, but with habits of the most truculent militarism towards the public, acquired in their Baltic, Silesian, and anti-Bolshevist campaigns."[31] These "Baltic" Brigades were in camp within easy march of Berlin. On March 10, 1920, General von Lüttwitz visited President Ebert to present a virtual ultimatum with regard to the German military program. For one thing, the General was emphatic that there should be no disbanding and no diminution of officers' salaries or privileges. He demanded new elections for the Reichstag, a plebiscite for election of the President, and a Cabinet of experts. Gustav Noske, who had quelled the "revolution" in the German naval bases at the end of World War I, warned von Lüttwitz that, if orders of the government were disobeyed and military force were used against the Republic, the government would declare a general strike. This had little effect on the General, and he was shortly afterward removed from his office as head of the Berlin Reichswehr.[32]

In the meantime a warrant was out for the arrest of Dr. Kapp and his chief associates, but the police force was so riddled with Kappists that the execution of these warrants met with all kinds of interference. Friday, March 12, saw the Baltic Brigades start their march on Berlin. The Ebert government, learning that the Berlin Reichswehr was on Kapp's side, made a rapid move to Dresden and then to Stuttgart, where it issued an emergency call for an immediate meeting of the National Assembly. At the same time a call went out for a general strike throughout Germany against the Kapp rebels. The proclamation declared: "There is but one means to prevent the return of Wilhelm II; the paralysis of all economic life. Not a hand must stir, not a worker give aid to the military dictatorship. General Strike all along the line."[33] Two facts show the concern which the people of Germany felt for the continuance of their existing government. The first was the amazing unity of support given the strike by non-Socialist parties of the Center and the "Democrats." This meant that the Catholic trade unions of the Rhineland and the so-called "yellow" unions of the "Democrats" were, for once, united in purpose with the two Socialist parties. The Communists acted with the

[31] H. G. Daniels, *The Rise of the German Republic* (New York: Scribner, 1928), pp. 124–31.

[32] Gustav Noske, *Von Kiel bis Kapp* (Berlin, 1920), p. 207.

[33] Karl Brammer, *Funf Tage Militardiktatur* (Berlin, 1920), p. 65; *The Times*, London, March 15, 1920.

others, but their purpose was questionable.[34] The second most significant fact was the surprising act of Carl Legien, head of the German Federation of Labor, famous for his earlier condemnation of the general strike weapon as "General strike, general nonsense." He appeared to recognize in this present crisis that all labor organization was at stake, and so issued a call for a general strike from the side of the trade unions. Unlike the government, Legien remained in Berlin, went underground, and from his hiding place directed the struggle. When the strike ended in Kapp's defeat, it was Legien as much as any who demanded punishment of the "Rebels."[35] Ruth Fischer outlined the crisis:

> This was perhaps the most complete political general strike in a modern industrial country. German economy was brought to a standstill. From one hour to the next no train ran, there was no gas, no electricity, only a limited water supply. The rebels had excellent artillery and machine guns, airplanes, well-trained and reliable troops, a well-conceived strategic plan for the conquest of Germany. But against the power of organized labor they were paralyzed; no army can function in a vacuum.[36]

Even before the official strike call had reached the workers, thousands had spontaneously ceased work. By Sunday, March 14, the general walkout was in full swing. Only the telephones remained in service. The attempt to overawe the working population by an overwhelming display of military might failed dismally. A split in the temporary Kapp cabinet on whether to negotiate with the workers' committees or to shoot the ringleaders was decided in favor of the latter. Clashes took place between the *Technical Emergency Corps* and the working population as the former went to and from their work in the water and light plants. The military were stoned in many districts, and replied with rifle fire, killing many.[37]

Kapp now sought a compromise with Ebert, including a common denunciation of the devastating general strike. Luckily for the German workers, Ebert was adamant in refusing even to consider such a compromise. In districts where there were no military forces Communists had already set up local "soviets." The food supply was hourly more precarious. On Wednesday, March 17, Wolfgang Kapp resigned and igno-

[34] Berlin *Vorwärts,* March 15, 1920.

[35] Ruth Fischer, *Stalin and German Communism* (Harvard University Press, 1948), p. 124.

[36] Ibid., p. 123. By permission.

[37] *Berliner Tageblatt,* March 24, 1920; Karl Brammer, op. cit., p. 22.

miniously fled to Sweden. Von Lüttwitz clung to his post. Kapp gave as his reason for flight the need for absolute union of all Germans against the "annihilating danger of Bolshevism."[38] Tension grew as rebel troops remained in command of Berlin and the strike was in no wise abated. Finally the Kapp government surrendered. Von Seeckt took over the Reichswehr and ordered the Baltic Brigades to withdraw immediately from Berlin. As they marched sullenly out they were treated to shrill and contemptuous whistles of the striking workers. Acting under orders, the rear guard opened fire at point-blank range, killing several workers.

The brunt of the strike fell on the workers. Casualties were almost as severe as in a battle; privation was great to all. When the Kappists surrendered there were barely four days' supplies of food left in Berlin. Vice Chancellor Schiffer, who had been left behind by Ebert as a kind of liaison Minister, had announced the surrender of the Kappists, and at the same time, on March 18, had called upon the German people to resume work. With the Kapp-Putsch defeated, at least for the moment, the workers who had borne the burden of the conflict rather naturally refused to return to work until the Ebert government had given them more definite evidence of its attitude towards the reactionary section of the nation. On Saturday, March 20, Legien announced that an agreement had been reached with the Ebert government that would permit the workers to call off the strike.[39] Dissatisfaction followed the publication of the settlement, and chaos reigned on the following Monday. Services were disorganized; the food supply was low; queues forming outside the bakers' and butchers' shops augured food riots.

The strike was finally and definitely called off on Monday at midnight, when the industrial councils and the shop stewards joined with the trade unions in an agreement with the govern-

---

[38] Karl Brammer, op. cit., p. 36; *The Times,* London, March 18, 19, 1920.

[39] The settlement terms included:

Nomination of state and Prussian cabinets by trade unions and the parties. Punishment of Kappist leaders. . . .

Framing of new social laws giving more rights . . . to civil servants.

Socialization of all industries ripe for it. . . .

Punishment of speculation in foodstuffs. Confiscation of agricultural products and of land improperly cultivated.

Dissolution of the Reichswehr. . . .

Resignation of Noske.

See *The Times,* London, March 22, 1920; *Vorwärts,* March 22, 1920.

ment. A further statement to this effect was issued by Legien, on the condition that if the government failed to keep its pledges the general strike would be resumed. A supplementary agreement included withdrawal of the troops, an end to the state of siege, a pledge that armed workers would not be attacked, and that negotiations would ensue to get workers incorporated in the *Sicherheitswehr* of Prussia.

In fact, the end was tragic. Where workers had retired from their strongholds as soon as the agreements with the Ebert government had been reached, the government troops' officers instituted a house-to-house search for arms, removed the workers' leaders, and in certain cases executed them after summary court-martial. The government granted to von Seeckt unlimited power to use the military court throughout the country. Yet when Kapp was in power Major-General von Seeckt had made no move to go to the aid of the Ebert government. "The striking workers and those who had risen in armed resistance had at a stroke become 'Spartacists' and 'Communists' who were striving for a Bolshevik dictatorship and therefore had to be crushed with a most brutal disregard."[40] In brief, the punishment of the Kappists became a farce. The Baltic Brigades were untouched. The penalty paid by the unhappy strikers who caused the failure of the Kapp-Putsch was bitter and unforgettable. It is a dangerous game for the workers to try to save their government by the general strike weapon, even if it succeeds.

(5) "JUNE DAYS" IN EAST GERMANY, 1953

Without any apparent warning to West or East Germany in 1953 a wild revolt of workers and middle class against the Grotewohl (Communist) government of East Germany broke out in East Berlin and throughout most of the other industrial centers and cities. Allied Intelligence, the Socialist Union party (East German Communist party), the Communist government, and the Soviet Occupation forces—one and all appear to have agreed on one thing, that the outbreak was completely unexpected.[41] This fact does not stand in the way of post facto search for the reasons for the outbreak of June 17, 1953.

For eight years the eighteen million population of East Germany had endured Russian occupation and Communist control. Occasional outbursts of sabotage had been the only overt form of protest against the oppression and confiscation carried

[40] Heinrich Strobel, *Die deutsche Revolution*, 4th ed. (Berlin: Der Firn, 1922), p. 192; *The Times*, London, March 29, 30, 1920.
[41] "After the Revolt," *Manchester Guardian Weekly*, August 27, 1953.

on by the puppet regime under the guns of Soviet Russia. Essential causes of the explosion can be suggested: Religious persecution of ministers, churches and church youth groups had reached a dangerous point, with Communist "Free German Youth" as one of the instruments of persecution. A second factor was the deterioration of the already intolerable food situation, fats and meat having become almost unobtainable, together with shortages of bread and potatoes. Furthermore, the Grotewohl government was fanatically pushing the final control over industry and agriculture, with the seizure of private businesses and co-operatives. These steps raised middle-class ire and brought despair to the farmers, who were fleeing to West Germany in great numbers. The igniting spark, however, was the government's call for immediate, higher productivity, at lower pay, from the factory workers of East Germany. This drive for lower overhead costs got under way in May, 1953, with specious newspaper items alleging that workers themselves had suggested this tightening up of the work "norms." At this juncture Mr. Semeonov, Ambassador to East Germany from Soviet Russia, and Soviet High Commissioner, took over absolute control of Eastern Germany. Disliking the effects of the steps already described, Semeonov appears to have inspired the Grotewohl government's "confession of error" and the reversal of its policy, with the sole exception of the raised "norms" of production. A week before the revolt, Grotewohl met the Church leaders and announced important concessions. Benefits to the middle class and the farmers were also pledged. Only the workers were left with no share in the handout, but with a ten per cent wage cut.[42]

East German workers were experienced in the trick of "norms": refinements of the "speed-up" granted to a worker who introduced an improvement which would raise the production norm. Four months at the old norm were his reward, while his fellows had to face pay cuts or comply with the new norm. Spontaneous and open resistance resulted. Workers unanimously rejected the new norm contracts. Others in large numbers absented themselves from their jobs. The arrest of protesting miners led to riots and the death and injury of several of the People's Police. The Soviet military were called into one plant.[43] These events occurred in 1951–52, so that the Grotewohl government could hardly claim to have been

[42] Terrance Prittie, "The Rising of June 17," *Manchester Guardian Weekly*, July 2, 16, 1953; Mark Arnold-Forster, "The June 17 Rising: Recoil of the Lies," *Manchester Guardian Weekly*, July 30, 1953.

[43] Theodore Lit, "Unions in Democratic and Soviet Germany," *Monthly Labor Review*, January 1953, p. 6 ff.

completely unaware of what their fanatical pressure for production would do to the East German workers.

* * * * *

(6) HAITI, 1956–57

Haiti in 1956–57 presented an unusual aspect of the general strike. This Negro nation of the Caribbean came near to
civil war at that time over the issue which of ten candidates
should be elected President. Business men led at least three
general strikes, unseating temporarily a military dictatorship.
The Republic of Haiti is the only French-speaking country in
Latin America, and with the Dominican Republic constitutes
the island of Haiti. On December 6, 1956, General Paul Magloire resigned as provisional Chief of State under pressure of
a nation-wide general strike, which was in protest against his
assumption of dictatorial powers. That only the army could
meet the terrorism rife on the island was his excuse.[44] The
rising against Magloire came after three days of general strike
in which most union labor quit, and the majority of stores,
plants, and offices closed. The Lawyers Association ceased
from pleading cases in court. "The people generally expressed
surprise at the effectiveness of the general strike as a substitute
for the violence usually employed to oust an unpopular Chief
of State."[45]

(7) GOLD COAST, 1949

Perhaps the most surprising thing about the general strike in
Africa is the relatively few actually recorded. In fact, however,
it should be recognized how predominantly rural are all but
the Northern and Southernmost portions of Africa. Usually
one connects the general strike with some degree of industrialism. In the case of the Gold Coast, industry on any large
scale is still in the future. Yet the main money crop, cocoa,
with a handful of American or British educated Negro leaders, together are likely to yield an intensely interesting experiment in the grafting of modern democracy upon the ancient
stem of tribal life and *Juju*. Barely 10 per cent of the population are literate; so the modern, young political leaders, such
as Kwame Nkrumah, intentionally live much more closely to
their people than did the old white and native officials of the
earlier British colonial days.

Unlike most one-crop colonial territories, the Gold Coast
has, under Nkrumah, been grimly saving the necessary capi-

[44] United Press wire, December 12, 1956; New York *Times*, December 13, 1956.
[45] Ibid. By permission.

tal that can modernize the country and bring to its people a healthier and perhaps more satisfying life. With a population almost 100 per cent Negro, modern political psychology and ancient tribal tradition have to be mingled with care and knowledge to achieve more than temporary progress. How successful Nkrumah has been in this tightrope walking can be seen in the story of the Gold Coast general strike of 1949.

Born over forty-five years ago on the Gold Coast, son of a goldsmith and a storekeeper, Nkrumah was educated in Roman Catholic mission schools, in Achimota College and then at Lincoln University in Pennsylvania, at the University of Pennsylvania and in London, England. Dr. Nkrumah returned to the Gold Coast late in 1947, to take part in the development of the U.G.C.C. (United Gold Coast Convention). Dr. Nkrumah found himself at odds with many of his U.G.C.C. colleagues, chiefly over the fact that the broadest basis of suffrage was not proposed, because, said the older leaders, the people were not yet ready for it.

A struggle with foreign store owners over the rising prices of the few goods the Gold Coast natives desired ended with Negro veterans being killed by the police. This roused such anger along the Gold Coast that much rioting occurred, and looting in the larger stores. The U.G.C.C. leaders petitioned London by cable to appoint a Commission of Inquiry. This was done by the British government, but the Gold Coast Governor arrested the leaders, and banished them to Northern territories, where they were separately incarcerated. When the Watson Commission sat, the imprisoned leaders were released to give evidence. The Commission reported that the old Constitution was outmoded. When the Governor appointed a constitutional committee of forty Africans, old and upper-class chiefs were chosen, and the younger leaders ignored. Dr. Nkrumah formed a youth committee and had them travel throughout the nation to rouse interest in universal suffrage, a fully elected legislature, and a representative cabinet. By this time a split had developed in the U.G.C.C. and a new organization, the Convention Peoples' party (C.P.P.) was established by Dr. Nkrumah with the purpose of starting a Gold Coast general strike. It was not so termed, but was referred to as "positive action based on non-violence," and was much akin to Gandhi's "civil disobedience" in Natal in 1913 and British India in 1930–31.

After some considerable negotiation between the government and Nkrumah, country-wide civil disobedience started on January 8, 1949. No one worked; buses and trucks were silent. Continuance of water, electricity and health services was agreed upon by the C.P.P. leaders. For twenty-one days this continued. Then Nkrumah and his leading colleagues were charged with sedition and imprisoned. The 1951 election for the Legislative Assembly gave Nkrumah thirty-five seats out of the thirty-eight involved. Thus the prisoner became the head of a dominant party, and ultimately the Premier of the Gold Coast. Not many general strikes in other parts of the world have contributed to such a reversal of power.[46]

On March 6, 1957, the Gold Coast became the independent nation of Ghana within the British Commonwealth. Ahead are grave problems of unity, since the Ashanti Province has an opposition party (N.L.M.—National Liberation Movement) with extreme states' rights theories. It is Nkrumah's task to unify the new nation of Ghana without dictatorship or civil war, and time may show that the general strike is a weapon relatively preferable to civil war.[47]

[46] Richard Wright, *Black Power* (New York: Harper, 1954), Chap. XI; John Gunther, *Inside Africa* (New York: Harper, 1955), p. 804, and *Collier's,* May 28, 1954; Barbara Ward, "An Answer to the Challenge of Africa," New York *Times,* October 31, 1954.

[47] "Morning After in Ghana," *Manchester Guardian Weekly,* March 21, 1957; William Clark, "Africans Face a Rugged Task," Washington *Post,* February 22, 1957.

13. Arthur Griffith:
THE RESURRECTION OF HUNGARY

The establishment of the Austro-Hungarian federation in 1867 has been cited by many as an excellent example of successful non-violent resistance in politics. Austrian-Hungarian relations in the middle of the nineteenth century were very complicated and it is impossible here to go into all their ramifications. In 1847, however, Hungary had been restive under Austrian rule and, under the leadership of Louis Kossuth, had demanded a greater measure of self-government. This the Austrians had refused, imprisoning Kossuth and other leaders.

With the revolutionary fervor of 1848 abroad in Western Europe, however, Eastern Europe could not be preserved against a similar spirit. There were demonstrations in Vienna and Budapest; and the Austrian Emperor, bowing to popular clamor, granted certain of the Hungarian demands for self-rule. Shortly thereafter, however, the situation was clouded by the resistance of several national groups in Hungary—Slovaks, Rumanians, Croats, and Serbs—who objected to the centralized nature of the new Hungarian self-governing institutions. Those among the Hungarians who advocated military suppression of the nationalities raised an army and sought to overcome their resistance. But the Austrians intervened and occupied Budapest. Once more the struggle became one between the Austrians and Hungarians. It was under these circumstances that an Hungarian Republic was proclaimed (in April, 1849).

The Hungarian national army now proceeded to conduct a military campaign against the Austrians, who then appealed to the Russians for help. In July of 1849, Russian troops entered Hungary and defeated the Hungarians. Kossuth, who had been instrumental in the military resurrection of Hungary, fled into exile abroad. Many Hungarian leaders who were unable to escape were executed by the Austrians, who instituted a regime of severe and violent repression.

It was under these circumstances that the events related in our reading took place. After violent measures against the Austrians had failed, Hungarians began to explore non-violent power. Their leader was Francis Deák, a remarkable political figure whose confidence in the possibilities of passive resistance seemed never to wane.[1] With Hungary utterly powerless in a military sense and rule by law abolished under Austrian domination, he advised his compatriots to offer no violence against Austrian agents but rather to refuse co-operation. They were to meet the tax-gatherer's demands with a polite but firm "no." They were to decline public positions. They were to demonstrate non-violently against Austrian rule and to ask for restoration of the Hungarian constitution.

In our reading, Arthur Griffith describes in some detail just how Deák and his followers went about their tasks. The long campaign, which extended over a period of more than a decade and a half, was filled with frustrations and disappointments. Eventually, however, it was substantially successful: Hungary was restored to a status of self-government in 1867 and was to participate jointly with Austria in a common parliament for the control of external and general matters. The agreement was known as the Austro-Hungarian Compromise, or *Ausgleich*.

The reader will note that passive resistance was not the only factor in producing this outcome. Austria during the sixties was having external difficulties—with Denmark and Prussia—and needed very much, therefore, to secure active Hungarian co-operation. When all this is admitted, however, the story of Deák and his campaign of non-violence remains an impressive one. Unfortunately, the Hungarians were not committed to non-violence on principle and some years later began to oppress their own subject nationalities.

Our reading is excerpted from Arthur Griffith's *The Resurrection of Hungary: A Parallel for Ireland* (Dublin: Whelan and Sons, 1918), pp. 1–68, with certain omissions. Griffith (1872–1922) was one of the great leaders of the Irish independence movement; and he saw in the non-violent movement of Hungary a model which he hoped his countrymen would emulate in their struggle with Britain.

[1] For a discussion of the internal political background of Deák's activities, see A. J. P. Taylor, *The Habsburg Monarchy, 1890–1918* (New York: Macmillan, 1942, rev. ed., 1949), Chaps. V to IX. Of Deák, Taylor remarks that "he was completely without ambition, except the ambition of seeing his country restored to freedom, and of a character so noble that in the last hundred years of Austrian history only the name of Masaryk is worthy to be placed beside that of Deák." (p. 118.)

I. THE MIGRATION OF DEAK

Francis Deák had been placed under arrest by the Austrians in an early stage of the war for declining to advise Kossuth and the members of the Hungarian Diet to unconditionally surrender. In the latter stage he had resided on his estate at Kehida. When the Hungarian flag had been trampled in the blood of its soldiers and Hungary lay prostrate, all her other leaders dead or in exile, Deák bethought himself it was time to sell his estate and move into town. So he sold his estate and moved up to town—to Pesth—and hired a bedroom and a sitting-room at the Queen of England Hotel, and walked about the streets, playing with children, giving alms to beggars, and conversing with all sorts and conditions of men. The Austrians regarded him doubtfully. "What did Deák sell his estate and come to Pesth for?" they asked each other. "Keep your eyes on him, my children," said the Austrian Prefect to the Austrian police.

But although they kept as many eyes on him as Argus had, still they could find nothing in Deák's conduct to warrant his arrest. They had taken away Hungary's constitution, they had taken away even Hungary's name, yet they could not construe playing with children, giving to beggars, and talking with men and women, into treason, and that was all Deák did. Still the uneasiness and mistrust of the Austrians grew. "It would be a good thing," at length said one brilliant Austrian statesman, "to make Deák a Grand Justiciary.[2] This would console the Hungarian people." And they made the offer to Deák. "When my country's Constitution is acknowledged I shall consider your offer," replied Deák. "What Constitution?" asked the Austrians. "The Constitution of 1848," said Deák.

*   *   *   *   *

"Deák wants the Constitution back," said the Austrians; "children cry for the moon." . . . In Deák's little room in the Pesth hotel every night a few friends gathered who puffed tobacco and drank moderately of wine. They had no passwords and no secrecy—they discoursed of Hungarian history, Hungarian literature, Hungarian industries, Hungarian economics, and the Hungarian Constitution, which they obstinately declined to oblige the Austrians by believing to be dead. "It is not dead, but sleepeth—owing to the illegal administering of a drug." Deák, who was a cheerful man, talked of the day when it would awaken, and made jokes. Visitors to Pesth from the country districts came to visit Deák. They stopped an evening, smoked a pipe and drank a glass of wine with him and with

[2] Judex Curiæ.

those who gathered in his sitting-room, and as they talked despair fell from them.

* * * * *

So far to hint at the policy Deák had conceived, a policy of Passive Resistance, which in eighteen years beat the Austrian Government to its knees. Deák stood by the Constitution of Hungary. He declined to argue or debate the merits of that Constitution or the "fitness" of his countrymen for it—good or bad, fit or unfit, it was Hungary's property and Hungary alone could relinquish it. He refused to go to Vienna or to go to Canossa. Pesth was the capital of his nation, and in Pesth he planted his flag. "Keep your eyes on your own country," he said to the people, from which it may be inferred that a policy of Passive Resistance and a policy of Parliamentarianism are very different things. . . .

II. HOW FRANCIS JOSEF VISITED PESTH

The light from the window of Francis Deák's room in the Pesth hotel irritated and alarmed the ministers of darkness. An Austrian garrison, politely called a police force . . . occupied Hungary. Its duties were . . . to keep the movements of Hungarian Nationalists under surveillance by day, to pay them domiciliary visits by night, to report or disperse any assembly of Hungarians whereat the National feeling was fearlessly voiced, to superintend with their bayonets the confiscation of the soil, and to seize and destroy Hungarian newspapers or prints which had courage enough to beard and denounce the Tyranny. An Austrian Lord Lieutenant sat in Pesth and erased the historic territorial divisions of Hungary, the Hungarian Parliament was declared dead as Cæsar, and a swarm of hungry Austrian bureaucrats ruled the land. Trial by jury was abolished, and Austrian removables, at 4,000 roubles per annum, manned the Bench. The Hungarian language was officially prohibited in the transaction of public business, and fired neck-and-crop out of the schools.

* * * * *

And yet Francis Deák, sitting on the Bridge of Buda-Pesth on a sunny afternoon, encouraging little boys to throw handsprings, . . . violently disturbed the equanimity of the bureaucrats in Pesth—yet why they could not say. The wave of disturbance rolled on to Vienna, and the statesmen there hit upon a subtle plan for the extinction of Hungarian Nationality beyond the power of all the Kossuths and the Deáks in the world to revive. This was to incorporate Hungary in the Germanic Confederation, so that if at any time Hungary again attempted to raise her head, not only Austria, but Prussia, Saxony, Bavaria and all the other countries of Germany would be bound to swoop down on her. But France intervened. Austria bluffed, but France remained firm. "We shall treat the attempt to obliterate Hungary as a casus belli," said the French Government, whereupon Austria caved in, and furthermore the State of Siege was abolished.

The abolition of the State of Siege was little change in one way—the bureaucracy still ruled the land, and the Constitution was still in abeyance—but it permitted Deák to carry out one side of his policy with greater freedom. The Kostelek or Agricultural Union which he had founded set itself to compete with Austrian farm produce and wipe it out of the home and foreign market; the Vedegylet or National Protective Union which Kossuth had founded was freer now to wage war on the Austrian manufacturer, and the National Academy was freer to preach love of Hungary's literature and Hungary's language, than hitherto.

*   *   *   *   *

Bach in Vienna was alarmed and disconcerted. He felt it necessary that Deák's influence should be destroyed, but how to destroy it puzzled him. At last he hit on an idea as brilliant and original as a modern Englishman himself could conceive —the idea of "a Royal Visit." "You must visit Pesth, sire," said he to Francis Josef. And Francis Josef prepared to visit Pesth. The Pesth newspapers were instructed to announce that a new era was about to dawn. Francis Josef was coming to Pesth— he was coming to restore the confiscated estates of the political offenders, and shower blessings on the people, and, therefore, he should be accorded a loyal and enthusiastic reception. Francis Deák would, of course, welcome him with open arms, for Deák was a loyal man. "I am," said Deák, "to the King of Hungary." "And, of course, the Emperor of Austria is King of Hungary," suggested the reptile Press. "He is entitled to be," said Deák, "when he complies with the law, swears to uphold the Constitution of Hungary, and is crowned with the crown of St. Stephen in Buda. I am a Hungarian—I owe allegiance to the King of Hungary—I owe none to the Emperor of Austria."[3]

The Emperor of Austria arrived in Pesth on the 4th of May, 1857, and was received with prolonged and enthusiastic cheers by the Viennese imported into Pesth for the occasion, by the plain-clothes policemen, the Austrian officials and the members of their families, and by the lion-and-unicorn shopkeepers. The

[3] According to Deák and his followers, the Austrian and Hungarian crowns were entirely separate, even though they might be worn by the same person.—Ed.

people looked on at the magnificent procession, which entered the city under a triumphal arch—erected by public subscription of the Austrian bureaucrats and their hangers-on in Pesth—bearing the inscription "God has sent You."

* * * * *

His Majesty the Emperor went to the Academy and expressed his admiration for the Hungarian language. "It is surely a New Era," said the Hungarian jellyfish; "let us present him with an address, Deák." "No," said Deák. "Not a grovelling address," urged the jellyfish; "an address pointing out the grievances under which we labour, and demanding their removal." Said Deák: "While Francis Josef violates the law and arbitrarily abrogates the Constitution Hungary cannot recognise him." But the loyal-addressers determined to present an address, and they did. . . .

* * * * *

A few months after the Deák-destroying visit of the Emperor Francis Josef, Bach realised that his grand scheme had been a fiasco—Hungary was as strong and as anti-Austrian as ever. "I must fix up Deák," said Bach, and he again invited him to come to Vienna to discuss the Constitution. "I know nothing of any Constitution, except the Hungarian Constitution; I can only treat on the basis of the Hungarian Constitution," replied Deák. "Come and let us discuss matters," urged Bach. "There can be no discussion, no argument, no compromise on the Hungarian Constitution. It still remains—and I remain in Pesth," said Deák. And so the year of Our Lord 1859 dawned for Hungary.

III. THE FALL OF BACH

In the spring of 1859 all Europe saw that war between France and Austria was imminent. Louis Napoleon engaged with the Hungarian exiles to make the Independence of Hungary one of the conditions of peace if he won the war—they in turn engaged to induce the Hungarian troops in the Austrian service to desert, and offered to make Napoleon's brother King of Hungary. But the French Emperor, after defeating Austria, broke his engagement on a plea of "the exigencies of the European situation."

Francis Josef came back from the wars in a chastened spirit. "My beloved subjects," he said to his people, "truth compels me to proclaim that we have been whipped," and, therefore, he announced he would devote his whole and uninterrupted attention to establish the "internal welfare and external power of Austria by a judicious development of its rich, moral, and material strength, and by making such improvements in the Legislature and Administration as are in accord with the spirit of the age." Next he fired out Bach. Thirdly, he invited Baron Josika, a Hungarian, to become Minister of the Interior. "Your Majesty," said Josika, "I am a Hungarian. I understand Hungarians. I do not understand Austrians. If you appointed an Austrian to govern us Hungarians, he could not govern us well because he is alien to us. Neither could I govern well your Austrians, since I am of a different race. I assure your Majesty that the man who pretends he can govern a people well, who does not belong to that people, or else who has not spent his lifetime among them, is a humbug." . . . Golouchowski, a Pole, was then offered and accepted the office declined by Josika. He and the Emperor put their heads together, and finally decided to increase the number of members in the Reichsrath—which then was the equivalent of what we know as the Privy Council—that they might better confer and consult with it as to how to fix up matters. Six members were summoned from Hungary. "What shall we do?" asked the summoned of Deák. "Don't go," said Deák. "If Francis Josef wants to consult Hungary, let him come to Pesth and consult her through her Parliament." Whereupon three of them refused to go, and three went and made eloquent speeches on the floor of the House, incited thereto by Count Desewffy, the loyal-addresser of 1857, who through attending tea-parties and, things organised by Rechberg and Von Hubner, two Austrian Union-of-Hearts statesmen, came to the conclusion that Deák was really the obstacle to the better understanding of two peoples whom God had created as the complement of each other, and Francis Deák, instigated by the devil, kept asunder. Poor Von Hubner, however, was an honest fellow, and in the exuberance of his New Eraian enthusiasm he grew quite sentimental about Hungary, with the result that the Emperor dismissed him from office. The Hungarian County Councils had been abolished in defiance of the Constitution, and the Emperor and Golouchowski concluded their first step in the Conciliation game should be to revive these Councils in defiance of the Constitution, since they dared not admit the right of the Hungarian Parliament. If they acted honestly, the thing was simple enough. The Hungarian Parliament need only be convoked, and the County Councils would be brought again into being by the command of that Parliament. But it was the last thing the Emperor or Golouchowski intended to do at this period. They had set out with the object of killing off the demand for an autonomous Hungary and drawing the fangs of Hungarian disloyalty by restoring her a strictly limited district control over her gas-and-water, and by saying kind things of the Hungarian people and offering jobs and titles to influential

Hungarians. "Let the dead past bury its dead," said Golouchowski—among the dead which it would bury being the Hungarian Constitution of 1848, a fact of which Golouchowski forgot to remind Hungary, but which Hungary did not forget.

* * * * *

The splendid allegiance of the people to Deák saved the Hungarians. Had they listened to the voices of the weaklings and the teachings of expediency, they would have got their County Councils—in exchange for their principle—and there was an end of Hungary. But Hungary had a statesman, not a politician, at her head. Deák's immobility and Hungary's solidity baffled Austria. Austria could not recede—her Imperial existence depended on reversing Bach's Absolutist policy. She could not advance—unless she paid Hungary toll. Deák had foreseen and knew—and smoking his pipe, waited. And the result was that Austria offered toll. By Royal Ordinance the County Councils were restored—Austria must needs save its face by making the restoration on the outside an Imperial affair—but at the same time the Hungarian Parliament was convoked. The wisdom of Deák was demonstrated even to the Wise Men, and Hungary not unnaturally was going to cheer when Deák told it not to. "Wait, my countrymen," said he, "until the Parliament opens, and we see what we shall see. There is abundant time to cheer afterwards." Deák knew his Austria, and Hungary sobered up, and in a calm and critical spirit awaited the now famous "Meeting of the Hungarian Diet of 1861."

IV. HOW THE HUNGARIANS REFUSED TO SEND REPRESENTATIVES TO THE "IMPERIAL PARLIAMENT"

The County Councils were re-established. Their first action was to dismiss the Austrian officials who had been planted on the counties during the Ten Years' Tyranny, their second to strike out the rate for supporting the Austrian Army, their third to order the tax-collectors to collect no taxes unless levied by authority of the Hungarian Parliament. "What is the object sought after by the Hungarian County Councils?" asked a Vienna journal indignantly. Its answer to its own question did not convey the truth half so well as the prompt reply of the County Council of Pesth: "To sweep away every trace of Austrian rule, and hold Hungary for the Hungarians." Francis Josef was disconcerted. He invited Deák to come and discuss matters with him, and Deák went. Francis Josef promised Deák that he would satisfactorily settle the Hungarian question, and assured Deák he might banish all suspi-

cion from his mind as to Francis Josef's bona-fides. Deák was
not bamboozled, but he decided to remove all pretext for
breaking faith from Francis Josef's grasp. Therefore Deák advised the County Councils to a less strenuous policy until the
Parliament met and they saw what kind of a Parliament it was
to be, and the County Councils bowed to Deák's statesmanship,
and tamed their hearts of fire. Suddenly the news came to
Pesth that Golouchowski had resigned and that Von Schmerling had succeeded him, and then came the news that Schmerling had a policy which was infallibly to settle the Hungarian
question and the Bohemian question and the Croatian question
and the other questions that disturbed the Austrian Empire.
. . . Schmerling proposed to establish, or re-establish, local
Parliaments in the different countries of the Empire, these Parliaments having control over internal affairs, but no control
over Imperial taxation, military matters, foreign affairs, and
soforth. An Imperial Parliament in Vienna was to control all
such things. This Imperial Parliament was to consist of 343
members, of whom Hungary was to have 85, Bohemia 56,
Transylvania 20, Moravia 22, Upper and Lower Austria 28,
Croatia and Slavonia 9, Styria 13, the Tyrol 12, and the smaller
States smaller numbers. Hungary received the Schmerling
policy with a cry of derision. . . . Excitement grew in Pesth,
and Deák had to use all his influence to restrain the people
from proceeding to acts of violence against the Home-Rule-
cum-Empire Party, which was almost wholly composed of Austrians or the sons of Austrians. "Be calm," said he to the people; "await the meeting of the Diet. A single false step and all
may be ruined." The Emperor's warrant for the convening of
the Diet was received, and Deák was immediately elected for
Pesth. Three hundred representatives in all were elected that
March of 1861, two hundred and seventy of them being avow-
edly anti-Austrian, and the handful hurlers on the ditch. When
they had been elected they refused to meet in the Castle of
Buda, whither they had been summoned. "The Constitution of
1848 fixed our meeting place in Pesth," they said, "and in
Pesth we meet or not at all." The Austrians fought, cajoled,
and gave way. . . . Then Francis Josef's message was read
by Francis Josef's Commissioner. His Majesty felt deeply, he
said, that mistrust and misunderstanding had arisen between
Austrians and Hungarians, and he wished to restore peace and
harmony. To that end he invited the Hungarian Legislature to
meet, look after Hungary's gas-and-water, and send representatives to the Imperial Parliament in Vienna. The hall re-
sounded with the scornful laughter of the deputies of the Hungarian people. Francis Deák calmed the tumult. It was sought,
he said, to have them transfer to a foreign assembly sitting in
the capital of a foreign country, and calling itself an Imperial

Parliament, the right of making laws for themselves and their children. Who would acquiesce?" "None!" shouted the representatives of Hungary with one voice. . . . Whereupon Deák drew up and the Hungarian Parliament adopted the famous "First Address of the Hungarian Diet of 1861 to His Imperial Majesty Francis Josef, Emperor of Austria, in reply to his Speech to the Parliament of the Free Kingdom of Hungary."

"The twelve years which have just elapsed," said the Address, "have been to us a period of severe suffering. Our ancient Constitution has been suspended. We have been grievously oppressed by a system of power hitherto unknown to us. . . . Each day brought new sufferings; each suffering tore from our bosom another fibre of faith and confidence." "We suffered," continued the Address, but in manly triumph added, "we were not untrue to ourselves"—hence Austria is forced to abandon Absolutism, and "We, the representatives of Hungary, assemble to recommence our constitutional activity. . . . If the independence of our country be menaced, it is our duty as men to raise our common voice against the attack." And it *is* threatened, continue the addressers—threatened by the very first step which *you*, Francis Josef, have taken in a Constitutional direction. It has been violated in that the Hungarian Constitution has been only re-established *conditionally*, deprived of its most essential attributes. It has been violated by the Diploma of October.

"That Diploma would rob Hungary for ever of the ancient provisions of her Constitution, which subject all questions concerning public taxation and the levying of troops throughout Hungary solely to Hungary's Parliament; it would deprive the nation of the right of passing, in concurrence with the King, its own laws on subjects affecting the most important material interests of the land. . . . —*Therefore, we declare that we will take part neither in the Imperial Parliament nor in any other assembly whatsoever of the representatives of the Empire; and, further, that we cannot recognise the right of the said Imperial Parliament to legislate on the affairs of Hungary*, and are only prepared to enter on special occasions into deliberation with the constitutional peoples of the hereditary States as one independent nation with another."

"Do you want to be crowned King of Hungary?" continued the Address in effect. "Very well; first comply with the law—cease to illegally suspend our Constitution, and then we shall arrange about your coronation."

*   *   *   *   *

On the 5th of July a messenger sped from Pesth to Vienna with the Address of the Hungarian Parliament to Francis Josef. . . .

V. AND HOW THE EMPEROR OF AUSTRIA
LOST HIS TEMPER

On the 21st of July the Emperor Francis Josef replied to the Address of the Hungarian Diet. "Faithful subjects," said he, "you are acting in an extremely silly manner. You want the right to decide on taxation and other matters for Hungary—why, I offer you the privilege of coming into our Imperial Parliament here in Vienna and deciding, in conjunction with my other faithful subjects, the taxation for the whole Empire. Your Little Hungary ideas are neither patriotic nor wise. Develop an Imperial soul, and get out of your parochial rut." . . .

These words were not the Emperor's exact words, but they give the true spirit of the reply. It was read to the Parliament at Pesth amid cries of anger. But Deák, cool and farseeing, held the fiercer spirits in check, and on the 12th of August the Deputies, on his motion, adopted the celebrated "Second Address of the Parliament of Hungary to Francis Josef." Deák was its author, of course, as he was the author of the preceding one. Calmly he examined each claim put forward on behalf of Austrian control of Hungary, and calmly he disproved each claim. He exhibited Francis Josef and his Ministers to the world as Violaters of the Law, Rebels to the Constitution. . .

On the 12th of August the Second Address of the fearless Hungarian Parliament was despatched to Francis Josef at Vienna. On the 21st Francis Josef replied by dissolving the Parliament. The Deputies declined to acknowledge his act as legal, and in solemn procession marched to the House, which was occupied by Austrian soldiers, who at the bayonet's point kept them out. Deák, turning from the House, lit a cigar and walked back to his hotel, where he joined in a game of bowls. "What is the news?" asked his landlord. "Austria," said Deák, as he knocked down the ninepins, "has declared war."

VI. THE BLOODLESS WAR

The Pesth County Council protested against the illegal dissolution of the Hungarian Parliament. The Emperor replied by ordering the Pesth County Council to be itself dissolved. The County Council disregarded the Emperor's order and continued to hold its meetings, until the Austrian soldiery entered the Council Chamber and turned them out by force. As the Councillors emerged into the streets they shouted with one voice: "Eljen a Magyar Huza!" "God save Hungary!" The shout was re-echoed by the people who had congregated outside, and who, raising the Councillors on their shoulders, carried them through the streets, singing the Hungarian National

Anthem. From the windows of his house the Chairman of the County Council addressed his fellow-citizens: "We have been dispersed by tyrannic force—but force shall never over-awe us," he said. "Austrians violate Justice and the Law, and then tell us we are disloyal subjects. When they restore what they have taken from us, then let them talk of loyalty." . . .

Every County Council throughout the land followed the ex-ample of the County Council of Pesth and shared its fate. The officials of the County Councils patriotically refused to trans-fer their services to the Austrians, and for a little time some-thing like anarchy prevailed in the land. Francis Josef ap-pointed a Hungarian renegado named Palffy military governor, and proclaimed a coercion regime. A Press censorship was established, all local governing bodies were superseded by Austrian officials, and trial by Removables instituted. "The dis-loyalty of the Hungarian local bodies pains my paternal heart," said Francis Josef. "I come here," said Palffy, "as a good chief and a kind friend." "Behold the good chief and kind friend," said a Pesth newspaper, "Palffy—the renegado. Judas, we sa-lute thee." Palffy suppressed the newspaper and resumed: "The welfare of Hungary has always been and always will be proportioned to the loyalty of its people to the Emperor. See? Those who preach otherwise are seditious, blasphemous, or harebrained persons. Be loyal and you will be happy." Where-upon a Hungarian humorist wrote a rude rhyme which he en-titled "The Austrian Thieves." "The Austrian Thieves" became a popular song in Hungary, and the tune to which it was sung was heard one day by Palffy played by a military band. There-upon he summoned all the military bandmasters before him. "In future," said he, "observe that no revolutionary tunes are played by your bands, and above all, take care not to play that seditious new song, 'The Austrian Thieves.'" "Your Excel-lency," said one bandmaster, bravely, "it is not a new song—it is a very old tune."

Deák admonished the people not to be betrayed into acts of violence nor to abandon the ground of legality. "This is the safe ground," he said, "on which, unarmed ourselves, we can hold our own against armed force. If suffering be necessary, suffer with dignity." . . . He had given the order to the coun-try—Passive Resistance—and the order was obeyed. When the Austrian tax-collector came to gather the taxes the people did not beat him or hoot him—they declined to pay him, assuring him he was a wholly illegal person. The tax-collector thereupon called in the police and the police seized the man's goods. Then the Hungarian auctioneer declined to auction them, and an Austrian of his profession had to be brought down. When he arrived he discovered he would have to bring bidders from Austria, also. The Austrian Government found in time that it

was costing more to fail to collect the taxes than the taxes, if
they were collected, would realise. In the hope of breaking
the spirit of the Hungarians, the Austrians decreed that soldiers should be billeted upon them. The Hungarians did not
resist the decree—but the Austrian soldier, after a little experience of the misery of living in the house of a man who despises
you, very strongly resisted it. And the Hungarians asserted that
from their enforced close acquaintance with the Austrian army
they found it to be an institution they could not permit their
sons, for their souls' sake, to enter, wherefore they proposed
that enlistment in the Austrian army was treason to Hungary,
and it was carried unanimously.

The eyes of Europe became centered on the struggle, and
when the "Imperial Parliament" met in Vienna without the
Hungarian representatives turning up to its deliberations, the
Prussian and French Press poked such fun at it that it became
a topic for laughter throughout Europe. So within nine months
of the illegal dissolution of the Hungarian Parliament of 1861,
Hungary, without striking a blow, had forced Austria into the
humiliating position of a butt for Europe's jests. "Austria can
wait and win," said Schmerling. "She can't wait half so long
as we can," replied Deák.

*   *   *   *   *

VII. THE FAILURE OF FORCE AND "CONCILIATION"

Austria strove to encounter the Passive Resistance of Hungary by ordaining, as England did in Ireland a generation later,
"exclusive trading" illegal. The Hungarians despised the ordinance and pursued their policy, occasioning much filling of
jails with "village ruffians," "demagogues," and other disrep-
utable people who disturb the peace of a country which a
stronger country desires to rob. Yet a few months of the jail-
filling process and Austria found herself in another cul-de-sac.
"The Hungarians are an emotional and generous people,"
thought Francis Josef; "I shall try the friendly monarch policy." And he amnestied all those whom but a few months before he had thrust into prison. But the Hungarians did not respond to the dodge and sing Alleluia for the generosity of the
royal gentleman in Vienna. They . . . added another satirical
stanza to "The Austrian Thieves."

In the meantime the Hungarian Deputies continued to meet,
not indeed as the Parliament of Hungary, but as the Hungarian Agricultural Union, The Hungarian Industrial League, the
Hungarian Archaeological and Literary Association, and soforth, and through their debates and discussions kept the peo-

ple of the country in the right road of National policy. There was no law, for instance, to compel Hungarians to support Hungarian manufactures to the exclusion of Austrian ones, but the economic wisdom of doing such a thing was emphasised in discussions at the admirable associations which we have named, and the results of these discussions had a force as binding as law upon the people. A succession of Hungarian gentlemen travelled Europe, seeking new fields for an Hungarian export trade, and keeping the Continental Press au courant with Hungarian affairs. At home, the Press was utilised to produce works of educational value to the Hungarian people—works National in tone and spirit, and the Hungarian historical novel became a feature of the time. A scarcity fell on the land in 1863, but the spirit of the Hungarian people tided them over what in Ireland's case in 1847 became an appalling disaster, and at the end of the year of famine, Francis Josef, baffled by the manly policy of a spirited people, attempted overtures for a reconciliation, and announced that it was his wish to satisfy Hungary "not only in material respects, but in other respects." But the Hungarians suspected him of insincerity and ignored his overtures—still continuing to refuse to recognise his kingship or his law, or his officials, or to pay his taxes, unless under compulsion.

*   *   *   *   *

Meanwhile Europe was scoffing at Austria's Imperial Parliament. The Bohemians, after spending two years in it, grew disgusted, recalled their representatives to Bohemia, and declined to recognise any laws passed in Vienna affecting Bohemia as binding. Thus repudiated and boycotted by the two chief countries of the Empire—Hungary and Bohemia—the "Imperial Parliament" became a standing jest for the politicians of the Continent. Francis Josef came back from the wars to find the name of Austria sinking lower day by day, and once again he caused overtures to be made to Hungary for reconciliation. Hungary's answer was the same—when she got what she demanded she would talk of friendship.

The friendship of Hungary had, however, become of urgent necessity to Austria, for Prussia was already quarrelling with Austria over the spoil of the Danish war [the war over Schleswig-Holstein].

*   *   *   *   *

VIII. THE ROYAL VISIT OF 1865

It is to be clearly understood that the visit of his Imperial Majesty, the Emperor Francis Josef, to Pesth, the capital of

disloyal Hungary, on the 6th of June, 1865, was wholly uncon-
nected with politics, and was in no wise prompted by the fact
that war between Austria and Prussia appeared inevitable. His
Majesty went to Pesth for the purpose of seeing the races. So
the journals of Vienna officially announced . . .

*   *   *   *   *

His Majesty returned from his trip to the Pesth Races with
the conviction that it would be decidedly dangerous to go to
war with Prussia just then, and to buy peace he handed over
one-half of the spoil he took in the Danish war—the Duchy of
Lauenberg—to Prussia . . . This eased the strain, for Prussia
affected to be contented, and the danger of war seemed to have
passed. Whereupon Austria turned to resume the coercing of
the Hungarians.

IX. AUSTRIA'S LAST CARD

Scarcely had the Treaty of Gastein, by which Austria ceded
Lauenberg to Prussia, been formally signed, than the Austrians
found reason to suspect that Prussia desired more than that
Duchy as the price of peace. Accordingly, coercion was suspended, soft words were spoken of the Hungarians, and an
amazing amount of virtue and innate loyalty to the Emperor
Francis Josef were discovered by the journalists of Austria to
exist in the souls of the countrymen of Deák and Kossuth. The
doubt of the Austrians as to Prussia's designs became a certainty after Lauenberg had been handed over, for when that
had been done the Prussians immediately asked for the remainder—Holstein—to surrender which to Prussia, under the
circumstances, would have been tantamount to Austria resigning the headship of the German Empire.

It was clearly no time for coercing the Hungarians—Prussia
was making friendly references through her Press both to that
country and to Bohemia, and was seeking to conclude an offensive alliance with Italy. . . .

*   *   *   *   *

There was clearly nothing for it but to "conciliate" Hungary. "Something must be done," said the Emperor. "Something must be done," his statesmen echoed.

*   *   *   *   *

The Manifesto of the 20th of September, 1865, was a
franker document than State documents usually are. First, it
abolished the Imperial Parliament, because as it admitted very
frankly, the machinery of the Imperial Parliament had been
upset since Hungary refused to send her representatives to Vi-

enna, and kept them at home instructing the people to ignore the laws made by the Imperial Parliament. The manifesto then acknowledged the right of Hungary, Bohemia, and the other countries to manage their own affairs and conserve their separate nationalities, and it wound up by declaring the authority of the Hungarian Parliament and the other countries' Parliaments restored. And the Emperor added he would do himself the honour of visiting Pesth in December to open the Parliament of Hungary.

"So far, so good," said Deák, "but this must not be a mock Parliament." . . .

X. THE MEETING OF THE HUNGARIAN DIET OF 1865

On the 14th December, 1865, the Emperor Francis Josef opened the Parliament of Hungary in state. His Majesty was dressed in Hungarian costume. He read his speech in the Hungarian language. The Hungarian Members of Parliament, clad also in the national costume, listened to it politely, and some cheered when he remarked that he came to talk to them with the "frank candour" that befitted a monarch discussing the commonweal with his people. Deák sat silent throughout. "There shall be no compromise," he had promised the people, and Deák knew his Austrian.

The Emperor's speech . . . pretended to give everything while in reality it gave little. It rallied the patriotic drum so much that a Hungarian Deputy drily observed that for using the expressions his Majesty used—and meaning them—five years before, his Majesty would have thrust a Hungarian into jail. At the end of the speech the Deputies applauded, and when the Press of Vienna next day exultantly proclaimed that Hungary had been appeased—and now—God be praised!—was with the Emperor—the Deputies politely explained that what they applauded was not the speech, but the admirable pronunciation of the Hungarian language the Emperor Francis Josef possessed—for a foreigner. . . .

Stripped of its casing, the speech of the Emperor meant that Austria was willing to erect a subordinate Parliament in Hungary with a limited control over home affairs, and to confer with Hungary on common affairs—in the Imperial Parliament —but the Constitution was not to be restored; the Laws of '48 were not to be recognised; the municipal institutions of the country were not to be re-erected.

*   *   *   *   *

The Emperor saw from his failure to deceive Deák that he could scarcely hope to humbug Hungary on this occasion.

. . . Parliament, after duly considering his speech, adopted an address in reply on the motion of Deák, who warned them "never to give up principle for expediency," which in courteous but firm language informed his Majesty that Hungary declined all compromise, and was neither to be intimidated nor cajoled into the surrender of her rights.

* * * * *

The address was presented to the Emperor at Buda. The Emperor, in a temper, replied that what he had said he had said, and he issued a rescript, to make an end of the matter, assuring his beloved Hungarians that he would firmly uphold the principles he had enunciated in his speech. . . . With a unanimous voice the Parliament presented a second Address to the Emperor Francis Josef, which they sent him within twenty-four hours of receiving his rescript. The second Address left nothing to be desired on the score of frankness. It told him that Hungary demanded the complete restoration of her Constitution, the recognition of her independence as a kingdom, the reconstitution of her municipalities, the acknowledgment of her territorial and political integrity, the acceptance of the Laws of 1848, and the absolute amnesty and compensation of every person who had been imprisoned or injured in consequence of the illegal government Austria had maintained in the land since 1848. And, it added, until Hungary got those things she declined to regard the Emperor Francis Josef as King of Hungary. . . . The Hungarian Parliament continued to meet as if nothing had occurred, and by the direction of Deák acted as if the Laws of '48 and the Constitution had never been suspended. And Austria was impotent, even if she had been strong enough to intervene, for Bismarck's subtle policy had succeeded: Prussia and Italy had formed an alliance. Austria knew it was no longer possible to avert war, and was feverishly arming to fight for the hegemony of the German Empire. In this dire strait Francis Josef swallowed his big words, and again made overtures to Deák. Deák's reply was concise and decisive. All the demands formulated by the Hungarian Parliament must be conceded. . . .

* * * * *

XI. THE AUSTRO-PRUSSIAN WAR

The Prussian army, within a few days of the declaration of war against Austria, overcame the resistance offered by the small German States which had thrown in their lot with the latter and advanced into Bohemia, where the Austrians under

Marshal Von Benedek, an Hungarian Imperialist, were assembled.

*   *   *   *   *

The occupation of Prague opened the road to Vienna, and
the Prussians prepared to march on the Austrian capital. In
this desperate strait, the Austrian Emperor purchased peace
from Italy by retroceding Venice, and the Austrian army
which had been engaged there under the Archduke Albrecht
hastened back to defend Vienna. Francis Josef then sent to
Pesth for Deák, and Deák on arriving at midnight in Vienna
was received by the Emperor, pale and haggard, in the palace.
"What am I to do now, Deák?" the monarch asked of his opponent. Deák's laconic reply is celebrated in Austrian history,
"Make peace, and restore Hungary her rights." "If I restore
Hungary her Constitution now, will Hungary help me to carry
on the war?" the Emperor inquired. The reply of Deák ex-
hibits the fearless and uncompromising character of the great
Magyar. It was in one word, "No." He would not make the
restoration of his country's rights a matter of barter. . . .

*   *   *   *   *

XII. COUNT BEUST

The Austrian Empire seemed doomed. The Imperialists
were demoralised—the oppressed exultant. . . . The Emperor
fired out Pouilly, and looking round for a serviceable man to
patch up things, fixed on Baron Beust, a foreigner of some
small reputation, to act as Austrian Foreign Minister—or in
plain English, to keep the concern from falling to pieces.

*   *   *   *   *

Beust's first step was to demand an agreement with the Hun-
garians. "On that," he said, "the continued existence of the
Empire depends," and even bigoted opponents of Hungarian
claims admitted, albeit reluctantly, that this was the case.
"Peace with Hungary means the existence or non-existence of
Austria, and it must be concluded without delay," said one
Austrian statesman publicly and frankly. . . .

*   *   *   *   *

XIII. THE SURRENDER OF AUSTRIA

On the 19th of November, 1866, the Hungarian Parliament
met, and received a rescript from the Emperor Francis Josef,
in which he declared he had resolved to give due "consideration to its demands and claims," and hinted at the appointment

of a responsible ministry and the introduction of responsible government in all parts of the Empire. Deák mistrusted the tone of the rescript. . . .

* * * * *

"None of your Majesty's proposals," he said, "will be taken into consideration by the Parliament of Hungary until all the demands made by the Parliament of Hungary are conceded, and a ministry responsible to it alone assumes power. . . . Between Absolutism and a nation deprived of its constitutional liberties, no compromise is possible."

This was the firm language of a patriot statesman speaking on behalf of his nation to the head of a power which oppressed it. Deák's firm reply evoked a despotic rejoinder. In the beginning of 1867, the Emperor issued a decree making military service compulsory on the Hungarians. Belcredi was on top. A shout of rage and defiance rang through all Hungary, and for a moment it seemed as if insurrection would break out. Only the strenuous efforts of Deák saved the situation. He saw that the crisis had come, but the last moves in the game had not been played. His voice was heard above the tumult and the Parliament, swayed by him, sent a deputation to the Emperor with "Hungary's Last Word," as it has been called—the reply to the Emperor's conscription decree—which had been drawn up by Deák himself, and in which he said, speaking in the name of the Parliament of Hungary—"Let your Majesty cancel the decree and all other measures sanctioned by Absolute power in defiance of our Constitution, let your Majesty restore our Constitution in its integrity, and that as speedily as may be." . . .

* * * * *

On the 7th of February, 1867, the Emperor . . . summoned Deák to Vienna, and in the Imperial Palace pledged his word to his old antagonist to concede all that had been demanded.

* * * * *

On the 18th of February, 1867, the Hungarian Parliament reassembled in Pesth to hear the reply to the "Last Word." It came in the form of a Royal rescript suspending the Conscription law and all other obnoxious laws until such time as the Hungarian Parliament declared itself willing to adopt them, and restoring the Constitution of Hungary. The reading of the rescript was followed by prolonged cheering from the Deputies, which, taken up by the waiting crowds outside, rolled and echoed through the streets like the roar of artillery. . . .

* * * * *

14. A. K. Jameson and Gene Sharp:
NON-VIOLENT RESISTANCE AND THE
NAZIS: THE CASE OF NORWAY

Those who insist that it is possible to resist non-violently ex-ternal aggression as well as internal social injustice are often asked, "But what would you do about enemies like the Nazis? Could they really be opposed effectively by non-violent means?" The answer is that there *was* considerable experience with exactly this problem during World War II. Denmark and Norway, in varying degrees and contexts, did utilize the tech-niques of non-violent resistance with rather notable results. To be sure, there was violent resistance also; and even where non-violent resistance was employed, it was not because principles like Gandhi's were consciously adopted but rather because other methods were not available. When all this has been ad-mitted, however, the record—particularly in Norway—is not un-impressive.

In Norway, the leadership of the Church, strongly supported by most clergymen and the laity, simply refused to co-operate in religious affairs with the Nazi occupation. When the Nazis established a new ecclesiastical leadership, the bulk of the old established Church ignored the orders of the new hierarchy. Through non-violent action, it preserved its integrity; and, as it stated in its manifesto of July 26, 1942, it possessed "no instru-ments of force, nor does it wish to employ such instruments."[1] Similarly, the Supreme Court resigned and there was wide-spread non-violent disobedience on the part of other groups, particularly the teachers. The morale of Nazi military forces was at many points undermined by those segments of the pop-ulation which, while formally correct in their relations with the soldiers, let it be known that in their capacity as soldiers they

[1] Bjarne Höye and Trygve M. Ager, *The Fight of the Norwegian Church against Nazism* (New York: Macmillan, 1943), p. 132. The whole book should be read to gain a more complete view of the non-violent non-co-operation used by the Church. See also Roy Walker, *People Who Loved Peace: The Norwegian Struggle against Nazism* (London: Gollancz, 1946).

were not welcome. Naturally, many Norwegians suffered for these acts; but their hardships seemed only to stiffen the non-violent resistance campaign.

This selection is divided into two sections. The first is a general survey of Norwegian resistance and a critical analysis of its non-violent phase, which lasted from 1940 to 1943 (after which violence assumed a larger role). The non-violent attitudes were in part the outcome of the Norwegian cultural background and at the same time were conditioned by the complete absence of the instruments of violence. Leaders had little knowledge of pacifist philosophy in a formal sense, and although certain elements in the Norwegian heritage make it a special case, the experience shows what can be done in the areas of religion, education, sports, and the professions by a nation largely untrained and yet determined.

The second section provides us with certain often dramatic details of the teachers' resistance in Norway.

The author of the first section, A. K. Jameson, was a writer for the British publication *Peace News,* and his account is taken from his *Peace News* pamphlet, *New Way in Norway* (1948), for which he relied on original sources—including Norwegians who had lived through the experience—as much as possible.

Gene Sharp, the author of the second section, has an M.A. in sociology from Ohio State University, has contributed articles on non-violence to such publications as the *Journal of Conflict Resolution,* and from 1955 to 1958 was an assistant editor of *Peace News,* in which the material included here originally appeared as a series of articles. More recently he has been conducting research on non-violence for the Institute for Social Research in Oslo, Norway.

A. K. Jameson: NEW WAY IN NORWAY?

There is a considerable amount of detailed information available about the Norwegian resistance. This Report attempts merely to summarize the facts very briefly and to see what can be deduced from them. Is it possible to conduct non-violent resistance and if so can such resistance be effective? The answer must obviously depend not only on the quality and amount of force to which resistance is offered, but also on the quality of the people resisting, which again depends on their previous history and the nature of their society at the moment of impact. The first section is, therefore, devoted to this last-mentioned question and subsequent sections to the actual course of the occupation.

I. ANTECEDENT CONDITIONS

The area of Norway is slightly larger than that of the British Isles, but it is spread over a length of 1,100 miles from north to south and consists largely of mountains with few and small valleys and long arms of the sea running far inland. Off the mainland lie no fewer than 150,000 islands of all sizes. As a result of this the country supports a population of only three million. Of this, one million is concentrated round Oslo fjord and the rest is scattered widely in small towns of ten to fifty thousand inhabitants and in villages and small isolated groups. Conditions of life are hard for the most part and call for courage, self-reliance, and co-operation within the group. Organized industry is of very recent growth and is located almost entirely round Oslo fjord; agriculture, dairy farming, forestry, fishing, are still the staple occupations employing the majority of the population.

These causes, combined with various historical factors, have resulted in the Norwegians being independent, enduring and resourceful as individuals, and also having a strong community feeling and a sense of social responsibility. There is great social solidarity and a democratic spirit much more pure and strong than is to be found in most other countries. The relations between employers and employed are generally amicable; serious trouble seldom arises, and disputes are settled by arbitration or other peaceful means. The Norwegian has a very great reverence for the law, which he regards as the only basis of an ordered society, and he takes his obligations under it seriously. Practically everyone is a member, not only of a political party, but also of several voluntary organizations for religion, culture, sport, etc. Local self-government is highly developed and plays a more important part in general administration than it does in this country. The level of education is high and the teaching profession is much honoured, teachers being largely chosen as representatives on political and economic councils.

Norway had no war between 1720 and 1940 except for a few small and unimportant episodes during the Napoleonic struggle from 1807 to 1814. Down to 1935 its armed forces were negligible. Peace was to the people as a whole the normal condition. In that year, alarmed at events in Germany, some steps were taken to increase the armed strength, but in only a half-hearted fashion which produced little effect. Vidkun Quisling had, indeed, been trying to introduce Nazi ideas and methods since 1933, but he met with no success. His party, the

Nasjonal Samling, at its greatest height never included more than 2 per cent of the population and even under proportional representation it never succeeded in returning a member to the Storting, the national parliament.

It should be noted, however, that although the national attitude was clearly against the violent solution of problems, the membership of organized pacifist movements was very small. I have not been able to get precise figures, but estimates made by the persons named on p. 16 show that there may have been about 500 members of the W.R.I., 100 of a clerical pacifist group, and 1,000 of the Norwegian Peace Society. Perhaps the very fact that most people regarded war as a barbarous and out-of-date method made them think it unnecessary to organize opposition to it.

II. THE OCCUPATION

1. Special Circumstances

The Nazis had persuaded themselves that the Norwegians, as pure Aryans, would welcome Nazi doctrine and would cooperate in building up the new order. They hoped not to have to fight at all, but if there were any resistance, they expected to crush it within a day or two. Even when they found resistance much stronger than they had expected, so that it cost them two months' hard fighting and quite heavy losses, they still adhered to their original attitude. They emphasized that they came as friends with the sole desire of rescuing Norway from the evils of democracy and initiating them into the glories of the new regime. Special instructions were given to the occupying troops as to their behaviour and everything possible was done not to arouse antagonism. The whole mechanism of Norwegian government was retained unchanged to begin with and the daily life of the people was interfered with as little as possible. The attack that had to be faced by the Norwegians was on the ideological plane, the attempt to substitute the aims and methods of National Socialism for those of democracy, to replace popular election and responsibility to the people by the leadership principle, the king as guardian of the law by the führer as maker of it.

2. First Stage, June–September, 1940

The Germans very nearly succeeded in their aim of annihilating any attempt at resistance on the day of the invasion, 9th April, 1940. Had they captured the king and the members of the government, as they hoped to do, it is probable that armed resistance would have broken down completely. As it was, these escaped by the skin of their teeth and formed a point round which the nation rallied. For a day or two there was uncertainty in the minds of the people, but then resistance came as an instinctive reaction rather than as a thought-out policy, spontaneously and not in response to orders from above. For the authorities were so completely taken by surprise that at first they could do little and it was only when the people of their own accord rallied to them that resistance was organized. What is said to have had more influence than anything else in causing this reaction was Quisling's impudent broadcast on the day of invasion, in which he proclaimed that the legal government had been deposed, that he had become Prime Minister, and called on all to stop further resistance. He had been so utterly discredited as a politician and as an individual that his words aroused violent indignation and made the people firmly determined to have nothing to do with a regime that used such instruments. The Germans realized their mistake and unceremoniously threw him aside four days later.

On 15th April some prominent Norwegians supported by T.U. and commercial organizations, with the consent of the German Commander-in-Chief, set up an Administrative Council to carry on affairs in the occupied territory. It was a temporary expedient to prevent the country from falling into chaos, which would have been an excuse for direct German administration. The Council had no political competence, although in fact it continued to function for six months, long after the fighting had ceased.

Surrender came exactly two months after the first landings, on 9th June after the king and members of the government had withdrawn to England. As we have said above, the Germans allowed things to go on as before with administration of civil affairs entirely in the hands of Norwegians. Employers and workers accepted the situation and carried on for a while without protest, accepting contracts from the German authorities even for military works, for in those first months of the occupation wages were higher than ever before and profits were large. The Trade Unions even allowed the Germans to replace the elected leaders by nominees of their own, fearing, if they resisted, that the organization built up by them over so many years might be altogether destroyed. In effect they withdrew from politics and concerned themselves solely with industrial affairs.

It was only in the political field that the Germans sought to impose their will. On 13th June they summoned the members of the Storting and gave them an ultimatum demanding that they depose the king, dismiss the government, and elect a State Council with full powers. The Storting refused to comply but agreed to write to the king asking him to abdicate voluntarily. He replied on 3rd July rejecting the proposal on the ground that the Storting was not a free agent but was acting under compulsion of the occupying authority. The Germans took no immediate action, but on 7th September they renewed the demands . . . Again the Storting refused . . . The Germans then abruptly broke off negotiations and on 25th September they issued a series of decrees.

These deposed the king and removed the government in London, dissolved all political parties except the Nasjonal Samling and confiscated their property, relieved the Administrative Council of its duties and in its place appointed thirteen acting Councillors of State in charge of various government departments all, except three well-known pro-Germans, members of the Nasjonal Samling. The Foreign Office and the Defence Ministry were abolished . . .

3. Second Stage, October, 1940–September, 1941

Although the government was nominally in the hands of the thirteen Norwegian Councillors, each had behind him a German official whose sanction was required for every order other than a routine one, so that in effect Terboven, the Reichskommissar, was the real ruler of the country. A new body, the Hird, was set up, equivalent to the German S.S. Corps, which took over more and more of the functions of the Norwegian police until the latter were practically confined to traffic-control and similar routine duties. . . .

The first attack was on the judicial system. The ordinary Courts were brought under the Quisling Minister of Justice, and a People's Court on Nazi lines was set up parallel to the existing ones. Decrees were issued by various Ministries which were in conflict with the law as it stood and when the Supreme Court objected to these arbitrary proceedings, Terboven said they were not competent to pass on the validity of any orders which he or the Ministers might issue. In consequence of this, all members of the Court resigned in December, 1940 and were eventually replaced by incompetent lawyers who were tempted to adhere to Quisling for the sake of the promotion.

During this same period an attempt was made to alter the system of local government by investing Mayors with dictatorial powers and depriving local Councillors of executive functions. In practice, however, these regulations were ignored and the system continued unchanged.

Norwegians are very much addicted to organized sports of all kinds and there is a large number of Sports Associations governed on strictly democratic principles. During this first winter of the occupation the Germans dissolved these and replaced them by others on the leadership principle to which they tried to compel the Norwegians to belong. The latter, however, refused to be dragooned in this way even when the premises and funds of their Associations were confiscated. So completely did they succeed in boycotting the new organizations that the few attempts they made to hold public competitions were a complete fiasco and during the whole of the occupation there were no organized sports meetings.

At the University the Students' Union was dissolved and a new Union on Nazi principles was set up, but this also died as the result of a boycott. One or two lecturers were appointed to teach Nazi doctrine, but as no one attended their classes they resigned before long.

A more serious attack was made on the Church by a decree that compelled pastors to reveal information given to them under the seal of the confessional if the police demanded it, the penalty for non-compliance being imprisonment.

In January, 1941 a strong protest was lodged with the Minister of Church Affairs signed by all the seven bishops. It pointed out that in Norway the Church is united with the State on the assumption that the latter upholds justice. This, they said, was now doubtful, and they adduced the illegalities which had resulted in the resignation of the Supreme Court, the decree violating the secrecy of the confessional and the conduct of the Hird, which was indulging unchecked in acts of increasing violence and lawlessness. The Minister's reply was regarded as entirely unsatisfactory and in February the whole correspondence was embodied in a Pastoral Letter which, in spite of prohibition by the authorities, was read in all churches and distributed as a printed leaflet. No action was taken by the authorities.

During this winter, decrees had also been issued making it compulsory to hang Quisling's portrait in all schools, to teach German instead of English as the second language, to eliminate all English text-books, to revise the teaching of history on Nazi lines, and to make instruction in Nazi doctrine compulsory. This resulted in February, 1941, in a widespread strike of teachers, supported by parents and the Church, and in face of this opposition the authorities gave way and either withdrew the obnoxious decrees or allowed them to lapse.

In two other departments of cultural life the Germans were similarly unsuccessful in imposing their ideology. During the summer of 1941 they became involved in quarrels with the doctors and the actors and in both cases they had to withdraw.

During the winter they had been trying to replace officials in central and local government offices by members of the Nasjonal Samling but without much success. In February, 1941, a decree was passed making membership a necessary condition of appointment to any government post. This at once produced a protest signed by representatives of twenty-two organizations of government servants, doctors, teachers, and other professions. As no reply was sent, another protest of a more comprehensive nature, embodying all the various illegalities perpetrated up to date, was sent in May, signed on behalf of forty-three organizations, which this time included various Trade Unions. The rank and file of the workers had realized the danger of acquiescing in the proceedings of the occupation authorities and it was owing to pressure from them that the leaders of the Unions joined in the protest.

At last the occupation authorities were compelled to take notice. Terboven summoned all the forty-three signatories to his presence on 18th June and, after a long and angry harangue, had five of the most prominent arrested on the spot and the remainder during the next few days. When he tried to appoint nominees of his own to the posts thus left vacant, the members of the associations resigned *en masse* rather than accept the new leadership. The National Labour Federation, the largest and most powerful of the workers' organizations, then lodged a further protest against interference in the internal affairs of the Unions.

The German authorities appeared to yield and released all the arrested men, but they succeeded in provoking the workers into striking on 8th September by refusing an increase of wages to compensate for the rise in prices and by cancelling the allowance of milk in the factories. The men's leaders saw the danger of this and induced them to go back on the 10th; but it was too late. A state of emergency had at once been declared. Two of the men's leaders were summarily shot, large numbers of workers as well as journalists and professional men were given long terms of imprisonment, the military and the Gestapo were placed in charge, and terror reigned for a week. The members of the T.U.C. were replaced by Quisling nominees who were given power to appoint controllers in the Unions, membership of which was made compulsory. Delegate meetings were abolished and election of officials forbidden. Similar measures were taken with the Employers' Federation, which had supported the men's protests.

This ended the second stage.

4. Third Stage, October, 1941–December, 1942

All pretence of collaboration was now at an end. The occupation authorities no longer withdrew when they met with opposition but did their utmost to break it down by violence. On the other hand, the resistance, which had hitherto been largely spontaneous and loosely organized, was tightened up and made much more efficient. Most of the leaders of the underground movement had been arrested during the week of terror, but others not known to the authorities took their places. An elaborate net-work of espionage was created so that the authorities' most secret documents and plans were known all over the country before they could be put into effect. In spite of the confiscation of wireless-sets in the autumn of 1941 the underground press, which was now organized and issued regular printed newspapers, was able to give news and advice received from London. Strategy was co-ordinated, an efficient system for concealing those wanted by the authorities and smuggling them out of the country was evolved. Officials, pastors, teachers, etc. dismissed from their posts were supported with their families by voluntary contributions. Although the entire resistance movement was very largely non-violent, many of those who escaped to England were specially trained for sabotage and were dropped into Norway by parachute. In the labour field, although there was never any attempt at open opposition except for the abortive strike of September, 1941, there was a good deal of quiet obstruction; machines mysteriously went out of action and work which should have taken weeks was spun out over months.

Nothing of importance happened for some little while. In February, 1942, a higher status was given to Quisling's government and he became Minister-President. His aim was to create a corporative state on Mussolini's model, and the first step towards this was the creation of Corporations. He began with that of the teaching profession. In February, decrees were issued reviving those which had been imposed and then withdrawn in 1941. In addition, the existing Teachers' Association was abolished and a new one set up on Nazi lines under a member of the Hird as Leader, membership of which was to be compulsory on all school teachers. At the same time a new Youth Movement was created on the model of the German one with compulsory membership for all between the ages of 10 and 18 and this was placed under the Labour Service Department.

There were then about 14,000 school teachers in Norway; of these over 12,000 refused to join the new Association and maintained their stand even when they were told that failure to join would be regarded as resignation, with consequent loss of pay and pension rights, and the liability of being drafted into forced labour. The parents supported them, and the schools had to be closed. The teachers were given till 15th March to come to a final decision and practically none accepted the terms. By the end of March 1,300 of them had been arrested and sent to concentration camps, where every effort was made to break their spirit by imposition of severe physical tasks and mental strain. When this proved unavailing, 500 of them were transported in the hold of an ancient steamer to Kirkenes in the extreme north and there subjected to brutal treatment. Still the number of defections was very small and the authorities had to admit defeat. Gradually, between May and October, all those arrested were released.

Meanwhile the schools had reopened on 8th April and it was announced that all teachers who took up work again would be regarded as having automatically joined the new Association and subscriptions would be deducted from their pay. Some preferred not to rejoin and taught privately; the majority resumed work, but only after signing a declaration that they did so in the interests of the children and that they refused to join the Association. The authorities then allowed the matter to drop and the new Association never actually came into being. By August the schools were in full swing again. The victory was obtained partly by the staunch support of the parents who overwhelmed the Education Department with written protests against the decrees.

There were similar protests against the Youth Movement and in these the Church joined on the ground that to compel children to join a movement in which doctrines were taught of which the parents might not approve, was a violation of parental rights. In this respect also the authorities were unsuccessful and the Movement never came into existence.

In order to enforce their protest, the seven bishops on 24th February resigned their administrative functions as officers of the State Church, though retaining their spiritual functions towards the people. The government countered by dismissing the bishops and prohibiting them from exercising any functions at all, spiritual or otherwise, and by arresting the Primus, the bishop of Oslo, and two others. Thereupon on 5th April, 797 out of 861 (93 per cent) of the clergy took action similar to that of the bishops. For some months bishops and clergy alike were subjected to harassment of all sorts, interference with their daily life and duties, prosecution for alleged offences, banishment from their homes, or confinement within them.

Quisling's next step was to arrogate to himself the right of the king as supreme bishop to appoint persons in the place of those dismissed, but the only ones he could find willing to accept were without the necessary qualifications. The Church replied by appointing a Provisional Council to carry on the work of the bishops and, although Quisling declared it illegal, he was forced in the end to recognize it and to negotiate with it. By the end of the year the Church was again functioning more or less normally.

Having failed with the Teachers' Corporation, Quisling next tried to institute a Labour Corporation. The workers, however, became aware of his intention before actual orders were issued and forestalled him by resigning from their Unions *en masse* so that the Corporation, if brought into being, would have represented only a handful of Quisling's supporters. The situation had become so ludicrous that Hitler personally intervened and ordered the whole project of setting up a Corporative State to be abandoned. At the same time, however, 100 of the men's leaders were arrested and the workers were told that, if they did not withdraw their resignations, those arrested would be shot. As the resignations had produced the desired result, the men consented to rejoin.

Although the new tactics of violence failed in their aim of compelling Norway to accept the new order, certain results had been achieved. All voluntary Associations had either been dissolved and their property confiscated or had been placed under Quisling control; press and radio were also under control and there was a considerable amount of infiltration of supporters of Quisling into key-posts in the administrative services. By the end of 1942, moreover, some 100 Norwegians had been executed, 7,000 were in concentration camps, and 1,000 had been deported to Poland.

5. Fourth Stage, 1943–44

The main struggle in this stage was for the mobilization of manpower. Since July, 1941, all ages and both sexes had been liable to undertake work of national importance—which meant in practice construction of fortifications and doing general war work. In the summer of 1942 there had been a strict comb-out of unessential industries and commercial firms. So far, however, there had been little difficulty in getting all the labour required, as wages for work of that sort were higher than elsewhere; but by 1943 they had been reduced to the same low level as others and transfer from one job to another was prohibited without permission. In February, 1943, compulsory registration for both men and women was introduced and a target of 75,000 additional workers was fixed. Wholesale opposition was at once declared. Obstructive tactics of various kinds so overwhelmed the authorities that few registrations could be effected, and when the police went with the calling-up notices of those who did register they seldom were able to deliver them; those affected had gone underground. The Oslo Registration Office with records of the entire country was burned down. By the end of summer only 6,000 had been rounded up. Stern measures were then taken. The police were given extra powers and special Courts were instituted in which offences against the labour laws were summarily dealt with and the death penalty was imposed for a large number of them. . . . But still only a handful of those wanted was obtained and the contest went on unceasingly until the Germans were finally defeated.

III. GENERAL CONCLUSIONS

From the facts as stated above it will be apparent that the resistance falls into two stages; the first, from 1940 to 1943, was mainly non-violent, the second, from 1943 till the final withdrawal of the Germans, became increasingly violent, chiefly through the agency of units specially trained in England and parachuted into Norway who carried out extensive sabotage of military objectives. It is the first, largely non-violent, stage which is of interest to pacifists.

The champions of resistance in that stage were the teachers and the clergy as a body and some of the more prominent men in other walks of life, journalists, professional men, Trade Union leaders, members of sports clubs and those who carried on the underground movement. The total number was less than 1 per cent of the population and they belonged mostly to the middle class.

The government and municipal services were also affected, but to a smaller degree. The authorities did, indeed, have to abandon their claim that membership of the Nasjonal Samling should be compulsory for all members of those services, but they were successful in imposing many of their practices and in replacing many officers of long standing by supporters of Quisling.

As regards commerce and industry, labour and domestic service, the books so far published say little and it is difficult to get at the facts. The reason is that those books are concerned to emphasize those aspects of the occupation in which the Germans were least successful in realizing their aims. It does seem certain, however, that, at least until 1943, the Germans had little difficulty in getting all the labour and service they required. Ake Fen,[2] writing in 1943, says: "On the whole the commercial and industrial life has been carried on along the old original lines, but the capacity is diminished. There is plenty of work, mostly for unprofitable ends—German ends." Up till that year the workers as a whole had acquiesced in the occupation. . . .

There was more opposition when in 1943 the occupation authorities were in difficulties for manual labour and tried to throw their net wider and to rope in sections of society which were not accustomed to it. Then resistance was offered and was successful to a considerable extent. It was, also, the first time that violence was used on a large scale. At no time, however, was any attempt made to paralyse the life of the country by refusal to work or by stoppage of transport. There were great shortages of food, fuel and consumer goods, but condi-

[2] *Nazis in Norway* (Penguin).

tions never reached the pitch of really acute general hardship.

It is obvious that the Norwegians were a peace-loving people whose instincts were all in favour of non-violence; but few of them were pacifists in the sense of holding a reasoned creed of pacifism based on abstract principles, religious, moral, or of any other nature. Hence when invasion came the great majority had no hesitation in resisting violently; but this violence was for the most part confined to the duly constituted armed forces and, once the army had surrendered, there was practically no civilian armed resistance, no "partisans" or "men of the maquis," such as came into existence in other countries. At first, it is true, there were isolated instances of the murder of German soldiers, but that was soon stopped, partly from expediency perhaps, but also because there was no desire to defeat the Nazis by stooping to their own methods. There was a genuine, widely spread and sustained effort to keep the whole resistance non-violent in which all sections of society co-operated. The violence which did come later was hardly at all the spontaneous product of the national will but a military technique inculcated in a foreign country. There was a general agreement to treat the Germans non-violently, but to avoid contact with them as far as possible and to leave them in no doubt about the universal detestation which they inspired. The icy aloofness which they experienced had a depressing effect which undermined their morale. It was practised by all, even by those who were working for them, except the two per cent of Quisling's followers and they were boycotted along with their masters and made to feel the contempt in which they were held by all the rest.

Another thing which differentiates the Norwegian resistance from that in most of the other occupied countries is that it was for the most part openly avowed without any attempt at concealment of those responsible for it. There was, of course, an underground movement, but it was used chiefly for the purpose of keeping the groups of resisters, widely scattered over a large area, in touch with one another, of co-ordinating effort and of sheltering those on the run from the occupation authorities. It was not used for hatching plots nor for carrying out reprisals for acts of oppression.

There was a very remarkable degree of solidarity among all social classes and the greatest fidelity in carrying out the instructions received from the leaders. The high moral tone of the whole movement is clearly shown in the way the black market was run. Producers of foodstuffs were supposed to hand over all their produce to government distributing agencies, but in fact they succeeded in keeping back quite a lot. In contrast to what happened elsewhere, however, this store was sold secretly at prices very little higher than those officially

fixed and much of it was bought up by employers for the benefit of their employees and by individuals for maintenance of
those in hiding from the authorities. Practically no private
profit was made from these transactions and hence the market
had not the same demoralizing effects as it had in other occupied countries, and it ceased the moment the occupation was
over.

If the question is asked whether the Norwegian experience
goes to prove that the technique of non-violence offers an efficient substitute for violence and can be successful in producing the desired results, the answer would appear to be that it
does and can in the moral and ideological realm. That is to
say, the occupying authorities completely failed to impose
their new order on Church, education, professional, and sporting organizations. These organizations were, with their funds
and buildings, taken over by the authorities and handed to
the two per cent of the population who collaborated with
them; but it was only the material shell which was handed
over. As regards the spirit, that was kept untouched and untouchable and to the end Church and schools continued to
preach and teach on the same lines as before the occupation.
It was a magnificent demonstration of faithfulness to an ideal
and of staunchness in face of physical suffering carried out
over a period of years during which the occupying authorities
seemed to be all-powerful and almost unchallenged in their
career of conquest. The moral and physical strain must have
been intense and the steadfastness displayed is worthy of the
highest praise.

At the same time it must be observed that Norway's success
is no guarantee that the method would be equally successful if
tried elsewhere or in other circumstances. That success was
due largely to the character of the Norwegians, their history
and the nature of their social arrangements. Not every nation
has precisely their qualities, their innately democratic outlook
which ensured solidarity among all classes, nor their combination of strong individualism with capability of close co-operation and willingness to carry out the instructions of a trusted
leader. Their high standard of education, their long tradition
of freedom from war and of peaceful solution of domestic
differences must undoubtedly have helped to keep them non-
violent.

The exact circumstances of the occupation might not recur.
The Germans came ostensibly as friends and, after the actual
fighting was over, they genuinely did their best to win the Norwegians to the new order by relatively peaceful means. For
the first eighteen months such violence as did occur was
mainly from Norwegians themselves, Quisling's Hird, and during that period the Germans accepted one defeat after an-

other without retaliation. An invaluable breathing-space was thus given to the Norwegian people in which to recover from the first shock of invasion, and the fact that they were able, during that time, successfully to prevent the Germans from imposing their system, strengthened their courage and enabled them better to endure the harder trials which came later. It is by no means certain that, if extreme measures had been put into operation by the Germans right from the start, the results would have been the same. It should also be remarked that during this same initial period the nation as a whole was being continually heartened and encouraged in resistance by broadcasts from the Norwegian government in London, for wireless-sets were not confiscated till autumn 1941. There can be no doubt that these had a very great effect in sustaining morale and again it may be that, without such encouragement, the will to resist might not have been so strong.

It is, however, only in the comparatively limited spheres of Church, schools, professions, and sports and with reference to moral and ideological ends that the Norwegian experience offers any evidence about the power of non-violence. For, while with few exceptions non-violence was observed by the people as a whole in their individual relations with the Germans, no attempt was made to use it as a mass weapon outside those spheres in order to compel them to withdraw or even to regard the wishes of the Norwegians.

A satisfactory feature of the years of occupation is that they seem to have generated no lasting hate of the Germans. Within a very few months of the end of the occupation Norway was sending generous support in food and clothing to her late enemies, and people who have visited Norway in the last eighteen months say that there is a general desire to forget the past and to go forward to a co-operative future. A certain number of their own war criminals (or persons so designated) have been punished, but here also there is a tendency to let bygones be bygones, to wipe the slate clean and to start afresh.

* * * * *

Gene Sharp: TYRANNY COULD NOT QUELL THEM

The basic points at which the teachers would resist had already been decided. After the old teachers' organisation had been abolished in June, 1941, following mass resignations when the Nazis sought to take it over, a new anonymous leadership arose.

This illegal group of teachers formulated a list of four points of resistance:

(1) Any demand for the teachers to become members of Quisling's party, the *Nasjonal Samling;*

(2) Any attempt to introduce *Nasjonal Samling* propaganda in the schools;

(3) Any order from outside the school authorities;

(4) Any collaboration with the *Nasjonal Samling* youth movement.

These four points, spread among the teachers in December and January, were to be kept in mind and not discussed.

Even if the teachers were imprisoned for their resistance, they should not give way on these issues.

They viewed Quisling's new organisation as part of a larger plan to reorganise teaching methods, and saw that they would soon be expected to indoctrinate their pupils with the Nazi ideology.

On February 11 and 12, 1942, there was a secret meeting of resistance leaders in Oslo. They too saw Quisling's step as the moment they had been waiting for and shared the view of the teachers: if they accepted this beginning, there would be no clear later point of resistance. They would finally have to accept the logical consequences of the first step.

It was decided that the teachers should refuse to become members of the new organisation. Each teacher would be asked to write to the Education Department of Quisling's Government informing it of his refusal to be part of the new teachers' organisation.

A statement, short, simple and easy to remember, was drafted which every teacher was asked to use.

LEADERS AROSE

Mr. Holmboe described the kind of methods used to spread these orders.

"A friend telephoned me one afternoon," he said, "and asked me to meet him at the railway station. There he gave me a small box of matches.

"He told me we teachers were to follow the lead of those who had met in Oslo, and that all the possible consequences had been discussed."

Then his friend caught the train and was gone.

"The box of matches contained the statement. My job was to circulate it secretly among the teachers in my district. That was all I knew. I didn't know who the 'leaders' were who met in Oslo."

In the teachers' resistance no leaders were specially selected. They just arose from the situation. Generally, those who had an idea of something to be done were accepted and obeyed.

"In the middle of the fight we never knew from whom the

orders came," Mr. Holmboe said. "They were obeyed because they came through people who had put themselves in charge."

CONSCIENCE IN REVOLT

This was the statement he found in the match-box:

"I declare that I cannot take part in the education of the youth of Norway along those lines which have been outlined for the *Nasjonal Samling* Youth Service, this being against my conscience.

"According to what the Leader of the new teachers' organisation has said membership of this organisation will mean an obligation for me to assist in such education, and also would force me to do other acts which are in conflict with the obligations of my profession.

"I find that I must declare that I cannot regard myself as a member of the new teachers' organisation."

Every teacher was to write this statement himself, sign it with his own name and post it himself to the Education Department of Quisling's Government.

The idea of having all of the letters in a particular school district gathered together and posted as a group so that everyone could know that the other teachers had also written was discussed and rejected.

Mr. Holmboe told me that there was an inarticulate feeling among the teachers that "this type of passive reaction is of course dangerous and 'they' have their ways of stopping us, but it is the only way we have to express our opposition and we must do it."

Isolated teachers in the mountains tried to keep contact with teachers in other districts, but whether this was possible or not each was to take personal responsibility for his own action.

One nervous teacher in the mountains before posting his letter telephoned long distance to Mr. Holmboe to be sure that everyone else was really carrying out the plan—despite the probability that the telephone was tapped.

The letters were all to be posted on the same day, February 20, 1942.

MASS ARRESTS

Of the 12,000 teachers in Norway, between 8,000 and 10,000 responded to the call and wrote to Quisling's Education Department dissociating themselves from his new teachers' organisation.

*   *   *   *   *

On the same day 150 university professors also protested against the N.S. Youth Front.

GOVERNMENT TACTICS

On February 25 the authorities announced that the teachers' protest would be regarded as official resignations of their appointments and if they persisted they would be fined.

The same day the Education Department announced that all schools would be closed for a month "for lack of fuel."

The falsity of this excuse was obvious. Wood is a usual fuel in Norway, and the forests stretch almost the whole length of the country. Further, the weather had become mild after a severe cold spell.

The Quisling Government, Mr. Holmboe explained, was "panic-stricken." By closing the schools and thus dispersing the teachers it hoped to weaken their solidarity and break their resistance.

From all over the country came offers of fuel to keep the schools open.

Actually the "fuel holiday" proved to be the means of spreading the news of what had happened, for the official newspapers had published nothing about the teachers' resistance. People began asking why the schools had *really* closed. The facts got around.

FINANCING REBELLION

The Leader of Quisling's new teachers' organisation then announced that in such and such districts 100 per cent. of the teachers had become members. But many knew these were isolated school districts which had only one or two teachers.

On March 7 the official newspapers announced that 300 teachers would be called to do "some kind of social work in the north of Norway."

March 15 was set as the deadline for compliance, and resisting teachers were threatened with loss of jobs, pay and pensions. The official newspapers finally referred to the protest, while playing it down as much as possible, but the warnings were issued only in circulars from the Education Department addressed to the teachers.

In response to this threat, preparations were made for financial difficulties teachers and their families might face. Most of them had already been contributing two per cent. of their incomes for financing the resistance. Other people now joined this plan.

*   *   *   *   *

LETTERS OF PROTEST

Tens of thousands of letters of protest from parents, and some from others, were posted on March 6 to the Education Department. This move was probably organised by the resistance leaders. Reliable figures are not available, but probably somewhat less than ten per cent. of all the parents of pupils in the country took part.

Heavily burdened, but smiling, postmen carried bag after bag of protest letters to Quisling's Education Department. By signing their own names, Mr. Holmboe said, the parents made a personal contribution and became "committed to resistance."

March 15—the deadline for compliance—came and went. The teachers remained defiant.

On March 20 and the few days following about 1,000 teachers were arrested. There were no women among them. The arrests did not terrorise the people.

The policeman who came to arrest Mr. Holmboe was an ordinary Norwegian policeman, not a member of Quisling's party. He was "very decent" and waited an hour for Mr. Holmboe to make preparations.

Whether or not ordinary Norwegian policemen ought to have carried out such orders for arrests and other instructions from the Quisling Government has been often discussed since.

The selection of teachers for arrest appeared haphazard. The authorities did not always arrest those whom they feared most. Apparently, they thought the weaker ones would be easier to break down, and therefore some should be included in the arrests.

What Quisling's régime most wanted was to compel the teachers to abandon their resistance publicly.

It was often left to the police to decide whom to arrest. And where the police were not *Nasjonal Samling* members, they sometimes consulted the teachers first.

In one school the police telephoned the principal to say they had orders to arrest eight teachers. The teachers held a meeting to decide who should go, considering such factors as age, health and dependants. Then the principal telephoned their names to the police.

After the arrests, the clergy made a statement in the churches at Easter about the relationship between parents and their children and nearly all resigned.

Mr. Holmboe spent over a week in the local prison at Hamar with about 20 other teachers, eight of whom were from his own school. The rektor (principal) had also been arrested.

The approximately 650 teachers arrested in southern and

western Norway were then transferred from local prisons to Grini concentration camp.

Throughout their detention the teachers' families received "from somewhere" the equivalent of their former salaries. In face of an ultimatum at the camp three teachers gave in. The rest stood firm.

Four days later came another warning: Unless they withdrew their protests, in future they would receive no professional positions, but instead would become part of a labour force.

The German commander of Grini concentration camp, *Sturmbannführer* (SS Commander) Koch, was nicknamed by the prisoners *Stormfyrsten*—"the tempestuous prince." He always carried a whip and was accompanied by a large dog.

On one occasion the teachers received an expression of sympathy from an unexpected quarter, following an harangue by Koch which concluded with the words:

"You must not think you will be martyrs, or that a few dirty teachers will be able to stop the New Order for Europe!"

At that point the dog vomited.

NAZI CAMP TREATMENT

On March 31 the teachers were taken from Grini concentration camp to Jørstadmoen camp, near Lillehammer, about 200 kilometres from Oslo.

*   *   *   *   *

THE GESTAPO

When they arrived there were some bedsteads but no mattresses or bedding; cooking vessels had to be salvaged from a junk heap; tools for shovelling snow had to be improvised by the prisoners.

Mr. Holmboe was part of a small group that reached Jørstadmoen on March 30 directly from local prisons. A second group arrived next evening.

On April 1 the great bulk of prisoners arrived from Grini, making a total of 687.

That day and the next the Germans organised the camp. Teachers were divided into age groups and assigned to barracks. German-speaking teachers were selected as group leaders. The Germans chose Mr. Holmboe as their interpreter.

During these days he became recognised by the teachers as their spokesman and leader.

The Gestapo created an atmosphere of fear. Orders were

crossly shouted. Teachers were kicked on the slightest pretext and were forced to run rapidly wherever they went.

This intimidation was aimed at producing nervousness and insecurity among the teachers.

WHAT DAY IS THIS?

On the third morning there seemed not to be a single German in the camp. No one knew what was going to happen. Uncertainty and tenseness spread.

For prisoners whose fate lies in the hands of others this is the difficult time. "The hardest things," said Mr. Holmboe, "are not those that happen, but those that might happen, and the time waiting for things to happen."

What were "they" going to do to the teachers? Would it be better to give in? Was it all worth what might happen?

The tenseness grew.

Then one of the teachers said: "Do you remember what day this is?" And someone said: "Is this a good day for us to resign from small sufferings? Remember what Christ endured."

It was Good Friday.

That afternoon the "terrorism" began. It was not the extreme individual torture for which the Nazi régime was notorious—including in Norway—but a more gradual and prolonged "treatment" designed to wear down the teachers' ability to resist.

THE HUNGER WEAPON

Hunger and weariness were the chief weapons. In the morning they received a cup of synthetic coffee. At noon a cup of hot water soup—for the German staff had "organised" (the camp slang for stealing) most of the few vegetables allotted for prisoners.

Each was given 150 grams of bread a day—one-fifth of a small loaf of about 1½ lbs. This made four small slices.

They received it at night, and had no more until the following night. Therefore if they were to have anything to eat next morning they had to exercise extreme restraint and eat only two thin slices at night despite their hunger.

Some were unable to do this and therefore went hungry the next morning. A few so disciplined themselves that they put aside a little of their daily ration of bread for a possible time when there would be no food at all.

Each morning there were 1½ hours [of] "torture gymnastics," including crawling and running in very deep snow. Men up to 59 years old were treated "more or less as young people."

Then followed 1½ hours heavy work—"idiotic work" the teachers called it—much of which was shovelling heavy snow. This was followed by another 1½ hours crawling and running in the snow.

People who have never run in snow reaching well above the knees cannot know how much effort it requires.

After 4½ hours "treatment" there was an hour's break and lunch—one cup of hot water soup.

On that first Saturday afternoon while the rest of the teachers were being put through the afternoon session, the 76 older teachers—aged 55 to 59—were interrogated. Before the questioning the younger teachers made it clear that if the older ones wished to back down because of their age it would be understood and not held against them.

Mr. Holmboe said that as the older men were brought in one by one the Germans were really surprised as each refused to withdraw his protest.

The meaning was clear: if the older men had not yet broken down there was little chance that the younger men would.

And so the treatment was resumed. No one knew how long it would last.

While the older men were being questioned that afternoon the usual afternoon treatment continued for the others: two or three hours repeat of the morning session.

Meanwhile, in the outside world, the Quisling authorities prepared to re-open the schools.

They announced that all who began working would automatically be registered as having joined the new organisation and their subscriptions would be deducted from their pay. The opening in Oslo and Aker was delayed, but the rest opened on April 8.

But on reporting for work the teachers repudiated membership of Quisling's new teachers' organisation, and made a statement in their classes on the first day.

Mrs. Holmboe herself was one of these teachers. She said there was tenseness, then each teacher, before the class "spoke of conscience, the spirit of truth and our responsibility to the children."

But, she said, she was not worried about her own possible arrest. The feeling of solidarity was so strong that she knew someone would take care of her two children.

COLLAPSED

Meanwhile, the treatment of the prisoners continued.

Two cases of pneumonia developed. The prisoners were not clothed for snowy weather and there were no facilities for drying clothes.

One of the teachers collapsed during a session of the "treatment" and was carried to the medical centre. It was rumoured that he was dead.

A German officer came storming in demanding of the teacher lying on the floor: What is this? Why are you behaving in this way? The teacher, regaining consciousness, replied that there was "too little food, too much to do."

But if only you give in, everything will be all right. Why do you persist?

"Because I am a Norwegian."

LIKE MARTYRS

The "terrorism" had continued, Sunday and Monday and Tuesday. After 11 a.m. Tuesday various groups were taken from their work for questioning: "Will you sign . . . ?"

The old men were marched in, refused to retract their protests, and were marched out again. Then the men began saying "No" as they entered the room, giving the Germans no chance even to question them.

"They were like martyrs going to their persecution," Mr. Holmboe said.

At least one of the most determined of the teachers was a pacifist; pacifists and non-pacifists stood solidly together.

Only 32 out of the 687 gave in and were brought out of the camp. With this the Germans' theory that the teachers' determined resistance was caused by one section intimidating the rest collapsed.

The terrorism resumed: torture gymnastics, hard work, almost no food.

INTO THE ARCTIC

In the "outside world" the other teachers who had not been arrested and were still defying Quisling's demands were facing a difficult time.

Rumours began to spread that the Gestapo were going to shoot ten of the teachers held at Jørstadmoen; or one in every ten; that they were going to be sent to no-man's land in the far north between the German and the Russian armies to destroy the land-mines, and to certain death.

"I know someone who works at the Minister's office and . . ." "I know people at the office of the German headquarters and they told me . . ." "I know . . ."

*   *   *   *   *

THE WIVES' PROBLEM

The teachers who had not been arrested wrestled with the problem: should they give in, or should they maintain their protests, taking the chance that their action might mean the execution of friends and husbands? "We didn't know what to do," Mrs. Holmboe told me.

Then they made their decision. "I went as a wife," Mrs. Holmboe said, "to one man who wanted to give in and said, 'The wives don't want you to give in. We will take the chance.'"

Mr. Holmboe said their action made "the greatest impression on me of anything in the whole struggle. We who were arrested didn't feel we'd done very much, but our colleagues in the schools stood firm in spite of this heavy pressure." He was glad the decision had not been his to make.

CATTLE-TRUCK JOURNEY

The terrorism, which had begun on Good Friday, had continued through the following Wednesday. The pace on Thursday was a little slower with only the heavy "idiotic work" and no "torture gymnastics." On Friday there was nothing.

Mr. Holmboe did not know what the teachers in Jørstadmoen camp would have done if the treatment had gone on two or three days more, or until the first ten died from it. "Or, if they'd shot ten—what then?"

But they did not have to face that problem. For the treatment there was ended. All of them were taken away from Jørstadmoen; 499 began their journey north. The others were taken back to Grini.

Mr. Holmboe would have been the 500th to go north, but, ill with pneumonia, he was left behind temporarily.

The 499 began their cattle-truck rail journey northwards to Trondheim at midnight on April 12, 1942.

The slow train trip across southern Norway was a dramatic event for the whole country. The refusal of the teachers to give in had a great effect on the people as a whole," Mr. Holmboe said.

As the train passed through the mountains, farmers came to the stations where the prison train stopped briefly, offering milk for the teachers, but the German guards drove them away.

MEDICINES REFUSED

After 17 cold hours in the cattle-trucks the train arrived at Trondheim. The 499 were then crammed into a small steamer

—the *Skjerstad*—which had been built to carry 100 passengers.

A doctor—a member of Quisling's party—examined the conditions on the boat and was horrified. He telegraphed Quisling asking that the voyage be stopped. His request was ignored.

There was illness among the teachers; they asked the Gestapo authorities for medicines or a doctor. The request was refused.

The Red Cross tried to provide help, but the medical supplies were seized by the Gestapo guards.

WILL THEY DROWN US?

The teachers knew nothing of their fate. Many thought the over-loaded boat would be put to sea and sunk, the blame being laid on Allied submarines or bombers.

"The days before things happen are more terrible than the days they happen," Mr. Holmboe reminded me. A few suffered emotional breakdown from fear. Some would have withdrawn their protests then, but the Germans did not ask them to.

On April 15 the steamer left Trondheim and began its long and very hazardous voyage to the far North of Norway. Still the teachers did not know their fate. The voyage took 13 days, stopping three times, and the food was very poor.

Yet even in these surroundings the prisoners organised lectures and choirs to occupy themselves.

Several smaller ships—carrying supplies and ammunition for the Germans, it was thought—accompanied the *Skjerstad*, for their own protection, not that of the teachers, as the Allies knew of the teachers' boat.

On April 28 it arrived at Kirkenes, a small town near the Finnish (now Russian) border, and far beyond the Arctic Circle—close to the German-Russian front. The weather was cold and rough.

In three days the teachers were transferred from the control of the Gestapo to the authority of the *Wehrmacht*—the German army.

Meanwhile, back at Grini on April 26, after once more refusing to give in, 153 teachers began their journey to Kirkenes, by cattle-truck train, and then in a small steamer called the *Finmarken*.

Several extremely sick, feeble and crippled teachers remained at Grini.

PACIFISTS SEIZED

When the *Finmarken* stopped briefly at Tromsø, about May 8, a representative of the local Gestapo told the teachers of a circular issued on April 25 by Quisling's Education Department.

This was a long and wordy statement, saying in effect that all was settled, that all activities of the new teachers' organisation would stop, and that the schools would re-open.

The teachers on the *Finmarken* were asked what would be their reaction *if* they were given an opportunity to answer the circular. They said they would sign no retraction of their protests.

Afterwards three of the teachers—two of them pacifists—were locked up on the boat for having been especially vigorous in opposing any concession. One of these declared that his pacifism was the reason why he would sign no such statement, and the Germans mistakenly supposed him to be one of the leaders.

Nothing further happened on the *Finmarken* about the circular. The boat docked at Kirkenes on May 11, with 147 teachers—six had been left at hospitals on the way.

At Kirkenes the first group of teachers were told of the circular about Quisling's new teachers' organisation. The teachers interpreted the circular as an attempt by the Quisling régime to save face while at the same time saying that the new teachers' organisation would be dropped.

As events turned out, the new organisation never actually came into being, and the announced membership fees were never deducted from the teachers' salaries.

They sent a telegram to the Education Department on May 13 saying that with reference to the circular of April 25 they wished to resume their teaching positions. There was no reply.

Meanwhile, the schools in Oslo had finally re-opened on May 7 and the teachers had presented a declaration dissociating themselves from the new organisation.

HAY FOR BEDDING

At Kirkenes there were no beds, bedding, mattresses or furniture for the teachers. They slept for a while in barracks built for German soldiers. Only a few teachers had brought sleeping bags with them when arrested. Later there were stoves for heating.

Mr. Holmboe asked the German officer if the teachers could take some hay from a nearby haystack for bedding. He refused. A sympathetic German soldier showed Mr. Holmboe how to remove the old straw from the top of the haystack, take the necessary supply of fresh straw, and then replace the old so that the appearance was unchanged.

With very few Gestapo men among the German soldiers, the treatment was less severe than at Jørstadmoen. A few of the Germans were sympathetic and helpful, but the teachers' plight was not easy.

QUISLING ADMITS DEFEAT

In June most of the teachers were moved to another camp which had originally been a silver fox farm. Instead of barracks, they now lived in 17 octagonal huts made of heavy but untreated cardboard with wooden floors.

Only one of them had a window. The roofs were tarred, but when the walls became wet they lost their grip from the frames. The teachers nicknamed the camp *pappenheim*—cardboard home.

A few preferred the fox cages, which consisted of wire netting—top, bottom and sides—and a wooden frame. These teachers were regarded as more sporting than the rest.

About 300 others were housed in stables. In the barns there was hardly room even to lie down. Forty slept in a row, with about a foot's width each, so they all had to turn over at once.

DANGEROUS WORK

At Kirkenes the teachers were required to work. Despite their lack of experience, they were set to unloading from ships large oil drums and heavy crates of supplies.

These supplies sometimes included ammunition, and there was discussion among the teachers as to whether they ought to do this work. They finally decided, however, to proceed but to "go slow."

They were divided into shifts which worked day and night seven days a week. Considering their lack of training it was extremely risky; one teacher was killed, two men lost an eye each, one broke a leg and both arms.

*   *   *   *   *

EFFECT ON THE PEOPLE

While at Kirkenes the teachers did not feel particularly heroic nor much concerned with victory or defeat. They were too much "concerned with immediate affairs."

They were badly equipped for the cold. Some, Mr. Holmboe thought, would have withdrawn their protests after a month or two of this, but after their transit from the south they were given no chance.

While it was thus impossible for them to have given in if they had wanted to, the Norwegian people regarded them as heroes for maintaining their resistance. "In many ways our victory was organised by the enemy," Mr. Holmboe said.

The teachers' deportation to Kirkenes had had an enormous effect on both the Norwegian people and the Quisling régime.

"YOU'VE DESTROYED EVERYTHING"

While it consolidated the opposition of the people to the occupation and the puppet government, Quisling and his followers became furious.

Quisling knew that if he took harsher measures against the teachers he might irrevocably increase public antagonism against the régime.

Quisling had good reason to be angry.

The new teachers' organisation had been the pilot project of his whole plan for instituting the Corporate State, and the teachers had thwarted it.

This was shown better than anywhere else at the village of Stabekk on May 22.

Vidkun Quisling arrived by car at the Stabekk *gymnasium* (high school). His Minister of Education and the head of the police for the whole country accompanied him. Twenty members of the Hird (Norwegian Gestapo) surrounded the school.

"ARREST US, TOO"

The teachers were called together. Quisling stormed and raged and shouted at them. His voice could be clearly heard outside the building.

He ended with the words: "You teachers have destroyed everything for me!"

"That sentence was a triumph for us," Mr. Holmboe said. "It became a slogan and was taken up and quoted everywhere afterwards." It meant, he said, the teachers had blocked Quisling's whole plan of organising the new Corporate State.

Quisling ordered the arrest of all the teachers at that school. Next day, a few teachers who had been absent during Quisling's visit, went to the prison where their fellow teachers were held.

"We should be arrested, too," they said.

At Kirkenes the days, weeks and months passed. The brief Arctic summer came and went, and the weather turned cold again.

THE TEACHERS' RETURN

The days and weeks and months passed—for the people in the "outside world." But for the teachers, as for all prisoners, time was counted in minutes and hours and days. But finally, even for them, the days grew into weeks and the weeks into months.

While the time passed slowly for the prisoners at Kirkenes camp, the Norwegian people did not forget them. Their spirit rose as they spoke of the sufferings and the bravery of the teachers, and their resistance stiffened.

The intransigence of the authorities increased the impact of the protest.

The longer the teachers were kept at Kirkenes the more the nation remembered them. The authorities thus "helped us to put up a much longer and braver fight than otherwise would have been possible," Mr. Holmboe told me.

The spring grew into summer, and that became autumn. Still the teachers unloaded the boats and tried to keep warm.

Although living in misery, they organised lectures, composed songs and sang, although there were no musical instruments. Others drew sketches and some painted (with paints smuggled into the camp).

As autumn wore on and winter approached the weather became very cold, for they were well beyond the Arctic Circle.

Despite the hardships and the cold, there was practically no serious illness in the camp. Some attributed this to the Arctic air killing disease-causing bacteria.

DOCTOR'S REPORT

Yet there were less serious illnesses, and a considerable number of teachers were no longer able to work. A German doctor examined them. Perhaps as a result of his report, it was announced that the Germans were willing to send back those who were unfit.

The teachers were surprised.

The German doctor followed the advice of the representatives of the teachers and selected 150 who were to be sent home.

But the night before they were to depart the German authorities announced that before they left they must sign a declaration that they were willing to resume their positions in the schools as members of the new Nazi teachers' organisation (which had actually not come into being).

What should they do? They were ill. Although only late August the weather was gradually becoming colder and colder. The winter was coming, and they did not have adequate clothing.

Yet, after five months of resistance, should they give in now?

HARD DECISION

The rest of the teachers held a meeting. The discussion was earnest. It was a difficult problem.

Some argued that each person must make his own decision, but they could not personally sign such a statement.

Others argued that just as in a war it is sometimes necessary to withdraw and for the injured and ill to leave the front lines as non-combatants, while others continue the fight, so it was now.

This view was supported by Mr. Holmboe. In addition, the statement they were asked to sign was in German, and this particular struggle was not against the German Army but against the Quisling régime.

The majority concurred. They recommended that the teachers who were ill sign the statement. They did so.

Those papers, however, never left the Kirkenes camp, and were never used for propaganda against the teachers.

NO STATEMENT SIGNED

So it was that about 150 teachers were sent home and re-leased. One of them took a sketch, made at the camp, home to Mr. Holmboe's family.

Then on September 16 a second group of about 100—who had signed no statement—were sent back.

Mr. Holmboe was among the group which still remained at Kirkenes. They did not know their fate. Even if the Germans intended to send them back as well the time was short.

There was a shortage of shipping. If they did not leave Kirkenes before December they might not be able to leave before spring. Although the sea generally does not freeze at Kirkenes, shipping would soon be extremely dangerous. The "dark time" of the year with no sunshine in the Arctic was approaching, and the black-out of lighthouses along Norway's jagged coastline spelt danger to all shipping.

The teachers became nervous. The temperature dropped 20 degrees (C) below freezing. Then on November 4 the approximately 400 remaining teachers were put on a steamer, and began a 16-day trip south to home.

They also had signed no statement.

As the teachers were released the news travelled rapidly over the country that the men—who had become national heroes—were coming back without having given in to Quisling.

TRIUMPHANT RETURN

People met the train at the railway station. The ex-prisoners were given free lodging at the best hotels. Flowers and food—which was very scarce—poured into their homes.

Mr. Holmboe arrived home on November 20—exactly eight months after his arrest. Congratulations poured in, including some from people he did not know personally, who wanted to demonstrate their support.

Despite the stresses of the past months his wife remained calm. In 1939, when her husband had been called into the neutrality service to guard against the belligerents' violating Norway's neutrality, "I felt my knees were cut off," she told me. "Later, when the war came, and he was arrested twice, I felt more and more quiet."

No one had known what would happen when the teachers began their protest, Mr. Holmboe told me, but "the experience showed to everyone the strength of non-violent resistance."

The teachers had won more than a small skirmish. After Quisling had encountered further difficulties in his effort to impose the Corporate State, Hitler personally intervened and ordered that the whole project of setting up a Corporate State in Norway should be abandoned.

*   *   *   *   *

The 1942 Norwegian teachers' resistance does not prove that non-violent resistance is always successful, or that it can always bring a totalitarian State to its knees. There were circumstances operating in the teachers' favour which are not always present.

But the "Kirkenes Journey" does prove a point which is often denied; that non-violent resistance can be successful under occupation by such a régime as Hitler's Nazi Germany.

*   *   *   *   *

15. Joseph Scholmer: VORKUTA: STRIKE IN A CONCENTRATION CAMP

In the summer of 1953, as is detailed in this reading, a great strike broke out in a Soviet forced-labor camp. On the part of the miners working there, it was largely non-violent and its leaders hoped to make it completely so.

Joseph Scholmer, author of our account, was a prisoner at Vorkuta and had a good opportunity to study the psychology and sociology of the strike at first hand. The refusal to work was motivated by the desire to gain reduction of sentences and to improve camp conditions. Although the concessions eventually granted by the authorities were relatively minor, Scholmer suggests that had the strike been emulated by other communities, industrial production would have declined drastically and with it might have come a collapse of the political system itself.

The reading illustrates at least three important problems which arise in connection with any non-violent resistance movement. First of all, we note the importance of the context within which non-violent conflict is waged: at Vorkuta, this included such events as the recent death of Stalin, the uncertainty of his successors as to their future, the wave of strikes in East Germany and Poland, and the general atmosphere of hope that appeared to pervade the world after the passing of the dictator. Secondly, Vorkuta exemplifies nicely the measures likely to be used by the authorities to break up any non-violent resistance; and in this connection it will be noted that most employees of the camp never lost their humanity, often exhibiting considerable understanding of the strikers. A third and very vital observation is one stressed by Scholmer himself—that the strike was carried out by men who were inexperienced and who, had they been more experienced, might have achieved greater success.

When all the frustrations of Vorkuta are enumerated, it still remains true that it demonstrated the possibilities of a largely non-violent strike even under adverse conditions. If it failed to achieve major objectives of the strikers, it should be remembered that a very high percentage of violent struggles have also failed: thus a militarily well-prepared Germany in World War I went down to defeat, as did a highly militarized Japan in World War II. In fact, the record of failure in violent struggle —using "success" here in its conventional sense—is a very long one.

The reading is reprinted from Chapter XI of Joseph Scholmer's *Vorkuta*, translated by Robert Kee (New York: Holt, 1955).

———

During the first three years of my stay in the Soviet Union I had experienced a number of improbable things. But it had never occurred to me that in the Fatherland of the Workers, the home of the victorious proletariat, I would live to see a regular full-blown strike. A strike of more than 10,000 miners lasting for several weeks with all the usual paraphernalia-strike committees, slogans, pamphlets, and, of course, black-legs—a strike similar in every respect to that other historic strike, in the Lena Goldfields Company's mines in Siberia in 1912, when the Tsarist police fired into the strikers just as the Communists were to do in 1953.

This strike would not of course have been possible if the underground resistance groups had not already been in existence. These groups were not formed specifically for the strike. They were already there. But they provided the personnel and the necessary technical basis for any sort of offensive action. The strike leaders were to some extent identical with the leaders of the resistance groups and in the camps in which this was not so they were at least chosen and approved by them. The strike had at its disposal a piece of machinery which had been built up with the greatest care and could be relied upon to function smoothly.

It is also difficult to say whether the strike would have taken place without the example of the strike in the Russian Zone on June 17, 1953. Before June 17 the possibility of a mass strike had not been considered by the prisoners, nor had the leaders of the resistance groups laid any plans for one. All their preparations were for the eventuality of war. June 17 revolutionized the situation. The prisoners suddenly saw that there was something they could do. For a war—their one hope so far—they were dependent on the West, but they could bring about a strike themselves. It took some time for this realization to sink in. It was the ordinary man in the camp who had to bear the day to day burden of the strike. The necessary thought process had to have time to develop.

As things were, this process of fermentation took from June 17 to the end of July. It is, however, quite certain that if June 17 had led to a general strike in the Eastern Zone, lasting as long as a week, the strike at Vorkuta would have broken out immediately, without any interval. The situation was quite tense enough as it was; everyone felt instinctively that it could not be long before the explosion came.

*   *   *   *   *

It was nearly midnight on a warm summer's night in July 1953. The drying room in my block was almost empty. At a little table in the corner two prisoners were playing dominoes. I could let my fire go out. It hadn't rained all day, nothing had to be dried.

I told the two prisoners that I was going out to see a friend in another block. (In fact all the doors were supposed to be shut, but the guards often used to be careless and leave them open.)

'Don't worry, we'll see that nothing gets stolen.'

I found Georg sitting on a bench in front of his block.

'Good evening, Comrade *sushilchik!*'

'Good evening, dear colleague!' said Georg.

Georg was an engineer. We had made our odyssey through the various brigades together. We had dug in the foundations together, we had slung bricks, mixed concrete, carried mortar, and unloaded tree-trunks. But now all that was behind us. We were safe at last. Our health had been ruined over the years and we were on the disabled list. And we sat together on a bench in front of one of the blocks and looked out towards the beauty of the tundra on this long midsummer night.

'Would you like some tea?' asked Georg.

'Yes, please.'

A few hundred yards away lay the road which led up to the north-western camps. Behind it lay the railway. The railway forked at that point: one line went to the pits, the other continued straight on and disappeared over the horizon into the tundra. It ended at a port on the Arctic Ocean, about fifty miles to the north.

'I can't make it out,' said Georg. 'Not a single coal truck has come out of those pits since yesterday evening. There's not a sign of life there. The engines are taking empty trucks up but bringing no coal back.'

'Perhaps there's a technical hitch.'

'I don't think so. If it were only a question of one pit, perhaps—but three!'

About half-past one people came back from the night shift in the pit and reported that a strike had broken out in Pit Number 7. An engine driver who had been in Number 7 and was taking loaded trucks out of our pit told them about it.

The news was electrifying. We stood there discussing it for hours.

The next day a whole collection of further details started coming in. These consisted largely of *parásha,* or lavatory rumours. Many such idiotic rumours had probably been put about by the NKVD to cause confusion.

One thing, however, remained quite clear, and that was that Pit Number 7 had struck. But the engines were still bringing down the odd truck loaded with coal. Did this mean that the other pits on the same stretch of line were still working?

A rumour came in that a strike had also broken out in Pit Number 40, the largest and most modern of all the pits at Vorkuta. The next day the camps in the immediate vicinity of the town were said to be striking.

All these rumours were backed up with concrete details as to source and origin.

A 'free' man working in the pit, whose wife had been into the town that day had told the brigade-leader in Number 6 seam that the strike had spread to Pit Number 1.

In the course of the day—so rumour had it—there had been shooting in Pit Number 40 and a number of people had been killed and wounded. That evening—still according to rumour— Pit Number 8 stopped work.

At first it was impossible to get any clear picture of what was happening. Then things slowly began to fall into shape. Pits Numbers 7, 14/16 and 29 were on strike for certain. In addition, the prisoners working on the site of the big new electric station in the vicinity of the striking pits had also come out on strike.

The prelude to these events turned out to have been something of which we had had a glimpse from our own camp.

A few nights before, a special prisoner train from the direction of Vorkuta had come slowly past our camp. Behind the iron bars of the little windows we had just been able to make out the faces of the prisoners.

'*Otkúda?* Where are you from?' asked our people.

'Karaganda.'

The train moved slowly round the great bend which led up towards Pit Number 7 and halted in one of the sidings.

The next day the train came back empty.

Three days later the strike broke out in Pit Number 7. It was the people from Karaganda who had started it off.

This was what had happened:

The prisoners in the Karaganda area lived under rather better conditions than we did, both from the point of view of climate and in other respects. But the main thing about Karaganda was that there was no long murderous Arctic winter there. When the shortage of labour at Vorkuta became acute owing to the increasing amount of building projects and the increasing amount of disablement among the prisoners, the NKVD Central Office in Moscow decided to send reinforcements of labour to Vorkuta from Karaganda. These reinforcements consisted of prisoners who had been living in Karaganda under semi-free conditions; most of them had been engaged on building projects. And the enrolment for Vorkuta took place on a voluntary basis. Volunteers were promised better pay than in Karaganda and settlement as 'free' population.

And now on their arrival in Vorkuta they had been put into one of the usual special camps. Their living conditions were in no way different from those of any of the other prisoners in Vorkuta. And there could be no question of settling them as 'free' population, for the practical facilities were not available.

Whereupon the Karaganda people were so disappointed and enraged that they refused to do a stroke of work from the moment they arrived in the camp. On being officially informed that the authorities at Vorkuta could not hold themselves responsible for any promises that might have been made to them in Karaganda, they set about stirring up trouble among the other inhabitants of the camp. They found the general situation more than promising. The old inhabitants of the camp declared their solidarity with the people from Karaganda.

And so a few days later Camp 7 was living through a general strike. Neither the pit workers nor the brigades on the building sites outside the camp went out to work. From Camp 7 the strike spread to Camps 14/16 and Camp 29. Our camp, Number 6, was to be the fourth to join the strike.

Some of the prisoners in our camp who had previously been in Camp 7 described the atmosphere to us. They said that the prisoners were a mixture of intellectuals and simple men of action. It was more like 9/10 than 6. The prisoners were tougher; as in 9/10, many of them were the survivors of a process of biological selection. Within a few days it became possible to piece together what had been going on there.

The camp had first elected an official strike committee which made the following demand to the camp authorities: a plenipotentiary was to be sent at once from the Ministerial Council of the USSR or from the Politburo. They refused to deal with anyone who had not come direct from the Kremlin.

Attempts to make the prisoners return to work proved a complete failure. General Derevianko, the military commander, appeared and held a meeting at which he tried to get them to abandon the strike. The prisoners used the meeting to put forward propaganda for themselves. A speaker stepped up and asked the General whether the prisoners' demand for a plenipotentiary to be sent from Moscow was being agreed to. When the General answered 'No,' the speaker broke up the meeting with the words:

'We have nothing to discuss with you. We will only treat with a responsible authority from Moscow.'

A second attempt proved equally fruitless. Then this camp, like the others which had struck, was surrounded and put in a state of siege.

The prisoners' demands, as presented by their strike committees in the different camps, all concentrated round one main point: the quashing of, or at least reduction of, the decade-long sentences that had been inflicted on them. The exact way in which this demand was formulated by the different groups varied considerably from camp to camp.

Some, for instance, demanded an immediate review of all political trials including sentences. Others demanded simply a considerable reduction of the sentences without bothering about the form of judicial procedure. Others demanded to be settled as 'free' population, and declared themselves ready to stay on in Vorkuta. They were in fact ready to continue working in the pits there until coal production should be put on a different basis, either by securing voluntary labour from the Soviet Union with sufficiently attractive financial offers, or by making it obligatory for the *kómsomóls* to spend a year of service in the northern pits. Perhaps the most drastic demand was best formulated by the members of a building brigade in Camp 14/16 who, ordered to go to work by a guard on the second day of the strike, merely asked him if the barbed wire were still there, and declared that they wouldn't go back to work until it had been taken away.

The majority of the prisoners were clear from the beginning that the Soviet Government would never accept their demands in full. They were hoping for some sort of compromise, such as that sentences would be scaled down by one-third or one-fifth, starting with the first year. Only very few of the prisoners realized that it was quite impossible for the Government to comply with the prisoners' demands even to this extent.

Immediately after the outbreak of the strike in Camp 7 the authorities issued the following notice to all special camps in Vorkuta:

1. The prisoners will no longer be shut in at nights.
2. The bars in front of the windows are to be removed.
3. Numbers worn on the left arm and the right knee are to be removed.

4. Henceforth every prisoner is entitled to write one letter a month to his family instead of two letters a year.

5. With the permission of the officer in charge of all special camps at Vorkuta, General Derevianko, all prisoners whose work and conduct is satisfactory may, on application to, and with the approval of, the Commandant of their camp, receive one visit a year from members of their families.

6. Every prisoner has the right to address applications for the revision of interrogation and trial proceedings to the Chairman of the Special Commission sent from Moscow, General Maslennikov.

This notice was taken round all the special camps by special messenger on the second day of the strike. The prisoners began delightedly pulling the hinges off the heavy iron bars which were laid across the doors of the blocks at night, accompanying their action with a lot of swearing. The bars were wrenched from the windows and the numbers were torn off their clothes. As far as the concession about receiving visits from relatives was concerned the prisoners realized well enough that it was of no practical significance. Which of their relatives was in a position to come two thousand miles or more from the Ukraine, the Baltic States or Siberia, at their own expense, in order to spend a few hours daily with a member of their family for a period of three days or so?

As to the last point: one-third of the 3,500 prisoners of Camp 6 addressed petitions for a revision of their proceedings in accordance with this announcement to Colonel General Maslennikov or to the State Prosecutor-General of the Soviet Union, General Rudenko (former Soviet prosecutor at Nuremberg). In every single case they were turned down with the same stereotyped formula:

'Your petition of such and such a date has been examined. The sentence is hereby confirmed. There is no occasion for a revision of the proceedings. After you have served your sentence you will be released.'

It was in fact quite impossible for the Government to abandon the system of labour or even to modify it to meet the strikers' limited demands. To have done so would have had a paralysing effect on Soviet industry. The labour camps are an essential component in the industrial life of the Soviet Union. Their role is to supply raw materials. Prisoners, who had been employed in the industrial ministries before their arrest, estimated that half of the entire coal production of the Soviet Union and eighty per cent of the wood supply is provided by forced labour. In other words, without this labour, the Soviet Union's industrial production would be brought to a standstill. The Kremlin is a prisoner of its own prison system.

*   *   *   *   *

Camp 6 was one of the relatively quiet camps at Vorkuta. It seemed doubtful if it would join in the strike at all. And in fact it was exactly a week from the arrival of the first reliable information about the outbreak of the strike in the other camps to the moment when the proper psychological atmosphere for a strike in Number 6 had been created. All through this week the underground resistance groups in the camp had been laying their preparations. During this week too the NKVD did all it could to paralyse the prisoners' growing determination to strike, by filling the camp with rumours.

For instance we heard that:

A widespread amnesty was imminent. By striking the prisoners were merely annoying the Government and interfering with the arrangements for the amnesty.

Or everyone who went on strike would be sent before a special tribunal which would sentence him to a further twenty-five years. This rumour of course made no impression on those who had twenty-five years already, but those who had only a few years of their sentence left, or were just about to be released, could not help paying attention to it.

Or again: those who had struck in other camps had been taken to Vorkuta and shot after a drum-head court-martial. Everyone whose life meant anything to him paid attention to that. But the rumour was exploded when, a few days later, an enormous column of prisoners was seen marching back from Vorkuta to Camp 7. They waved and shouted:

'Damói! Damói! We're going back home! The *peresílka*'s overflowing; there's no more room for us!'

So those who went on strike were merely being taken to the *peresílka*.

Or again: all those who struck would have their mail stopped. That exercised a considerable moral pressure.

But when in spite of all these rumours the NKVD realised that things were not looking so good for them, they made a few preventive arrests of prisoners whom they considered capable of playing a prominent role in the event of a strike: three Russians and two Jews. These arrests throw an interesting light on the informer system in the camps. The Russian informers were only in a position to report on Russians and Jews. They had been unable to make any contact with the real leaders who were nearly all Ukrainians and Lithuanians.

One important step taken by the NKVD had been to isolate the camp. Normally the camps at Vorkuta keep in touch with each other whenever parties of prisoners are transferred from one camp to another. These transfers were stopped at once. Another opportunity for exchanging information is offered by the collaboration of brigades from different camps on the same working projects, on the railway, or on the roads, or in the gravel pits. In this way it is possible to keep up a regular correspondence between camps. Messages are deposited at certain agreed points and are then picked up by the other brigade. This source was also cut off. The outside brigades were stopped from leaving the camp.

The first concrete piece of information about the strike in Camp 7 and the order to join the strike came from one of the railway personnel. An engine driver whose engine had brought full coal trucks down from some of the other camps said to the people working in the goods yards:

'I am to tell you to start as soon as you can. Camp 7 is expecting you to join the strike.'

During the night the underground strike committee, which was dominated by Ukrainians and Lithuanians, gave out the order that the strike was to begin the next morning. The heads of the individual national groups informed their own men. The instructions were not to fall in for *rasvód*, the outside roll-call, but to return to the blocks after breakfast.

We were woken at five o'clock as usual. The prisoners dressed and went over to the *stolóvaya*. While they were eating, soldiers formed up outside and barred the way back to the blocks. They forced the prisoners to fall in for *rasvód* at the guard-house nearby. The prisoners didn't dare to come to grips with the guards. The guards on their side knew that any assault on the prisoners could easily bring the issue to a head. They were polite but firm. They succeeded in assembling the whole of the first shift at the main gate.

Then the officers made their first attempt to scare the prisoners into going to work.

The strikers' names were called out individually and they were asked if they were willing to go to work or not. Those who refused were taken over to the door of the guard-house and kept there for the time being. Those who agreed to go to work—a small group largely composed of technical personnel —were formed up into a column and marched over to the pit. Finally, after a lot of effort, the officers succeeded in getting a second larger group out of the camp into the pit.

But once there the prisoners refused to put on their working clothes. The number of guards round the pit-head was increased. They tried to persuade the prisoners to start work. Those who refused to do so were taken into a room where an officer from the NKVD legal department was sitting.

'Why don't you want to work?'

The prisoners answered evasively. Most of them said something like:

'Because the others are not working.'

In front of the officer lay a fat book with pages divided into two columns: one for those who were willing to work and the

other for those who were not. He tried to get the prisoners to
sign in one or the other of the two columns. The prisoners
had the uncomfortable feeling that they were going to be put
down in the book in any case and refused. Many hid in
the area round the pit-head and were chased by the guards.
That evening my friend Seryosha told me that he had played
hide and seek with the guards all day.

After the experiences of the morning, the afternoon shift refused to go to lunch in the *stolóvaya*. The brigades sent people
to fetch the bread, but apart from that, lived off their slender
supplies of sugar, cheap sweets and margarine. The Lithuanians distributed their bacon to non-Lithuanians—an otherwise
unheard of event. This was an extraordinary demonstration
of the Lithuanians' solidarity with the other nationalities.

After about an hour three guards arrived to summon us to
work. They were very polite. They had orders to try and persuade the brigades to go to work. They did their best to carry
out these orders, although they knew quite well that they would
have no success. The prisoners knew that the guards were
acting on the orders of the Commandant, and the guards in
turn knew that the prisoners understood their position.

So the ensuing conversation took place entirely according to
the rules. None of the soldiers asked why the prisoners were
striking. None of the prisoners made any provocative remarks.
The blocks refused to go out to work—all right. The soldiers
let a decent interval elapse, without making any further attempt to carry out their orders. The prisoners understood that
the soldiers couldn't very well go back to the Kommandantur
at once. They had been told to try and persuade the prisoners.
They were using silent methods of persuasion, that was all.

The prisoners offered them stools to sit down on, but the
soldiers declined the offer. This was going too far. Finally they
moved over to the door and stared out into space. The long
avenues of the camp were deserted. The faces of the other
prisoners could be seen behind the barred windows of the
other blocks. The other guards were now beginning to wander
back from these blocks. They had been equally unsuccessful.

'Right,' said the guards. They laid the heavy iron bars across
the outside of the door again and went back to the Kommandantur.

At this time of year it can be very hot at Vorkuta. It was
stifling in the block. All the windows had been opened. The
prisoners lay on their beds stripped to the waist. Some of them
read, others slept, others sat drinking hot water. Gradually the
heat became unbearable. Three Ukrainians took out the window of the lavatory, pulled the bars out of the window frame
and climbed outside. They were followed by ten, twenty, thirty

or more others. They sat down in the sun and stared out into the tundra. Pit Number 7 was still not working.

Then Mironenkov, one of the senior NCOs of 'the Blues,' arrived in the camp and started going round the blocks testing doors and windows to see that they were properly shut. When he came to the emergency exit of the block next door he rattled it to make sure that it was fast. Suddenly it opened from the inside and a voice said: 'Well, what's the news?'

'Yob tvóiu mutch,' said Mironenkov, and saw that all the nails in the door had really been pulled out and that what looked like nails from the outside were merely dummies. He went over to the carpenter's shop to fetch a dozen long nails and began nailing up the door of the block again.

Then he turned round to us:

'How did you get there?'

Someone said:

'Well, we were outside anyway but the door was locked and we couldn't get in again.'

Mironenkov tested the bars of the window of the lavatory which had been temporarily put back again, and they came away in his hand. Someone called out:

'Mind out the whole window doesn't fall on top of you!'

Mironenkov took the whole window out.

'Davái!' he said. 'Everyone back inside.'

The prisoners climbed back into the lavatory. Mironenkov fetched some more nails and started trying to hammer the bars back into position. Someone called to him:

'I bet you never thought the day would come when you would have to work and we would sit and watch you.'

It was a thoroughly 'Russian' atmosphere. The whole afternoon passed like some scene out of a comedy by Ostrovski.

The atmosphere was less placid in the block in which the prisoners who ran the 'ventilation' of the pit were living. The 'ventilation' brigade was badly needed in the pit for technical reasons. All the pits at Vorkuta contain coal-gas, but Pit Number 6 is particularly bad. The ventilation had to be kept going if the pit was to remain workable. The attempts to get these brigades to go to work were therefore correspondingly more insistent. Not three, but seven guards appeared. The prisoners maintained their attitude. In the course of the discussion that followed one of the guards took hold of a prisoner by the leg and tried to pull him out of bed. He was immediately set upon by the man's neighbours. A few sharp blows soon put him in his place again.

'You've no right to lay hands on us!'

The atmosphere was tense. The seven guards decided to beat a retreat.

Half an hour later the Deputy Commandant arrived accompanied by the Deputy Security Officer. It so happened that both their superiors were on leave.

The conversation which followed was of a quite grotesque politeness. It gave a perfect indication of the state of mind of the Government in whose interest these two representatives were acting. Both officers adopted a fatherly tone. They talked to the prisoners as if they were naughty children.

'Haven't we done enough for you? Think of the terrible years before 1948. We've built new blocks for you. The food is better. Have any of you ever been badly treated by us? Can anyone say he has never seen me strike a prisoner? You must understand the pit has its norm to fulfil. If you don't work now you'll only have to make up for it later.'

The two of them understood the prisoners' mentality. The Deputy Commandant, unlike the Commandant, Schilin, was in fact hated by no one. The prisoners saw that it was an awkward situation for the Deputy Commandant. Perhaps his whole future depended on his ability to get the camp to abandon the strike. Perhaps Derevianko had said to him on the telephone:

'See that you bring this strike to an end at once. Otherwise no more promotion for you.'

But the 'ventilation' brigade remained firm. A Ukrainian said:

'We've nothing against you. We know you've never struck a prisoner and that conditions in the camp have improved and that we're not hungry any more. But that's no reason why we should agree to sit here for another twenty-five years. The strike isn't directed against you—it's about other things. We stand solid with our comrades. We're striking for something fundamental.'

The Deputy Commandant left the camp without success.

Only five of the thirteen special camps at Vorkuta joined the strike. The others were restrained mainly by the preventive measures which the NKVD took on the basis of their experience in the five camps which struck. After each camp had been hermetically sealed off, the NKVD took certain steps to deceive those which had not struck. In Camp 6, for instance, they let the empty trucks go on running between the pit-head and the slag-heap for three days after the strike had begun, so that every camp within range would think that the pit was still working.

The three women's camps at Vorkuta did not strike, because they were not well enough organized politically, although there were individual cases of women refusing to work.

Those prisoners who had been arrested in the striking camps were mostly sent to Camp 11, where they were kept separate from the main body of the other prisoners there. Others were taken to the cells in the main prison in Camp 1. In Camp 11 they lived under a particularly strict régime. They were set a twelve-hour day, and given lower rations than usual. They received no pay, all their mail was stopped; and they were allowed neither radio nor newspapers. Guards accompanied them from the blocks to the *stolóvaya*, from the *stolóvaya* to the pit, and back again to the blocks after work. The blocks were kept locked all the time and the windows were barred. In fact they refused to produce any more coal than was required for the camp's internal needs.

* * * * *

On the evening of the second day of the strike in our camp I had a long conversation with Amstislavski. He was a perfect example of the typical Soviet civil servant, a Party member, without any mind of his own. There were about fifty such prisoners in the camp, former Party officials or members of the administrative machine, ex-officers, engineers or technicians of one sort or another. It was delightful to watch them in this new situation. They were absolutely dismayed. This was the first strike that had ever taken place in the Soviet Union. The effect on their political consciousness was that of an atom bomb. Deliberate reasoned opposition to the State was something that had never crossed their minds as possible before. They had lost their whole feeling of security: who could say what would happen next? They were terrified of incidents and secretly sent messages to the camp authorities conveying their loyalty.

* * * * *

The same military precautions were taken immediately against all the camps that joined the strike. The soldiers in the special reserve in Vorkuta stood by in readiness from the moment the strike began. One night they started setting up machine-gun nests round Camp 6. It was like manoeuvres for them. When they had finished with their machine-guns they started putting mortars into position.

'What will the soldiers do? Do you think they'll shoot?'

Everywhere the same conversation. On the whole people felt that in the present situation, that is to say, in the absence of any positive factor to affect their political morale, the soldiers would probably shoot if ordered to. The strike leaders were determined that the strike should be carried out without bloodshed if possible.

This war that was no war soon began to bore the soldiers. They lay about in the tundra trying to protect themselves from the millions of flies that were biting them. The tundra is a boggy place. Every now and again it rained and the foxholes which the soldiers had dug for themselves filled with water. We could hear them complaining about their wet feet.

One evening a soldier was patrolling up and down on the duck-boards on the other side of the wire. Georg and I were sitting together and he was telling me about the flora of the tundra. Just beside the duck-boards, where the sentry was marching up and down, was a large, purple, trumpet-like flower.

'What a pity!' said Georg. 'It only blooms at this time of year and then in only one or two places. So far nine of the brigades working outside have been able to bring me one.'

We discussed what we could do about it. In the end I had a word with the soldier.

'Excuse me, sir,' I said to him with exaggerated politeness. 'We'd very much like to have that flower that's blooming just there beside the duck-boards—the purple one.'

The sentry looked round. He knew he wasn't allowed to talk to prisoners. But he was perfectly friendly.

'What do you want it for?' he asked.

'We're botanists. We're interested in it.'

'Are you Germans?'

'Yes.'

He went on marching up and down thinking it over. It seemed a strange request. Should he give these Germans the purple flower or not? After a minute or two he said:

'How can I get it over to you?'

'That's very simple,' we said. 'We'll throw a stone over wrapped up in a bit of paper. Wrap the flower around the stone, put the stone back in the paper and throw it back to us.'

And this was what he did.

This incident gives a very good idea of the mood of the soldiers at the time. We realized that in the present situation if ordered to shoot by Derevianko, they would certainly shoot. On the other hand the system had been unable to immunize them completely against the ordinary temptations of being human.

On the whole it was obvious that the sympathies of most of the soldiers were with the prisoners and, certainly in our camp, with the exception of the incident in the 'ventilation' block, nothing happened to disturb the good relations between the two parties. The guards could easily have shown hostility, or have made their antagonism clear to us. But they didn't. They didn't raise a finger to do anything more than they were ordered to do. And if their officers had not been there to supervise them they would not have done even that.

The strikers took careful note of this.

* * * * *

. . . The Kremlin did the only thing it could have done in the circumstances: it sent a commission of inquiry to Vorkuta to make a rapid and comprehensive investigation of the whole situation.

This commission consisted of about thirty officers and arrived by air on the little aerodrome at Vorkuta. . . .

*   *   *   *   *

The commission worked for about eight days and then flew away again.

Then came a day when we heard heavy tommy-gun and rifle fire quite clearly in the distance. It came from the direction of the three pits, Numbers 7, 14/16 and 29, ahead of us. At that time we didn't know which of these three camps the shooting was coming from.

The same evening one of the two surgeons in our camp, Blagodatov, was sent off by himself to an unknown destination. When he came back a week later I heard from him an account of the dramatic events which had been taking place at Pit Number 29.

There it had not been just a question of the prisoners refusing to go to work. Their first action had been to hold a public meeting and choose a camp committee of their own, in which all nations were represented.

This committee then went to the Commandant and informed him that the prisoners were at once taking over control of the camp themselves. They guaranteed the preservation of law and order and demanded that to avoid unnecessary complications he should immediately withdraw his officers and men from the camp.

This the Commandant proceeded to do.

A camp police was organized from among the prisoners. Those who were in the *bur* for refusing to go to work or other non-criminal offences were released. The most notorious NKVD informers in the camp were locked up for their own protection and guarded by members of the new camp police.

A survey was then made of the food supplies in the camp and it was found that there was enough for four weeks. New increased rations on a uniform scale were fixed for all prisoners. The store sold all its reserves to the prisoners. The proceeds were handed to the Commandant. Five pigs which had been living off the swill from the kitchen were slaughtered. (An immediate consequence of this was that when our strike broke out in Camp 6 one of the first measures taken by the authorities was to bring the pigs to safety.)

In Camp 29 the prisoners' demands were essentially much the same as in the other camps: removal of the barbed wire, review of all political trials and a reduction of sentences. But the camp committee, like the strike committee in Camp 7, refused to deal with the local authorities in Vorkuta. They demanded to deal directly with a plenipotentiary of the Central Committee of the Communist Party or of the Soviet Government. Two attempts by General Derevianko to harangue a public meeting of prisoners proved a complete failure. The camp committee merely seized the opportunity to strengthen the morale of the striking prisoners.

In the meantime the camp was surrounded by a military formation in battle order. Machine-gun posts were built, and mortars put into position. As neither of the two parties would give in, a compromise between the prisoners' demands and the authorities' offer was out of the question. The situation moved relentlessly towards its bloody climax.

As soon as the military preparations for the occupation of the camp, which had been carried out under the personal supervision of General Derevianko himself, were complete—we saw a large number of lorries filled with infantry moving up in the direction of the striking camps during the night—an emissary was sent into the camp in the General's name demanding the prisoners' surrender. This emissary, an officer, behaved in such a provocative manner that he was set upon by the prisoners. The prisoners were once again called upon to surrender, this time by loudspeaker; but they refused. They assembled at the main gate, linked arms and formed themselves into a solid phalanx. There were loud cries of:

'Go on, shoot! It is better to die than to go on living like this!'

The Ukrainians sang their national songs.

Derevianko gave the order to storm the camp.

The soldiers moved forward.

The main gate was battered in. They found the prisoners massed before them an easy target.

It was at this point that the surgeon, Blagodatov, was ordered to Camp 29.

'When I arrived at the camp,' he told me, 'I found about 200 seriously wounded still alive, most of them hit in the chest and stomach. There were about a dozen Germans among them. Sixty-four prisoners had been killed on the spot, including four Germans. There wasn't much chance of saving many of the wounded, first because they had no resistance left to deal with wound infections, and secondly because there weren't enough instruments or bandages, or facilities for operating, or trained personnel.

'We operated for a whole week. We did what we could, but they were dying from their wounds all the time.'

A fortnight after the start of the strike in Camp 7 the General also delivered an ultimatum to the strikers there: either they must march out and form up in the tundra or else the camp would be taken by storm.

To prevent bloodshed the strikers decided to obey Derevianko's orders. The gates were opened and a long column of prisoners marched out. A few hundred yards away they were all surrounded like a flock of sheep. One by one they were made to file past the camp commandant, the head of the NKVD, his officers and his crowd of informers. With the help of the informers all strikers who could possibly be suspected of having had anything to do with the leadership of the strike, were weeded out. These amounted to between four and five hundred prisoners. They were loaded into lorries and driven away. The remainder were sent back into the camp. This action in fact eliminated the entire strike committee though they were not known individually. All the active elements in the camp were now missing. The masses were leaderless. The morale of the strikers had been broken. Work began in the pit again next day.

* * * * *

. . . Although the concessions made by the Government were in the end infinitesimal compared with the strikers' practical demands, even the most infinitesimal concession represented, in the circumstances, something tremendous. The strike was a sensational success for this one reason alone: it proved that it is possible to use the weapon of the strike with relative impunity in the Soviet Union itself—in the 'workers' paradise' in which it should by definition be impossible.

* * * * *

. . . This had been an underground strike; it had been carried out under the very noses of the NKVD. The conditions for it were in every way more difficult than for a strike in a capitalist country. None of the strikers themselves had any strike experience. These workers were striking for the first time in their lives. . . . They had the simple inexperience of the workers in the early days of capitalism, of the Chartists, or of the Russian workers' groups in 1880. Not one of the leaders had ever seen a strike before in his life, let alone taken part in one or led one. They improvised their strike technique as they went along. Moreover, this technique had to develop independently in each camp. The camps had no chance of learning from another's experience. Thus the strike took a completely different course in each camp.

And undoubtedly mistakes were made.

In not one of the camps did the leaders make use of that form of strike which, throughout the history of strikes, has

always proved the most effective: the sit-down strike. They let
everything be thrashed out in the camp itself instead of in the
pit. That is where the main battleground of the strike should
have been, for the simple reason that the pit is the exclusive
preserve of the prisoners.

*   *   *   *   *

Inside the pit it would have been possible to carry on open
and effective strike propaganda. Small meetings, impossible in
the camp because of the informer system, could have been
held. And the strikers' shock troops could have got possession
of technical key points such as the main production lift and
the coal trucks, and from there have exercised control over the
whole pit.

The fact that the prisoners stayed in the camps gave the
NKVD their chance to sort out, isolate and remove the most
active elements in the strike.

*   *   *   *   *

The most important thing about the strike was that it ever
took place at all. It had a profound effect not only on the prisoners but also on the civilian population in other parts of the
Soviet Union. Two months later we had some students from
the Leningrad mining institute working in the pit.

'We soon got to know you were on strike,' they told us. 'The
drop in coal was noticeable at once. We don't have any reserves. There's just the plan, that's all. And everyone knows
how vulnerable plans are.'

*   *   *   *   *

This strike had been the first visible positive demonstration
against the Government since the sailors' mutiny at Kronstadt
in 1921. It had destroyed the myth that the system was un-
assailable. The system is in fact wide open to attack the moment the workers start using against its ruling classes those very
methods which its ruling classes recommend to the workers in
'capitalist' countries. In addition to this, the planned economic
system of the Soviet Union is far more vulnerable to such a
form of attack than 'capitalist' society. This army of millions
of prisoners literally controls the supply of basic raw materials
(50 per cent of the coal and 80 per cent of the wood).
A strike, not only in Vorkuta, but in every region administered
by the NKVD would certainly have the effect of shaking the
Soviet economic system to its foundations.

PART III

NON-VIOLENT POWER
WITH EXPRESS PRINCIPLE

.

In contrast to the readings in Part II, those in Part III are concerned with deliberate, conscious, and principled non-violence. While the cases presented in Part II did on occasion approach the theory of non-violence, those in this part deal with situations and experiments based upon more or less well-articulated philosophies, and with the quest for ways of defending group autonomy and achieving social justice through basically non-violent power.

Only one large community in history has ever sought consciously and over a long period of time to dispense with military force as a method of defending itself against aggression and infringements of its rights. It is, therefore, appropriate that this section begins with an account of the unarmed politics of colonial Pennsylvania. Although Pennsylvania was a part of the British Empire and was therefore nominally defended by British troops, throughout most of its history no such troops were available near at hand for defense against the Indians or others. Nor did the colony desire such defense; unlike the other colonies, it refused to raise its own army or militia. It claimed to found its domestic and international policies on principles of exact justice, which it believed would serve as a better defense than armed might; and although its later history is filled with dubious compromises, it remains an undisputed fact that so long as seventeenth-century Quaker views predominated and a large proportion of the population adhered to that faith, the community was never menaced by Indians. During the same period most of the other colonies had many difficulties with the tribes, and some suffered cruel wars.

Pennsylvania constitutes a good example, too, of an effort to distinguish between the legitimate employment of physical force and what the founders regarded as its illegitimate use; and although they never worked out a complete theory, certain doctrines can be inferred. Thus, restraint of individuals through police action and mild punishments (mild at least in relation to seventeenth-century views) were deemed compatible with Quaker conceptions of non-violence, while the indiscriminate force employed in war was not.

This first reading is followed by John Fiske's history of the Dominican missionary Las Casas and his transformation of the "Land of War" into a "Land of Peace," an account that illuminates the theories behind both Las Casas' attitude to human relations and Fiske's own belief that human progress consists in the development of non-retaliatory responses to violence. The remaining readings treat of principled efforts to utilize strategies of non-violent power in the modern world. Of these, Reading 18 is perhaps the most basic, for it deals with the concrete application of Satyagraha in Indian politics and, because of the influence of Gandhi's ideas in the West, deserves particularly careful perusal. In a sense, South Africa, the subject of Reading 19, occupies the same place with respect to Satyagraha that India held a generation or more ago: the doctrine's application on a mass scale is in its beginning stages.

The most obvious application of Satyagraha and other theories of non-violent resistance in recent American experience has been the Negroes' struggle for equality. Reading 20 takes up this theme. While Gandhi's influence has been important in this conflict, we should also remember native American precedents, among them non-violent resistance to the Fugitive Slave Laws before the Civil War and the history of the feminist movement, which employed many tactics that might come under the heading of non-violent resistance or coercion.

It seems appropriate to follow with a brief reading describing strategies and tactics of non-violent direct action against preparation for war. The theory that informs these strategies grows out of the belief that, while orthodox methods of peacemaking are usually acceptable as far as they go, they are not enough. Governments, "democratic" no less than "totalitarian," are weighted down with a kind of inertia that seems to take them, despite the professions of their leaders to the contrary, down the road to war. As though in an hypnotic trance, societies become captives of slogans ("peace through strength," "armament build-ups for negotiation") and of a traditional reliance on violence. The non-violent direct actionist seeks to break through this inertia, to dramatize his doubt about the slogans, and to challenge the very assumptions of the existing international order.

Finally, we are invited in Reading 22 to imagine a nation converted to ideas resembling those of William Penn and Gandhi. It would, of course, abolish its military defenses and seek to use only non-violent resistance to oppose and frustrate invasion. In specific terms, how would it do this and what kinds of preparation would be required? What changes in attitude would be entailed? What results could be expected?

In answering questions of this kind one cannot, of course, reply with any great certainty; for most men appear to think that as individuals they can do little or nothing to prevent war, and no large modern nation has ever renounced military defense. The basis for our replies must, therefore, be general ethical and psychological considerations and the indirect experience afforded by the case studies examined in earlier readings.

It might be observed, however, that advocacy of unilateral disarmament is no longer a vision of wild dreamers. In recent years, it has been seriously supported in Great Britain. Thus Stephen King-Hall, a former commander in the British Navy, suggested a version of it for Britain in 1958.[1] Walter Millis, America's noted military historian, speaks of the "uselessness of military power,"[2] and he goes on to assert that were the United States to divest itself of its arms unilaterally it would be far safer than it is today. Professor Charles Osgood of the University of Illinois, while not advocating unilateral disarmament, has pressed the case for "unilateral initiatives" that would relax the international atmosphere and make genuine negotiations possible. Finally, the present writer has worked out a scheme for phased unilateral disarmament by the United States.[3] It would involve such measures as complete nuclear and non-nuclear disarmament within six years; simultaneous development of an organized system for non-violent resistance to invasion; diversion of resources now used to support the military to economic and social development; and a planned program for re-employment of those now working in armaments and supporting industries.

Reading 22 is in effect saying that we should be searching for realistic methods of national defense and discarding such unrealistic means as military power.

[1] Stephen King-Hall, *Defence in the Nuclear Age* (London: Gollancz, 1958).

[2] "The Uselessness of Military Power," in *America Armed: Essays on United States Military Policy,* ed. by Robert A. Goldwin (Chicago: Rand McNally, 1963).

[3] Mulford Sibley, *Unilateral Initiatives and Disarmament* (Philadelphia: American Friends Service Committee, 1962).

16. Isaac Sharpless: COLONIAL PENNSYL-VANIA: THE QUEST FOR NON-VIOLENCE

In 1654, Oliver Cromwell received an unusual letter from the Quaker George Fox. In the letter, Fox said:[1]

> God is my witness, by whom I am moved to give this forth for the Truth's sake, from him whom the world calls George Fox; who is the son of God who is sent to stand a witness against all violence and against all the works of darkness, and to turn people from the darkness to the light, and to bring them from the occasion of the war and from the occasion of the magistrate's sword. . . .

In effect, as Frederick Tolles remarks, on this and other occasions Fox was "demanding nothing less than that the military ruler of all England should forthwith disavow all violence and all coercion, make Christ's law of love the supreme law of the land, and substitute the mild dictates of the Sermon on the Mount for the Instrument of Government by which he ruled."[2]

But Cromwell, of course, remained unconvinced.

Later on, however, another Quaker, William Penn, initiated the famous "Holy Experiment" in Pennsylvania. In it, he sought to apply Quaker principles to the sphere of politics and government and to demonstrate that a non-violent society could indeed be established. Colonial Pennsylvania down to 1756—when Quakers surrendered control of the Provincial Assembly—became one of the most remarkable efforts in the history of mankind to build a warless community in which exact equity would prevent violence and coercion would be reduced to a bare minimum. The present reading deals at some length with this experiment, concentrating on Indian relations and on problems of maintaining intact the Quaker "testimony" against military violence.

Pennsylvania was founded on the proposition that if Indians

[1] *The Journal of George Fox*, rev. ed. by John L. Nickalls (Cambridge University Press, 1952), pp. 274–75, 197–98.

[2] Frederick B. Tolles, *Quakerism and Politics* (Guilford College, North Carolina, 1956), p. 4.

were amply compensated for their lands and were treated on a basis of equality with white men, Indian wars and massacres would not occur. The difficulties were, of course, many, and were complicated by the colony's internal politics and by the demands of the British government. As time went on, the principles of the colony's founders became increasingly difficult to apply, and the society never attained the level of Fox's ethic. Yet these compromises should not be exaggerated. When all is said that can be said against the obfuscations and evasions of the Quaker Assembly, it did succeed in building a workable non-violent commonwealth and in living at peace with the Indians for about seventy years, and few political societies in history can boast a comparable record. When at last external factors brought the "Holy Experiment" to an end, the Quaker majority in the Assembly resigned, for they saw that they could make no further compromises without undermining their basic convictions about non-violence and the nature of man.

The author of the reading, Isaac Sharpless (1848–1920), was for many years a leading Quaker educator, who became dean and later president of Haverford College. The material is taken from Chapters VI and VII of his book *A Quaker Experiment in Government.* (Philadelphia: A. J. Ferris, 1898)

THE INDIANS

No phase of early Pennsylvania history needs less defense than the Indian policy of the colonists. The "Great Treaty" at Shackamaxon has been immortalized by West on canvas and Voltaire in print, and historians have not hesitated to do it ample justice. The resulting seventy years of peace and friendship, as contrasted with the harassing and exterminating wars on the boundaries of nearly all the other colonies, attest its practical utility. The date of the treaty is more or less uncertain, its place rests on tradition, and its objects are not positively known.[3] It seems probable that it occurred in June, 1683, under the elm tree whose location is now marked by a stone, and that it was held for the double purpose of making a league of friendship and of purchasing lands.

There can be no doubt of Penn's benevolent intentions regarding the Indians. The Quaker doctrine of universal divine light seemed to give encouragement to do missionary work among them. George Fox again and again in his letters

[3] *Pennsylvania Magazine,* Vol. VI., pp. 217–38. Article by Frederick D. Stone, which is frequently used in the succeeding pages.

urges ministers to convey to the Indians the messages of Christ's life and death, and God's love for them.[4] The Indians responded as if they knew the reality of the indwelling of the Great Spirit. On that point their theory and that of the Quakers agreed, and this may have been the basis of the bond of sympathy which existed between them.

On the "18th of the Eighth month (October), 1681," the Proprietor sent by his cousin and deputy, William Markham, a letter[5] to the Indians, simple, brief and kindly, admirably adapted to dispose them favorably to him. He had been authorized by his charter "to reduce the savage nations by gentle and just manners to the love of civil society and Christian religion." He was evidently greatly interested in them, as his long and elaborate descriptions sent home on the basis of rather insufficient knowledge testify; and he seems to have had great hopes of making acquisitions to Christianity among them.

He saw, however, that Christian sentiment alone would not advance the standard or even prevent the degradation of Indian morality. He knew at least partly the character of frontier traders, the valuable bargains to be obtained from a drunken Indian, and the weakness of Indian character in the face of sensual temptations. Whatever he could do to lessen these evils he stood ready to attempt. He refused an advantageous offer when he needed money badly lest he should barter authority to irresponsible people to the disadvantage of the Indian. "I did refuse a great temptation last Second-day, which was £6000

---

[4] "You must instruct and teach your Indians and negroes and all others how that Christ by the grace of God tasted death for every man, and gave himself a ransom for all men, and is the propitiation not for the sins of Christians only but for the sins of the whole world."—G. F., in 1679.

"And God hath poured out his spirit upon all flesh, and so the Indians must receive God's spirit. . . . And so let them know that they have a day of salvation, grace and favor of God offered unto them; if they will receive it it will be their blessing."—G. F., in 1688.

[5] "My Friends: There is a great God and power that hath made the world and all things therein, to whom you and I and all people owe their being and well-being; to whom you and I must one day give an account for all that we do in the world.

"This great God hath written his law in our hearts, by which we are commanded to live and help and do good to one another. Now this great God hath been pleased to make me concerned in your part of the world, and the King of the country where I live hath given me a great province therein, but I desire to enjoy it with your love and consent, that we may always live together as neighbors and friends. . . ."

. . . to have wholly to itself the Indian trade from south to north between the Susquehanna and Delaware Rivers. . . . But as the Lord gave it to me over all and great opposition . . . I would not abuse His love nor act unworthy of His providence, and so defile what came to me clean."[6]

There is additional proof of the correctness of this statement in a letter of one of the intending purchasers, James Claypoole: "He (W. P.) is offered great things,—£6,000 for a monopoly in trade, which he refused. . . . I believe truly he does aim more at justice and righteousness and spreading of truth than at his own particular gain."

*   *   *   *   *

William Penn had paid King Charles £16,000 for Pennsylvania. He recognized, however, the Indian claims to the same territory, and was ready to purchase them. Moreover, as he determined never to engage in warfare with the natives, and was trustful in the efficacy of justice and reason to settle all disputes, he would begin with a friendly bargain with them for the land he was to occupy.

The purchase of lands of the Indians was no new thing. . . .

*   *   *   *   *

What seems to have impressed the Indians was the fact that Penn insisted on purchase at the first and all subsequent agreements as being an act of justice, to which both parties were to give their assent voluntarily. They also felt that the price paid was ample to extinguish their claims, and that no advantages were taken by plying them with drink or cheating them with false maps. . . .

*   *   *   *   *

Practically the whole of Pennsylvania was purchased of the Indians, some of it several times over. . . .

*   *   *   *   *

During Penn's lifetime the relations continued so good that there was no difficulty in restraining unruly Indians. We find in the early minutes of the Council several complaints against Indians for stealing the settlers' hogs. The kings were sent for and presumably settled the matter.

Penn writes, in 1685, of the Indians:

If any of them break our laws they submit to be punished by them; and to this they have tied themselves by an obligation under their hands.

[6] Hazard's *Annals of Pennsylvania*, p. 522.

He was equally desirous to punish white trespassers on Indian rights. The great difficulty was to keep settlers off lands not already purchased. During his lifetime, he bought so far in advance of settlement that he managed to avoid any sense of injury on the part of the Indians. Later in the history of the Colony the problem became a serious one.

Another cause of complaint was the demoralization wrought by rum. . . .

The Friends who had settled at Burlington in advance of Penn's purchase of Pennsylvania had very early seen the effects of the sale. By 1685 the Yearly Meeting was convinced on the subject, and "doth unanimously agree, and give as their judgment, that it is not consistent with the honor of Truth for any that make profession thereof to sell rum or other strong liquors to the Indians . . .

The Indian chiefs were sensible of the honesty of these efforts. In a conference held about 1687, one of them spoke as follows:[7]

> The strong liquor was first sold us by the Dutch, and they are blind; they had no eyes, they did not see it was for our hurt. The next people that came among us were the Swedes, who continued the sale of the strong liquors to us; they were also blind, they had no eyes . . . But now there is a people come to live among us that have eyes; they see it to be for our hurt; they are willing to deny themselves the profit of it for our good.

*   *   *   *   *

At the time of the death of Penn the relations between the whites and Indians could not well be improved. While there were individual outrages on the Indians, and individual stealings from the whites, they were punished as completely as the circumstances would admit, and never produced ill feeling. The frontier was safe from marauders, tomahawks and scalping knives were unknown, and traders carried on their business with safety. A perfect confidence in the fairness of Penn and the Quakers existed among the Indians, which in time deepened into an abiding respect.

As lands became more in demand for settlement, difficulties increased. But it was a different spirit in the white negotiators, rather than inherent perplexities, which drove the red men first to estrangement, then to hostility, then to bloody revenge, making them an easy prey to French machinations. Much was said at the time about the peace policy of the Quakers making the Province insecure against French and Indian attack. A more

[7] Janney's *Life of William Penn,* p. 123.

profound study would indicate that that insecurity was primarily caused by rank injustice to the Indians at the hands of the sons and successors of William Penn. A policy of peace and one of justice combined may be successful; it is hardly fair, however, to provoke attack by iniquity and then saddle the inevitable consequences upon the lack of preparation for military resistance. Had the sons of Penn maintained the confidence and friendship of the Indians, an effective buffer against all hostile French designs would have existed, and Pennsylvania been spared the horrors of 1755 and succeeding years. This friendship, notwithstanding the increasing pressure on the Indian lands, might have been maintained, had there been no deceitful measures which left the red man quiet but sullen, with a brooding sense of wrong, and desire for revenge. Even then he seems to have understood that the Quaker was his friend and shielded him in his frontier raids. It is said that only three members of that sect were killed by the Indians in the Pennsylvania troubles, and they had so far abandoned their ordinary trustful attitude as to carry guns in defense.[8]

There were inherent difficulties in preventing rum being furnished to the Indians, and in keeping settlers off their hands. Charles Thomson[9] says, in the case of the rum, that while ample promises were held out to them, they were never kept. In 1722 the Indians told Governor Keith that they "could live contentedly and grow rich if it were not for the quantities of rum that is suffered to come among them contrary to what William Penn promised them." Again in 1727 they complain of traders who cheat them, and give them rum and not powder and shot, so that the Indians nearly starve. The Governor in reply to this said he could not control traders, that Indians and whites all would cheat, and that they were at liberty to break in the heads of all rum casks. . . . The Scotch-Irish and Germans were pressing in at a tremendous rate and cared nothing for Indian titles. It seemed to them absurd to allow Indians a great stretch of fertile land for hunting purposes only. Sometimes the settlers were removed, at other times the Indians were satisfied by payments, but they still felt aggrieved as they saw their lands melting away before the ubiquitous whites.

These causes, while adding to the general discontent, would not with proper management have produced serious disaffection had they not been re-enforced by a few cases of glaring

[8] Dymond, *Essay on War.*

[9] *An Enquiry into the Cause of the Alienation of the Indians,* 1759. The facts which follow are mainly derived from this book. C. T. was afterwards secretary of the Continental Congress and author of a translation of the Bible.

injustice. The first of these was the notorious "Walking Purchase."

In a treaty in 1728 James Logan said that William Penn never allowed lands to be settled till purchased of the Indians. Ten years before he had shown to their chiefs deeds covering all lands from Duck Creek, in Delaware, to the "Forks of the Delaware,"[10] and extending back along the "Lechoy Hills" to the Susquehanna. The Indians admitted this and confirmed the deeds, but objected to the settlers crowding into the fertile lands within the forks occupied by the Minisink tribe of the Delaware Indians. Logan accordingly forbade any surveying in the Minisink country. White settlers, however, were not restrained, and the Indians became still more uneasy. A tract of 10,000 acres sold by the Penns to be taken up anywhere in the unoccupied lands of the Province, was chosen here and opened for settlement. A lottery was established by the Proprietors, the successful tickets calling for amounts of land down to 200 acres, and many of these were assigned in the Forks, without Indian consent.

In order to secure undisputed possession and drive out the Delawares, who it must be remembered had always been more than friendly, a despicable artifice was resorted to, which will always disgrace the name of Thomas Penn. A deed of 1686 of doubtful authenticity was produced, confirming to William Penn a plot of ground beginning on the Delaware River a short distance above Trenton, running west to Wrightstown, in Bucks county, thence northwest parallel to the Delaware River as far as a man could walk in a day and a half, which was no doubt intended to extend to the Lehigh Hills, thence eastward by an undefined line, left blank in the deed, presumably along the hills to the Delaware River at Easton. It was one of numerous purchases of a similar character which in the aggregate conveyed to William Penn all southeastern Pennsylvania, and had with his careful constructions made no trouble. The walk, however, had never been taken, and in 1737 the Proprietors brought out the old agreement as a means of securing a title to the Minisink country.

The route was surveyed, underbrush cleared away, horses stationed to convey the walkers across the rivers, two athletic young men trained for the purpose, and conveyances provided for their baggage and provisions. Indians attended at the beginning, but after repeatedly calling to the men to walk, not run, retired in disgust. Far from stopping at the Lehigh Hills, they covered about sixty miles and extended the line thirty miles beyond the Lehigh River. Then to crown the infamy, in-

[10] Between the Delaware and Lehigh rivers, where Easton now stands.

stead of running the northern line by any reasonable course they slanted it to the northeast and included all the Minisink country. It was a gross travesty on the original purchase, an outrageous fraud on the Indians, which they very properly refused to submit to. They remained in their ancestral homes, and sent notice they would resist removal by force. There unfortunately seems to be no doubt of the iniquity of the transaction. There is the testimony of at least two witnesses to the walk. It appears to have been a common subject of remark. Indifferent men treated it as sharp practice, and honest men were ashamed. But the Proprietors had a sort of a title to the fertile lands along the Delaware.

* * * * *

Finally the Penns concluded at one stroke to extinguish all Indian titles to Western Pennsylvania. The rest was practically their own. The Indian chiefs were collected at Albany, and by means which will not bear examination were induced to sign the contract. . . .

* * * * , *

The victory over Braddock turned all doubtful Indians into the ranks of the hostiles. The fall of 1755 and spring of 1756 were dire seasons for the frontiers of Pennsylvania. The burning of houses, the shooting down of men, the outrages on women and children, the flight to places of safety, the demands for protection from government and friendly Indians,—from all these things the policy of William Penn had shielded the settlers for seventy-three years. The very tribes with which he had formed his treaties, which were always so warm in their friendships for him, which had been the victims of the "Walking Purchase," been branded as women by the Six Nations, and moved about from place to place,—the Delawares and the Shawnees,—now proved as fierce as any. All that the brilliant author of the History of the Conspiracy of Pontiac has said of their general peacefulness was disproved. When ill-treated they had their bloody revenge, exactly as in New England. They showed no lack of Indian spirit. Hitherto overcome by the superior numbers and organization of the Iroquois, they now under French tutelage and a sense of wrong turned on their oppressors and proved their equality in endurance, in resource and in cruelty. That Pennsylvania was saved by the just and pacific policy of the first settlers, and would have suffered just as the other colonies did by the reverse, seems as probable as any historical conclusion.

* * * * *

MILITARY MATTERS

Of all Friendly ideas the most difficult to incorporate practically into government machinery was that of peace. The uncompromising views which most Quakers held as to the iniquity of all war, seemed to those outside the Society utopian if not absurd, and did not command the united support of its own membership. That justice and courtesy should characterize all dealings with other states, that no aggressive war could ever be justified, that in almost every case war could be honorably avoided, all were willing to endorse and practice, but a minority, probably a small minority, held that circumstances might arise when war like defense was necessary and proper, and that the Sermon on the Mount was not to be interpreted any more literally when it commanded "Resist not evil" than when it commanded "Lay not up treasures on earth."

The general tenor of authoritative Quaker teaching, however, admitted no such interpretation. It is not found in the writings of Fox, Barclay, Penington or Penn. Their language is always unequivocal in opposition to all war. The Quaker converts among Cromwell's soldiers, of whom there were not a few, left the ranks for conscience' sake as uniformly and as unhesitatingly as the Christian converts of the early centuries abandoned the Roman armies, with the plea, "I am a Christian, and therefore cannot fight."

"Not fighting, but suffering," says William Penn[11] in 1694, "is another testimony peculiar to this people. . . . Thus as truth-speaking succeeded swearing, so faith and patience succeed fighting in the doctrine and practice of this people. Nor ought they for this to be obnoxious to civil government; since if they cannot fight for it neither can they fight against it, which is no mean security to any state. Nor is it reasonable that people should be blamed for not doing more for others than they can do for themselves."

We have important testimony to Penn's position in the unsympathetic statement of James Logan.[12] After expressing his own view that all government was founded on force, he says: "I was therefore the more surprised when I found my master on a particular occasion on our voyage hither (in 1699), though coming over to exercise the powers of it here in his own person, showed his sentiments were otherwise." He adds that "Friends had laid it down as their principle, that bearing of arms, even for self-defense, is unlawful."

There seems therefore no doubt that the Society had with

11 *The Rise and Progress of the People Called Quakers.*
12 *Pennsylvania Magazine*, Vol. VI., p. 404.

practical unanimity accepted military non-resistance in its most extreme form.

*   *   *   *   *

It was easy to hold peace views as an academic proposition, supported by the spirit and letter of the New Testament; but when the actual problems of government arose how was this non-resistant principle to be applied to the protection of society against criminals? This logical difficulty does not seem to have troubled the early Pennsylvanians. So far as appears they drew a line between police and military measures, making one effective and barring out the other. There was to them no contradiction to call for explanation. With strict logic they might have been driven to the position of Count Tolstoi,[13] who carries his non-resistance so far as to object to all government, and all restraint on criminals. Or the line might be supposed to be drawn on the sacredness of human life, but, as we have seen, opposition to capital punishment, *per se,* never arose before the Revolution. Probably if pressed for an answer to the question why it was right to resist a street mob of subjects with police and not to resist an attacking force with soldiers, they would have replied that one act was in defense of life and property under authority of civil powers "ordained of God," and involving no iniquitous means, while all military measures necessarily included the destruction of life and property, of innocent as well as of guilty, and reversed the established rules of morality in sanctioning stealing, lying, and killing those who were not personally offenders.

The Quaker Assembly of 1740, in their ethical controversy with Governor Thomas, argued thus: "And yet it is easy to discover the difference between killing a soldier fighting (perhaps) in obedience to the commands of his sovereign, and who may possibly think himself in the discharge of his duty, and executing a burglar who broke into our houses, plundered us of our goods, and perhaps would have murdered too if he could not otherwise have accomplished his ends, who must know at the time of the commission of the act, it was a violation of laws, human and divine, and that he thereby justly rendered himself obnoxious to the punishment which ensued."[14]

Penn did not hesitate to commend force in civil affairs when necessary. "If lenitives would not do, coercives should be tried; but though men would naturally begin with the former, yet wisdom had often sanctioned the latter as remedies which,

[13] See, for example, Leo Tolstoy's novel *Resurrection* and his essay *The Kingdom of God Is Within You.—Ed.*

[14] *Colonial Records,* Vol. IV., p. 373.

however, were never to be adopted without regret," he wrote in 1700.[15] The whole machinery of courts and police was intended to be effective in resisting crime and criminals. All prisons were more or less work-houses, and the reformation idea had larger vogue than in some places, but there was no hesitation apparent to secure by force the ascendency of law.

The position they took was probably this: We will never do an injustice, provoke a war, or attack an enemy. If attacked we will, therefore, always be in the right. We cannot do wrong even to defend the right, but will trust that having done our duty, Providence will protect us. Beyond this we cannot go.[16]

Penn had authority by his Charter "to levy, muster and train all sorts of men of what condition or wheresoever born in the said province of Pennsylvania for the time being, and to make war and pursue the enemies and robbers aforesaid as well by sea as by land, yea even without the limits of said province, and by God's assistance to vanquish and take them, and being taken to put them to death by the law of war, or save them at their pleasure, and to do all and every act or thing which to the charge and office of a Captain-general belongeth, as fully and freely as any Captain-general of an army hath ever had the same."

These powers were doubtless ample for a peaceable Quaker. He could not exercise them himself without trampling on the views to which he was indelibly committed. The power to use them implied the power to transmit them, and this is just what Penn did.

He was in a delicate position. He was, as feudal lord of the province, liable to be called upon to support Britain's causes by force of arms against Britain's enemies. This he could not personally do, but if the Deputy-Governor had no conscience in the matter, Penn would not interpose to prevent obedience to the commands of the Crown. He selected non-Quaker deputies, and doubtless this consideration had its effect in inducing the choice. If some were inclined to criticize him for appointing others to perform acts he could not do himself, it must be remembered that deeds concerning whose culpability differences may properly exist, are evil or good for an individual,

[15] Janney's *Life of Penn*, p. 441.

[16] In a pamphlet printed in 1748, entitled *The Doctrine of Christianity as held by the people called Quakers Vindicated*, in answer to Gilbert Tennent's sermon on the "Lawfulness of War," substantially this position was taken. The pamphlet appeared anonymously, but is known to have been written by a Friend of prominence, closely connected with James Logan, who doubtless was expressing the recognized views of the Society. A copy is in the Philadelphia Library.

dependent on the attitude of his own conscience. The Friends never asked a man to violate conscience, and recognized the differences due to education, enlightenment and mental constitution. If others honestly thought war right, it was right for them. Hence the actions of the Deputy were not of the character which involved evil-doing on his part, even though the same actions would have been evil for Penn himself. Such was Paul's attitude, and such was probably Penn's argument. . . .

* * * * *

The first trial of Quaker faith had, however, occurred prior to this, in 1689. The Crown had suggested that in order to defend the Colony against an attempted attack by the French, a militia should be formed. Governor Blackwell urged this, and he was supported by Markham and the non-Quaker portion of the Council. The Friends refused to have anything to do with it. They told the Governor that if he desired a militia he had power to create one, and they would not interfere if it did not offend any consciences.

John Simcock said: "I see no danger but from bears and wolves. We are well and in peace and quiet; let us keep ourselves so. I know not but a peaceable spirit and that will do well. For my part I am against it clearly."

Samuel Carpenter said: "I am not against those that will put themselves into defense, but it being contrary to the judgment of a great part of the people, and my own, too, I cannot advise the thing nor express my liking for it. . . ."

After much discussion the five Quaker members of Council asked leave to retire for a conference. On their return they announced, "We would not tie others' hands, but we cannot act. We would not take upon us to hinder any, and do not think the Governor need call us together in this matter. . . . We say nothing against it, and regard it as a matter of conscience to us. . . . I had rather be ruined than violate my conscience in this case."[17] The matter was dropped.

Again in 1693, Governor Fletcher, who was also Governor of New York, in the interval of Penn's deposition, asked the Assembly for money to support a war against the French and Indians of Canada, which had been raging on their frontiers. He knew the difficulties. "If there be any among you that scruple the giving of money to support war, there are a great many other charges in that government for the support thereof, as officers' salaries. . . . Your money shall be converted into

[17] *Colonial Records,* Vol. II., p. 470. Samuel Carpenter, who expressed this sentiment, was adjudged the richest man in the Province.

these uses and shall not be dipt in blood."[18] Upon the basis of this promise, after some delay, the money was voted.

In May, 1695, a requisition was made on Pennsylvania for eighty men with officers for the defense of New York. The Council advised calling together the Assembly, but not until harvest was over. The Assembly united with the Council in refusing the bald request, reminding the Governor of Fletcher's promise that the last appropriation should not "be dipt in blood," but should be used "to feed the hungry and clothe the naked" Indians, and suggested that such of it as had not been used as promised should go towards the present emergency. The Council finally offered two bills, one to make an appropriation, and one to demand a return to Penn's Frame of Government, which was held in abeyance since his return to power. As the Governor had to take both or neither he dissolved the Assembly. A year later he was willing to make the required concession, and urged that the money was needed in New York "for food and raiment to be given to those nations of Indians that have lately suffered extremely by the French. . . ." The Assembly made the necessary vote and the Constitution of 1696 was obtained in payment.

The next time the pacific principles of the Assembly were tried was in 1701, when the English Government asked for £350 for the purpose of erecting forts on the frontiers of New York on the plea that they were for the general defense. Penn, who was then in the Province, faithfully observed his promise "to transmit," but declined to give any advice to the Assembly. The members were evidently greatly agitated, and repeatedly asked copies of his speech, which was in fact only the King's letter. After some fencing two reports appeared. One, from the Pennsylvania delegates, urged their poverty, owing to taxes and quit-rents, also the lack of contributions of other colonies, but added plainly, "We desire the Proprietor would candidly represent our conditions to the King, and assure him of our readiness (according to our abilities) to acquiesce with and answer his commands *so far as our religious persuasions shall permit,* as becomes loyal and faithful subjects so to do."[19] The other answer came from the Delaware portion of the Assembly, excusing themselves because they had no forts of their own.

When the Assembly met, a month later, Penn again referred to the King's letter, but nothing was done, and the matter was not pressed.

[18] *Colonial Records,* Vol. I., p. 361.
[19] Ibid., Vol. II., p. 26.

Governor Evans made several attempts to establish a militia, but the Assembly refused any sanction, and the voluntary organizations were failures.

The military question came up in 1709 in a more serious form. An order came from the Queen to the various colonies to furnish quotas of men at their own expense towards an army to invade Canada. New York was to supply 800, Connecticut 350, Jersey 200, and Pennsylvania 150. In transmitting the order Governor Gookin, who evidently anticipated difficulty, suggested that the total charge would be about £4,000. He says, "Perhaps it may seem difficult to raise such a number of men in a country where most of the inhabitants are of such principles as will not allow them the use of arms; but if you will raise the sum for the support of government, I don't doubt getting the number of men desired whose principles will allow the use of arms."[20]

This was too manifest an evasion for the Assembly to adopt. Its first answer was to send in a bill of grievances. The opportunity was too good to be lost, and David Lloyd, then Speaker, made the most of it.

In the meantime the Quaker members of the Council met some of their co-religionists of the Assembly "and there debated their opinions freely and unanimously to those of the House, that notwithstanding their profession and principles would not by any means allow them to bear arms, yet it was their duty to support the government of their sovereign, the Queen, and to contribute out of their estates according to the exigencies of her public affairs, and therefore they might and ought to present the Queen with a proper sum of money."[21]

The Assembly the next day sent an address to the Governor which said, "Though we cannot for conscience' sake comply with the furnishing a supply for such a defense as thou proposest, yet in point of gratitude of the Queen for her great and many favors to us we have resolved to raise a present of £500 which we humbly hope she will be pleased to accept, etc., etc."[22]

To this the Governor replied that he would not sign the bill. If the Assembly would not hire men to fight, there was no scruple which would prevent a more liberal subscription to the Queen's needs. The Assembly was immovable, and asked to be allowed to adjourn, as harvest time was approaching.

The Governor refused consent, when the House abruptly terminated the whole matter.

[20] Ibid., p. 740.
[21] Ibid., p. 478.
[22] Ibid., p. 479.

Resolved, N.C.D., That this House cannot agree to the Governor's proposal, directly or indirectly, for the expedition to Canada, for the reasons formerly given.

Resolved, N.C.D., That the House do continue their resolution of raising £500 as a present for the Queen, and do intend to prepare a bill for that purpose at their next meeting on the 15th of August next, and not before.[23]

The House then adjourned without waiting for the Governor's consent.

* * * * *

In 1711 a similar request was made by the Government, and in response £2,000 was voted for the Queen's use. This money never aided any military expedition, but was appropriated by a succeeding Governor to his own use, and the fact was used as an argument in 1740 against similar grants.[24]

* * * * *

Then followed the thirty-years peace, when no calls for military service or money were made. Occasionally the Governor would think it necessary to establish a militia, when the Assembly would caution him to make it purely voluntary and force no conscience. There were friendly relations with the Indians. No European troubles necessitated money or troops for Canadian attack or defense. But, beginning with 1737, the gradual alienation of the Indian tribes made a disturbed frontier ready to be dangerous at the first outbreak of war, and new conditions prevailed.

Hitherto the relation of the Friends to these inevitable military solicitations had been largely that of passivity. They would not interfere with the movements of those who desired to form military companies. If the Governor chose to engage in the arming and drilling of voluntary militia, he had his commission from the Proprietors, and they from the Charter of Charles II. It was no matter for the Assembly. The meeting organizations would endeavor to keep all Quakers from any participation in these un-Friendly proceedings, and the Quaker Assemblymen had their own consciences to answer to, as well as their ecclesiastical authorities, if they violated pacific principles.

When it came to voting money in lieu of personal service, the legislators had a difficult road to follow. If the government needed aid, it was their duty, in common with the other colonies, to supply it. Even though the need was the direct result of war, as nearly all national taxes are, they were ready to assume their share of the burden. Cæsar must have his dues

[23] *Colonial Records,* Vol. II., p. 486.
[24] Ibid., Vol. IV., p. 366, et seq.

as well as God, and a call for money, except when coupled directly with a proposition to use it for military attack or defense, was generally responded to, after its potency as an agent in procuring a little more liberty was exhausted. They would not vote money for an expedition to Canada or to erect forts, but they would for "the King's use," using all possible securities to have it appropriated to something else than war expenses. The responsibility of expenditure rested on the King. There were legitimate expenses of government, and if these were so inextricably mingled with warlike outlay that the Assembly could not separate them, they would still support the Government.

It is easy to accuse them of inconsistency in the proceedings which follow. It was a most unpleasant alternative thrust before honest men. The responsibility of government was upon them as the honorable recipients of the popular votes. Great principles, the greatest of all in their minds being freedom of conscience, were at stake. Each call for troops or supplies they fondly hoped would be the last. Their predecessors' actions had secured the blessings of peace and liberty to Pennsylvania for sixty years, and if they were unreasonably stringent, their English enemies held over their heads the threat to drive them from power by the imposition of an oath. Then the persecutions of themselves and their friends, which their forefathers had left England to avoid, might be meted out to them, and the Holy Experiment brought to an end.

Nor is it necessary to assume that their motives were entirely unselfish. They had ruled the Province well, and were proficients in government. Their leaders doubtless loved the power and influence they legitimately possessed, and they did not care to give it away unnecessarily. They tried to find a middle ground between shutting their eyes to all questions of defense on the one side, and direct participation in war on the other. This they sought by a refusal for themselves and their friends to do any service personally, and a further refusal to vote money except in a general way for the use of the government. If any one comes to the conclusion that during the latter part of the period of sixteen years now under consideration the evasion was rather a bald one, it is exactly the conclusion the Quakers themselves came to, and they resigned their places as a consequence. The iniquities of others over whom they had no control brought about a condition where Quaker principles would not work, and they refused to modify them in the vain attempt. For a time rather weakly halting, when the crucial nature of the question became clear, and either place or principle had to be sacrificed, their decision was in favor of the sanctity of principle.

They were on the popular side of the questions of the day,

in close association with Benjamin Franklin and others. The fact that these allies in their other battles were unwilling to stand by them on this question made their position especially difficult. They, however, always carried the popular Assembly against all combinations.

In 1739, urged by the Proprietors, the Governor presented to the Assembly the dangers of the defenseless condition of the Province in the approaching war with Spain and asked for the establishment of a militia.

This opened the way to an interchange of long argumentative papers between Governor and Assembly in which the positions of the two parties were laid down with considerable ability. The Assembly said: "As very many of the inhabitants of this Province are of the people called Quakers, who, though they do not as the world is now circumstanced condemn the use of arms in others, yet are principled against it themselves. . . ."[25]

* * * * *

To this the Governor replied that no religious opinions would protect the country against an invading force, and as representatives of the whole people, not of a denomination, they must defend the Province from external enemies as they did from criminals within, and that there was no intention to force any one's conscience.

* * * * *

The Assembly reminded him that the Province had prospered under Quaker management for a number of years before he had anything to do with it, and would in the future, if his misrepresentations should not prevail in England, even "though some Governors have been as uneasy and as willing and ready to find fault and suggest dangers as himself."

The Governor in despair replies: "If your principles will not allow you to pass a bill for establishing a militia, if they will not allow you to secure the navigation of a river by building a fort, if they will not allow you to provide arms for the defense of the inhabitants, if they will not allow you to raise men for his Majesty's service for distressing an insolent enemy . . . is it a calumny to say your principles are inconsistent with the ends of government?"

After pages of argument, . . . the Assembly refused to do anything.

Governor Thomas, under royal instructions, approached the same subject a year later with a similar result. . . .

* * * * *

[25] *Colonial Records,* Vol. IV., p. 366, et seq.

In 1744 he used his authority as Captain-General in organizing a voluntary force said by Franklin to amount to 10,000 men. On this the Assembly took no action.

The next year the Governor asked them to aid New England in an attack on Cape Breton. They told him they had no interest in the matter. He called them together again in harvest time to ask them to join in an expedition against Louisburg. A week later came word that Louisburg had surrendered, and the request was transferred to a call for aid in garrisoning the place, and in supplying provisions and powder. The Assembly replied that the "peaceable principles professed by divers members of the present Assembly do not permit them to join in raising of men or providing arms and ammunition, yet we have ever held it our duty to render tribute to Cæsar."[26] They therefore appropriated £4,000 for "bread, beef, pork, flour, wheat or other grain." The Governor was advised not to accept the grant, as provisions were not needed. He replied that the "other grain" meant gunpowder, and so expended a large portion of the money.[27] There is probably no evidence that the Assembly sanctioned this construction, though they never so far as appears made any protest.

Again in 1746 aid was asked of the Assembly towards an expedition against Canada. After forcing the Governor to yield the point as to how the money should be raised, they appropriated £5,000 "for the King's use."

This seems to have been the attitude of the Quaker Assembly for the ten years to come. . . .

* * * * *

In 1754 the Governor, at the instance of the Proprietors, who anticipated the French and Indian troubles on the western frontier, endeavored to induce the Assembly to pass a bill for compulsory military service for those not conscientious about bearing arms.[28] He evidently did not expect much. . . .

* * * * *

This was after the Assembly had voted £10,000, but coupled the grant with conditions the Governor would not accept.

While they were debating the question Braddock came into the country as commander of the combined forces in an expedition against Fort DuQuesne. Pressure came down strong and heavy on the Quaker Assembly. Their own frontier was invaded. Their own Indians, as a result of the wicked and fool-

[26] Ibid., p. 769.
[27] This is on the authority of Franklin.
[28] *Pennsylvania Archives,* Vol. II., p. 189.

ish policy of their executive, were in league with the invaders. All classes were excited. To aid the great expedition which at one stroke was to break the French power and close the troubles was felt to be a duty. Franklin diligently fanned the warlike spirit, procuring wagons for the transfer of army stores, and was extremely valuable to the expedition at some cost to himself.

* * * * *

Braddock was defeated. The Indians were let loose on the frontiers. Daily accounts of harrowing scenes came up to the Council and Assembly.[29] Settlers moved into the towns and many districts were depopulated. Strong were the expressions of wrath against the Quakers, who were held responsible for the defenseless state of the Province.[30]

This was hardly a just charge, even from the standpoint of those who favored military defense, for the Assembly had signified its willingness to vote £50,000, an unprecedented amount, to be provided by "a tax on all the real and personal estates within the Province," which the Governor refused to accept. While the matter was in abeyance the time for the new election of Assemblymen came around, and both parties, except the stricter Quakers, who were becoming alarmed, put forth their greatest exertions. The old Assembly was sustained, the Friends, with those closely associated with them, having twenty-six out of the thirty-six members.

The new House went on with the work of the old. They adopted a militia law for those "willing and desirous" of joining companies for the defense of the Province. This is prefaced by the usual declaration: "Whereas this Province was settled (and a majority of the Assembly have ever since been) of the people called Quakers, who though they do not as the world is now circumstanced condemn the use of arms in others, yet are principled against bearing arms themselves,"[31] explaining also that they are representatives of the Province and not of a denomination, they proceed to lay down rules for the organization of the volunteers. After the Proprietors had given their £5,000 the Assembly also voted £55,000 for the relief of friendly Indians and distressed frontiersmen, "and other purposes," without any disguise to the fact that much of

29 *Votes of Assembly,* Vol. IV., pp. 481, 699.

30 The people exclaim against the Quakers, and some are scarce restrained from burning the houses of those few who are in this town (Reading).—Letter of Edmund Biddle, *Colonial Records,* Vol. VI., p. 705.

31 *Pennsylvania Archives,* Vol. I., p. 516.

it was intended for military defense, though it was not so stated in the bill. Before this was done, while they were still insisting on taxing the Penn estates, in answer to the charge that they were neglectful of public interests, secure in the confidence of their constituents just most liberally given, they say: "In fine we have the most sensible concern for the poor distressed inhabitants of the frontiers. We have taken every step in our power, consistent with the just rights of the freemen of Pennsylvania, for their relief, and we have reason to believe that in the midst of their distresses they themselves do not wish to go further. *Those who would give up essential liberty to purchase a little temporary safety, deserve neither liberty nor safety.*"[32] Their position definitely was, We will vote money liberally for defensive purposes, but we will take care to secure our rights as freemen, and we will not require any one to give personal service against his conscience.

The money was largely spent in erecting and garrisoning a chain of forts extending along the Kittatinny hills from the Delaware River to the Maryland frontier.[33]

The amount of defense the Assembly had provided, while probably expressing the will of their constituents, did not satisfy the more peace-loving of the Friends on the one hand, nor the advocates of proprietary interests on the other.

In Eleventh month 1755 twenty Friends, including Anthony Morris, Israel and John Pemberton, Anthony Benezet, John Churchman, and others, representing the most influential and "weighty" members of the Yearly Meeting, addressed the Assembly. They say they are very willing to contribute to taxes to cultivate friendship with Indians, to relieve distress, or other benevolent purposes, but to expect them to be taxed for funds which are placed in the hands of committees to be expended for war, is inconsistent with their peaceable testimony, and an infringement of their religious liberties. Many Friends will have to refuse to pay such a tax and suffer distraint of goods,[34] and thus "that free enjoyment of liberty of conscience for the sake of which our forefathers left their native country and settled this then a wilderness by degrees be violated." . . .

* * * * *

As the Assembly was composed, this was an earnest plea from the responsible Friends to their fellow religionists to

[32] *Votes of Assembly,* Vol. IV., p. 501.

[33] *Pennsylvania Magazine,* July 1896. Dr. Stillé on "The Frontier Forts of Pennsylvania."

[34] This afterwards happened in numerous cases.

stand uncompromisingly by their principles. It was not very kindly received. . . .

* * * * *

In the minds of the Friends the crisis was reached when the Governor and Council (William Logan, son of James Logan, only dissenting) in the spring of 1756 declared war against the Delaware Indians, the old allies and friends of William Penn, but now in league with the French and killing and plundering on the frontiers. They were quite sure that peaceful and just measures would detach the Indians from their alliance, and that war was unnecessary. The lines were becoming more closely drawn, and the middle ground was narrowing, so that it was impossible to stand upon it. Either the principle of the iniquity of war must be maintained in its entirety, or war must be vigorously upheld and prosecuted. Some Friends with Franklin took the latter position, but the great majority closed up their ranks around the principle of peace in its integrity. . . . In the same fall several . . . Friends declined re-election, and after the next House assembled four others, Mahlon Kirkbride, William Hoyl, Peter Dicks and Nathaniel Pennock, also resigned. "Understanding that the ministry have requested the Quakers, who from the first settlement of the Colony have been the majority of the Assemblies of this Province, to suffer their seats during the difficult situation of the affairs of the Colonies to be filled by members of other denominations in such manner as to perform without any scruples all such laws as may be necessary to be enacted for the defense of the Province in whatever manner they may judge best suited to the circumstances of it; and notwithstanding we think this has been pretty fully complied with at the last election, yet at the request of our friends, being willing to take off all possible objection, we who have (without any solicitation on our part) been returned as representatives in this Assembly, request we may be excused, and suffered to withdraw ourselves and vacate our seats in such manner as may be attended with the least trouble and most satisfactory to this honorable House."[35]

The places of all these Friends were filled by members of other religious denominations, and Quaker control over and responsibility for the Pennsylvania Assembly closed with 1756 and was never resumed.

* * * * *

[35] *Votes of Assembly*, Vol. IV., p. 626.

17. John Fiske: LAS CASAS AND THE LAND OF WAR

Bartolomé de Las Casas (1474–1566) was a remarkable Dominican missionary who devoted a large part of his life to protecting Latin American Indians against servitude and mistreatment at the hands of Spanish adventurers. He believed firmly in a universal human quality that would make even so-called savages respond favorably to gentle, sincere, and just treatment. In this famous essay, the eminent nineteenth-century American historian, John Fiske, describes Las Casas' journey to the community of Indians just north of Guatemala, whose ferocity had caused the Spaniards to name the place the "Land of War."

Las Casas regarded the "Land of War" as a great challenge to his moral convictions, and the story of how he persuaded its inhabitants to give up human sacrifice and live at peace with their neighbors is a dramatic one to which Fiske, because of his own beliefs, brought great sympathy. The style in which it is told may seem somewhat overly romantic to modern readers, but the episode remains a startling one in the history of colonization.

Fiske (1842–1901) was the author of many significant works in philosophy, history, and political theory. This account is taken from his *The Discovery of America* (Boston: Houghton, 1892), pp. 464–73.

———————

While in the monastery at San Domingo, Las Casas had written his famous Latin treatise *De unico vocationis modo,* or the only proper method of calling men to Christianity. In these years of trial his mind had been growing in clearness and grasp. He had got beyond all sophistical distinctions between men of one colour and faith and men of another,—a wonderful progress for a Spaniard born eight years before the Moor was driven from Granada. He had come to see what was really involved in the Christian assumption of the brotherhood of men; and accordingly he maintained that to make war upon infidels or heathen, merely because they are infidels or heathen, is sinful; and that the only right and lawful way of bringing men to Christ is the way of reason and persuasion. To set forth such a doctrine at that time and still keep clear of the Inquisition required consummate skilfulness in statement. This little book was never printed, but manuscript copies of the original Latin and of a Spanish translation were circulated, and called forth much comment. The illustrations drawn from American affairs exasperated the Spanish colonists, and they taunted Las Casas. He was only a vain theorizer, they said; the gospel of peace would be all very well in a world already perfect, but in our world the only practicable gospel is the gospel of kicks and blows. Go to, let this apostle try himself to convert a tribe of Indians and make them keep the peace; he will soon find that something more is needed than words of love. So said the scoffers, as they wagged their heads.

Las Casas presently took them at their word. The province of Tuzulutlan, just to the north of Guatemala and bordering upon the peninsula of Yucatan, was called by the Spaniards the "Land of War." It was an inaccessible country of beetling crags, abysmal gorges, raging torrents, and impenetrable forest. In their grade of culture the inhabitants seem to have resembled the Aztecs. They had idols and human sacrifices, and were desperate fighters. The Spaniards had three times invaded this country, and three times had been hurled back . . . It could hardly be called a promising field, but this it was that Las Casas chose for his experiment.[1]

Let us note well his manner of proceeding, for there are those to-day who maintain that the type of character which Victor Hugo has sketched in Monseigneur Bienvenu is not calculated to achieve success in the world. The example of Las Casas, however, tends to confirm us in the opinion that when combined with sufficient intelligence, that type of character is the most indomitable and masterful of all. And in this I seem to see good promise for the future of humanity. The wisdom of the serpent, when wedded to the innocence of the dove, is of all things the most winning and irresistible, as Las Casas now proceeded to prove.

Alvarado, the fierce governor of Guatemala, was absent in Spain. Las Casas talked with the temporary governor, Alonzo de Maldonado, and the result of their talk was the following agreement, signed May 2, 1537. It was agreed that "if Las Casas, or any of his monks, can bring these Indians into conditions of peace, so that they should recognize the Spanish monarch for their lord paramount, and pay him any moderate tribute, he, the governor, would place those provinces under

[1] A full account of the work of Las Casas in Tuzulutlan is in Remesal's *Historia de Chiapa*, lib. iii., cap. ix–xi, xv–xviii.

his majesty in chief, and would not give them to any private Spaniard in *encomienda*. Moreover, no lay Spaniard, under heavy penalties, except the governor himself in person, should be allowed for five years to enter into that territory."[2] Ojedas and other such sinners were now, if possible, to be kept at a distance. No doubt Maldonado smiled in his sleeve when he signed his name to this agreement. Of course it could never come to anything.

Thus guaranteed against interference, the good monks went to work, and after a due amount of preliminary fasting and prayer they began by putting into Quiché verses an epitome of Christian doctrine simple enough for children to apprehend, —the story of the fall of man, the life and death of Christ, the resurrection of the dead, and the final judgment. It is a pity that these verses have not been preserved, but no doubt Las Casas, whose great heart knew so well how to touch the secret springs of the Indian mind, knew how to make the story as attractive and as moving as possible. The verses were nicely balanced in couplets, so as to aid the memory, and were set to music so that they might be chanted to the accompaniment of the rude Indian instruments. Then the monks found four Indian traders, who were in the habit of travelling now and then through the "Land of War" with goods to barter. They spent many weeks in winning the affection of these Indians and teaching them their sacred poem, explaining everything with endless patience, until the new converts knew it all by heart and felt able to answer simple questions about it. When the monks felt sure that the work was thoroughly done, they despatched the four traders on their missionary errand to the pueblo of the most powerful cacique in that country, taking care to provide them with an ample store of mirrors, bells, Spanish knives, and other stuff attractive to barbarians.

When the traders arrived at their destination they were hospitably received, and, according to custom, were lodged in the tecpan. They were zealous in their work, and obeyed their instructions faithfully. After vending their wares as usual, they called for some Mexican drums or timbrels, and proceeded to chant their sacred couplets. They were well received. Indians uttering such strange sweet words must have seemed miraculously inspired, and so the audience thought. For several days the performance was repeated, and the traders were beset with questions. After a while they drew pictures of the tonsured monks, and said that they learned these mysteries from these holy men, who, although white men, were not like other Spaniards, for they spent their lives in doing good, they had no wives, they treated all women with respect, they cared nothing

2 Arthur Helps, *Spanish Conquest,* Vol. III, p. 337.

for gold, and they taught that the time had come for abolishing human sacrifices. The cacique became so interested as to send his younger brother back to Guatemala with the Indian traders, charging him to watch the Dominicans narrowly, and if he should find them answering to the description that had been given of them he might invite them to visit Tuzulutlan.

Thus the ice was broken. It is needless to say that the young chieftain was well received, or that he was satisfied with what he saw. The invitation was given, and one of the Dominicans, the noble Luis de Barbastro, who was the most fluent of the four in the Quiché language, now made his way into the inaccessible fastnesses of Tuzulutlan, escorted by the young chief and the Indian traders. By the first of November, six months after the beginning of the enterprise, Father Luis had converted the cacique and several clan chiefs, a rude church had been built, and human sacrifices prohibited by vote of the tribal council. Then Las Casas, with another monk, arrived upon the scene. There was much excitement among the tawny people of Tuzulutlan. The hideous priests of the war-god were wild with rage. They reminded the people, says Remesal, that the flesh of these white men, dressed with chile sauce, would make a dainty dish. Some secret incendiary burned the church, but as the cacique and so many clan chiefs had been gained, there was no open rebellion. Before another year had elapsed the Indians had voluntarily destroyed their idols, renounced cannibalism, and promised to desist from warfare unless actually invaded. And now were to be seen the fruits of the masterly diplomacy of Las Casas. Though the cacique had thrice defeated the Spaniards, he knew well how formidable they were. By acknowledging the supremacy of Charles V.—a sovereign as far off as the sky—and paying a merely nominal tribute, he had the word of Las Casas, which no Indian ever doubted, that not a Spaniard, without the express permission of the Dominicans, should set foot upon his territory. This arrangement was made, the peaceful victory was won, and Las Casas returned to Guatemala, taking with him the cacique, to visit Alvarado, who had just returned from Spain.

This rough soldier, it will be remembered, was the man who by his ill-judged brutality had precipitated the catastrophe of the Spaniards in the city of Mexico on the May festival of 1520. In his hard heart there was, however, a gallant spot. He knew a hero when he saw him, and he well knew that, with all his military qualities, he could never have done what Las Casas had just done. So when the stern conqueror and lord of Guatemala, coming forth to greet Las Casas and the Indian king, took off his plumed and jewelled cap, and bent his head in reverence, it seems to me one of the beautiful moments in history, one of the moments that comfort us with the thought of what may yet be done with frail humanity when the spirit of Christ shall have come to be better understood. Of course Alvarado confirmed the agreement that no lay Spaniard should be allowed to enter Tuzulutlan; was he not glad enough thus to secure peace on this difficult and dangerous frontier?

Las Casas now, in 1539, went to Spain and had the agreement confirmed in a most solemn and peremptory order from Charles V. The order was obeyed. The "Land of War" was left unmolested and became thenceforth a land of peace. Not only did it cease to trouble the Spaniards, but it became a potent centre for missionary work and a valuable means of diffusing Christian influences among other Indian communities. The work was permanent. Las Casas had come, he had seen, and he had conquered; and not a drop of human blood had been shed!

18. Krishnalal Shridharani:
APPLIED SATYAGRAHA IN INDIA

In Reading 5, we saw how Gandhi came to evolve the principle of Satyagraha during his struggles in South Africa. But the practical application and development of the principle was the work of the Indian independence movement during the twenties, thirties, and forties, and it is this work that is discussed in the present reading.

In it, Krishnalal Shridharani, an Indian journalist and sociologist who knew the independence movement at firsthand, offers a general description of Satyagrahi activities between the First and Second World Wars.

He stresses the supreme importance of adequate preparation and discipline for non-violent struggle, evident from the Indian experiences. Because this was found to be so vital to effectiveness and because the movement depended so heavily on Gandhi, it seems worth while to look more closely at Gandhi's ideas about the course that non-violent resistance movements ideally should take.

The practice of Satyagraha could result in a new form of war—a non-violent, non-retaliatory war. But before this stage was reached, Gandhi maintained, all avenues for peaceful resolution of the conflict had to be explored, for there was no room in the spirit of non-violent movements for stubborn pride or refusal to confer. One ought to respect one's opponent and avoid open breaks if possible. The program, as Gandhi saw it, had five stages, and groups carrying on non-violent campaigns should exhaust all the possibilities of each before proceeding to the next.

The first stage called for a utilization of all the regular constitutional machinery available, including legislative debates, arbitration by third parties, and direct negotiations (provided that the other side was open to them). If, after a reasonable period, this seemed fruitless, the movement was to pass into the stage of agitation, taking the cause to the people with pamphlets and speeches to develop a heightened awareness of what the conflict was about. Gandhi was aware that in totalitarian societies methods of agitation would have to be different from those possible under a more liberal government, probably performed through a network of communications built up outside the normal channels.

If agitation failed to open the opponent's mind, Gandhi recommended an ultimatum, a document drawn up by the leaders with the consent of the movement's representatives, listing the people's needs and stating that continued opposition would produce some sort of direct action. It was hoped that this would shock the opponent into a realization of the possible consequences of his position, but if this, too, was unsuccessful, the members of the movement would have to begin the preparations for direct action. This phase Gandhi called self-purification, and its purpose was to develop *ahimsa,* or the spirit of harmlessness, the prerequisite to action untainted with self-interest. Satyagrahis were to pray and fast, seeking to discover whether perhaps their own deficiencies were in part responsible for the evils they wished to abolish. They were to ask themselves whether they were not too lacking in self-respect to command the respect of the opposition, and ponder how they could avoid the pitfall of reducing both sides to mere things instead of human beings.

The last stage of the campaign was some form of direct action: economic boycott, sit-down strikes, non-payment of taxes, mass resignation from public office, deliberate and organized disobedience to certain laws, etc. Some combination of these measures would, it was hoped, so cripple the society that the opponent would be forced to open channels for discussion. Gandhi counted heavily on his opponent's lack of preparation for non-violent methods and bewilderment about how to meet them, coupled with the sympathy such tactics could arouse in servants of authority like the police. The ultimate result, if the opponent held out until the bitter end, would be a complete collapse of all order, and power would pass to the Satyagrahis, who could constitute a new government.

Gandhi insisted that the training of a Satyagrahi should be as rigorous as that of any soldier, and it is interesting that the experience of the Indian movement shows that a military tradition does not, in spite of what is generally believed, build up habits that disqualify men for non-violent campaigns. Some of the most disciplined Satyagrahis in the Indian movement were Pathans, traditionally fierce warriors. Under the leadership of Abdul Ghaffar Khan many of them became active in the Indian Congress movement, and sources agree that they were among the most ardent in embracing the non-retaliatory ethic. Perhaps their very tradition of discipline helped them to accept the severe training and self-restraint essential for Satyagraha.

By the outbreak of the Second World War, Satyagraha campaigns had already resulted in many concessions from Great Britain, but Britain's declaring India at war with Germany without even consulting the Indian legislative body showed how much yet remained to be done and led to other non-violent struggles. Throughout the war a large number of Indian leaders were in jail, but although those free to carry on were many fewer than in the thirties, the basic techniques were the same. The final granting of Indian independence in 1947 was due to many factors, among them anti-imperialist sentiment in Britain itself and its weakened position after the war, which meant that the continued maintenance of its rule in India was increasingly an economic burden. But the success of the Satyagraha campaigns, although difficult to assess exactly, was undoubtedly one of the major causes.

Our excerpt is from Krishnalal Shridharani, *War Without Violence: A Study of Gandhi's Method and Its Accomplishments* (New York: Harcourt, 1939), Chapters IV and V.[1]

A. COMMUNITY VERSUS THE STATE

* * * * *

Violent overthrow of the government has been the only method popular with revolutionists irrespective of their creed, nationality or race. Almost to a single instance, all revolutions have resulted in carnage. What is even more significant, violence has never stopped at the conclusion of a revolution. It has had to be employed even during the aftermath, that is, when the replacement of the established order by the people's government has taken place. Born in a welter of blood, revolution also has to be consummated in blood.

In this carefully plotted and well-established pattern of revolution, the Gandhi struggle is perhaps the first and only variation. . . .

* * * * *

Instances of the employment of non-violent direct action on such a gigantic scale have been naturally few and far between.

[1] For a recent detailed study of Gandhi's techniques, see Joan V. Bondurant, *Conquest of Violence* (Princeton University Press, 1958).

In fact there have been only two well-marked periods in the history of the *Swaraj* movement when Satyagraha has served as the instrument of the entire Indian community in its struggle against the state. The All-India Non-violent Non-co-operation Movement began in 1920, and continued up to the middle of 1922. Then followed the expected period of demoralization and despondency. It was, however, soon over, and various groups engaged themselves in spasmodic outbursts of Satyagraha. Their activities were restricted to small communities and the issues fought over were either local or secondary. It was not until 1930 that a call for general "mobilization" was sent to the four corners of India. The nation-wide struggle that ensued perfected the various techniques and demonstrated the workability of Satyagraha as a form of concerted action on a national scale. The struggle reached its triumphant apex in the form of the Gandhi-Irwin pact of March 5, 1931.

1. Non-co-operation Movement, 1920–1922

As our chief concern here is to comprehend Satyagraha in practice, our interest in the nationalist movement itself is secondary. The pros and cons of issues and claims involved, therefore, bother us little if at all. To acquire a proper background for understanding the particular forms taken by non-violent direct action, however, a brief account of the various conflicts which precipitated the crisis on a national scale is necessary.

The beginning of the Indo-British relationship dates back to the closing decades of the seventeenth century. Attracted by the fabulous wealth of India, which also inspired the epoch-making voyage of Columbus, the directors of the East India Company decided around 1686 to "establish . . . a large, well-grounded, sure English domination in India for all time to come." Consequently, they obtained trading rights in Bombay, Calcutta and Madras from the Indian authorities. They began to purchase land, and without provocation or permission from the rulers of India, started the fortification of their trading posts. The latter were manned by armed British troops and by cannons, thus violating the trust of the natives. The subsequent friction led to the rise of Robert Clive who proposed stern measures against the resisting natives. In 1757, Clive defeated the Bengal forces at Plassey and appropriated a large portion of Indian territory in the interests of the Company.

Then ensued an era of unscrupulous plunder and exploitation by the Company men. . . .

* * * * *

Swelling resentment finally broke down the endurance of the long-suffering natives. What was left of the Indian soldiery rallied in 1857, and struck at the British forces in India. The English retaliated with organized strength and with the aid of Christian converts turned out by various missions. The rebellion of the natives was crushed with "medieval ferocity"; some 100,000 Indian lives were taken during the struggle as well as during the aftermath. The incident came to be known as the "Sepoy Mutiny" because it was a revolution which failed. India went under the authority of the British Parliament as a result, and was completely disarmed.

The resentment remained. The hearts of the people refused to be tamed. As another armed revolt was impossible, the energies and the discontent of the populace found an outlet in "parliamentary pursuit." This new trend resulted in the formation of the Indian National Congress in 1885.

*   *   *   *   *

The main activity of these leaders consisted of an annual meeting held to pass formal resolutions. Their purely parliamentary activities received their first contact with militancy in 1905. That year, the ruling Britons decided to divide the province of Bengal into two parts. The "Partition of Bengal" was to be effected with a view to securing the most beautiful and fertile land of India for the sole enjoyment of the British immigrants. This aroused the fury of the *Bengalis,* who, backed by the whole of India, called a vigorous boycott on British-manufactured goods. The struggle sent many to prison. Some were severely beaten, and quite a few disabled for the rest of their lives. This was the first time the Indian gentry had experienced the rigors of direct action. The agitation of the leaders and the vigorous use of economic pressure by the people at large were not in vain. The partition plan was repealed.

The success of the movement gave the Indian a taste of his own potential strength, which resulted in corresponding changes in his attitudes and aspirations. These, however, were soon to be vastly modified by the extraordinary situation created by the World War in Europe. India was called upon to do her duty by the Allies. The tone of the British Parliament as well as that of the bureaucracy in India was unrecognizably changed. Commands were tempered, and a volley of requests and appeals replaced them. Great promises of Dominion Status and war booty were given to India if she discharged her duty in the Empire's hour of trial.

India rose to the occasion. Men and money were rushed to the aid of the Allies. Later, when a serious crisis arose in the World War, India was again approached for additional aid. The prospects for the Allied cause seemed dark indeed, and unless more men and money came to their aid, there was no hope for victory. At this point, Lord Chelmsford, then

Viceroy of India, invited various leaders to Delhi to join him in emergency deliberations. The purpose of this War Conference was to devise ways and means by which more Indians could be sent to the battlefields and additional Indian money poured into the coffers of the Allies. For this, the populace at large had to be enthused and aroused to the pitch of frenzy. War propaganda could not be accomplished solely by officials or pro-British half-Indians. It could only be done with the aid of the popular leaders. Consequently, Gandhi, by this time the acclaimed leader of the masses, also had to be invited and utilized in spite of his Home Rule tendencies. Moreover, Gandhi was a personal friend of Lord Chelmsford, and the Viceroy had a deep-rooted faith in his sincerity. In those days the would-be rebel "prided in being and being called a British subject."

Gandhi attended the War Conference at the invitation of the Viceroy and supported the resolution drafted to help the Empire in its hour of danger. He apparently felt his course to be a short-cut to Home Rule for India. His position is made clear by the following paragraph taken from his letter to the Viceroy in connection with the above-mentioned conference.

"I recognize," Gandhi wrote, "that in the hour of its danger we must give, as we have decided to give, ungrudging and unequivocal support to the Empire of which we aspire in the near future to be partners in the same sense as the Dominions overseas. But it is the simple truth that our response is due to the expectations that our goal will be reached all the more speedily. I do not bargain for its fulfillment, but you should know, that disappointment of hope means disillusion."

All in all, India contributed $500,000,000 to the Allied war machine. War loans to the value of $700,000,000 were purchased by India in addition. Finished products to the value of $1,250,000,000 were sent to the Allies' side from India. The sacrifice of India's manhood was still greater.

*   *   *   *   *

The conclusion of the War, however, changed the whole picture. India was not only denied any part of the War booty but she was even denied admission to the League of Nations. The gullible American [Woodrow Wilson] was convinced by British statesmen that the demand for membership in the League came from a few malcontents and that the populace at large was quite satisfied with the existing arrangement. And whose business was India, an internal problem of the Empire? Cruelest cut of all, India was not to receive Dominion Status as promised during the War.

Discontent grew by leaps and bounds. At this point, broken soldiers returned from the trenches with accounts of injustices and unequal treatment. In spite of unprecedented heroism and military acumen, no Indian received a commission—simply because he was an Indian. And all of them, they reported, were discriminated against by Europeans irrespective of rank and station. In India itself, the war boom was over and there was a general state of unemployment. Manufacturing tycoons, who had doubled and tripled their wealth overnight, forgot their abnormal profits of war-time and began to reduce wages and personnel. Consequently, the rumbling of discontent among the proletariat, audible in pre-war days, grew louder. The teeming farming population of upper India, especially inhabitants of the Punjab, were resentful of the ravages made on their male population by enforced enlistment in the British Army. Even the upper middle class, savoring the fast-fading taste of power and profit, was resentful of the turn of events. The inevitable disillusionment had come at last, and India was again a seething volcano.

As if to add fuel to the fire, the report of the Rowlatt Committee was published at this critical moment. This committee was appointed by the government to ascertain whether special emergency actions were necessary to stamp out the revolutionary spirit of the people. The commission, composed of all Englishmen and no Indian, recommended drastic measures to deal with the growing unrest. The Rowlatt Committee advised the government to curtail the people's right to gather in large assemblies. Freedom of speech and assembly as well as freedom of the press were to be greatly reduced and in many cases forfeited. Imprisonment without trial, a distinct breach of the *Habeas Corpus Act,* was to be a common practice with the police and civil authorities. All India was aghast and aroused to the pitch of frenzy. Was that the reward of their services during the World War, they asked?

When this report reached Gandhi, he was still an invalid from overwork on behalf of the Allies. He felt himself and India betrayed by the Britons. He was mortally wounded. It was at his behest, according to his own self-condemnation, that India had made such tremendous sacrifices during the War. Gandhi realized that he had misled the people in his ignorance of British duplicity. Consequently, he felt it his duty to the Indian people to keep the Rowlatt Report from becoming a law. First from his sickbed and subsequently from innumerable platforms he denounced the bill as a breach of the *Habeas Corpus Act* and urged the people to resist it at every step. The government, however, forced it through the council and appended it to the laws of the land.

Driven to desperation, Gandhi called upon the people to

offer a Satyagraha. A day was appointed for complete *Hartal* as a sign of mourning. Each village and every city in the country was to stop all normal activity for twenty-four hours and every adult was to observe a fast. Streets were deserted and shop windows shrouded. Mass meetings were held in the evening to denounce the act. Individuals were asked at these meetings to sign a Satyagraha pledge which bound them to disobey the act and such other laws as would be recommended by the nationalist high command. Finally huge processions marched through the "main streets" of India shouting revolutionary slogans.

The government struck back at the Satyagrahis in order to nip their revolt in the bud. Processions were stopped by the military at various places and large crowds were fired on at Delhi, Calcutta and Amritsar. Reports reached Gandhi that there was serious trouble brewing in the Punjab. At the invitation of the Punjab leaders, Gandhi started out for that province on a peace mission. He was arrested *en route* and brought back to Bombay. The Amritsar *Punjabis*, disappointed by the news of Gandhi's arrest, called a meeting to voice their protest. Two leading local leaders, consequently, were arrested and imprisoned. The undaunted populace, nevertheless, held a protest meeting on the 18th of April, 1919. Some 20,000 unsuspecting men, women and children gathered together in the Jallianwalla Bag, a walled-in garden with only one exit. All were peaceful and pledged to non-violence, and none among them was armed with even so much as a stick. Suddenly, General Dyer, a British military officer, arrived on the scene with fifty picked soldiers armed with machine guns. He posted his troops at the only exit of the walled-in garden so that no one could escape. Without a word of warning, he gave orders to fire. About 1,650 rounds of ammunition were leveled at the peaceful gathering of men, women, and children at close range. The holocaust was over in a few minutes. When Dyer withdrew, some 1,200 dead and 3,600 wounded were lying in the garden.

When this news broke, India was stunned. The leaders felt at loss to find words strong enough to denounce the barbarous brutality of the government, and the people were numbed and sickened by the tragic picture of carnage. When the first horror of the incident was over, sympathetic spokesmen of public opinion rallied around Gandhi to devise ways and means of "compelling repentance" on the part of the powers that be. The first few steps, suggested by Gandhi, included: huge processions singing national songs and shouting slogans; mass meetings codifying their protest to the government action; and picketing of government buildings by women. The authorities, as expected, tried to suppress the growing tension by such coercive measures as arrests of the Satyagrahis, *lathi*-charges (cracking heads open with bamboo sticks), firing on crowds, and wholesale massacres. The next move of the Satyagrahis, therefore, was to dramatize their suffering and sacrifices. Then came Gandhi's call for non-co-operation. The people were asked to withdraw their aid and support which made the administration possible. Those who had been rewarded by the government with titles and honorary offices were to surrender their privileges. Rich people were to refrain from buying government loans and the poor were asked to refuse any petty service to the local authorities. Lawyers suspended their practice and disputes were settled outside the courts. Government schools were deserted as the students decided either to go to "national institutions" or to the villages to carry on the *Swaraj* propaganda. Benches in legislative councils were unoccupied because the leaders were out among the people instigating non-violent revolution. A militant boycott of British goods was promulgated, coupled with a petition to the public to patronize indigenous products. Finally, Indians in government service, from high officials to petty tax-collectors, were asked to resign from their posts. Complete paralysis of the administration was the objective. This program was further bolstered by the nationalist propaganda at work in the Indian Army. Soldiers were persuaded to sever connections with the undesirable aliens.

Momentarily, everything seemed to be going on smoothly. There was panic in government quarters and many of the administrative departments were at a virtual standstill. The cable wire between Delhi and Ten Downing Street hummed frantically day and night. George Lloyd, then Governor of Bombay, confessed later on: "Gandhi's was the most colossal experiment in world history; and it came within an inch of succeeding."

True to the pattern of Satyagraha, more militant maneuvers were to follow. After non-co-operation had partly paralyzed the administration, the actual business of destroying the existing order was planned. This finesse was to be accomplished by non-payment of the government taxes and by civil disobedience of repressive laws. Bans on nationalist literature were to be disregarded, and the government monopoly of salt manufacture was to be broken by mass action. The Rowlatt Act, the immediate cause of all this friction, was to be completely shattered.

But this could not be. In spite of Gandhi's constant and eloquent appeals to his countrymen to refrain from hatred and violence, in spite of his own peerless example, violence broke out. The reports reached him that the mob was beyond control of his Satyagrahis in several places. Riots had occurred in Ahmedabad and Viramgam. At Chauri Chaura, especially, the crowds, unaccustomed to non-violence, went mad and committed atrocities. Gandhi was stunned by this news, and in deep agony of spirit, concluded that the time was not yet ripe for mass non-violence. Then he decided upon the drastic step of calling a halt! This decision produced the utmost consternation within the ranks of his colleagues. Many regarded it as a sacrifice of the people's cause on the altar of an individual's ideals. However, Gandhi's decision prevailed and the Satyagraha was called off.

After a lapse of time, on March 18, 1922, Gandhi was arrested and tried on the charge of instigating the people to violence. He pleaded guilty in the following words: "The only course open to you, the Judge and the Assessors, is either to resign your posts and thus disassociate yourselves from evil if you feel that the law you are called upon to administer is an evil and that in reality I am innocent, or inflict upon me the severest penalty if you believe that the system and the law you are assisting to administer are good for the people of this country and that my activity is therefore injurious to the public weal."[2] The English judge imposed upon Gandhi the sentence of six years' rigorous imprisonment. He, however, added: "If the course of events should make it possible for the government to reduce the period and release you, no one will be better pleased than I."

Thus the first experiment with non-violent direct action on a national scale suffered an abortive end. Although it failed to obtain its immediate objective, it was immensely successful in awakening India to the consciousness of her own potential power. Moreover, the experience gathered during this non-co-operation movement paved the way for India's next great movement of 1930.

2. Civil Disobedience Movement, 1930–1934

A lengthy period of reaction followed the apparent failure of the non-co-operation movement of 1920–22. On one hand the people of India were brooding over the future of the *Swaraj* movement and on the other the British bureaucracy was tightening its grip over public affairs. It was, indeed, almost a clenched fist. What is more significant from our point of view, the efficacy of Satyagraha was seriously disputed. The radical youth groups and the labor parties were not convinced of the "compelling power" of non-violent direct action. Leaders of public opinion and philosophers began to discover, one

[2] Krishnadas, *Seven Months with Mahatma Gandhi* (Bihar, 1928), Vol. II, Appendix B, p. 18.

by one, many loopholes in the ideology of Satyagraha. It aroused widespread academic interest and discussion. Books were published either defending or denouncing Satyagraha and *Gandhism* in general. Gandhi contended that the failure was due to the inadequate "preparedness" on the part of the people, but after his release from jail he kept silent and retired to his *Ashrama*. This period of reflection and uncertainty, however, brought to the people a greater realization of the implications of Satyagraha and of its various potentialities.

The period of demoralization over, new organizations and new trends began to revive the spirits of the people. Inspired by the Soviet *Five-Year Plan,* the urban workers were waiting for a Messiah from the steppes. The All-India Trade Union Congress, founded in 1921, was a powerful group by this time. On the farmers' front, the National Congress party was making a heroic effort to expand its activities and to seek recruits by the thousands from among agriculturists.

The labor movement came to a head in 1929. Strikes occurred all over India. The Bombay Textile Labor Union was the first. A general strike of the jute workers followed in Bengal. The Iron Works at Jamshedpur, one of the largest in the world, was the next to be threatened by a labor war. The Iron Plate Works in the same industrial town, connected with the Burma Oil Company, succeeded in suppressing the walkout before it reached large proportions. The labor movement was becoming *class conscious* for the first time in India's short industrial history.

Meanwhile, the struggle on the nationalist front was reaching its climax. There were local Satyagrahas in the farming districts of Gujarat and Maharashtra. The conspicuous success of the Bardoli Satyagraha of 1928, already described in the previous chapter, infused new hope in the people and revived a general confidence in Gandhi's method. The absence of any Indian representative on the Simon Commission[3] drew the "Liberal" and the "Moderate" elements to the Congress fold. Thus the nation was again all energy and enthusiasm.

About this time, a new element was gaining in importance in the Indian political mosaic. The youth of India was demanding a hearing. Their organizations spread like wildfire, and by 1928, there was hardly a town of any size in India without its unit of politically-minded young men. These societies were sincerely radical. Their guiding spirits were nationalists with overtones of Socialism. They advocated that

[3] Composed of Englishmen only and presided over by Sir John Simon, this commission was appointed by the British Parliament to recommend constitutional changes in the Government of India.

either Gandhi launch the nation once more in direct action or give up his leadership.

With the intuition of a born leader, Gandhi felt that the time was ripe for direct action against the British government of India. The situation called for a strong Congress president who could swing the youth leagues and the workers behind that body. Gandhi's choice was Pandit Jawaharlal Nehru. One year previously, the Indian National Congress in its annual meeting at Calcutta had given an ultimatum to the government to confer Dominion Status in twelve months' time. The government failed to comply. Thereupon, in 1930, under the younger man's inspiration, India declared her independence on the memorable 26th of January. It was again a revolution, albeit non-violent; the community was rising against the state.

To fulfill its new goal, viz., Complete Independence, the Congress Executive authorized civil disobedience. It also appointed Gandhi as the nation's "Dictator." Upon Gandhi's arrest, it was decided that Pandit Nehru was to occupy the vacated position. A list of Dictators was prepared but kept secret. The struggle, however, was not to start until Gandhi published his detailed plan of attack and gave a signal.

When the plans were ready and the scene set, it was announced to the waiting nation that civil disobedience would be inaugurated on March 12, 1930. Ten days prior to this scheduled date, however, Gandhi, conforming to the pattern of Satyagraha, had sent the *Ultimatum* to the Viceroy and requested a prompt answer. The people were advised accordingly to maintain a state of non-committal "preparedness" pending the response of the government to Gandhi's final challenge. In this communication were listed the minimum demands of the Congress to be fulfilled in a maximum period of time.

The Viceroy's answer was unsatisfactory. Now it was incumbent upon the Satyagrahis to acquire by direct action what they failed to secure through parliamentary procedure. Taking up the challenge, Gandhi started on his famous *March to the Sea* with a handful of his nearest and dearest. Upon arrival at Port Dandi, Gandhi and his "first batch" violated the Salt Act by preparing salt from the sea water. That was the signal the country awaited. The very next day witnessed India's transformation into one vast battlefield. The community and the state at last openly faced each other as enemies and in the following months, laws were regularly broken by the citizenry and punishment was meted out by the state.

The Satyagrahis attacked on many fronts and employed a variety of tactics. In big cities, they organized and led huge processions in defiance of police orders and prohibitory notices served by the warrant officers. In village and town alike, public meetings and conferences of local leaders were held in spite of the government ban. The usual boycott of British goods coupled with intensive picketing by women became general. Pickets were posted even at the gates of British banks, insurance companies, mints and bullion exchanges. As the press was now forbidden by the authorities to print campaign notices and news regarding government repression, the Satyagrahis issued their own bulletins and leaflets. Although these were regarded as illegal and revolutionary, they were freely distributed among the masses. Even more serious was the work of printing and selling proscribed literature. Stuccoed walls and sometimes the paved streets served as a bulletin board. Foreign correspondents never failed to marvel at the spectacle of the sympathetic pedestrians carefully picking their way around the elaborate Congress announcements chalked on the sidewalks.

When the movement gathered momentum, certain more drastic stratagems were included in the general program. A boycott was called on all state-owned post offices, telegraph systems, trams and ship lines. Public saluting of the National Flag, instead of the Union Jack, and displaying the National Flag on public buildings as well as over civil and criminal courts was another maneuver employed by the civil resisters in order to provoke further government friction. Non-violent volunteers were wont to refuse to make parole rounds to the police, and others defied restraint orders served on them by the courts. Attempts were made to reoccupy Congress offices which had been seized by the police.

Civil disobedience of unjust laws, however, was the principal feature of the strategy. The Salt Act was taken as the symbol of British exploitation of the masses and made a test case. The most formidable forces, therefore, were arrayed against the government monopoly of salt manufacture. In the wake of the violation of the Salt Act followed a redoubtable attack on the Forest Laws. And then came a general attack on as many obnoxious statutes of the state as were found vulnerable. Picketing of liquor and opium shops ate an alarming hole in the government earnings. Finally, the city-dwelling businessmen and manufacturers were called upon to withhold certain taxes, and village farmers were asked not to pay land revenue.

Meanwhile, the bureaucracy had set free all the repressive and coercive powers at its command. First, the ranking leaders were rounded up and imprisoned. All Congress offices were decreed illegal and confiscated. However, new leaders sprang from the people, and more offices were opened in outlying areas. Then followed wholesale arrests of groups and volunteer corps. When the jails and improvised "detention camps" were filled to capacity, baton charges on peaceful pickets and processions became the order of the day. Women Satyagrahis were insulted and ill-treated. Prisoners were subject to inhuman cruelties in the jails. Next on the program of suppression was the confiscation of the Satyagrahis' property. Finally, firing on unarmed crowds became a common spectacle.

The toll of suffering was tremendous. According to nationalist sources, during the one year of non-violent direct action (from March 12, 1930, when Satyagraha was inaugurated, to March 5, 1931, when the truce was signed), 100,000 Indians cheerfully forfeited their liberty to enter His Majesty's numerous prisons, detention camps and improvised jails. A modest estimate shows that no less than 17,000 women also underwent various terms of imprisonment.[4] A score of them were expectant mothers when they found themselves behind prison bars. Consequently, these "war babies" of India were born in prison.

The number of the "lathi charges" mounted somewhere in the hundreds, and unarmed crowds were fired on without warning. Thousands were wounded and hundreds killed. Despite this "reign of terror," the people of India displayed a remarkable degree of restraint and non-violent discipline. What is more important, slaughter and mutilation failed to repress the movement or intimidate the people. On the contrary, it exhausted the government itself. The coercive arms of the state were paralyzed by the Satyagrahic tactics of the opponents. After a full year of struggle, the government gave in and began negotiations with the Congress high command. Gandhi and the members of the Working Committee of the Congress were released from jail and the former was invited to Delhi.

For the first time in history, on March 5, 1931, the representative of His Majesty signed a truce treaty with Gandhi, the erstwhile "rebel." Satyagraha on a national scale had now come to a successful ending. The main demands of the people were granted in the treaty thereafter known as the "Gandhi-Irwin Pact," and the stage was set for further negotiation with a view to evolving a free India. Gandhi was invited to London for the Round Table Conference.

Now that Gandhi was in London and the other leaders in-

---

[4] Figures as quoted in *Condition of India, being a report of the Delegation sent by the India League in 1932* (London, 1934). The government has generally evaded stating exact figures concerning its repressive measures. Whenever stated, however, these figures fall far short of the nationalist estimates.

active, with the "non-violent army" disbanded and agitation discontinued, now that people were rejoicing in their triumph and consequently were off guard—the government broke its promises. So when Gandhi landed in Bombay, he found his pact with Irwin, now Lord Halifax, violated by the government. He also discovered that the bureaucracy was in a belligerent mood and did not mean to carry out the terms of the treaty. Thereupon, Gandhi was forced to revive Satyagraha. The renewed movement, however, died a natural death in 1934. Meanwhile, the new constitution, a substantial if unsatisfactory result of the nationalist struggle, was completed. Later it became the law of the land.

Thus the second nation-wide attempt at securing complete independence was, at best, a partial success. The movement, however, further prepared the country in the art of government and made the people confident of their strength and ability. According to all observers, foreign as well as domestic, it was a reborn India at the conclusion of the Civil Disobedience Movement. This angle has a great bearing on our special interest here, the fact that Satyagraha was proven to be an effective instrument of achieving political ends even when employed on a nation-wide scale. For the actual Satyagrahic engagement of the opponent culminated in the triumph of the nationalists as epitomized in the "Gandhi-Irwin Pact." The subsequent violation of the truce treaty by the Britons can in no way be regarded as a weakness or a failure of Satyagraha as such. It might have, at the most, exposed a flagrant lack of statesmanship in the nationalist high command.[5]

Triumphant in a conflict between the community and the state, and between groups, Satyagraha has given evidence of being an effective mode of revolution or civil war. The Indian movement had even greater implications. It was not merely a struggle between the community on one hand and the state on the other, but it was also a conflict between a people and an alien government. To be sure, the British bureaucrats and the army in India had the might of England and her Dominions behind them. It cannot be denied that this

[5] The magnitude of the success of the 1930–1934 Satyagraha, however, cannot be grasped without considering the present political situation in India. The nationalists have now complete control over seven out of the eleven great Provinces of India, with partial control over two more Provinces under coalition ministries. Even in the remaining two Provinces, the National Congress party has single largest groups in the legislatures. Thus the Satyagrahi "ex-convicts" are today Premiers and Ministers in India's several Provinces. [This note refers to the period immediately before World War II.—Ed.]

power was utilized in the attempt to stamp out the nationalist uprising. Thus the Indian struggle had many characteristics of a conflict between two nations; it was waged, in a way, on an international scale. When viewed in that light, the success of the 1930 Satyagraha indicates that non-violent direct action might prove to be an effective means of settling a conflict involving even different states. There has been, moreover, one instance in Europe of the use of the non-violent method in a conflict between two governments. The struggle took place between Norway and Sweden in the early part of the nineteenth century. The Treaty of Kiel, concluded in 1814, stipulated that Norway should be ceded to the kingdom of Sweden. In order to effect this part of the treaty, Bernadotte invaded Norway. Surprisingly enough, no resistance was forthcoming. So after weeks of military inactivity, Bernadotte indicated that he was ready to enter negotiations. Unity of the two countries was the result. Even when, after a century of partnership, the Norwegians decided by a majority vote to secede from Sweden and become independent, the latter accepted the decision without bloodshed. The unsullied record of peaceful accord between the two countries is still the envy of other nations.

B. ORGANIZATION AND DISCIPLINE

The successes of Satyagraha, particularly those with a national bearing, have come not merely from the employment of a novel and surprising strategy, but they are made possible also by the existence in India of a lusty organization to back and to conduct the actual operations of non-violent direct action. In fact, no technique of mass mobilization, however sound and logically tenable, can ever achieve anything worth while without being utilized in an organized manner and without being checked and controlled by strict discipline. How much more should such be the case of Satyagraha which aspires to be an equivalent of war, an institution operative both during peaceful periods and when force is matched with force. It is essential, therefore, to look into the organizational set-up of the *Swaraj* movement in India.

1. The Indian National Congress

The Indian National Congress, whose banners herald Complete Independence for India's millions, is a country-wide organization counting millions in its membership. Aimed directly at *Purna Swaraj* (complete independence), it is founded on the theory of non-violence; Satyagraha and Satyagraha alone is its creed of action. The Congress cuts across the distinctions of color, caste and creed. It is even above class stratification. Consequently it gives entrée to the purest Brahmin priest and lowliest untouchable. Hindus, Mohammedans, Christians, Sikhs, Buddhists, Jainas, Parsees and even the aboriginal Bhils find a mutual bond in the National Congress. The industrial magnates of Bombay and Calcutta sit cheek by jowl with dispossessed Indian villagers at each annual session.

* * * * *

Congress offices were established in as many villages as the leaders could manage. The shrewd eyes of Gandhi had noticed that there are over 700,000 villages in India, and about two-thirds of them are in territory directly ruled by the British. Seventy-one per cent of the population, roughly 224,000,000 Indians, live in these little settlements. In order to make Satyagraha a mass movement, the Congress had to rely heavily upon the loyalty of rural India. It would be difficult to estimate the exact number of villages that have a Congress office today, but the wholehearted response which Gandhi's call in 1930 received from these areas, indicates that one hamlet out of three is thoroughly indoctrinated in the credo of Satyagraha and has a Congress office of its own.[6] During times of peace, this village unit is busy with the "constructive program" of the Congress as formulated by Gandhi. Over and above corralling new converts to the cause, the village unit seeks to control and direct the civic life of the community, thereby replacing the government functionaries. It distributes Satyagraha's free literature, and has among its personnel men and women who can spread Congress propaganda with oratory and songs. Village leaders give night courses in village economy with emphasis on the fact that an increase in local products would be a telling blow to British commercial interests. Besides these general activities, the Village Congress Office directs:

1. the propagation of hand spinning,
2. a campaign against drugs and intoxicants,
3. the propagation of Hindustani as the *Lingua Franca* of India,
4. the elimination of untouchability,
5. welfare activities such as relief and reconstruction, and
6. Hindu-Mohammedan unity.

When on a war footing, that is, when a call for civil disobedience or non-co-operation has been received from the

---

[6] Sir Samuel Hoare declared in the House of Commons during the hectic days of 1930, that only one village out of ten had taken to civil disobedience. Even at that, Sir Samuel's *"official version"* concedes the Congress some 50,000 villages, and over five million rural Indians.

Congress high command, the village organization rallies the community against paying its land revenue or similar taxes, and advises the villagers when they come to the point of breaking laws and boycotting government functionaries. The resignation of the *Mukhi* (the governmental representative who collects the taxes) has often been effected by village party workers, and when the *Mukhi* resigns, the only tie binding the village to the British *Raj* at Delhi is broken.

* * * * *

Elected every year, the Congress President stands at the apex of this pyramid whose base, as we have seen, is sunk deep in rural India. There is also a permanent secretariat of the Congress at *Swaraj Bhavan,* Allahabad, to maintain the continuity of the work.

During peacetime it is the duty of the President (*Rastrapati* = Ruler of the Nation) and the *Working Committee* to carry out the dictates of the plenary session, and to set in action the "constructive program" drawn up at the convention. They are organizers and disciplinarians, covering the country in preparation for the emergencies of Satyagraha.

On a wartime basis, that is, when the Congress resorts to direct action, the President becomes a *dictator,*[7] and names a man who must take his place should the acting President be imprisoned. Sometimes a list of succession is prepared which will replace any loss in high command. Wartime authority is vested in men who hold key positions, and in "war councils" which replace village units.

2. The Hindustani Sevadal

The Congress organization is supplemented by a permanent corps of *Swayamsevakas,* or volunteers. *Hindustani Sevadal* (The Corps of Servants of India) is a modern innovation, but it has been an inestimably important factor in the successful campaigns of recent years. These volunteers, steeped in nonviolence, are experts in Satyagrahic strategy and discipline. In times of direct action, they are assigned the job of shaping and disciplining that horde of raw, adventurous recruits who form the bulk of any mass movement. The *Sevadal* has thus supplied what is known in military language as commissioned officers.

[7] Although Pandit Jawaharlal Nehru was the Congress President in 1930, it was Gandhi who was made the first dictator. After all, Gandhi, the inventor of the new weapon of Satyagraha, was the only man at first who understood his invention, and the only one who could put it into practical use. The Pandit was the next dictator.

* * * * *

The general discipline of the volunteer officers as well as of the rank and file of recruits during a campaign of non-violent direct action is governed by the credo of non-violence. Gandhi, in order to avoid any misunderstanding on this point, and after being empowered to do so by a resolution of the Working Committee in February, 1930, postulated a set of rules governing the behavior of Satyagrahis, or civil resisters, in the *Young India* of February 27, 1930. Published on the eve of the Civil Disobedience Movement of 1930, it was Gandhi's attempt to codify his conception of how the ideal Satyagrahi should behave. [Here are his commandments in his own words]:

As an Individual

1. A Satyagrahi, i.e., a civil resister, will harbor no anger.
2. He will suffer the anger of the opponent.
3. In doing so he will put up with assaults from the opponent, never retaliate; but he will not submit, out of fear of punishment or the like, to any order given in anger.
4. When any person in authority seeks to arrest a civil resister, he will voluntarily submit to the arrest, and he will not resist the attachment or removal of his own property, if any, when it is sought to be confiscated by the authorities.
5. If a civil resister has any property in his possession as a trustee, he will refuse to surrender it, even though in defending it he might lose his life. He will, however, never retaliate.
6. Non-retaliation excludes swearing and cursing.
7. Therefore a civil resister will never insult his opponent. . . .
8. A civil resister will not salute the Union Jack, nor will he insult it or officials, English or Indian.
9. In course of the struggle if one insults an official or commits an assault upon him, a civil resister will protect such official or officials from the insult or attack even at the risk of his life.

As a Prisoner

10. As a prisoner, a civil resister will behave courteously toward prison officials, and will observe all such discipline of the prison as is not contrary to self-respect. . . .
11. A civil resister will make no distinction between an ordinary prisoner and himself, will in no way regard himself as superior to the rest. . . .
12. A civil resister may not fast for want of conveniences whose deprivation does not involve any injury to one's self-respect.

As a Unit

13. A civil resister will joyfully obey all the orders issued by the leader of the corps, whether they please him or not.

14. He will carry out orders in the first instance even though they appear to him to be insulting, inimical or foolish, and then appeal to higher authority. . . .

15. No civil resister is to expect maintenance for his dependents. It would be an accident if any such provision is made. A civil resister entrusts his dependents to the care of God. Even in ordinary warfare wherein hundreds of thousands give themselves up to it, they are able to make no previous provision. How much more, then, should such be the case in Satyagraha? It is the universal experience that in such times hardly anybody is left to starve.

*   *   *   *   *

19. Leo Kuper and Albert Luthuli:
SOUTH AFRICA: THE BEGINNING OF NON-VIOLENT RESISTANCE

We now turn to the great 1952 passive resistance or "Defiance" campaign in South Africa. Non-violent resistance had subsided after Gandhi left South Africa but again in 1946 Indians in South Africa turned to it to protest injustice by the South African Government. Until 1952, however, there was no united non-violent resistance movement. That is to say, while the Indian community under Gandhi and after World War II had employed non-violent tactics, there had been no effort to unite Indians with other non-whites. The 1952 campaign for the first time evoked joint endeavors by the Indians, "Natives," and "Coloreds" (racially mixed groups). The African National Congress spearheaded the effort for the Native or African population.

In 1952 the white (English and Boer) population of South Africa, only about 20 per cent of the total, enjoyed a dominant legal, economic, and social position. For many years there had been an effort to keep the races apart and South African governments, whatever their political hue, did not differ fundamentally from one another in their attitudes to the problem. After 1948, however, with the triumph of the Nationalists (largely of Dutch descent), legislation to separate the races (apartheid) and to guarantee white supremacy became ever more common, and indeed, scarcely a year has passed since without some new restriction on Native, Indian, or Colored populations. Thus today a whole network of deliberately contrived legislation keeps the majority racial groups in permanent subjection to the tiny white minority.

The pattern of subjection had become quite clear by 1952. It consisted basically of three kinds of laws and customs: (1) devices for separating the races in ever more rigid ways; (2) delegation of wide discretionary powers to the Native Affairs Department so that the control of matters affecting the Natives reposed more and more in autocratic administration; and (3) schemes to make certain that only the whites would have the legal right to initiate and control social change.

Naturally, laws had eliminated the possibility of marriage between Europeans and non-Europeans. Statutes had also been enacted to provide severe penalties for any "carnal knowledge" between the races (Alan Paton's novel *Cry the Beloved Country* deals in part with this theme, it will be remembered). Long before the advent of the Nationalists, Color Bar Acts had limited the kinds of occupations open to Natives in industry and elsewhere, and segregation statutes tried to separate the races in the use of such public utilities as the railways. In 1950, the Suppression of Communism Act defined Communism so broadly and imposed such restrictions on ordinary civil liberties that many activities fully acceptable in other countries became punishable in South Africa. Natives were required to possess passes in order to move about the country and failure to produce one on demand by a policeman could result in imprisonment.

As the Nationalists multiplied acts of this kind and made punishments more and more severe, Natives, Coloreds, and Indians became desperate. They had little or no direct parliamentary representation, and that which remained from an earlier day was under attack by the Nationalist Government. Most of the best land originally possessed by the Natives had been taken away by the whites and now, under the Nationalists, they were beginning to be told that many of them must return from the cities in which they had been working to their poor native "reserves." Had they been armed, there is no doubt that some would have turned to violence. As it was, their only recourse appeared to be some form of non-violent resistance.

But it was not only because they had few weapons that they resorted to non-violence. Gandhi's teachings had made a deep impression on both Indian and Native leaders, and the Christian backgrounds of several of the latter were also profoundly influential. Zulu Chief Albert Luthuli, one of the leaders of the African National Congress and winner of the Nobel Peace Prize for 1960, tells us in his recent autobiography[1] that his religious beliefs played a large role in his emphasis on non-violent action. The whole resistance campaign of 1952, therefore, is an example of deliberate non-violence; an effort was made to plan each step in the strategy of resistance, and those participating were to be carefully trained in the non-violent techniques.

[1] Albert Luthuli, *Let My People Go* (New York: McGraw-Hill, 1962).

In the first section of this reading, Leo Kuper, a white South African, describes the campaign and assesses the progress made, which was so great that it thoroughly alarmed the white minority. The movement was very well controlled and enlisted the enthusiastic co-operation of thousands, and Chief Luthuli has written that the challenge of such disciplined non-violence was more than the leaders of the whites could meet, since, as he says, "it robbed them of the initiative."[2] Details of what followed are not clear, for the government, in an obvious attempt to protect itself, later refused to appoint a commission to investigate the facts, but evidence points strongly to the employment of *agents provocateurs* by the whites in the Port Elizabeth and Kimberley areas, in an attempt to induce violence and thus regain control of the situation. (This is, of course, a familiar technique of authoritarian regimes faced with non-violent resistance, and was employed in, among other places, Czarist Russia.) Chief Luthuli flatly asserts that when the violence came it was set in motion by the government itself.[3]

Kuper, as the reader will see, does not claim enormous success for the campaign, pointing out that one result was to stiffen the government's attitude and drive the races even farther apart. Chief Luthuli, however, having in mind long-range consequences rather than immediate positive effects, believes that it constituted a turning point in the struggle for liberation by establishing a precedent for large-scale non-violent protest that gathered weight as it went, creating among Africans "a new climate" and a spirit of militant defiance.[4] Furthermore, it can be said to have given rise to a new and important feeling of self-confidence, by demonstrating that the activities of unarmed men and women (for women were among the most active) could indeed disturb a powerful ruling class. This growing self-confidence was a long step toward the elimination of slavery, which must begin in the mind of the slave.

Chief Luthuli's book gives many examples of more limited non-violent resistance, and that, despite increasingly repressive legislation. In 1957 a very successful bus boycott was carried out, not as a result of the African National Congress' leadership, but as the spontaneous act of an aroused population. A bus company's decision to increase fares threatened to thrust

2 Luthuli, op. cit., p. 127.
3 Ibid., p. 126–28.
4 Ibid., p. 136.

its riders down even further below the line of precarious existence, and the response, in both Johannesburg and Pretoria, was a clear and swift one. In Johannesburg, the riders unanimously decided simply to walk to work, and many of them walked twenty miles or more each day rather than meekly submit to further exploitation. Although many whites were sure they would soon tire, they persisted, even in the face of police intimidation. Some of the boycotters who turned to bicycles had their tires deflated by the police, and the Native Pass system was also used to harass both walkers and cyclists. Their lot aroused the sympathies of many white people, some of whom, despite police threats, gave lifts to the protesters, thus coming into direct contact, often for the first time, with Natives who were not their servants and seeing firsthand the meaning of non-violent resistance in terms of individual suffering. The upshot was the Chambers of Commerce's decision to subsidize the bus company so that fares would not have to rise.[5]

Other examples of the spirit encouraged by the 1952 resistance were: the great demonstrations carried out by Native women against the Pass laws, during which, in 1958, 2000 women were arrested in Johannesburg alone; the boycott of potatoes in 1959, which paralyzed the potato industry dependent as it was on the forced labor of Pass offenders; and the Pass burning campaign of 1960.

The natives of South Africa are still a long way from liberation, but one must remember the generation that elapsed in India between the first non-violent resistance campaigns and the achievement of independence. Moreover, the Africans' behavior indicates that those prerequisites for freedom—self-respect and willingness to undergo voluntary suffering—are developing. Most of the leaders of the African National Congress believe that non-violent struggle of some kind is the key to ultimate emancipation. Nor are their reasons based solely on moral considerations. As Chief Luthuli has put it, "we shall not jeopardize the South Africa of tomorrow by precipitating violence today."[6]

In the second section of the reading, Chief Luthuli offers an apologia for his break with "moderation" in the South African struggle. After his active participation in the campaign of 1952, the South African Government removed him from the

[5] Ibid., p. 177.
[6] Ibid., pp. 219–20.

chieftainship of his tribe. His response was the public statement reprinted here.

The first selection is excerpted from Leo Kuper's *Passive
Resistance in South Africa* (Yale University Press, 1957). The
author, a sociologist, was born in 1908 in Johannesburg and
was awarded a Ph.D. by the University of Birmingham. Cur-
rently he is dean of the faculty of social science at Natal University in South Africa.

Leo Kuper: *PASSIVE RESISTANCE IN SOUTH AFRICA*

Notwithstanding the many restraints, it was largely through
public meetings that the leaders spread the message of the
passive resistance campaign among the non-white masses.
These meetings were often the starting-point for acts in defiance of the law. Since the situation evoked such conflicting
images and interpretations, an account of a resistance meeting,
and of the sequence of acts which constitute passive resistance,
will help to define more concretely the subject matter of our
discussion. I have selected for the following description a meeting I attended in Durban.

This meeting had been called by the Natal branch of the
African National Congress and the Natal Indian Congress for
November 9th, 1952, at Nicol (Red) Square, Durban, but
the City Council had forbidden the use of the land. Not
knowing this, people arrived to find the square empty, except
for a few armed policemen on motor-cycles. On a nearby
corner, as though in warning, was a hoarding with the words
5 KILLED 39 INJURED IN EAST LONDON RIOTS.[7]

People moved on to Lakhani Chambers, the headquarters of
the Natal Indian Congress, realizing that a decision as to the
venue of the meeting would be taken there. The leaders of
the resistance movement were already in consultation. The
decision rested with the President of the Natal Indian Congress, Dr. G. M. Naicker, and other leaders. Dr. Naicker is
firmly dedicated to non-violence, in the tradition of Mahatma
Gandhi, and has served terms of imprisonment in two passive
resistance campaigns.

With Dr. Naicker was the secretary of the Natal Indian
Congress, Mr. J. N. Singh, a handsome man with military car-
riage, trained at the University of the Witwatersrand, and
practising as a lawyer in Durban. Mr. Singh had been selected
to lead a corps of volunteers in the defiance of law that very
afternoon. Someone asked him cheerfully whether he had

[7] This was the second disturbance in the Cape Eastern Province.

taken his vitamins and he replied that he had. Dr. Naicker explained to me that resisters went into training so as to ensure that they were physically fit to withstand the rigours of a term of imprisonment. Resisters were punished by the loss of a meal, if they displeased the warders, 'and they are easily displeased with us.' A young student who had recently served his resistance term added that resisters were set to breaking stones or digging rubble, and were penalized by the loss of a meal if the task were not completed at the end of the day. He spoke with revulsion of the prison diet (which he described as mealie-meal in the morning with one teaspoon of sugar, one quarter-loaf of bread with a teaspoonful of fat for lunch, mealie-rice with boiled beans for supper) and his difficulty in following the advice of the long-term prisoners to 'press it down.'

Meanwhile, a number of resisters both African and Indian, who were to participate in the meeting as stewards, speakers or volunteers, were active on a variety of missions. As they passed each other on the stairs or in the corridors, they exchanged the resistance movement's greeting. This takes the form of the call '*Afrika*,' the 'a' pronounced as in English 'bath,' with a resolute emphasis on the first and third syllables. At the same time, the right fist is clenched, with thumb held erect, and moved up towards the shoulder. Word and gesture symbolize the unity of the peoples, and the return of the country to them. Some of the men wore armbands, which signified that they had served, or were about to serve, terms of imprisonment for defiance of the laws.

The decision in regard to the venue of the meeting was difficult to take and long delayed. Too ready a compliance with official edicts would make it impossible for the leaders to function publicly, and would indeed undermine the spirit of resistance. On the other hand, the pattern of recent disturbances in East London and other parts of the country, resulting in considerable loss of life and destruction of property, might be repeated in Durban, if the resisters attempted to meet on the forbidden Red Square. Inevitably some measure of responsibility would attach to the resisters, even though they themselves behaved with disciplined non-violence.

Finally, Dr. Naicker announced that the meeting would be held on a privately-owned piece of ground, not subject to the City Council's control.

* * * * *

The crowd was composed of Africans and Indians of all ages, men and women, the Indian women in colourful *saris,* the African women in various European-styled clothing. On the outskirts stood a 'ricksha boy' in gorgeous beadwork, his head adorned with plumes and painted ox-horns. The narrow street was lined by a few cars, in one of which sat a number of white men from the political section of the South African police. A huge flag, with the symbolic colours of the African National Congress, black for the people, green for the land, and gold for the wealth, marked the platform, a wagon.

From the beginning, the first act as it were, the organizers asserted the peaceful nature of the meeting. One of the vice-presidents of the Natal Indian Congress, who had already served a term of imprisonment, mounted the platform and exhorted the crowd to sit. The meeting could not begin, he called, till everyone was seated. To stand would create an impression of disorderliness which had to be avoided. This was a peaceful meeting; the campaign was non-violent. Gradually, leisurely, most of the people sat down on the ground. This seemed to create a feeling of good-humoured relaxation and of solidarity.

Almost immediately, a deep bass voice from somewhere in the crowd began a Zulu chant 'Mayibuy' IAfrika.' The whole crowd, Indians as well as Africans, joined in this song of the resistance movement, and instead of Amen, shouted 'Afrika!' Throughout the meeting 'Afrika' was used in this way—a fervent affirmation whenever a speaker emphasized the principles of the defiance campaign, or attacked discrimination or indeed made a good joke.

MAYIBUY' IAFRIKA!

Thina sizwe esinsundu,
Sikhalel 'iAfrika,

Eyathathwa amaNgisi;

Sisesebumnyameni.

Chorus: Mayibuye, mayibuye,
Mayibuy'iAfrika!

Eyathathwa ama-
Ngisi;
Sisesebumnyameni.

Chorus: Mayibuye mayibuye,
Mayibuy'iAfrika!

Eyagqilazwa ama-
Bunu;
Sisesebumnyameni.

LET AFRICA RETURN!

We black people,
We cry for Africa,

Which was taken by the English,
While we were still in darkness.

Let it return, let it return,
Let Africa return!

Which was taken by the English,
While we were still in darkness.

Let it return, let it return,
Let Africa return!

Which was enslaved by the Boers
While we were still in darkness!

* * * * *

Then they took up '*S'yayifun'inkululeko*' (We want freedom) and '*Vula Malani*' (Open, Malan).

S'YAYIFUN'INKULULEKO	WE WANT FREEDOM
S'yayifun'inkululeko; (twice)	We want freedom; (twice)
S'yayifuna, s'yayifuna!	We want it, we want it!
S'yayifun'inkululeko.	We want freedom.
We! Malani.	Listen! Malan.
S'yayifun'inkululeko; (twice)	We want freedom; (twice)
S'yayifuna, s'yayifuna!	We want it, we want it!
S'yayifun'inkululeko	We want freedom.
We! Verwoerdi.	Listen! Verwoerd.

(Etc., all Cabinet Ministers sung to in turn.)

VULA, MALANI!	OPEN, MALAN!
Vula Malan, siyangqongqoza: (four times)	Open Malan, we are knock-ing: (four times)

* * * * *

The ready good humour and the rich spontaneous song gave
an impression of strength and solidarity. The sentiments
seemed to be rooted in the emotions and music of these people, and not something foreign, peddled by agitators.

* * * * *

Dr. Naicker came to the wagon and took up the theme of
non-violence, while Mr. M. B. Yengwa, secretary of the Natal
branch of the African National Congress, interpreted into Zulu.
Dr. Naicker began by saying that as he looked at the faces
round him, he saw on them no violence, yet the meeting had
been prohibited on the Red Square.

* * * * *

He spoke of the need for racial co-operation, and of the
deliberate unreliability of the White press. 'In to-day's paper,'
he said, 'there is another white lie. I'm not sure whether this
means the same as when a European talks of white lies. I'm
not sure what sort of lies those are, saying that India is giving
two million pounds to our campaign. This is an attempt to
make this movement appear to be directed from outside, led
by Nehru, backed by non-South Africans. This is done to divide us non-Europeans and destroy the unity and friendship
which we are steadily building. England, America and India
are sending us money, but only token sums, not to support us
financially, but to show their sympathy with us. . . . It is said

that at first the Europeans had all the Bible and the non-Europeans had all the land, but now the non-Europeans have all the Bible, and the Europeans have all the land. Yet we will not take it by force; we do not use nor advocate force.[8]

At one stage, a police officer came up to the platform, and Dr. Naicker, after a few minutes, announced that there were complaints about noise, and asked that the loud-speakers should be toned down. Someone in the crowd swore. His neighbours turned quickly on him.

Indian and African speakers alternated, and the speaker after Dr. Naicker was from the African National Congress. He developed a favourite theme with non-white political audiences, the deceit of the white man. . . . He described the poverty of the reserves, and the effect that culling the cattle would have on an already land-hungry, cattle-hungry people. With ironical humour, he commented on the white man's myth that the discriminatory laws are for the benefit of the people discriminated against. 'The laws they say are good for us. The pass-laws—they are good for us. When they take away our cattle—it is good for us. When they take our houses—good for us. They say, no rights till you're civilized. It's like saying you can't go into the water until you can swim perfectly.' . . .

Mr. J. N. Singh was then announced as 'leader of to-day's batch,' and he stepped forward to the microphone. 'We are civilized men,' he declared, 'not barbarians, and we must not rest until the Europeans respect us and our women.' Standing quite still a little behind him were his wife and her sister and Mrs. Naicker, a matron draped in deep red. 'We will not let ourselves be terrorized, nor will we accept moral degradation. In Port Elizabeth and Kimberley, East London and Johannesburg, the police have shot and killed our people like animals. I ask you to stand and think for a short time of those who have died and to sing softly in prayer.'

The crowd sang and, when the song ended, Mr. Singh discussed the rights of non-whites to live like human beings. This, and not lawlessness, he said, was the aim of the campaign of defiance against unjust laws.

Dr. Naicker stood up and spoke with clear emphasis: 'I want you all to listen very carefully. Mr. Singh and his batch are now going to walk to the Berea Road station to be arrested. None of you must follow him. Demonstrations are no longer allowed under the Riotous Assemblies Act. Stay here peacefully till the meeting is over.' As Mr. Singh and his company moved away, accompanied by an observer from the

---

[8] Notes were taken in longhand throughout the meeting and, though the quotations are not verbatim, they are very close to what was said.

meeting, the crowd watched without stirring from the ground. A police car drove slowly off.

A youth-leader of the African National Congress stepped jauntily up to the microphone. His words, aggressively self-assured and demagogic, were very different in tone from those of previous speakers. 'We must not look to the past,' he cried, 'but forward. *Afrika!*' . . .

* * * * *

A loud noise, like a shot, suddenly rang out, once and again. The crowd tensed, heads turned. A police car moved slowly round. Eyes showed the unspoken fears. I understood then how easily a crowd can stampede to action and self-destruction.

But the speaker was unperturbed. After commenting on events in Kenya and other parts of Africa, he ended on a note of triumph: 'To you who are young and whose blood is hot, we say catch the bull by its horns. *Afrika!*'

At this stage, Dr. Naicker announced the arrest of the re-sisters. 'I rejoice to tell you that our people have been safely arrested. *Afrika!*' The crowd relaxed. Then Dr. Naicker commented on the position of the governing Nationalist Party and of the opposition United Party, the similarity of outlook on the non-European question, and the United Party's pandering to race-prejudice to catch votes; and he predicted that the United Party had already lost the next election, because it had no policy. 'If the Nationalist Party told the United Party to go to the toilet, it would go. [Laughter.] *Afrika!*'

* * * * *

The crowd sang 'Let Africa Return,' and all the time men and women moved forward and made their contributions. Then they sang the African anthem, *Nkosi Sikelel'iAfrika.*

NKOSI SIKELEL'IAFRIKA	LORD BLESS AFRICA
Nkosi Sikelel'iAfrika!	Lord bless Africa!
Maluphakanyis'udumo lwayo!	Exalted be its fame!
Yizwa imithandawo yethu!	Hear our prayers!
Nkosi Sikelela!	Lord grant thy blessing!
Woza, moya,	Come, spirit,
woza, woza,	come, come.

* * * * *

The arrest of Mr. Singh was the second act in the development of the drama of passive resistance, and, since it took place off-stage, I am giving an account of a subsequent arrest at the Berea Road railway station, a favoured area in Durban for the defiance of apartheid laws.

In Durban, the resisters had a 'Gentleman's agreement' to notify the railway police in advance of the intention to commit a breach of railway apartheid regulations, so that the arrest would be effected with a minimum of disorganization. On the following Sunday, Mr. Ismail Meer, one of the vice-presidents of the Natal Indian Congress, led a batch of resisters from the meeting-place to the Berea Road station, only to find the entrance barred by the police. In a truck near by were more police fully armed and there were also police in the cars which had followed the resisters from the meeting-place. Since it was impossible to enter the European waiting-room peacefully, Mr. Meer returned with his fellow resisters to the meeting, and reported what had happened. He described the incident as a breach of faith, and as a victory over apartheid. The non-Europeans were now so politically conscious that the South African Government was obliged to use the police in order to prevent non-Europeans entering the European section.

* * * * *

Far from being complacent in their 'victory,' and relieved that it had been gained without suffering, the resisters felt frustrated by the miscarriage of their plans, and resolved to repeat their act of defiance, without first notifying the police. On the next day or the day after, they drove up to the Berea Road station in two cars. No policemen barred the entrance, and Mr. Meer led fourteen resisters without hindrance into the waiting-room marked 'Europeans Only, *Alleen vir Blankes.*' There were seven Indian men, apart from Mr. Meer, and seven Africans—four men and three women. . . .

At first, the resisters were restrained, sitting very still and occasionally speaking quietly. Then, as the minutes passed and nothing happened, there were obvious signs of tension. Some wiped perspiration from their brows; they began to smoke; they responded quickly to unexpected noises outside the waiting-room, clearly bracing themselves for arrest. Then after a time they seemed to relax a little, and moved around talking to each other, or they read, trying to appear unconcerned. At one stage an African, with a beautifully dressed baby in his arms, seeing non-Europeans in the waiting-room, almost came and sat down, but someone called out to him and he quickly removed himself.

At last, after the resisters had waited almost an hour, three white policemen, armed with revolvers, suddenly marched into the waiting-room. They asked for the leader and Mr. Meer stood up and spoke quietly to them. The police then placed all the resisters under arrest for trespassing in the European waiting-room. . . .

From then on, the resisters were under the control of the police, and the next acts followed the ordinary process of law. The resisters did not ask to be released on bail, but spent the night in the cells. The following morning they were brought up for trial before a magistrate. The court was packed with a mixed group of supporters. There were also two Europeans, but the usual apartheid in seating arrangements was not observed. The Clerk of the Court read the charge, and the resisters all admitted guilt. Mr. Meer was asked whether he had anything to say, and, following precedent, he explained the reasons for the defiance of apartheid regulations. Then the magistrate sentenced Mr. Meer to seven days' imprisonment and the other accused to fourteen days' imprisonment, with the option of a fine, which they all declined.[9] The resisters were removed from court, and the crowd slowly dispersed, having been prohibited from demonstrating support.

The separate acts, which together constituted passive resistance, were familiar to South African society. The non-European political meeting, with its analysis of white domination, its aspirations for 'liberation', was not new. So too, prosecutions for minor statutory offences are a familiar aspect of the structure of South African race relations: every week, the South African courts dispose of thousands of non-European statutory offenders. Even the arrangements for the imprisonment of short-term offenders sufficed also for the passive resisters.

The motives of the resisters were, however, profoundly different from those of the ordinary statutory offender. They felt themselves to be dedicated. They deliberately defied the laws, and the breach of statutory regulations became charged with new meaning. They voluntarily sought imprisonment, and imprisonment became a mark of achievement. It was to this spirit of resistance that the whites responded with active emotions of hate or sympathy and not with their normal indifference to non-European statutory offenders. For the whites, too, the breach of statutory regulations became charged with new meaning.

* * * * *

During the three years between the coming to power of the Nationalist Party and the passive resistance campaign in

[9] This was an unusual sentence. The more usual sentence in Durban for this offence was either twenty-one days' or one month's imprisonment, and it was not the practice to show more leniency to the leaders. Mr. Meer later spoke of his sentence with obvious embarrassment. Ready to sacrifice himself, subjected to the strains of uncertain police and Government retaliation, the leniency of his sentence came as an anti-climax, almost as a humiliation.

1952, the political organizations of the non-whites experimented with the boycott and large-scale demonstrations. The 1949 Conference of the African National Congress accepted generally the policy of uncompromising non-collaboration with the Government and agreed specifically to boycott Advisory Boards, the Natives' Representative Council, and indirect parliamentary representation. Dr. A. B. Xuma, the President-General of the African National Congress, opposed this policy on the grounds that there were sufficient collaborators to ensure the perfect working of these institutions, and therefore urged that Congress should use the available machinery for its own purposes. He was overruled, and replaced, as President-General, by Dr. James S. Moroka, who firmly pledged himself to the boycott.

Three major demonstrations were held in 1950. The first, a Freedom of Speech Convention, was opened by Dr. Moroka in Johannesburg. This was followed by May Day or Freedom Day demonstrations against discrimination, in which the Communist Party played an active, sponsoring role. Africans, Indians and Coloureds took part, and many children stayed away from school. Disturbances broke out in the late afternoon and evening, and the demonstrators suffered heavy casualties. The third demonstration, called by Dr. Moroka, was a National Day of Protest against the Group Areas Bill and the Suppression of Communism Bill, and a day of mourning for Africans who had lost their lives in the struggle for liberation.

*   *   *   *   *

In the following year, 1951, the proposed removal of coloured voters from the common roll by the Separate Representation of Voters Bill spread the struggle further. Coloureds formed the Franchise Action Council to oppose the Bill, and on May 7th staged an effective strike in Port Elizabeth and the Cape Peninsula, with some support from Africans and Indians; again, many children stayed away from school.

The broadening of the struggle, and mounting apartheid legislation, provided a favourable setting for concerted action. A conference of the national executives of the African National Congress and the South African Indian Congress, with representatives of the Franchise Action Council, met in July 1951, and appointed a Joint Planning Council. It was given the task of co-ordinating the efforts of the national organizations of the African, Indian and Coloured peoples in a mass campaign for the repeal of the Pass Laws, the Group Areas Act, the Separate Representation of Voters Act, and the Bantu Authorities Act, and for the withdrawal of the 'so-called' rural rehabilitation scheme, including the policy of stock-limitation. The plan submitted by this Council, as amended by the African National Congress, forms the basis of the passive resistance campaign.

Blue-print for Resistance

The Joint Planning Council, reporting in November 1951, recommended that the African National Congress, supported by the South African Indian Congress and other democratic organizations, should call upon the Government to take steps for the repeal of the offending laws and policies. Failing repeal, the two Congresses should embark 'upon mass action for a redress of the just and legitimate grievances of the majority of the South African people.'

Two alternative dates, April 6th and June 26th, 1952, were suggested for the commencement of the struggle. April 6th was chosen because it was the day set aside by the white population for the tercentenary celebrations of Van Riebeeck's landing at the Cape. From the point of view of the Joint Planning Council, it marked

'one of the greatest turning points in South African history by the advent of European settlers in the country, followed by colonial and imperialist exploitation which has degraded, humiliated and kept in bondage the vast masses of the non-white people'

* * * * *

The Council recommended that the struggle should take the form of defiance of unjust laws, that is, the deliberate breach 'of certain selected laws and regulations which are undemocratic, unjust, racially discriminatory and repugnant to the natural rights of man.' Three stages of defiance were suggested: first, selected and trained persons to go into action in the big centres, such as Johannesburg, Cape Town, Bloemfontein, Port Elizabeth and Durban; second, an increase in the number of volunteer corps and centres of operation; and, third, mass action on a country-wide scale, embracing both urban and rural areas.

Two factors, the degree of obnoxiousness of the law and the possibility of defying it, determined the selection of specific acts of resistance. Africans are not vitally affected by the Group Areas Act; their obvious targets are the many deeply resented restrictions on freedom of movement imposed by the Pass Laws, which lend themselves easily to defiance. The very existence of Indians is threatened by the Group Areas Act, which can only be defied when steps are taken to impose racial separation; Indians are not restricted by the Pass Laws, though they are denied free movement across provincial borders. The Coloureds are not so adversely affected by the plans for racial segregation as the Indians, and enjoy a freedom of movement denied the Africans. All three groups suffer more or less equally under discrimination in public services and amenities.

These considerations explain the recommendations of the Joint Planning Council in regard to acts of resistance. Defiance of the Pass Laws was suggested for the African National Congress. For the South African Indian Congress, the planners recommended action against provincial barriers, apartheid laws such as train, post-office and railway station segregation, and the Group Areas Act, *if and when possible,* while general apartheid segregation and the Group Areas Act, *if and when possible,* were held out as targets for the Franchise Action Council.

Similarly, differences in the type of discrimination against the various sections of the non-white peoples influenced the organization of volunteers. The plan called for a number of volunteer corps, each in charge of a leader, responsible for the maintenance of order and discipline and for leading the corps into action when called upon to do so. The membership of each volunteer corps was restricted to the members of a particular racial group (to the members of the African National Congress, or of the South African Indian Congress, or of the Franchise Action Council or other organization of Coloureds). Only in cases where the law or regulation applied 'commonly to all groups' would racially mixed units be allowed.

The effective organization of the campaign posed the problem of finding a focus of resistance which would involve the rural African population in struggles initiated by the politically more sophisticated urban dwellers. This was all the more urgent, since the ready reserve of labour in the rural areas and the migrant-labour system place the urban passive resisters at the mercy of their white employers. Mahatma Gandhi found a focus of mass resistance in the apparently trivial issue of the Indian salt tax. Pandit Nehru certainly did not anticipate the success of the struggle against the salt tax, unrelated as it was to the movement for national independence.[10] The task of the Joint Planning Council was to select targets of resistance which would serve as a South African counterpart to the salt tax, and carry resistance to the masses.

[10] *Nehru on Gandhi* (New York: Day, 1948), p. 54. 'Salt suddenly became a mysterious word, a word of power. The salt tax was to be attacked, the salt laws were to be broken. We were quite bewildered and could not quite fit in a national struggle with common salt. . . . What was the point of making a list of some political and social reforms—good in themselves no doubt—when we Were talking in terms of independence?'

The planners sought these targets in the Government policy of stock-limitation, and in the Population Registration Act. They recommended that during the struggle against the Pass Laws the rural Africans should be asked not to co-operate with the authorities in culling cattle or limiting livestock; and they suggested, as a possible means for carrying the struggle from the second to the mass phase, the organized resistance of all sections against registration under the Population Registration Act. Stock-limitation must have seemed a most appropriate focus for resistance, since cattle are a source of prestige among rural Africans, a symbol of wealth, and intimately connected with the rights and obligations of families. Yet the salt tax fired the imagination of rural Indians, while stock-limitation has indeed given rise to bitterness, but only to sporadic resistance. The explanation of these different reactions would seem to lie partly in the spiritual inspiration of Mahatma Gandhi, and partly in the fact that the South African Government has not prosecuted its stock-limitation policy with vigour. Similarly, the Population Registration Act must have seemed a likely target; it imposes a general duty to register, and lends itself readily to passive resistance on a mass scale. Again, hopes of a mass response have not been realized. Registration proceeds with no sign of resistance.

The choice of passive resistance as a form of struggle appears to have been governed by considerations of expediency rather than by the ethic of Satyagraha.

* * * * *

The members of the Joint Planning Council would be well aware of the danger that their liberation movement might be blunted if the struggle were directed against specific incidents of discrimination, instead of against the principle of discrimination as such. Hence, they related the campaign to the broad principles of democracy on the following terms:

> All people irrespective of the national groups they may belong to, and irrespective of the colour of their skin, are entitled to live a full and free life on the basis of the fullest equality. Full democratic rights with a direct say in the affairs of the Government are the inalienable rights of every man—a right which in South Africa must be realized now if the country is to be saved from social chaos and tyranny and from the evils arising out of the existing denial of franchise to vast masses of the population on grounds of race and colour. . . .

At the same time, the planners drew a distinction between these final objectives of the struggle for freedom and the immediate objectives of the resistance movement, which they declared to be the repeal of the unjust laws mentioned in their terms of reference. They conceived the campaign as a first step in the progressive extension of democratic rights to the non-whites.

An Exchange of Letters

The African National Congress, at its annual meeting in December 1951, adopted the report of the Joint Planning Council and selected April 6th, 1952, for the beginning of the struggle. The South African Indian Congress resolved to support the African National Congress; and the third partner, the Franchise Action Council, pledged its support of the demonstrations scheduled for April 6th.

In accordance with the blue-print for passive resistance, prepared by the Joint Planning Council, the African National Congress sent a letter (undated) to the Prime Minister, Dr. D. F. Malan. It was signed by Dr. J. S. Moroka and Mr. W. M. Sisulu, the President-General and Secretary-General, and took the form of a legal demand: '. . . Conference unanimously resolved to call upon your Government, as we hereby do, to repeal the aforementioned Acts,[11] by NOT LATER THAN THE 29TH DAY OF FEBRUARY 1952, failing which the African National Congress will hold protest demonstrations and meetings on the 6th day of April 1952, as a prelude to the implementation of the plan for the defiance of unjust laws.'

The preamble to the demand drew attention to the founding of the African National Congress in 1912,

'to protect and advance the interests of the African people in all matters affecting them and to attain their freedom from all discriminatory laws whatsoever. To this end, the African National Congress has, since its establishment, endeavoured by every constitutional method to bring to the notice of the Government the legitimate demands of the African people and has repeatedly pressed, in particular, their inherent right to be directly represented in Parliament, Provincial and Municipal Councils and in all councils of state.' The Government, 'through its repressive policy of trusteeship, segregation and apartheid,[12] and through legislation that continues to insult

[11] Pass Laws, Stock Limitation, the Suppression of Communism Act of 1950, the Group Areas Act of 1950, the Bantu Authorities Act of 1951, and the Separate Representation of Voters Act of 1951.

[12] It is an indication of the political outlook of the writers that trusteeship, segregation, and apartheid are treated as different labels for the same commodity—race domination.

and degrade the African people by depriving them of fundamental human rights enjoyed in all democratic communities, have categorically rejected our offer of co-operation.' In consequence, there has been a gradual worsening of the social, economic and political position of the African people, aggravated by recent legislation. 'The African National Congress as the National Organization of the African people cannot remain quiet on an issue that is a matter of life and death to the people; to do so would be a betrayal of the trust and confidence placed upon it by the African people.'

*   *   *   *   *

THE CAMPAIGN

Heralded by a day of prayer in many locations throughout the Union, the campaign was launched on June 26th, 1952. Disciplined volunteer corps, pledged to the aims of the resistance movement and under the control of trained leaders, deliberately committed acts of civil disobedience. These acts, in general, took one or other of the following forms:

Entering a location without a permit.
Being out at night without a curfew pass.
Sitting on railway seats marked 'Europeans only.'
Entering the European waiting-room on railway stations.
Travelling in railway coaches reserved for Europeans.
Entering the European section of the post office.

In other words, the only law directly challenged was the Pass Law, symbol of domination for the whites, and of subjection for the Africans. For the rest, the resisters' acts attacked apartheid regulations, mainly on the railways.

The movement developed in the main urban centres, as recommended by the Joint Planning Council for the first phase of the struggle. The Witwatersrand area and Port Elizabeth entered the campaign on the opening date, and they were followed by the major South African cities. Two of these, Cape Town and Durban, delayed their entry, and there was an uneven pattern of participation in the different regions. In the provinces of Natal and the Orange Free State, the only active centres were Durban and Bloemfontein, each contributing a small quota of resisters. The whole of the Cape Western area was relatively inactive, and even the Transvaal, the industrial core of the Union with an immense urban African proletariat, did not participate as fully as might have been expected. In contrast, the Eastern Cape, which includes the port cities of

East London and Port Elizabeth, provided the main body of support. This appears from the following figures showing the regional distribution of resisters:

Eastern Cape	5,719
Western Cape, Mafeking, Kimberley	423
Transvaal	1,911
Natal	246
Free State	258
	8,557

(The Secretarial Report to the 21st Conference of the South African Indian Congress, July 9th–11th, 1954.)

The reasons for these differences are not at all clear. The level of participation in Natal was exceedingly low, when compared with the extent of Indian resistance in the 1946 campaign. . . .

*   *   *   *   *

The months of August, September and October mark the peak periods of resistance. In the last five days of June, 146 volunteered, in July, 1,504, in August, 2,015, in September, 2,258, in October, 2,354, and in November and December only 280. . . . The first stage of the resistance movement was completed in October; selected groups of volunteers had defied the laws in the main centres, and resistance had, indeed, already spread to some of the smaller towns. Thereafter, resistance, far from developing in the rural areas according to plan, declined precipitately.

Conduct of the Campaign

While the plan of the Joint Planning Council was shaped by tactical considerations, the Satyagraha form of passive resistance clearly influenced the actual conduct of the campaign.

The activities were open and public. No attempt was made to conceal intentions or to deceive the authorities. On the contrary, the resisters co-operated fully with the police and the Government. Thus Mr. Nelson Mandela, a lawyer and one of the leaders of the African National Congress, handed the following letter to the Magistrate at Boksburg on the date of the commencement of the campaign:

SIR,—We have been directed by the Joint Action Committee of the African National Congress, Transvaal, and the Transvaal Indian Congress, to advise you that in terms of the decision of the Congresses the persons in the list attached herein will defy the permit regulations and deliberately court imprisonment by entering Boksburg Location today at 2.30 p.m. without obtaining the necessary permits. Mr. Nana Sita, President of the Transvaal Indian Congress, will lead the batch.

Yours faithfully,
N. THANDRAY, Secretary, Transvaal Indian Congress.
S. SELLO, Secretary, African National Congress (Transvaal).

(Preparatory Examination of W. M. Sisulu and 19 others, p. 286.)

* * * * *

Because of this influence of the Satyagraha type of resistance, the resisters cheerfully lined up for arrest, and sought to sustain arrest, trial and imprisonment with good humour. Hence, too, when the police made no arrest, the resisters offered themselves again and again. Mr. Ismail Meer's batch was obliged to repeat its attempt to enter the European section of the Berea Road railway station, and Dr. Wilson Conco, Chairman of the African National Congress (Natal), with his group of volunteers, paraded the streets for two nights, soliciting arrest.

* * * * *

. . . Under the inspiration of Satyagraha, the resisters generally sought to minimize bitterness by their selection of defiance acts. The Berea Road railway station in Durban and the New Brighton railway station in Port Elizabeth are largely used by non-whites; entry into the waiting-room reserved for Europeans at these stations would directly affect few white passengers. Walking the streets without a curfew pass and going into an African location without a permit are acts purely domestic to the non-whites themselves; were it not for police action and the newspapers, the ruling group would be completely unaware of any change in the pattern of South African life.

When sentenced, the resisters, with few exceptions, chose imprisonment, rejecting the tempting option of a fine. Nor did they plead in mitigation. Instead, following precedent in India, the resisters used the court as a platform from which they might reach out to the conscience of the ruling class. . . .

* * * * *

It is not difficult to understand the magistrate's impatient reaction to protests against the laws which he is obliged to administer. Many of these protests took the almost routine form of a direct indictment of unjust laws, and gave reasoned explanations of the motives for deliberate defiance and the voluntary submission to punishment. Others touched deeper chords of emotion and of the yearning for freedom. The statement read by Mr. S. Mokoena, Bloemfontein Volunteer-in-Chief, to

276 NON-VIOLENT POWER WITH EXPRESS PRINCIPLE

the Bloemfontein magistrate is a moving example of the court
literature of the resistance movement:

'We have decided voluntarily, and without any form of
compulsion having been exerted upon us, to defy the laws
which not only we non-Europeans regard as extremely unjust, but also a growing number of Europeans in this
country.

'It has been suggested by our European administrators,
Your Worship included, that we should ventilate our
grievances through the "proper channels" . . . You will
be the first to agree, Your Worship, that we have exhausted all attempts to air our genuine sufferings through
the so-called "proper channels."

'The history of our struggle for liberation is a sad story
of unfulfilled or broken promises by our White administrators. It is a history characterized by obsequious representations and cap-in-hand deputations. The Natives'
Representative Council was a "proper channel"—albeit an
ineffective one—through which we could draw the attention of the Government to our sorry lot. The Council is
now no more. The Location Advisory Boards and the
Bungas, toy telephones that they actually are, are also
some of the oft-spoken "proper channels."

'Theirs is an ineffectual voice. Our so-called European
Native representatives in Parliament are yet other "proper
channels." These representatives were the first to admit
that theirs was a voice in the wilderness as they were bat-
tling against "a stone wall of colour prejudice" in Parliament. . . .

* * * * *

'It is interesting to speculate, Your Worship, what the
reaction of the European would be, were he, just by sheer
miracle, to discover himself an African just overnight and
thus be subjected to the thousand and one irksome discriminatory laws that our people have borne for centuries
with Christian-like fortitude. This I say, because just recently two South African Members of Parliament protested strongly against alleged discrimination, real or im-
aginary, to which, so they said, they were subjected in
India; discrimination which by mere comparison with
what is our daily dose of this satanic doctrine is not
worthy of the name. And, to come nearer home, Europeans are up in arms in South Africa against the introduction of the population registration measure which they
regard as the extension of the pass system to them.

'The local curfew regulation which is one of our tar-

gets of defiance is extremely unfair. Hitherto, our movements in town were limited up to 10 p.m. But recently the
Minister of Native Affairs, with the approval of the City
Council, brought down the time to 9 p.m., and this notwithstanding the protestations of the "proper channel,"
the local Native Advisory Board, that is. The majority of
trains leave the station long after 9 p.m., and many an
African man or woman has been arrested for the "crime"
of having gone to see somebody off at the station after
9 p.m.

*   *   *   *   *

'We do not quarrel with Your Worship when you say
you have no alternative but to punish us for deliberately
breaking the unjust laws; that is the unenviable duty you
are bound to carry out. But, with due respect to Your
Worship, we wish to state that punishment, no matter how
severe, can be no deterrent to us. We have undertaken
this campaign fully expecting such punishment. We have
steeled and braced ourselves up to bear whatever punishment may come our way. And, happily, we derive encouragement and inspiration from the knowledge that
practically the whole of the African population in Bloemfontein is four-square behind us, if not actively, then at
least morally.' (The *Bantu World,* November 15th,
1952.)

But the Courts were not an effective forum for reaching the
great white public. Only brief depersonalized accounts of the
proceedings appeared in the newspapers circulating among
white readers. The protest statements were rarely mentioned;
laconic news items, 40 ARRESTED FOR DEFYING APARTHEID
LAWS, 88 MORE ARRESTS, engulfed the individual strivings and
aspirations, inevitably perhaps in view of the many resistance
acts and consequent decline in news value.

The resisters were therefore thrown back on their own resources to make known the sacrifices of the resistance movement, and for the most part reached only sections of the non-
whites themselves. Mimeographed news-sheets, such as *Afrika*
and *Flash,* filled in the skeleton outlines provided by the national Press. More effective were the meetings associated with
different stages of civil disobedience acts; the dispatch of the
volunteers (as when Mr. J. N. Singh's batch left the public
meeting at Durban to defy railway apartheid regulations), the
trial and the return from gaol.

*   *   *   *   *

The prayer meetings, most marked in the Eastern Cape, the
symbolism of flags and slogans, the resistance songs and the

speeches, the vicarious participation in the suffering of the resisters, served to spread among non-whites the meaning of passive resistance, and to heighten its political and spiritual significance.

The resistance leaders might well feel that the campaign was
a great success. Six thousand volunteers had defied the laws
in the first hundred days of the campaign. A firm control by
the leaders and discipline and good humour among the followers demonstrated the increasing strength of the non-white
organizations. There were occasional outbursts of bitterness,
but remarkably few incidents between the resisters and the
police.

* * * * *

It was precisely at this stage, at the high peak of a successful
campaign, at a time most inauspicious for the aspirations of
the non-whites and most convenient for the Government, that
a series of riots broke out.

The Riots

The immediate causes of the riots are by no means clear.
The Government refused to hold a commission of inquiry; not
that a Government commission would necessarily add to our
understanding. Facts vary with the political viewpoint, especially in Government commissions.

* * * * *

The police and official versions of the riots were given prominence in the national Press. The first disturbance was at Port
Elizabeth, on the afternoon of October 18th, 1952, when a
railway constable at New Brighton station attempted to arrest
two Africans suspected of stealing a drum of paint. According
to the constable's account, the men resisted arrest and other
Africans came to their assistance. In the immediate and ensuing struggle, the constable shot one of the suspected men
who attacked him with a long knife, hit another assailant in
the right breast, fired a shot which glanced off the temple of a
third assailant, wounded in the arm a woman attempting to set
the ticket office alight, and thereafter fired other shots at different groups, who were stoning the station. All told, he admitted
to firing twenty-one shots. (Evidence at the Preparatory Examination of William Gova and 126 Others, Magistrate's
Court, Port Elizabeth, pp. 3–7. At the subsequent trial of some
of the accused, in the case of Regina v. William Gova and 10
Others, the Judge commended the constable for his great courage and devotion to duty in the midst of large numbers of
hostile Africans and in the face of a serious threat to life and
property.)

Police reinforcements arrived to find a crowd of between 2,000 and 3,000 Africans throwing stones at the railway station. They fired a few warning shots in the direction of the crowd, since verbal warnings would have been useless because of the noise. The crowd diminished: some of its members left; others took refuge behind buildings, running out to hurl stones at the police. The latter, a small force, fired on their attackers, action which the Judge held was well within the rights of the police. When there was a lull, the police divided into two bands, one returning to the police station in case it should be attacked, and the other moving on to the railway station. About an hour later, in response to a message, the police entered New Brighton Location. A big crowd was throwing stones at some buildings and burning an overturned lorry. The police fired a few shots at the foremost of the stone-throwers, causing the crowd to scatter, and then discovered the first white fatality, a man with head battered in, clothing torn and covered with blood. There were no further attacks; the police officer went back to the police station with most of his men, and re-entered New Brighton some two hours later in time to rescue a white woman. The cinema was burning, and three white men lay dead on the other side of the road. (Preparatory Examination, pp. 23–9, and Judgment in Regina v. William Gova and 10 Others.)

One company of police fired some fifty shots, the second company about forty shots. The African casualties were seven dead and twenty-seven injured, according to official accounts. . . . The only serious injury to a European policeman was a stone injury on the shin. (Preparatory Examination, pp. 28–9.) Much damage was done to property.

The second incident was at the Denver Native Hostel on November 3rd, 1952, when the residents, who had resolved not to pay an increase in rental from eleven shillings to one pound per month, rushed at a tenant who tendered the rental, shouting that he should be 'hit' and 'killed.' The municipal police took the tenant into the administrative offices, and the crowd threw stones through the windows. Police arrived; the crowd severely damaged a car belonging to the acting superintendent of the hostel and stoned police vehicles and the hostel building. The police fired some shots outside the building, but apparently without injuring the rioters. Later they fired again, this time into the hostel, from the protection of a tunnel or portico and from behind a double iron gate. The regional magistrate, in his judgment at the trial of Moathludi and others on a charge of public violence, held that the first shootings were justified, since there was real danger to life. He was, however, not prepared to take the same view of the later shootings into the hostel, which caused the casualties. He failed to see how anyone who stood behind the gates could have been in danger of life or limb from missiles. (This account of the events is taken from the magistrate's reasons for judgment in Regina *v.* Moathludi and Others, Case No. M.6/53, in the Court of the Regional Magistrate, Southern Transvaal.)

Three Africans were shot dead and four were wounded. One constable received an injury from a missile which struck his collar bone. In evidence, a police constable stated that 'our instructions are to shoot to hit where stones are being thrown. This was done with a view to injure us.' (P. 108 of the Preparatory Examination.) Other constables told the Court that they were instructed to, and did, shoot to kill; the officer-in-charge, on the other hand, contended that his instructions were to wound and not to kill. (See the magistrate's reasons for judgment.)

On November 8th, 1952, at No. 2 Location, Kimberley, three young Africans bought beer at the municipal beer hall, and when they had finished drinking, stood up, shouted '*Afrika!*', threw the beer mugs in the air, and tramped on them. When they were ordered out, most of the other beer-drinkers followed them. A crowd gathered and started to stone the building. Members of the Municipal police, who attempted to drive them off, were obliged to take refuge in the hall, where they were trapped. (Evidence of a beer-hall employee, and summing up of the magistrate at the inquest proceedings on the African dead; *Natal Daily News,* November 26th, 1952, and December 3rd, 1952.) A small police contingent arrived, were stoned, and opened fire under instructions 'not to shoot women and children if this could be avoided and to shoot only those actually stoning the bus or police.' The mob scattered, re-formed, continued throwing stones, and the police withdrew when ammunition ran low. 'Attacks were repelled only by shooting. Warnings had no effect.' (Police account, the *Natal Mercury,* November 26th, 1952.)

The beer hall and administrative block were now on fire. The police returned with a force of seventy men, and, under a heavy rain of stones, fired only at selected targets. . . .

The magistrate came to the conclusion that the police on all occasions had fired in self-defence. . . .

*   *   *   *   *

In contrast to the official versions, little has been heard of the views of the Africans as to the immediate causes of the riots. Some laid responsibility on *agents provocateurs.* (For example, Dr. W. F. Nkomo, as quoted in the *Bantu World,* November 29th, 1952.) In this connection, a comment of the director of the South African Institute of Race Relations has some relevance. 'In both Port Elizabeth and Kimberley, Eu-

ropeans stated that strangers had come into the neighbour-
hood previously to the riots. The implication is that strangers
to the cities concerned might have been deliberate immediate
causes—"not our own Natives".' (Report by the Director on
visits to Port Elizabeth, East London and Kimberley in connection with the riots, R.R.9/53, January 12th, 1953.)

Others commented on the fact that anti-social elements, and
more particularly *tsotsis,* took advantage of the situation to
express their destructive proclivities, and that the Government,
by its suppression of responsible African leaders, was handing
over the leadership of the Africans to the *tsotsis.* These *tsotsis*
are maladjusted juveniles, frustrated by the general conditions
of urban African life and the lack of facilities for schooling
and employment. Some evidence of the extent to which juveniles were thought to be involved in the East London riots
is given by the numbers charged before the Courts—forty-eight
of a total of ninety-one. (W. B. Ngakane, *Investigation into
Case Histories of African Juveniles involved in the East London Riots.* Report by the South African Institute of Race Relations, R.R.41/53, April 21st, 1953.)

Another source lays responsibility squarely on the police,
emphasizing the way in which the role of the police had been
re-defined by the Minister of Justice, and seeking to demonstrate that the readiness of the police to shoot precipitated the
riots. According to this source, the people in East London location were holding a *bona-fide* prayer meeting. While the
preacher was reading about the oppression of the Israelites, a
police officer in charge of two lorry-loads of armed police decided that he could not permit such subversive theology and
ordered the crowd to disperse within five minutes. The meeting immediately broke up. In less than two minutes, while people were walking away, the police officer is said to have ordered a charge, a second charge, then shots were fired, and a
man was killed. The police thereupon climbed into their lorries and drove up and down the main streets of the location
firing at people and into houses. Nobody had attacked the
police—it would have been suicide to do so. There are reported to be bullet holes all over the location, many far from
the scene of the disturbances.[13]

*   *   *   *   *

The deeper causes of the riots are to be found in the social
and economic conditions of the African people and in the

[13] I cannot take the matter any further than the presentation of
the official version and an unofficial counterversion. Alexander
Campbell, in *The Heart of Africa* (New York: Knopf, 1954),
Chapter IV, gives an account of his own inquiries into the events of
the East London riots.

policy and application of white domination. The immediate causes will never be known, but it seems reasonably clear that in Port Elizabeth and East London the taking of the lives of innocent white people, the destruction and the brutality were a mob reaction of a type all too familiar throughout the world, and a retaliation for the police shooting of their own people; that this retaliation was anti-white, directed against the few white people in the locations, and the buildings which symbolized the white man's world; and that the relationship between the police and the African people is one of deep antagonism and a threat to the peace of the country. There can be no doubt of the violence of the mobs, once aroused, and of the need for firm police action. But I find it difficult to understand how the police themselves escaped with sc few injuries if the threat to life was dangerous enough to justify the drastic measures they used.

*   *   *   *   *

Suspension of the Campaign

Though the immediate causes of the riots are obscure, their effects were to damp down the spirit of resistance. It is, of course, conceivable that the campaign had reached its peak prior to the riots, and was, in any event, in process of decline.

The resistance leaders vigorously denied the charge that they were responsible for the riots, and their conduct was entirely consistent with innocence. Dr. Moroka immediately issued a statement on behalf of the African National Congress and the African people, strongly condemning the violent disturbances at Port Elizabeth. Both Congresses demanded an impartial commission of inquiry. They showed no anxiety whatever that the findings might possibly be against them and they could not have known that the Government would refuse to set up the usual routine public investigations, after events of such magnitude.

Nor did the Congresses hesitate to charge the Government and police with responsibility for the riots. Dr. J. L. Z. Njongwe, President of the African National Congress (Cape), emphasized that the seven Africans shot dead at Port Elizabeth were killed before a single European had been harmed, and demanded an inquiry so that the facts could be brought into the open. (*Press Digest,* No. 45, October 30th, 1952, p. 451.) The Natal branches of the Congresses called upon the Ministers of Justice and of Lands to stop creating social tension by talking about batons, guns and blood. 'No matter what Nationalist spokesmen say about the Defiance Campaign, the fact remains that our campaign is based on the noble ethics of non-violence and peace. We challenge the Government to prove the contrary. . . . The concept of violence and bloodshed is being spread by the Nationalists and nobody else.' (*Advance*, November 20th, 1952.)

In the same issue, *Advance* reported the contents of a leaflet distributed by the National Action Committee of the two Congresses. The shootings at Kimberley, East London and Denver were described as part of the Government's plot to weaken the defiance campaign and to ruthlessly oppress the non-European people.

'The Government wants—
'to create race riots between European and non-European, Indian and African, and African and Coloured;
'to use the riots and general disturbances to cause panic among the Europeans so as to drive them into the arms of the Nationalists;
'to declare a state of national emergency, to seize absolute power, to cut off the leaders from the people and to impose a fascist dictatorship on the country.

'Its methods are—
'to send out agents among the people to provoke incidents which can be used by the police as a pretext for shooting and to incite and preach race hatred; to accuse the Indians, blame the Africans and praise the Coloureds;
'to use the police for the purpose of inciting racial strife between the Africans and Indians and for the distribution of literature propagating apartheid.'

Non-Europeans were warned not to be provoked, not to 'listen to those who talk against any section of our population—anyone who speaks against the Indian, the Coloured, the Chinese, the African or European is an enemy of the people and an agent of the Government.'

Challenging the Government to hold an inquiry into the recent disturbances, the National Action Committee of the African National Congress and the South African Indian Congress stated that authentic reports strongly suggested that the disturbances were engineered by *provocateurs* and that the 'shooting order' of the Minister of Justice played a major part; failure to hold an inquiry indicated that these riots and disturbances were deliberately incited and provoked by the Government. (*Advance*, November 20th, 1952.)

*   *   *   *   *

. . . So little abashed was the African National Congress at allegations of complicity in the riots, and so little intimidated by threats of drastic action, that on November 10th, 1952, it

organized in Port Elizabeth a one-day strike against the imposition of a curfew. The Coloureds did not participate, but as
far as the Africans were concerned, 'the strike was 96% successful and brought to Port Elizabeth industrialists the realization that the African community had a power of organization
which they could not afford to ignore, particularly in such a
vulnerable industrial port as Port Elizabeth.' (Report of the
South African Institute of Race Relations, R.R.9/53.)

Yet notwithstanding all these activities after the Port Elizabeth riots, and the determination of the leaders, the resistance
movement was tailing off into suspension.

* * * * *

In Cape Town, four white resisters, three of them University students, marched into the non-European booths of the
General Post Office, and began writing telegrams to Dr.
Malan. They were arrested and removed by the police. A
week later, a white trade union organizer defied the apartheid
regulations in a Johannesburg post office; presumably his
telegram to the Minister of Justice, calling for the abolition of
colour discrimination, has not yet been dispatched.

Congress leaders welcomed this participation of white resisters, partly as a demonstration to their own followers that
all whites are not oppressors, and partly as a means of placing
the struggle on the clear basis of principle, rather than of race
conflict.

* * * * *

Possibly the impending general elections were a factor in
the final suspension of the movement. While the resistance
leaders did not distinguish between the election programmes
of the Government and opposition parties—the non-European
policies of the two parties were not fundamentally different—
they nevertheless did not wish to do anything which would
ensure the return of the Nationalist Party to power. Thus they
refrained from taking advantage of the Appellate Court decision in the case of Regina v. Lusu (March 1953), when they
might have flooded, with impunity, many of the amenities reserved for whites.

Certainly, the arrest of the leaders must have contributed to
the decline of the campaign. The new laws were also an important factor, as stated by Chief Albert Luthuli, the recently
elected President-General of the African National Congress.
'Round about November,' he said, 'there was a Government
Proclamation which made certain things illegal. Parliament
later passed the Public Safety and the Criminal Law Amendment Acts. In the light of that, it was necessary for the organization to take stock of the situation. It meant studying our

programme and the new situation to adapt our plans and to see what we could do.' (The *Leader*, April 24th, 1953.) Clearly the riots played a decisive role. . . .

June 26th, 1953, the first anniversary of the launching of the campaign, was observed as a day of commemoration and rededication. In a message to Africans and their allies, Chief Luthuli appealed for the lighting of bonfires or candles or lanterns outside their homes, 'as a symbol of the spark of freedom which we are determined to keep alive in our hearts, and as a sign to freedom-lovers that we are keeping the vigil on that night.' Older members of each household should tell the younger 'the story, so far as they know it, of the struggle of the African people in particular, and the non-Europeans in general, for their liberation.' (The *Leader*, June 26th, 1953.)

The passive resistance campaign was already passing into the history of the liberation movement.

Chief Albert Luthuli: THE ROAD TO FREEDOM IS VIA THE CROSS

I have been dismissed from the Chieftainship of the Abase-Makolweni Tribe in the Groutville Mission Reserve. I presume that this has been done by the Governor-General in his capacity as Supreme Chief of the "Native" people of the Union of South Africa save those of the Cape Province. I was democratically elected to this position in 1935 by the people of Groutville Mission Reserve and was duly approved and appointed by the Governor-General.

Path of Moderation

Previous to being a chief I was a school teacher for about seventeen years. In these past thirty years or so I have striven with tremendous zeal and patience to work for the progress and welfare of my people and for their harmonious relations with other sections of our multi-racial society in the Union of South Africa. In this effort I always pursued what liberal-minded people rightly regarded as the path of moderation. Over this great length of time I have, year after year, gladly spent hours of my time with such organisations as the Church and its various agencies such as the Christian Council of South Africa, the Joint Council of Europeans and Africans and the now defunct Native Representative Council.

* * * * *

What have been the fruits of my many years of moderation? Has there been any reciprocal tolerance or moderation from the Government, be it Nationalist or United Party? No! On the contrary, the past thirty years have seen the greatest number of Laws restricting our rights and progress until to-day we have reached a stage where we have almost no rights at all: no adequate land for our occupation, our only asset, cattle, dwindling, no security of homes, no decent and re-munerative employment, more restrictions to freedom of movement through passes, curfew regulations, influx control measures; in short we have witnessed in these years an intensi-fication of our subjection to ensure and protect white su-premacy.

A New Spirit

It is with this background and with a full sense of responsi-bility that, under the auspices of the African National Con-gress (Natal), I have joined my people in the new spirit that moves them to-day, the spirit that revolts openly and boldly against injustice and expresses itself in a determined and non-violent manner. Because of my association with the African National Congress in this new spirit which has found an effec-tive and legitimate way of expression in the non-violent Passive Resistance Campaign, I was given a two-week limit ultimatum by the Secretary for Native Affairs calling upon me to choose between the African National Congress and the chieftainship of the Groutville Mission Reserve. He alleged that my associa-tion with Congress in its non-violent Passive Resistance Cam-paign was an act of disloyalty to the State. I did not, and do not, agree with this view. Viewing non-Violent Passive Re-sistance as a non-revolutionary and, therefore, a most legiti-mate and humane political pressure technique for a people denied all effective forms of constitutional striving, I saw no real conflict in my dual leadership of my people: leader of this tribe as chief and political leader in Congress.

Servant of People

I saw no cause to resign from either. . . .

* * * * *

I do not wish to challenge my dismissal, but I would like to suggest that in the interest of the institution of chieftainship in these modern times of democracy, the Government should de-fine more precisely and make more widely known the status, functions and privileges of chiefs.

My view has been, and still is, that a chief is primarily a servant of his people. . . .

* * * * *

Laws and conditions that tend to debase human personality —a God-given force—be they brought about by the State or other individuals, must be relentlessly opposed in the spirit of defiance shown by St. Peter when he said to the rulers of his day: "Shall we obey God or man?" No one can deny that in so far as non-Whites are concerned in the Union of South Africa, laws and conditions that debase human personality abound. Any chief worthy of his position must fight fearlessly against such debasing conditions and laws.

* * * * *

Even Death

As for myself, with a full sense of responsibility and a clear conviction, I decided to remain in the struggle for extending democratic rights and responsibilities to all sections of the South African community. I have embraced the non-Violent Passive Resistance technique in fighting for freedom because I am convinced it is the only non-revolutionary, legitimate and humane way that could be used by people denied, as we are, effective constitutional means to further aspirations.

The wisdom or foolishness of this decision I place in the hands of the Almighty.

* * * * *

My only painful concern at times is that of the welfare of my family but I try even in this regard, in a spirit of trust and surrender to God's will as I see it, to say: "God will provide."

It is inevitable that in working for Freedom some individuals and some families must take the lead and suffer: The Road to Freedom is via the CROSS.

MAYIBUYE!

Afrika! Afrika! Afrika!

20. C. Eric Lincoln and Martin Luther King, Jr.:
NON-VIOLENCE AND THE AMERICAN NEGRO

In 1954 the United States Supreme Court decided that racial segregation in public schools was unconstitutional, and other decisions have held the same with respect to segregation in interstate transportation. The court's tendency over a period of years has been to hold that racial segregation in public facilities of all type is contrary to basic law. But while the old doctrine of "separate but equal" has thus been overthrown in form, it still remains very much in effect in practice. Local governments continue to enforce ordinances even after they have been declared unconstitutional, and local customs and traditions—even without the formal sanction of law—sustain separation of the races against an increasingly keen moral consciousness that condemns it. How can one fully implement the law and break down traditions and local customs that, in both North and South, violate the standards of equity sustained by the insights of millions? To many critics it has appeared that authorities are often unable or unwilling to do much about this issue, and the sense of injustice felt by minority groups continues to grow.

The problem is gradually being answered by a remarkable development of the theory and practice of non-violent resistance. A classic example is the 1955–56 bus boycott in Montgomery, Alabama, which in many respects resembles the South African bus boycott (see pp. 258–59). Thousands of Negroes walked often long distances to work, rather than ride on the segregated buses. The boycotters, well-disciplined and thoroughly imbued with Gandhi-like principles of non-violence, were finally successful in attaining their objectives.

Meanwhile, organizations like the Congress of Racial Equality (C.O.R.E.) and the Fellowship of Reconciliation were preparing the ground for other challenges. Long before the mid-fifties, many individuals—some of them close students of Gandhi—had used Satyagraha-like methods in attempting to obtain non-discriminatory service in restaurants and other public services. For the most part, these efforts did not receive much public notice, although they were often quite successful. During World War II, non-violent resistance techniques used by conscientious objectors in prison sometimes prepared the way for the breakdown of segregation in penal institutions. Even in pre-Civil War America, Negroes had used non-violent direct action to secure non-discriminatory treatment on the railroads of certain northern states.

But it was in 1960 and 1961 that the whole problem of non-violent resistance in race relations was most highly dramatized. The time appeared to be ripe for a nearly universal response by the Negro community; federal law was favorable, and there was widespread concern about what "image" the United States would have abroad were segregation to continue. Moreover, the economic position of the Negro, bad as it continued to be, was improving. A new sense of self-confidence, too, was abroad among members of the younger generation, many of them now attending college; and fresh leadership within the ranks of Negro ministers—witness the career of the Reverend Dr. Martin Luther King, Jr.—initiated an often deep religious commitment to non-violence.

So the great wave of Sit-Ins and "Freedom Rides" came about. Thousands of Negroes, mostly very young, deliberately sat down in restaurants and asked for service on equal terms with white patrons. The jails were sometimes too full to hold all the "violators of public order" arrested for such innocuous acts; and in some areas the overflow was accommodated in crude stockades or other improvised quarters. From Northern as well as Southern communities came "Freedom Riders" who challenged segregation in waiting rooms, in buses, and in other facilities. Intellectuals and non-intellectuals alike participated, and those who sympathized but could not themselves share in the direct activities contributed financial support.

To the cursory reader of newspapers, all this activity may have seemed purely spontaneous; and, indeed, some of it was undoubtedly a rather unstructured response to a widely felt need. But behind most of it were carefully laid plans built upon conscious adaptations of Gandhian theories. Training centers for non-violent resistance were attended by would-be Sit-Inners and "Freedom Riders." Thus in 1962, the Congress of Racial Equality distributed a brochure announcing an Interracial Action Institute to be held in Houston, Texas. Cost of the three-week course was $150.00; and the brochure described the nature of the training:

> "Learn nonviolence through using it in action" is the theme of the Institute. To do this, Institute members will take part in testing eating places and theatres. In cases where Negroes are refused service, the usual steps of negotiation and then peaceful, direct action will be followed.
>
> It is the essence of nonviolence that it proceed step-by-step. Where discrimination can be ended through negotiation, more drastic steps are not used.
>
> Institute participants—Negro and white, student and adult, from South and North—will learn by doing. Institute members will live interracially. . . . Participants will also receive training in community organization, group discipline, and the theory and meaning of nonviolence.

The reader will note the strong resemblance of these principles to the steps in Gandhian Satyagraha (see pp. 236–37) and also their affinity with the ideas animating non-violent resistance in South Africa.

Our reading consists of two sections. In the first, C. Eric Lincoln, who teaches social philosophy at Clark College, Atlanta, illustrates the strategy of a Sit-In in Atlanta. Following this we re-print the code of conduct used by non-violent direct actionists in Nashville—standards which were widely observed.

It is highly appropriate that our reading conclude with a selection from Dr. Martin Luther King, Jr., who summarizes his view of the relation between the Negro's struggle for freedom and the theory and practice of non-violence. Now co-pastor of the Ebenezer Baptist Church in Atlanta, Dr. King was a strong intellectual and spiritual force in the Montgomery bus boycott of 1955–56; and the Sit-Inners and "Freedom Riders" looked to him for inspiration and counsel.

The product of a Protestant theological training, he originally had as his major academic interest systematic theology and philosophy, but later his central concern became social ethics. At the seminary he felt the influence of Walter Rauschenbusch's doctrine of the social gospel; at the same time he was dubious about the power of love as a solution for social problems. "The 'turn the other cheek' philosophy and the 'love your enemies' philosophy are only valid, I felt, when individuals are in conflict with other individuals; when racial groups and nations are in conflict a more realistic approach is necessary."[1]

His doubt began to disappear when he read the works of Gandhi: "As I delved deeper into the philosophy of Gandhi my skepticism concerning the power of love gradually diminished. . . ." He came to believe that the Gandhian method of non-violence could become one of the most potent weapons available in the struggle of exploited men for liberty. When he went to Montgomery as a pastor, this intellectual conviction was greatly strengthened by actual experience in the bus boycott. Non-violence became not merely a method but, as he put it, a "commitment to a way of life." After his visit to India, this belief was reinforced, and Dr. King was particularly impressed by the absence of bitterness between the British and the Indians, a fact he attributed to the methods the Indians had used in their struggle. By 1960 he had become convinced that the idea of non-violent resistance was applicable in the international sphere as well as in the integration conflict. The alternative was not, he thought, between violence and non-violence. It was "either non-violence or non-existence."[2]

The selection from C. Eric Lincoln appeared in the *Reporter*, January 5, 1961; the Nashville code in the New York *Times*, March 2, 1960; and the article by Dr. King in the New York *Times Magazine*, September 10, 1961.

C. Eric Lincoln: THE STRATEGY OF A SIT-IN

ATLANTA

If no wool-hat politicians from the rural counties are loitering about with their ears cocked for subversive conversation, both Negro and white natives are apt to boast that Atlanta is "the New York of the South."

One morning last March, sophisticated Atlanta was rudely jarred by the realization that it was like New York in ways it had never particularly noticed before: its Negro minority was not at all timid about expressing its dissatisfaction and demanding action in no uncertain terms. In fact, there in the morning Atlanta *Constitution* was a full-page advertisement entitled "An Appeal for Human Rights," and the list of rights the Negroes said they wanted ranged all the way from the right of attending the public schools of Georgia on a non-

[1] Martin Luther King, Jr., "Pilgrimage to Nonviolence," *Christian Century*, April 13, 1960, p. 440.
[2] Ibid., p. 44.

segregated basis to being admitted to hospitals, concerts, and restaurants on the same basis as anybody else. The home-bound commuters got the same message in a full-page advertisement in the evening *Journal,* which, according to its masthead, "Covers Dixie Like the Dew."

The advertisement, signed by six Negro students representing the six Negro colleges in Atlanta, said in part:

"We, the students of the six affiliated institutions forming the Atlanta University Center—Clark, Morehouse, Morris Brown and Spelman colleges, Atlanta University and the Interdenominational Theological Center—have joined our hearts, minds and bodies in the cause of gaining those rights which are inherently ours as members of the human race and as citizens of the United States . . .

"We do not intend to wait placidly for those rights which are already legally and morally ours. . . . Today's youth will not sit by submissively, while being denied all rights, privileges, and joys of life. . . .

"We must say in all candor that we plan to use every legal and non-violent means at our disposal to secure full citizenship rights as members of this great Democracy. . . ."

The reaction in Atlanta, a city known for its more or less amicable race relations, was swift and vigorous. In the white community there was genuine amazement over the dissatisfaction of the Negro students. After all, in Atlanta many Negroes own expensive homes, run substantial businesses, and practice the professions with a high degree of respect in the community at large.

Predictably, white reaction polarized along urban-rural political lines. Mayor William B. Hartsfield, whose qualifications as a hardheaded Southern liberal are rated high by many of the most militant advocates of Negro rights, praised the statement and said that it "performs the constructive service of letting the white community know what others are thinking."

But a few blocks away in the state capitol, Governor Ernest Vandiver denounced the student appeal as a "left-wing statement . . . calculated to breed dissatisfaction, discontent, discord and evil." The Georgia governor had been elected on a platform of total segregation by a predominantly rural electorate voting under Georgia's so-called county-unit system. Under the county-unit rules, a vote cast by a semi-literate sharecropper in rural Echols County (with a population of 2,494) has ninety-odd times the value of a vote cast by an Emory University professor voting in Atlanta, which has a metropolitan population of more than one million. The governor did go so far as to admit that the appeal for human rights was "skillfully prepared"—so well prepared in fact, that "Obviously, it was not written by students." According to Governor Vandiver, "It did not sound like it was prepared in *any* Georgia school or college." (The italics are mine but the grammar is his.)

The governor could have been more generous in his estimate of the quality of education in Georgia. As far as Negroes are concerned, Atlanta, with six private and church-related institutions of higher learning, has long been a unique educational center. It is estimated that at least ten per cent of all Negro Ph.D.s in America received their undergraduate training in Atlanta. And the students of the Atlanta University Center were soon to exhibit a remarkable degree of skill at dramatizing their determination to have the rights to which they feel entitled.

The sit-in movement in Atlanta was born in a corner drugstore opposite the Atlanta University Center, when a handful of students from the several Negro colleges found themselves discussing the sit-ins already in progress in North Carolina and elsewhere. A mass meeting at Atlanta University early last March resulted in the formation of a Committee on Appeal for Human Rights, which several days later drew up the statement enumerating their grievances and calling upon "all people in authority . . . all leaders in civic life . . . and all people of goodwill to assert themselves and abolish these injustices."

To test the receptiveness of white Atlantans to the attempted desegregation of public and semi-public facilities, the students sought to attend a musical at the city auditorium with tickets for orchestra seats ordered in advance; and they "sat in" for service at a lunch counter at Rich's, the largest department store in the Southeast. At the municipal auditorium they were permitted to occupy the seats for which they held tickets, but the section in which they sat was promptly designated a Negro section by the management, and seating continued on a *de facto* segregated basis. At Rich's the students were served on March 3 and 4, but thereafter, and without prior notice, they were refused. The Appeal for Human Rights followed, but neither the newspaper advertisements nor attempts at negotiation with Rich's and the other major downtown stores produced results.

At Rich's—which stretches almost a full block on either side of Forsyth Street—one can buy anything from a packet of pins to a passage to Paris. It is generally assumed that from seventy to ninety per cent of the Negroes in Atlanta's business and professional class have maintained accounts there. When no satisfactory agreement could be reached with the management of the store, the students threw picket lines in front of it and urged all Negroes to cancel their accounts and practice "selective purchasing"—that is, to spend their money somewhere else. This was to be the first in a series of skirmishes with the giant store, a kind of field maneuver in preparation for an all-out campaign in the fall.

By the time the colleges were closed for summer vacation, the student movement had taken on some of the aspects of a permanent organization. The Committee on Appeal for Human Rights had developed into a kind of general staff, and several operating committees with specific functions had been set up under its aegis. A Student-Adult Liaison Committee had been established to interpret the student movement to the Negro community and to enlist its support. On this committee were business executives, college presidents, professors, lawyers, other Negro leaders, and students.

The adult members of the liaison committee also served in an advisory capacity on request, but they were excluded from all student meetings dealing with policy and strategy. As one student leader has explained, "We preferred not to embarrass or otherwise discompose our adult leaders; they may have vested interests or personal obligations which may make it difficult for them to share directly in our deliberations, or in our strategy and the implementation of policy." Nonetheless, the sit-ins got overwhelming support from Negro adults, both direct and indirect. For one thing, during the summer a great many adults learned to get along without the convenience of charge accounts at the downtown stores. One group of businessmen underwrote a modest newspaper called the Atlanta *Inquirer,* edited by a college professor and largely staffed by students.

After most of the college students had scattered for their summer vacations, a switch in tactics directed the summer "field maneuvers" at chain grocery stores that have outlets in Negro neighborhoods but discriminate against Negroes in their employment practices. Except for "selective purchasing," the main campaign against the downtown stores was postponed until fall.

The summer "maneuvers" were directed mainly at units of Colonial Stores and at some smaller businesses located in areas with from ninety-five to one hundred per cent Negro patronage. When the stores refused to negotiate with the students on the question of hiring Negroes above the level of menials, picket lines were organized and a selective purchasing campaign was urged upon Negro housewives. The chief target, a Colonial store near the heart of the Negro business district on the city's Northwest Side, suddenly "closed for remodeling." A few days later it reopened with Negroes upgraded in three departments. Shortly thereafter a second store in the Colonial chain hired a Negro cashier and a Negro butcher. Two smaller stores had either already employed Negro salespersons or did so immediately after Colonial changed its policies.

What came to be referred to as the "Fall Campaign" got under way immediately after the reopening of the colleges in mid-September. This time the main sit-in targets were in the heart of the Atlanta shopping district. Because of its size and its alleged "leadership" in the maintenance of segregated facilities, Rich's became once again the prime objective. Encouraged, however, by the fact that in the seven months since the sit-ins had begun in Greensboro, North Carolina, 112 Southern cities had desegregated lunch counters. The students added Davison-Paxon, the second largest store in Atlanta, as well as drug chains such as Lane-Rexall and Walgreen and the dime and variety stores, including Woolworth, Kress, W. T. Grant, McCrory, Newberry, and H. L. Green. Accommodations were requested at *all* facilities—lunch counters, rest rooms, and in the case of the department stores, restaurants and dining rooms.

The stores refused to negotiate with the students, and beginning on October 19 a succession of sit-ins harassed the downtown merchants and brought out scores of extra police and plainclothes detectives. By Friday, October 21, hundreds of students had launched attacks in co-ordinated waves. Service to *anyone* at eating facilities in the stores involved had all but ended, and sixty-one students, one white heckler, and Dr. Martin Luther King were all in jail. Under a truce called by Mayor Hartsfield everyone was out of jail by Sunday morning except Dr. King. Negotiations between the merchants and the Students-Adult Liaison Committee were promised on the initiative of the mayor. When the truce ended thirty days later, no progress had been made in settling the impasse, and on November 25, the all-out attack was resumed. By mid-December, Christmas buying was down sixteen per cent—almost $10 million below normal.

Both the Atlanta police and the merchants have been baffled by the students' apparent ability to appear out of nowhere armed with picket signs, and by the high degree of co-ordination with which simultaneous attacks were mounted against several stores at once. Even members of the Ku Klux Klan, dressed in full regalia and prepared to counterdemonstrate against the students, frequently found themselves wandering around the downtown streets bemused—always a jump or two behind the sit-in students. The secret of their easy mobility lay in the organization the students had perfected in anticipation of an extended siege.

Much of the credit for the development of the organizational scheme belongs to Lonnie King, a Morehouse student who is the recognized leader of the student movement in

Atlanta, and his immediate "general staff." Policymaking is done by a board of about fifteen students, constituting the Committee on Appeal for Human Rights, which interprets and tries to make effective the wishes of the students of the six colleges who are loosely joined together in what is known as the Atlanta Student Movement. The committee is co-chaired by Lonnie King and Herschelle Sullivan, a twenty-two-year-old senior at Spelman College. Its executive officer has the rather whimsical title of *"le Commandante."*

Le Commandante is Fred C. Bennette, a pre-theology student at Morris Brown College. The headquarters of the movement are in the basement of a church near the University Center, and Bennette arrives there promptly at seven o'clock each morning and goes through a stack of neatly typed reports covering the previous day's operations. On the basis of these reports, the strategy for the day is planned.

By eight o'clock the first contingent of volunteers for the day's assignment has arrived; there may be anywhere between twenty-five and a hundred students present. There is a brief devotional period, which usually concludes with a prayer that the white people of Georgia and throughout the United States will learn to overcome their prejudices, and that the students will be restrained, non-violent, and loving in their attempts to establish human dignity in Georgia. After the devotions, the student volunteers may go to the church kitchen for coffee and doughnuts provided by various adult organizations. They are then likely to scatter about the church looking for places to study until they are summoned for duty.

Meanwhile, *le Commandante* and his staff are in conference. Robert ("Tex") Felder, Deputy Chief of Operations and a second-year student at the Interdenominational Theological Center, will have arrived, as will a fellow student, the Reverend Otis Moss, who serves as field commander for the committee. Morris J. Dillard of Morehouse and James Felder of Clark College, who serve as co-chairmen of a subcommittee on public relations, will be on hand, and *le Commandante* will also expect to hear a report from a Clark College senior, Benjamin Brown, who keeps the organization's books and acts as its treasurer. Telephoned reports from Senior Intelligence Officer Daniel Mitchell, a Clark junior (already at his post downtown), will describe the nature of the flow of traffic at each potential target.

The general staff having concluded its deliberations, a number of pickets selected on the basis of their class schedules and the nature of the day's objectives will be assembled and briefed by Deputy Commander Robert Felder. A large map dividing the downtown district into five areas is invariably consulted and an Area Commander is appointed for each operational district. Assignments fall into three categories: pickets (called by the students "picketeers"), sit-ins, and a sort of flying squad called "sit-and-runs." The objective of the sit-and-runs is simply to close lunch counters by putting in an appearance and requesting service. When the merchants discontinue service to all rather than serve the Negroes, the sit-and-runs move on to another target. The group designated "sit-ins" are prepared to contest their right to be served and are willing to go to jail if need be. Those volunteering for sit-in duty agree not to request bail if they are arrested.

By now it is nine or nine-thirty, and transportation has arrived. Cars provided without charge by funeral homes or other businesses as well as by individual housewives and some students are waiting to be loaded. The Deputy Commander provides each driver with a driver's orientation sheet outlining in detail the route to be followed by each driver, and the places where each of the respective groups of students are to be let out. The Area Commanders are given final instructions concerning the synchronization of the attack, and the cars move off, following different routes into the city.

In one of the last cars to leave headquarters will be the Deputy Field Commander, who with a selected squad of "stand-bys" will be driven to his "field headquarters" on the "Ramparts," a designation referring to the steps of the Post Office annex across the street from Rich's department store.

Meanwhile, Field Commander Otis Moss is checking a communications code with Ernest Brown, an eighteen-year-old Morehouse junior, or one of the five other licensed radio operators who man a short-wave radio set up in the church nursery. When this has been attended to, Commander Moss climbs into an ancient automobile equipped with a short-wave sending and receiving unit and heads for the downtown shopping district. He is accompanied by Robert Allen, eighteen, a Morehouse junior majoring in physics, whose job it will be to man the mobile radio unit.

The students have scarcely been deployed before a delivery truck arrives with a crate of apples and a dozen loaves of bread. These are from a small storekeeper who wants to contribute to the cause. Other gifts of food, cigarettes, and soft drinks arrive during the course of the morning. A housewife brings in a half-dozen pies; an insurance executive calls to say that he will underwrite the cost of $115 worth of printing the students have contracted for. A small service station will give a hundred gallons of gasoline. All such gifts are recorded and notes of thanks are written to the donors by members of a subcommittee on community support. By eleven o'clock a group of churchwomen have arrived to prepare lunch for the students.

Reports from the Field and Area Commanders begin to trickle in by radio and telephone. As the lunch hour nears, the volume of reports will increase to one every two or three minutes. The reports are typed and dated and placed on the desk of *le Commandante* by a corps of young women who serve as "Communications Aides." Duplicates are posted on the bulletin board and the students remaining at headquarters crowd around to watch the fortunes of their colleagues downtown. Here are two actual reports taken from the files and approved for publication by the Security Officer:

11/26/60   11:05 AM
From: Captain Lenora Tait
To: le Commandante
Lunch counters at Rich's closed. Proceeded to alternative objective. Counters at Woolworth's also closed. Back to Rich's for picket duty. Ku Klux Klan circling Rich's in night gowns and dunce caps. "Looking good!"

From: Gwendolyn Lee
To: le Commandante
Sign has been torn from the back of one of our white picketers. He got another sign and returned to the line. Morale of white picketers very good. Known heckler, an old man in a gray suit, is on the scene. White opposition increasing. Plainclothes detective made co-ordinator keep moving. All picketers now in front of Rich's.

The white pickets referred to were from Emory University, a segregated Methodist college in Atlanta. White students from the University of Georgia have also joined the Negro students in the picket lines.

Negro students have sometimes been kicked and beaten, and one student, Elroy Emory of Morris Brown College, has been repeatedly singled out for attack by a group of black-jacketed young white men who come regularly to heckle the Negro pickets. The Ku Klux Klan has mounted counterdemonstrations on at least two occasions, and has threatened to call a white boycott against any store that desegregates its eating facilities.

The downtown merchants and the Atlanta police have deplored the Klan's meddling, as have the Atlanta newspapers. It has been the Negro students who have insisted that the Klan's right to demonstrate ought to be protected. When the Klan turned out in force on Saturday, December 10—red, white, and green satin gowns, hoods and all—to demonstrate against the students and the newspapers, the students called a mass meeting for six o'clock the next morning "to pray for our white brothers of the Ku Klux Klan." Nearly five thousand students and adults made their way to Herndon Stadium before daylight, and stood bareheaded in a cold rain to be led in prayer by the Reverend William Holmes Borders for the spiritual enlightenment of the Ku Klux Klan. That night a bomb wrecked a Negro elementary school a few blocks from the scene of the early-morning prayer meeting.

The sit-ins continue, a somber prelude to the school desegregation problems Atlanta will have to face next September. Support from adult Negroes is firm and consistent, and professional men and women have joined the students in the picket lines on "Doctors' Day," "Nurses' Day," and even "Professors' Day."

In some cases the students have been encouraged by white clerks and other personnel working in the very stores against which the sit-ins are directed. At least one sympathetic white woman living in Atlanta's exclusive Buckhead section fired her maid when the maid admitted that she had crossed the picket line at Rich's to buy a dress. Another white woman who had been watching the New Orleans spectacle on television called an official at one of the Negro colleges to ask that the Negroes continue to pray that the white race be forgiven for its behavior toward Negroes and that the students be encouraged to continue their efforts.

There seems little doubt that the efforts will be continued. The Negro students and their white and black allies are determined to keep on sitting in, sitting and running, and picketing until their battle is won.

THE NEGRO STUDENTS' CODE[3]

Acknowledging the teachings of Jesus Christ and Mohandas K. Gandhi, and looking to the Reverend Martin Luther King, Jr. for counsel, college students in Nashville, Tennessee drew up the code below to govern student conduct in "sit-in" protests at lunch counters discriminating against Negroes.

Don't strike back or curse if abused.

Don't laugh out.

Don't hold conversations with floor workers.

Don't leave your seats until your leader has given you instruction to do so.

Don't block entrances to the stores and the aisles.

Show yourself courteous and friendly at all times.

[3] From the New York *Times,* March 2, 1960.

Sit straight and always face the counter.

Report all serious incidents to your leader.

Refer all information to your leader in a polite manner.

Remember love and non-violence.

May God bless each of you.

Martin Luther King, Jr.: THE TIME FOR FREEDOM HAS COME

On a chill morning in the autumn of 1958, an elderly, toil-worn Negro woman in Montgomery, Ala., began her slow, painful four-mile walk to her job. It was the tenth month of the Montgomery bus boycott, which had begun with a life expectancy of one week. The old woman's difficult progress led a passer-by to inquire sympathetically if her feet were tired. Her simple answer became the boycotters' watchword. "Yes, friend, my feet is real tired, but my soul is rested."

Five years passed and once more Montgomery arrested the world's attention. Now the symbolic segregationist is not a stubborn, rude bus driver. He emerges in 1961 as a hoodlum stomping the bleeding face of a Freedom Rider. But neither is the Negro today an elderly woman whose grammar is uncertain; rather, he is college-bred, Ivy League-clad, youthful, articulate and resolute. He has the imagination and drive of the young, tamed by discipline and commitment. The nation and the world have reacted with astonishment at these students cast from a new mold, unaware that a chain reaction was accumulating explosive force behind a strangely different facade.

Generating these changes is a phenomenon Victor Hugo described in these words: "There is no greater power on earth than an idea whose time has come." In the decade of the Sixties the time for freedom for the Negro has come. This simple truth illuminates the motivations, the tactics and the objectives of the students' daring and imaginative movement.

The young Negro is not in revolt, as some have suggested, against a single pattern of timid, fumbling, conservative leadership. Nor is his conduct to be explained in terms of youth's excesses. He is carrying forward a revolutionary destiny of a whole people consciously and deliberately. Hence the extraordinary willingness to fill the jails as if they were honors classes and the boldness to absorb brutality, even to the point of death, and remain non-violent. His inner strength derives from his goal of freedom and the leadership role he has grasped even at a time when some of his white counterparts still grope in philosophical confusion searching for a personal goal with human values, searching for security from economic instability, and seeking relief from the haunting fear of nuclear destruction.

* * * * *

Part of the impatience of Negro youth stems from their observation that change is taking place rapidly in Africa and other parts of the world, but comparatively slowly in the South. When the United States Supreme Court handed down its historic desegregation decision in 1954, many of us, perhaps naïvely, thought that great and sweeping school integration would ensue. Yet, today, seven years later, only 7 per cent of the Negro children of the South have been placed in desegregated schools. At the current rate it will take ninety-three more years to desegregate the public schools of the South. The collegians say, "We can't wait that long" or simply, "We won't wait!"

Negro students are coming to understand that education and learning have become tools for shaping the future and not devices of privilege for an exclusive few. Behind this spiritual explosion is the shattering of a material atom.

The future of the Negro college student has long been locked within the narrow walls of limited opportunity. Only a few professions could be practiced by Negroes and, but for a few exceptions, behind barriers of segregation in the North as well as the South. Few frustrations can compare with the experience of struggling with complex academic subjects, straining to absorb concepts which may never be used, or only half-utilized under conditions insulting to the trained mind.

A Negro interne blurted out to me shortly after his patient died, "I wish I were not so well trained because then I would never know how many of these people need not die for lack of proper equipment, adequate post-operative care and timely admission. I'm not practicing good medicine. I'm presiding over tragedies which the absence of good medicine creates."

* * * * *

There is another respect in which the Negro student is benefiting, and simultaneously contributing to, society as a whole. He is learning social responsibility; he is learning to earn, through his own direct sacrifice, the result he seeks. There are those who would make him soft, pliable and conformist—a mechanical organization man or an uncreative status seeker. But the experience of Negro youth is as harsh and demanding as that of the pioneer on the untamed frontier. Because his struggle is complex, there is no place in it for the frivolous or rowdy. Knowledge and discipline are as indispensable as courage and self-sacrifice. Hence the forging of priceless qualities of character is taking place daily as a high moral goal is pursued.

Inevitably there will emerge from this caldron a mature man, experienced in life's lessons, socially aware, unafraid of experimentation and, most of all, imbued with the spirit of service and dedication to a great ideal. The movement therefore gives to its participants a double education—academic learning from books and classes, and life's lessons from responsible participation in social action. Indeed, the answer to the quest for a more mature, educated American, to compete successfully with the young people of other lands, may be present in this new movement.

Of course, not every student in our struggle has gained from it. This would be more than any humanly designed plan could realize. For some, the opportunity for personal advantage presented itself and their character was not equal to the challenge. A small percentage of students have found it convenient to escape from their own inadequacies by identifying with the sit-ins and other activities. They are, however, relatively few because this is a form of escape in which the flight from responsibility imposes even greater responsibilities and risks.

It is not a solemn life, for all of its seriousness. During a vigorous debate among a group of students discussing the moral and practical soundness of non-violence, a majority rejected the employment of force. As the minority dwindled to a single student, he finally declared, "All I know is that, if rabbits could throw rocks, there would be fewer hunters in the forest."

This is more than a witty remark to relieve the tensions of serious and even grim discussion. It expresses some of the pent-up impatience, some of the discontent and some of the despair produced by minute corrections in the face of enormous evil. Students necessarily have conflicting reactions. It is understandable that violence presents itself as a quick, effective answer for a few.

For the large majority, however, non-violent, direct action has emerged as the better and more successful way out. It does not require that they abandon their discontent. This discontent is a sound, healthy social response to the injustice and brutality they see around them. Non-violence offers a method by which they can fight the evil with which they cannot live. It offers a unique weapon which, without firing a single bullet, disarms the adversary. It exposes his moral defenses, weakens his morale, and at the same time works on his conscience.

Another weapon which Negro students have employed creatively in their non-violent struggle is satire. It has enabled them to avoid corrosive anger while pressing the cutting edge of ridicule against the opponent. When they have been admonished to "go slow," patiently to wait for gradual change, with a straight face they will assure you that they are diligently searching for the happy medium between the two extremes of moderation and gradualism.

It is perhaps the special quality of non-violent direct action, which sublimates anger, that explains why so few students are attracted to extreme nationalist sects advocating black supremacy. The students have anger under controlling bonds of discipline. Hence they can answer appeals for cooling-off periods by advocating cooling-off for those who are hot with anger and violence.

Much has been made of the willingness of these devotees of non-violent social action to break the law. Paradoxically, although they have embraced Thoreau's and Gandhi's civil disobedience on a scale dwarfing any past experience in American history, they do respect law. They feel a moral responsibility to obey just laws. But they recognize that there are also unjust laws.

From a purely moral point of view, an unjust law is one that is out of harmony with the moral law of the universe. More concretely, an unjust law is one in which the minority is compelled to observe a code that is not binding on the majority. An unjust law is one in which people are required to obey a code that they had no part in making because they were denied the right to vote.

In disobeying such unjust laws, the students do so peacefully, openly and non-violently. Most important, they willingly accept the penalty, whatever it is, for in this way the public comes to re-examine the law in question and will thus decide whether it uplifts or degrades man.

This distinguishes their position on civil disobedience from the "uncivil disobedience" of the segregationist. In the face of laws they consider unjust, the racists seek to defy, evade and circumvent the law, and they are unwilling to accept the penalty. The end result of their defiance is anarchy and disrespect for the law. The students, on the other hand, believe that he who openly disobeys a law, a law conscience tells him is unjust, and then willingly accepts the penalty, gives evidence thereby that he so respects that law that he belongs in jail until it is changed. Their appeal is to the conscience.

Beyond this, the students appear to have perceived what an older generation overlooked in the role of law. The law tends to declare rights—it does not deliver them. A catalyst is needed to breathe life experience into a judicial decision by the persistent exercise of the rights until they become usual and ordinary in human conduct. They have offered their energies, their bodies to effect this result. They see themselves the obstetricians at the birth of a new order. It is in this manner that the students have related themselves to and materialized "the idea whose time has come."

In a sense, the victories of the past two years have been spectacular and considerable. Because of the student sitters, more than 150 cities in the South have integrated their lunch counters. Actually, the current break-throughs have come about partly as a result of the patient legal, civil and social ground clearing of the previous decades. Then, too, but slowly, the national Government is realizing that our so-called domestic race relations are a major force in our foreign relations. Our image abroad reflects our behavior at home.

Many liberals, of the North as well as the South, when they list the unprecedented progress of the past few years, yearn for a "cooling off" period; not too fast, they say, we may lose all that we have gained if we push faster than the violent ones can be persuaded to yield.

This view, though understandable, is a misreading of the goals of the young Negroes. They are not after "mere tokens" of integration ("tokenism," they call it); rather theirs is a revolt against the whole system of Jim Crow and they are prepared to sit-in, kneel-in, wade-in and stand-in until every waiting room, rest room, theatre and other facility throughout the nation that is supposedly open to the public is in fact open to Negroes, Mexicans, Indians, Jews or what-have-you. Theirs is total commitment to this goal of equality and dignity. And for this achievement they are prepared to pay the costs—whatever they are—in suffering and hardship as long as may be necessary.

*   *   *   *   *

21. Neil Haworth and *Peace News:*
DIRECT ACTION AGAINST
PREPARATION FOR WAR

As the arms race between the United States and the Soviet Union accelerated through the 1950s and one disarmament conference followed another, always without any real success, many people in the United States, Britain, and Western Europe began to look about for ways of dramatizing the peril in which the world found itself. Their object was twofold: to break through inertia and awaken world opinion to the dangers, and to halt the arms race through direct action of their own.

Non-violent resistance took many different forms. There were vigils before the White House and the Prime Minister's residence in London. The Committee for Nuclear Disarmament in Britain sponsored gigantic marches and demonstrations. Some, like Bertrand Russell, simply sat down in the streets, compelling the police to remove them, as a protest against existing trends. Numbers of people in the United States refused to pay income taxes, or at least the portion of their tax that presumably would be used for military defense.

Outright civil disobedience was also employed. Men and women defied New York law by deliberately refusing to take cover during the annual Civil Defense air raid drills, protesting both the futility of Civil Defense and its role in making the American people war-minded. Many were arrested and fined or jailed. In Omaha, Nebraska, a number invited arrest by peacefully invading a missile base, and in New London, Connecticut, an organized group from time to time boarded—or attempted to board—Polaris submarines under construction there, while others distributed leaflets protesting military preparations and what they considered to be the illusion of military defense. Activities of this kind in the United States are under the auspices of such organizations as the Committee for Non-violent Action, and the War Resisters League, in which most of the leadership is strongly imbued with Gandhian ideas.

One of the most dramatic types of non-violent direct action against preparation for war was the series of efforts to send ships into ocean areas where the United States was testing nu-clear weapons. These included the voyages of the *Golden Rule* and the *Phoenix* in the fifties and of the *Everyman* (I, II, and III) series in the early sixties.

The voyage of the *Golden Rule* was sponsored by the Com-mittee for Non-violent Action. The Captain was Albert Bige-low, a veteran of service in the United States Navy who had become disillusioned with the whole military system and was eager to protest against preparation for future war. Although at first he was reluctant to undertake the voyage into the test-ing area in the Pacific Ocean, after much persuasion he agreed to do so. The money was somehow raised. In addition to Bige-low, there was a crew of four persons, all of them active in various aspects of the non-violent direct action movement.

The ketch headed for Hawaii, which it reached on April 19, 1958, attracting considerable attention in Honolulu. The gov-ernment obtained a Federal District Court order restraining Bigelow from taking his ship beyond Hawaii. When the crew attempted to defy this injunction, they were arrested and, after serving a few days in jail, put on probation. The injunction and contempt citation were appealed to the Circuit Court of Ap-peals in San Francisco.

Another attempt to take the *Golden Rule* out to sea resulted in Captain Bigelow's second arrest, and when other members of the crew sought to sail the ship without him, they were sentenced to sixty days in the Honolulu jail. In acting after this fashion, Captain Bigelow argues, he and his crew were simply carrying on an old American tradition:

> Civil disobedience should properly be called *consider-ate* disobedience. The word "civil," in the phrase, means with civility, politeness, courtesy, or consideration. It is disobedience with loving-kindness. It is a deliberate act—undertaken after careful and prayerful deliberation. It is never mere revolt against authority.
>
> The only unusual thing about considerate disobedience is that Americans should think it unusual. We have a tra-dition of disobedience. We are rooted in many examples. Two instances are the Boston Tea Party and the assist-ance to runaway slaves. . . .[1]

The imprisonment of the *Golden Rule*'s crew attracted at-tention throughout the world and thus at least one objective of

[1] Albert Bigelow, *The Voyage of the* Golden Rule: *An Experi-ment with Truth* (Garden City, N.Y.: Doubleday, 1959), p. 143.

the voyage was attained: the protest against nuclear testing had been dramatized. In connection with the affair, the Atomic Energy Commission in Washington was picketed, and many of those who had contributed to the cause presented themselves to the Department of Justice for arrest as co-conspirators.

Another ship, the *Phoenix,* commanded by the anthropologist Earle Reynolds did manage to sail into the testing area in late June 1958.[2] There it was met by a Coast Guard cutter and forced to sail to Kwajalein, from where Reynolds was flown to Hawaii and convicted of violating the AEC regulation forbidding entry into the testing area—a rule of doubtful legality, since under international law the high seas are open to ships of all nations.

Although these direct non-violent actions did not result in the abandonment of testing at the time, they did have considerable success in arousing opinion and probably helped prepare the way for the nuclear testing moratorium of 1958–61.

This reading includes descriptions of two quite different applications of the idea of non-violent resistance to preparations for war. The first section, by Neil Haworth, a participant, tells of the vigil and civil disobedience at Newport News, Virginia, where a Polaris submarine was about to be commissioned. The protest was similar to those that were taking place almost continuously at New London, Connecticut, attracting a good deal of sympathetic attention.

The second section of our reading gives a brief account of the walk from San Francisco to Moscow of a small band of American non-violent resisters who were joined by many other demonstrators. When the University of Moscow authorities tried to halt their meeting (to fulfill a schedule), Russian students insisted that the discussion go on (it continued for two additional hours). The Manchester *Guardian* commented, October 7, 1961: "This is far from a trivial happening. In a dictatorship any public outbreak of forbidden ideas is significant; it becomes widely known even if nothing is reported in the press."

The first section is taken from the Committee for Nonviolent Action *Bulletin* for October 20, 1960 and the second from *Peace News Supplement* of October 20, 1961.

[2] See Earle L. Reynolds, *The Forbidden Voyage* (New York: McKay, 1961).

Neil Haworth: CIVIL DISOBEDIENCE AT NEWPORT NEWS

Prompted by a concern to carry resistance to the heart of U.S. Naval operations at the world's largest Naval base and to protest at the commissioning of the third Polaris sub Robert E. Lee, several of us started south from New London Sept. 7. We made preliminary investigations of the physical situation at the most important Naval installations, and of the ordinances in several towns. We began activity Friday afternoon, Sept. 9 with leaflet distribution at the Newport News Shipbuilding and Drydock Co., builders of Polaris subs, nuclear powered aircraft carriers and other vessels of destruction.

The distribution went amazingly well, with the majority of workers accepting leaflets, and very few discarded on the street. Our supply was exhausted just as the last of the day shift people were departing. As we prepared to leave we were approached by three police detectives. They had orders to stop our leaflet distribution and referred to a certain ordinance as prohibiting it. Joe Glynn had read the ordinance and pointed out that it referred only to advertising material. The detectives asked us to come to the police station to talk with the Chief. We agreed, but on arriving found the Chief busy and talked with the Assistant Chief instead. He was extraordinarily courteous but very firm in his insistence that section 70.2 of the Newport News ordinances prohibited the distribution of all sorts of political, religious and thought-provoking leaflets as well as advertising, although the language of the ordinance was quite clear. We tried to be equally polite and equally firm in insisting on our right to distribute the leaflets. We informed him of our plan to hold a vigil outside the shipyard from 6:30 AM Monday through 5 PM Tuesday. His response to this was to show us ordinance 70.7, which prohibited the painting or erection of any sort of sign on the paved portion of any street or sidewalk. We replied that this would not apply to our vigil since we would set up our sign on the grass strip beside the sidewalk outside the shipyard fence. The Assistant Chief said in his opinion it would still be a violation and suggested that we confer with the Chief before starting the vigil. We agreed to this despite the fact that it meant delaying the vigil since we would be unable to see the Chief before 8 AM on Monday.

On Saturday we held an all-day vigil outside the main gate of the Norfolk Naval Base, the world's largest and headquarters of the Atlantic submarine fleet. While there were few people to receive leaflets, our sign and vigilers were in plain sight of all cars entering the base or passing on the busy boulevard. Shortly after our arrival a security guard came out of the base and angrily ordered us to leave. When we politely but firmly refused, he knocked over and broke our sign. Then he decided we were not on Federal property and not under his jurisdiction, and he retreated back into the base.

Next, half a dozen Norfolk policemen moved in on our four vigilers and began asking questions. Their curiosity was exceeded by our patience, and after interrogating us for almost two hours, they were satisfied and withdrew, leaving two rather poorly disguised plainclothesmen to "protect" us from the Navy.

On Sunday we held another all-day vigil, this time at the Oceana Naval Air Station. There was no difficulty with the police, and after some initial confusion the Navy officials were friendly. The CO stopped to warn us of the approaching hurricane and asked if we had transportation and shelter available in an emergency. Two counter-demonstrators appeared briefly, and Joe Glynn and Peter Giffen spent two hours discussing disarmament in their car—a heavy rain having forced them to take shelter.

Plans for a vigil at the shipyard on Monday were disrupted by hurricane Donna. Damage in the area was heavy. The dory World Citizen narrowly escaped being crushed by a large tree which blew over in the back yard of a home in Virginia Beach where some of us were staying.

By early afternoon, the hurricane had passed and we went to Newport News to begin the vigil. Our conference with the Chief of Police was brief. He reaffirmed that if we set up a sign or distributed leaflets we would be arrested. We replied that we felt our demonstration was legal, even under Newport News ordinances cited by the police, and we would proceed. Considering our limited manpower, it seemed best if only one person were arrested at that time. Joe Glynn volunteered and began the vigil.

Since we feared the signs might be confiscated, only one of the two was displayed at first. For more than an hour, several policemen stood by as the vigil proceeded. As the change of shifts approached, Joe decided to set up the other sign. Immediately, the police moved in and said he was violating the law. Joe stood firm and was arrested. Eventually he was taken away after the proceeding had been observed by several hundred workers. The sign was left under guard until picked up later amid comments such as "You mean you're going to lock the sign up too?"

At the police station we learned that Joe was being held under $300 bond, charged with violation of Ordinance 69. No one would show us a copy of it, however.

At his hearing next morning, Joe was represented by Ed

Dawley, Norfolk attorney of Jordan, Dawley & Holt, who are handling many integration cases, and have gained understanding of non-violence through working with CORE and the sit-ins. Dawley was unable to obtain a copy of Ordinance 69 until a court order was issued that one be given. Ordinance 69 was a part of the building code related to signs, with 39 sections and many subsections. No specific section was alleged to have been violated, so Dawley asked that the trial be postponed until the next day. The court agreed, ordered the prosecution to present a bill of particulars and reduced bond to $100. We furnished this in cash and Joe was released.

The bill of particulars had five charges, principally that Joe had failed to obtain a permit from the building inspector prior to erecting the sign. Our conferences with the police before the vigil did not seem to impress the judge and Joe was found guilty and fined $10 plus $2.75 costs. Joe decided to pay so he could continue in the action. The trial demonstrated to the city officials that we would not back down on our rights and in a later action in Newport News the police permitted us to leaflet and display a hand-held sign, a considerable change from their original position.

We arrived at the Shipyard about 10 AM. We got the boat down the cliff and soon had two men vigiling by water and others vigiling outside the gate just 200 feet from the Lee. Vigilers had numerous interviews with newsmen come to inspect the sub early.

We had scheduled an all-day vigil for Wednesday at Norfolk Naval Shipyard in Portsmouth. Portsmouth officials said we needed a permit to distribute leaflets but they did not grant us one. We examined the ordinances in question and found that no permit was in fact required for our type of leaflet, and in any case our Constitutional rights demanded that a permit be granted if required. The trial delayed the vigil, which was altered to concentrate on leaflet distribution at the afternoon shift change. There was no attempt to prevent this activity.

CIVIL DISOBEDIENCE

Friday, Sept. 16 was the major focus of the project. The Robert E. Lee was to be commissioned as the third Polaris sub, and we would confront it with civil disobedience and other techniques.

We had difficulty finding a place from which to launch the World Citizen which was to be used by those attempting to board the sub. The only nearby marina had refused to do business with us, apparently at the instigation of the FBI. The best possibility seemed to be to lower the boat down a 30-foot cliff to a beach 5 blocks from the Robert E. Lee's berth. We were apprehensive about possible harassment by Newport News police.

Plans for the demonstration were formulated Friday morning in a Norfolk parking lot. Saul Gottlieb and his two assistants were present to make movies for their documentary of Polaris Action. Four members were ready for civil disobedience—Victor Richman, Margaret Windus, Don Martin and Bill Henry. Four other members were to support them—Bob Berk, Joe Glynn, Adriaan Maas and myself.

During lunch hour workers congregated around us prior to returning to work. Our sign read WE SUPPORT CIVIL DISOBEDIENCE AGAINST WAR—POLARIS ACTION. A tense situation developed. Lighted cigarettes were thrown at Vic Richman, burning holes in his clothing. Someone broke the handle from the sign and made off with it. Joe Glynn asked that the sign, which he had built, be returned, and his answer was a violent body-block. The sign disappeared inside the fence. Another sign was hastily prepared. Soon a policeman with a dog arrived to "protect" us. This was the first such attack in the immediate presence of TV cameramen and security guards.

Meanwhile, the boat vigilers had discovered that logs attached to a cable had been placed across the mouth of the slip making it impossible to approach the Lee. I telephoned the shipyard president to give him details of our plans. He was cordial but uninterested in the details and seemed confident that we would not get near the sub.

The commissioning ceremony was to begin at 2 PM. We decided to send Margaret, Bill and Don in the World Citizen to land Margaret and Bill on the dock near the sub. Margaret would walk towards the Lee and Bill would be prepared to swim to it if blocked on foot. Don would row back to pick up Vic and Joe, and Joe would row to the log-and-cable barrier where Vic and Don would start swimming. But it was found that there were now two Coast Guard cutters, two tugboats and an outboard motorboat blocking the way. Therefore Margaret, Bill and Don decided to pick up Vic, intending that the three men would swim past the obstructing vessels and Margaret would row the World Citizen back.

With our boat blocked 100 feet from the barrier, the three men jumped in and headed toward the sub. Despite maneuvers by the cutters and tugs, all three swam past the barrier. Now the Coast Guard became frantic and ended by sending their own swimmers in pursuit. The C.G. swimmers, aided by the motorboat inside the barrier, overtook our men before any had gotten closer than 50 feet from the Robert E. Lee. Bill Henry was towed back by a rope around his chest and Vic was suspended by his hair, half out of the water, in the excitement.

Meanwhile, Margaret observed that there was an opportunity for her to row forward and land on the dock and begin a vigil on some low pilings at the end of the dock. She seized the opportunity, landed and pushed the boat out to Saul Gottlieb in a rented motorboat. Margaret's presence on shipyard property quite close to the Lee presented the officials with a problem. Since arrests were apparently ruled out, they were left with a choice of carrying her up a ladder and through the assembled dignitaries or in a boat; or of leaving her alone to continue the vigil. They chose this latter.

The Coast Guard, having taken our men on board, turned their attention to Saul Gottlieb who had moved in for some closer pictures. On the pretext of his having violated some marine regulation, the motorboat with the World Citizen attached, was taken in tow to a distant place.

The rest of us on shore had observed everything except Margaret's landing, and we assumed that the demonstration was ended. We drove off to locate the people in custody. The Coast Guard told us that there were no arrests and also told us where they would be unloaded. We arrived there to see our men dropped to a concrete dock. Adriaan Maas had remained vigiling at the shipyard. A car with Admiral Fitzhugh Lee, second in command of the Atlantic Fleet, stopped and the Admiral asked Adriaan to have a ride and talk. Adriaan went and they had a friendly talk although no very great areas of agreement were reached.

We had managed to get the World Citizen loaded back onto a car, but when we learned of Margaret's vigil we again lowered it down the cliff and Don, Bill and Vic rowed out to set up a supporting sea vigil. Others took up positions at the gate. Margaret remained on vigil until dusk when she came back in the dory. (Remaining longer was obviated by the high tide which covers the pilings with water.)

Peace News: THE WALK TO MOSCOW

Ten months on the road, walking 6,000 miles from the desert and mountains of the United States to the Russian steppes, crossing six national frontiers including the "Iron Curtain" dividing Germany—this is the outline of the march.

Sometimes hundreds or thousands of supporters joined, sometimes a dozen or less paced through deserted stretches alone. A hard core walked all the way, but many long-term personnel kept changing owing to illness, commitments or personal doubts. The attitude of the authorities and of the people in each country varied in both the Western and Eastern countries.

There is not one story of the march but thousands, seen

through the eyes of individual marchers of different ages, nationalities and background who saw different portions of the march; of the national organisers in each country and of the hosts in every town along the way; and also of the police, the pressmen, the mayors, the military and the ordinary people the marchers met.

* * * * *

The march started in San Francisco on December 1, 1960, and arrived in Moscow on October 3. The marchers spent six months crossing the United States—4,000 miles. A selected team of 13 Americans plus two photographers flew to London on June 1. After a rally in Trafalgar Square on June 4 the marchers—joined now by two other Americans, four British volunteers, two from Sweden, one from Norway, another from Finland and one from West Germany—walked via Aldermaston to Southampton, where they took a boat to Le Havre.

The French authorities would not allow them to land. Five of the marchers jumped overboard and swam ashore in protest; and the team had to return to England. They made a second attempt at entry ten days later, were again not allowed ashore, and sent back to England. The marchers then crossed over to Belgium, and on July 2 at the border town of Mouscron met with a group of Frenchmen, who had been carrying on the march through France in the face of continual obstruction and arrests by the police.

From Mouscron the main team of marchers resumed their journey and walked via Brussels to West Germany, crossing near Aachen on July 15. They were joined at this stage by a French girl volunteer and two Belgian students. Their route through West Germany took them through Bonn and Hannover to the East German crossing point at Helmstedt. Members of a "tributary" march through Holland from Amsterdam to the German border joined the main team near Osnabruck on July 29. During their time in West Germany, the marchers defied the ban on demonstrating at military bases and were arrested, but allowed to continue the march.

On August 7 the team, joined now by four more West Germans and a Dutch volunteer, crossed the border into East Germany. After marching for a week under strict surveillance, a crisis arose over the question of the team entering Berlin. The crisis in the team's relationship with the East German authorities coincided with and arose out of the beginning of the Berlin crisis. As the marchers refused to bypass Berlin they were "deported" back to Helmstedt.

The march was resumed on August 22 in Poland where the team had a warm welcome and a good deal of freedom. They were allowed to picket the Defence Ministry in Warsaw and made a pilgrimage to Auschwitz. On September 15 they crossed the Russian border at Brest.

In the USSR the march progressed at breakneck speed to cover the 660 miles between Brest and Moscow in three weeks. The team went through Minsk and Smolensk, met large crowds at each town and even in villages and at cross-roads, made many speeches and distributed thousands of leaflets. On the outskirts of Moscow they picketed a military barracks; on October 3 they held a vigil in Red Square. They also spoke at the University and had a meeting with Mrs. Khrushchev before leaving Moscow on October 8.

This is but a skeleton outline of the march. . . .

THE MARCHERS' LEAFLET

This is the leaflet—printed in six languages—which the marchers distributed along their route across Europe:

WE ARE WALKING TO MOSCOW

Some of us have walked from San Francisco, almost 4,000 miles, to the Capital of the United States—Washington D.C.

For we are equally opposed to the armaments of the East and West. We are marching for unconditional disarmament NOW.

The most effective way to any disarmament today, we believe, is for some nation to start scrapping its weapons. When one country disarms first, it opens the way for others to do the same. Some nation must find the courage to act first.

In each country we pass through we are calling on the government to give up nuclear weapons unconditionally and to discard military pacts based on them. These pacts intensify the Cold War.

H-bombs and missiles are totally evil. They can kill millions of people outright, destroy thousands more slowly from burns and radiation sickness, and harm future generations. We cannot without protest let our own governments use these weapons in our name. And any country which has H-bombs and missiles, for whatever reason, is in fact willing to use them.

In the nuclear age war is outdated. It cannot deal effectively with major conflicts, and any war is likely to become a nuclear war. Dependence on arms must therefore be rejected.

In this new situation we believe that non-violence such as Gandhi used for the freedom of India, and the Norwegian teachers used in resisting Hitler—can best defend and enlarge freedom and justice.

All governments should therefore end conscription, start to do away with armed forces, and turn to Gandhian non-violence to defend freedom and resist tyranny and oppression.

BREAD NOT BOMBS

The world is full of hunger, disease and poverty. We believe that the Soviet Union and the United States with other countries should pool their resources to remove such suffering—by using the money now wasted on weapons of destruction.

We are appealing above all to the ordinary people in every country we walk through to take personal action and to work for the unconditional renunciation of arms by their own country. In Moscow and in every capital city on our route we shall say what the American Marchers have already said in Washington, D.C., the capital of the United States:

"At this stage disarmament can be achieved if one nation is prepared to take a first step in giving up its arms as an example for others to follow."

WE CANNOT BE SILENT

Some of us act out of religious conviction, others out of commitment to ethical values, and we are united in opposing modern war. Because humanity is in such grave danger of destruction, we are determined to speak what we believe to be true. In our own countries we have all urged the renunciation of mass violence. And we shall continue to do this. Some of us have joined demonstrations for disarmament. Others have refused to pay taxes for war, or have refused military service, or have protested at missile bases and atomic plants, or refused to work in industries making arms. As a result some of us have been arrested in our own countries and have spent time in prison.

WE SHALL SPEAK

This is our record. These are our beliefs. We hope to be able to speak out freely wherever we go. Within each country we will insist on distributing our literature, holding our banners and talking with the people. Because we believe the discussion of our ideas is vital, we are prepared to go to prison if prevented from carrying out our march or spreading our beliefs.

We believe that peace can only come when nations give up dependence on military force and turn to the kind of power Gandhi used in India. We therefore urge you, according to your convictions, to act for peace now!

22. Jessie Wallace Hughan and Cecil Hinshaw:
TOWARD A NON-VIOLENT NATIONAL
DEFENSE

A central question usually put to those defending the efficacy of non-violent power is "What would you do in the event of invasion?" The second question quickly follows: "Would you simply surrender?"

By now, the general answers to these questions should be obvious. To the first, the reply would be, "Use non-violent power." To the second, the advocate of non-violence would respond: "No. I repudiate both the immorality and destructiveness of violent power and the cowardice and seeming indifference implied by 'surrender.' "

An attitude of this kind, of course, has far-reaching corollaries. It means that a nation pinning its faith on non-violent power would surrender everything likely to incite others to violence or apparently defendable only by violence. Thus, grossly disproportionate economic power, military bases and threats, experimentation for military destruction, and imperialist control of other peoples would have to go. Sole reliance on non-violent power would also imply a considerable reorganization of the domestic society and economy. For example, to establish adequate economic foundations for peace requires social planning. Many ancient shibboleths—such as the one which tends to identify national defense with possession of overwhelming military might—would necessarily be undermined.

Yet the revolution in thinking required for a commitment to non-violence is in many respects no greater than those through which we have in fact gone in other areas during the past generation—for example, in attitudes to social security and in sex practices.

It could be that the threat of annihilation implicit in the arms race and the possession of fifty megaton bombs, together with increasing awareness of the impossibility of military defense, will help generate a similar revolution with respect to use of violent power. We would then associate possession of military weapons with destruction rather than defense and would discard them whether others did so or not. We would embark on unilateral disarmament in the belief that it would cut through the arms race and set in motion a process of competitive disarmament, just as the arms race itself was initiated through unilateral acts and responses. And we would be prepared to resist invasion by non-violent power.

It is to questions of this kind that our present reading addresses itself. It consists of two essays, one by Dr. Jessie Wallace Hughan, written in 1942, and the other by Dr. Cecil E. Hinshaw, published in 1956. Although Dr. Hughan's statement was written twenty years ago, most of the issues it raises are exactly the questions that continue to be asked about non-violent defense. Hinshaw's essay addresses itself specifically to the conflict between Communist and Western worlds and stresses particularly some of the psychological dimensions involved in non-violent defense.

Neither essay, it will be noted, can guarantee the success of non-violent defense. But both suggest that it is more likely to be successful than twentieth-century military defense, which on the basis of the record has been highly ineffective.

Dr. Hughan was for many years associated with the work of the American War Resisters League and was also an active Socialist. Dr. Hinshaw is a graduate of the Boston University School of Theology and has been connected for a number of years with the peace education work of the American Friends Service Committee.

The Hughan selection is an edited version of her *Pacifism and Invasion* (New York: War Resisters League, 1942). The Hinshaw excerpt is from his *Non-violent Resistance: A Nation's Way to Peace*, Pendle Hill Pamphlet No. 88 (Wallingford, Pennsylvania: Pendle Hill, 1956).

Jessie W. Hughan: PACIFISM AND INVASION

* * * * *

The pacifist proposal is a clear cut and serious one, and we must be ready to meet the challenge "If our nation should renounce war and the preparation for war, would this necessitate 'lying down' before a hypothetical invader?" The present pamphlet is an attempt to answer this question.

Now fear can be dealt with in only one way, through looking it straight in the face. We are going to imagine the United States completely disarmed and invaded by a foreign foe; we will indicate the available measures of defense, and then try to evaluate the chances of success as compared with the time honored military method.

Of course we can give no guarantee of victory, and no assurance against losses and casualty lists. We can promise only one thing, that while military defense, at its best, means breaking all the Ten Commandments, unarmed defense, at its worst, involves no such necessity. Shall we demand of the second method, then, a guarantee of success which the first is unable to give? Shall we not rather look into its possibilities with what objectivity we can, and if we find a reasonable prospect that non-violent defense may accomplish its purpose with no greater loss and suffering than a war of corresponding magnitude, shall we not welcome the stern opportunity, just as decent individuals among us all would grasp at any dangers and hardships that might enable them to maintain their families without resort to manslaughter.

How Efficient Is Military Defense?

As the accounts of the present war are far from closed, let us take a look at the costs and efficiency of military defense as shown by a table of World War belligerents at the end of the war:

Country	Known Dead	Net Money Cost	Results
1. Great Britain	908,371	35 billions	Successful
2. Belgium	13,716		Unsuccessful
3. France	1,357,800	35 billions	Partially successful
4. Russia	1,700,000	22 billions	Unsuccessful
5. Germany	1,773,700	37 billions	Unsuccessful
6. Austro-Hungary	1,200,000	20 billions	Unsuccessful

Only two of the countries achieved even partial success. Failures meant the direct and indirect deaths of civilians, estimated as roughly equal to those in the armies, and a total of ten million refugees, one and a half million of these in Belgium and two million in France.

In considering the risks of military defense it is interesting to note that Belgium was well prepared against invasion in 1914. The peace strength of its army in 1913 was approximately 180,000 men, and the military estimates for that year amounted to 3,359,890 pounds sterling.

* * * * *

Belgium was protected also by ironclad treaties of alliance with Great Britain and France. Yet Belgium was as completely conquered by the German invaders as was Luxemburg, which possessed no army and put up no defense at all, both countries being eventually set free at the end of the war.

The tragedy of Czechoslovakia [in World War II] was an instance of unsuccessful defense through military preparedness, in the hope to avoid actual war. Fortified by the "second Maginot Line," supplied by the great Skoda munition works and relying, like Belgium, on the protection of two great powers, the Czech Republic, no more pacifist than Belgium, was forced to surrender without a battle.

The story of Poland, a traditionally belligerent nation with military forces of over a million, is even more tragic than that of Czechoslovakia, in so far as it declined to "lie down" before the aggressor until its men had been slaughtered and its cities bombed.

Finland, another heavily armed small country, succeeded for three months, aided by Arctic winter and difficult terrain, in beating back the Russian invasion. Its people were heroic; its defense included the famous Mannerheim Line; its Allies were Britain and France. Yet the terms forced upon it in March 1940, were even more severe than those it had scorned the previous December.

History contains no more tragic list of failures in defense than those of the years 1939–40. Six highly civilized nations, Norway, Denmark, Holland, Belgium, France and Greece have been invaded and conquered, leaving out of consideration countries such as Rumania and Hungary, which compromised with the aggressor as a ransom for survival.

Denmark, whose policy had been consistently anti-militarist though not pacifist, offered no resistance, but submitted without a struggle to German occupation.

Norway, Holland, Belgium, France and Greece put their trust in military defense and in the protection of their powerful ally, Britain. One by one they fell before the German blitzkrieg.

The Pacifist Proposal

In the light of this inadequacy of armed defense, the proposal is that . . . the United States take the first steps toward the goal of complete disarmament. In the event of an unprovoked invasion after this disarmament shall have taken place, we contend that the country will not be under the necessity of submitting to the invader, but will have at its command the tactics of non-violent non-cooperation, in other words, by a general strike raised to the nth power. Under this plan resistance would be carried on, not by professional soldiers but by the people as a whole, by refusing to obey the invaders or to assist them through personal service or the furnishing of supplies.

Removal of Incentive to Invasion

It is, of course, true that the chance of an unarmed United States being invaded is about that of an unarmed citizen being shot as he walks up Fifth Avenue—possible, but improbable. The motivation of conquest in the present day world, unless such a conquest is undertaken for the sake of gaining military advantage in a larger war, is almost wholly economic, the desire for undeveloped raw materials or vast new fields for the investment of capital. The prizes of imperialism are countries like Ethiopia or China, with untapped resources and industrially unsophisticated people. Our own country is developed up to the hilt and so overflowing with goods and capital as to offer no temptations to conquest. Before it disarms it will, of course, have removed all trade restrictions on its own raw materials and will have completed the process of setting free its few imperialist possessions.

The policy of settling disputes through the World Court, arbitration and conciliation will be extended to questions of every type, and knotty problems such as tariffs and currency will be committed without reservation on our part to international boards of adjustment. By concrete instances we will prove to the world the readiness of American business to accept financial losses for the sake of peace as formerly for the sake of carrying on war.

The signal for total disarmament would doubtless consist of the passage by Congress of the Amendment to the Constitution already introduced several times into the Senate, taking from government the power to prepare for, to declare or to carry on war. As pacifist opinion gained in the United States, however, the army and navy would gradually have been reduced to such negligible proportions that the final passage of the amendment would form the culmination of a process whose goal was definitely foreseen. Foreign nations would then be formally notified of the unconditional adherence of the United States to the Kellogg Pact, and would not fail to assure us in the honeyed words of diplomacy of their wholehearted cooperation and devotion to the cause of world peace. The following up of this proclamation by actual disarmament might indeed tax the credulity of foreign governments. . . . All doubts would be removed, however, by the immediate throwing open to inspection of our former military and naval posts and munition centers.

By the time that disarmament goes through, therefore, we shall be endangered by none of the undeveloped territory which has rendered Great Britain and France as choice targets as Ethiopia and China, and by no bristling armaments such as rallied the world against Germany in 1914 and have again driven the terrified nations into war.

*   *   *   *   *

It is to be remembered also that the modification of the social mind which brings disarmament will have brought also a radical change in our own conceptions of patriotism and national honor. Patriotism is already becoming a very concrete matter, under the stress of civilian defense, and is expressing itself less in verbal protestations than in obedience to law and protecting love for one's fellow citizens—young men of military age as well as women and children. . . . As complete disarmament approaches reality, anti-militarism will *pari passu* have emerged as a sacred national ideal, for which patriots will freely sacrifice personal interest and if necessary life itself. Our state department, therefore, will be held strictly accountable for preserving friendly international relations and its efficiency will be measured by the skill with which it prevents disputes with other nations from approaching the danger line of war. To this department, rather than to the military, will be entrusted the lives and property of the country.

If asked how we know that these radical changes in social psychology and diplomacy will have entered into the situation, we reply that they are essential to the earlier stages of pacifist policy, and cannot fail to be accomplished facts before any nation is ready to take the final step of renunciation of all war.

Facing the Hypothesis

Once more we repeat our hypothesis, that of a country which has voluntarily renounced all war and done away with armament, this step having been prepared for by years of reliance upon policies of international justice and friendship rather than upon force or the growing threat of force, and of an unprovoked invasion by a foreign foe. Chimerical as may seem the idea of a foreign invasion under these conditions, the problem before us is confessedly a fantastic one, which we have promised to face in all seriousness. The imagination can call up certain possibilities. A government bankrupted through armament might hope to reimburse itself by tribute levied upon Wall Street; a dictator might seek to retain power through the prestige of foreign conquest or through the spreading of Fascist ideals by fire and sword.

*   *   *   *   *

Since there could be no mobilization on our part to make haste imperative, the foreign government would, of course, begin with negotiations of one kind or another—demands for tribute, territory, or complete surrender of political existence.

These would be met by our government with diplomacy, with offers of arbitration and conciliation, and with formal recourse to the World Court. Only after deliberate defiance of world opinion could an enemy nation issue the ultimatum preliminary to invasion or proceed to a surprise attack without such notice.

We now have the United States faced with the alternative of resistance to the death or of "lying down" in submission. It is true that resistance is a lottery at best, and that even such absolute surrender as that of Germany in 1918 would have lost half its tragedy if it could have been put through in the summer of 1914, before a soldier had been mobilized. In the absence of revenge any tribute must be imposed by greed alone, and in that case might prove as stimulating to the surrendered country as the tribute paid by France after the Franco-Prussian war. Cultural ideas which run counter to group spirit can, of course, be enforced in name only, and there is evidence that a nation united in devotion to its traditions may maintain its own way of life even after nominal surrender.

How a Pacifist Nation Would "Prepare"

In the present discussion, however, we are disregarding the alternative of submission in any degree, and assuming a people firm in the determination to die rather than yield as individuals, or as a nation, to the demands of an invader. No surrender but resistance to the bitter end is the national policy.

The country is prepared for the conflict, having taken the bold step of disarmament, after years of mounting pacifism and in full anticipation of a possible test. Adventurous spirits have even looked forward to the chance of invasion as to the literal "war to end war" in which their nation might be the protagonist, with opportunities of heroism for every citizen undreamed of under the old regime.

The entire populace has been continually educated by all the resources of school, church and radio. Recognizing that its own country embodies liberty in such concrete forms as freedom of speech, freedom of assembly and freedom of conscience, it has centered its patriotism about these realities rather than such abstractions as empire and victory; accordingly it is alert to challenge any violation of civil liberty by friend or foe and to refuse even at serious sacrifice to submit to them. It has learned that while an individual can be restricted or punished, he can never be compelled to action against his will; its heroes have shifted from Caesar and Napoleon to such men as Socrates and Pastor Niemoeller. It has become a national ideal to despise anger and cruelty as pathological and to hold all human life sacred.

Most difficult of all, the masses have been trained in the exercise of individual courage, measured by the cool test of deliberate heroism rather than group recklessness. . . .

*   *   *   *   *

As pacifism gradually becomes the conviction of the majority of citizens, the soldier's task of killing the enemy will have lost the attraction it now holds, but the soldierly virtue of enduring hardship and death for one's country will have become the ideal, not of a single profession, but of an entire population. Government officials particularly, from the head of the state to the lowest civil servant, will realize themselves to be the successors of the army in its function of national defense, pledged, whatever their rank, to unswerving loyalty if crises should arise.

*   *   *   *   *

The present use of the word "defense" to designate services as far removed from the military as housing and teaching is an indication that the foundations for non-violent resistance on a national scale are already being laid.

Exploration and surveys, soil reclamation, civilian aviation, prevention of flood and disease, relief of suffering from natural disasters at home and abroad, all these can afford increasing scope for the trained abilities now set apart for destructive purposes. The coast guard, enlarged to furnish protection throughout all coasts and inland waters, and the fire department, developed in forest and rural districts to the efficiency already achieved in cities, are amply able to provide physical equivalents for war, and can be made equally reputable by assigning to them the rank, pay and pensions now reserved for military defenders. A similar rise in honor and compensation can elevate the police force, both local and national, to the level of dignity where the army and navy now stand.

*   *   *   *   *

It is upon these various defense services, their officers high in the counsels of government and their privates in close touch with citizens everywhere, that the pacifist nation will rely in such hypothetical dangers as invasion by a foreign foe.

The propaganda and intelligence departments would carry even more responsibility under a pacifist government than at present. In time of peace their duty will be to inform the world of each concrete measure of disarmament and to interpret our policy of international friendliness to foreign peoples as well as to their governments. Radio and the screen will be utilized for this purpose, and our consulates abroad will circulate countless bulletins making clear the application of our "good neighbor" policy to the country in question. In case of invasion those departments will keep both friendly and hostile nations in touch with every measure and event. The foreign press will be given all facilities for news getting, and battalions of daring aviators will be ready to shower leaflets upon the enemy country if access to the press is closed. As observers abroad will have no discrepancies to reconcile between the protestations of our government and its known policies before the crisis, emergency propaganda of this type will be able to carry conviction impossible under the present regime.

Physical preparations for defense will of course be made, far less expensive than in the case of military resistance, but not less essential. The first of these is obviously the destruction of all firearms and other weapons of offense, with the machinery for producing them. This pledge of good faith to other nations is also a necessary defense measure to obviate "sniping" and other provocative incidents. Moreover, it will be important for an invading army to know that we possess no stores of war munitions which it may seize. For some time an exception may have to be made of the rifles of professional hunters and of small arms in the hands of the police, but, when private sale has once been abolished, only a negligible supply of the latter need be retained. As military "atrocities" chiefly occur under conditions of intoxication, one of the first war measures will be to destroy all distilleries and supplies of liquor throughout the country. Food and other necessities will have been stored at strategic points. Other defense plans will relate to methods of communication, of speedy evacuation, of rehabilitation, and of rendering various districts capable of maintaining themselves in possible isolation. The suggestions of the present article are the merest foreshadowings of the defense tactics which may be adopted. . . .

The Principles of Unarmed Defense

Though we cannot pretend to a complete blueprint of the working of unarmed defense, the four main principles are already established:

1. No services or supplies to be furnished to invaders.
2. No orders to be obeyed except those of the constitutional civil authorities.
3. No insult or injury to be offered the invaders.
4. All public officials to be pledged to die rather than surrender.

A Battle Without Arms

Let us now envisage the situation presented by the fantastic hypothesis of an invasion, fantastic in view of the years of friendly international policy which have preceded it, but yet a possibility. The potential enemy has ignored proposals of conciliation, and has either issued a humiliating ultimatum or opened hostilities by a surprise attack upon our coast. The world has its ear to the radio, and our government and people, morally and physically prepared, brace themselves for the conflict. As defense involves not only those of military age, but every man, woman and child in the community, there is immediate evacuation from threatened localities of all persons likely to be incapacitated through fear or physical weakness. Provision is quickly made for emergency supplies and communication, according to plans thought out beforehand. Civil officials, including directors of public utilities, as well as of government, have accepted the full responsibilities and dangers of leadership; succession to each important office has been provided for in the event of death or imprisonment, and citizens are well acquainted with the order in which those names on the long list of honor will take the place of those who have fallen.

Meeting with no opposition other than the ordinary traffic regulations, the enemy commander, with an escort picked for courage, enters the City Hall and is received with courtesy by the Mayor. After diplomatic preliminaries the Mayor, following the precedent of the heroic Mayor of Vienna in 1934, refuses the order to surrender and is taken prisoner. The first vice-mayor automatically succeeds, but the invaders exclude him from the City Hall, setting in his place a traitor or an officer of their own. Executives and clerks continue to perform their duties, however, until commands arrive from the enemy usurper, when they either ignore the orders or cease work altogether, quietly destroying combinations and documents if opportunity offers.

The city departments of fire and police, with the public utility services of telegraph, telephone and electricity, continue to function under their regular heads until these receive enemy orders. At this point they, too, will disregard specific commands or declare an instantaneous strike. Workers in garages, gas stations, airports and railroads will go on serving the civil population until interfered with, and resume work if and when pressure is removed. If their chief is arrested, the workers automatically transfer obedience to his successor on the list, failing to report to duty under an enemy appointee, but ready at a moment's notice to rally to their authorized head.

Food and strategic materials, if not already publicly owned, are controlled by trustworthy officials directed to refuse all supplies to the invaders, but to conserve and distribute them for the benefit of civilians.

The citizens in general follow the same rigid program of passive resistance as public employees. No one insults the interlopers, but no one sells to them or works for them. The usurping commander issues orders which are firmly ignored, but strict obedience is given to those legitimate officers who remain in authority. Civilian occupations go on as usual till the enemy touches them. In that case, work stops by magic and that particular unit of industry remains frozen till further notice.

Everywhere the invaders meet the same conditions—no battles, no opposing armies, no dangers, no chances for heroism. On the other hand, no surrenders to figure in the dispatches, no peasants offering food, no sullenly obedient populace, no technicians or workers to man the utilities. The soldiers have nothing to do but to serve themselves by routine labor, varied by assaults upon unarmed citizens and ignominious robbing of shops and hen-roosts.

Neither army morale nor war fever in the aggressor nation is likely to hold out long against this reversal of all that makes the spirit of a campaign. Our propaganda works havoc with the foreign soldiers and their own opposition politics with the foreign citizens. Before many weeks or months elapse, it is probable that the enemy government will hasten to cover up its blunder by recalling the inglorious and unprofitable expedition. [Nevertheless, let us face frankly]—

The Hypothesis of Ruthlessness

After the first skirmish with the people, the foreign general will consult his government as to the alternatives, terrorism or compromise. He has power to torture striking workers, execute disobedient citizens and deliberately starve the resisting community.

* * * * *

In the enemy country the first hysteria has died down, for civilian war spirit, like that of the army, requires battles and heroism for its sustenance. The opposition to the ruling group, always present whether open or suppressed, begins to gather strength.

Furthermore, the nation must save its face with other powers by at least the pretence of justifiability. Since a military dictatorship is even more dependent than a normal government upon the maintenance of an emergency situation, it cannot fail to find its popular support seriously undermined. Accordingly . . . self-preservation will prescribe the more moderate course, to make the most of its nominal victory rather than risk political defeat through wantonly terroristic measures.

In this case the invaders, after a number of arrests and confiscations, will advance to their next objective, leaving behind them, in addition to the usual garrison, a complete corps of technicians and workers for essential services and communications. The citizens meanwhile will have returned more or less to normal life, hampered by the presence of the garrison, suffering occasional arrests and even executions when orders conflict, and subject to seizures of property when foraging necessity demands it. Their condition will be unenviable and even pitiable, but will differ more in degree than in kind from that of civilians under martial law in territory occupied by their own military defenders.

We are deliberately facing, however, the most fantastic hypothesis which can be devised, and must force our imaginations to a third possibility—that of extreme and gratuitous ruthlessness such as has never yet appeared in history. We are to envisage an implacable commander under an unscrupulous government, supported by a political party quite reckless of world or minority opinion. Conquest at all cost is the policy chosen; as civil officials refuse obedience they are one after the other arrested and executed, and recalcitrant workers are herded into concentration camps, their posts being filled by foreign soldiers. As enemy technicians are limited in number, only work necessary to the army will be performed and the public utilities will be largely cut off.

An actual battle is under way, between starvation and enemy violence on one hand and the will of a selected civilian population on the other. The food supply will of course constitute the chief point of strategy. Provisions for some days have been brought by the foreign transports, but these must be economized for an emergency while the army lives as far as possible upon the country. As part of its defense precautions the home government has avoided concentration of essential supplies where they may be seized, and the invaders proceed to the robbery of small stocks in the hands of retailers and individuals. Foraging parties break into homes and warehouses, carrying off what supplies they find, but the food industry, like other services, congeals into strikes as soon as interfered with. Dairy products, meat and fresh vegetables cannot be bought or requisitioned. The shop is closed, the dairy is uncared for, the crops are ungathered, and the stream of commodities which normally enters the city by train or truck is immediately cut off at its sources and turned by the government to other districts. A modern city is seldom distant more than a few days from famine, and in a very short time the limits of seizure have been reached. The army finds itself reduced to dependence upon imported supplies, in the midst of a populace kept from starvation only in so far as it is permitted to handle its own provisions unmolested.

At the first threat to the civilian food supply, on the other hand, the evacuation has begun of those persons who remained in the invaded region. By train and motor car until these are seized, and then on foot, they scatter over the country, destroying crops and stores as they go. . . .

Have there been casualties? There have—executions, imprisonments, deaths from exposure and starvation.

There is also the possibility that ruthlessness may do its worst, resorting to air and sea bombardment, high explosives and poison gas, to break the will of the people. Under military defense, on the other hand, attempts at bombardment are not a mere possibility but a certainty . . .

* * * * *

As is now made clear to civilian defense groups, the government in war time aims first to protect things—factories and military supplies—and second to protect people,[1] but restriction of funds sets definite limits to those efforts. A pacifist government, on the other hand, would not be hampered in this way, but could direct its entire resources to the defense of civilian life and property.

It would be comparatively easy also to effect the evacuation of threatened towns. . . . Military governments are strictly limited in these matters, as the conventional defense requires the concentration of soldiers at danger points, with civilians for essential services, but the non-violent state could arrange for the complete evacuation of danger zones, and would, of course, gain efficiency by being able to employ all its resources for the defense of civilians.

After making all allowances, the number of casualties is no easier to compute than in an old style conflict. . . . Is there any general sufficiently barbarous to decree even fifty per cent of this slaughter against unarmed civilians? It is possible, but improbable.

Between the two courses of nominal seizure of government and ruthless terrorism or bombardment there are of course

[1] The British Defence Ministry's 1957 White Paper gives first priority to air bases and admits that British cities cannot really be defended.—Ed.

countless degrees and modifications which would approach far more nearly a true forecast.

The Enemy Has Gained Nothing

Be the losses little or great, however, the important point is that the enemy has gained nothing by the engagement, whether in indemnity, supplies or capitulation. If an air force has been employed it will of course be unable to occupy the district, and an army attempting to follow up its advantage would meet in exaggerated form the conditions already indicated, a city stripped of supplies and of all inhabitants but an unyielding even if starving group of survivors.

In any case the invaders will proceed to press on into the interior, leaving a garrison behind them with workers for transport and communication.

Everywhere the invaders meet with communities of unyielding civilians, resolute in giving obedience to none but their own government; they receive no services of any kind from the population; and can secure supplies only from the forcible seizure of small stocks, which diminish and disappear in proportion to the degree of ruthlessness exerted.

The invading soldiers must depend upon imported supplies and as they advance into the interior transportation becomes a serious problem. In the World War, 100,000 men and 25,000 animals required the transportation of 780 to 2,100 tons daily, aside from ammunition. A present day authority, Major George Fielding Eliot, considers four tons of supplies necessary for every soldier, "plus eight tons for his equipment, etc."[2]; for an invading force of 100,000 this would require the transportation of 1,200,000 tons.

In order to avoid increasing the transportation problem by adding an immense force of laborers and technicians, invaders trust to the inhabitants for the bulk of their skilled and unskilled labor and since passive resistance by civilians has never constituted a feature of war, this has usually been practicable.

* * * * *

As unarmed defense . . . transfers resistance from the military to the civil population, the invaders of our hypothesis will have at their command no assistance of this type. Soldiers must not only attend personally to all their needs, but also man without native help all the railroads, telegraphs, and airports upon which the advance depends. At each stage, moreover, they must leave behind them a complete local government with gar-

[2] *The Ramparts We Watch* (New York: Reynal, 1938).

rison, technicians and workers, as the legitimate authorities
will have new groups of defenders always ready to take the
risks of restoring civil life at the rear of the invading forces.

It is, of course, unthinkable that the enemy would undertake the maintenance of public utilities and government upon
any peace time scale. In 1935 the railroad employees of the
United States numbered 1,013,000 and the federal civil service 824,259, amounting together to more than half the German or the Japanese army of that time, including reserves.
Even the skeleton service required for military purposes would
call for thousands of men, and we have taken in this estimate
no account of garrisons, food, service and utilities other than
the railroads. We cannot picture the advance of the invaders
as anything but costly from a financial point of view, precarious as far as permanent results are concerned, and dis-
tasteful to the large proportion of the army who are compelled to exchange uniforms for overalls for an indefinite
period.

* * * * *

Let us assume this advance of an invading force through a
first class country to continue for, say a month. The enemy
has cut a swath of nominal occupation on the one hand, or
of devastation on the other, through the country. They may
have reached the goal of our national capitol and burned it,
as happened in 1813 (a war which was followed by a most
successful peace). By landing several expeditions they may
even have laid waste three or four broad paths into the interior. The effect upon the civil life of these localities has been
that of a severe natural calamity; and persons and industry
have been transferred after many casualties to districts as yet
untouched.

The invaders, on the other hand, have achieved not
one of the objectives for which the expedition has been
launched. . . .

* * * * *

Any military advantages to the enemy must be only nominal. Naval and air bases have no meaning in the unarmed nation, and are worthless as stepping stones to new conquests
when the territory is itself of great extent.

Most important of all, any efforts to engraft a foreign fascism will encounter, not a people weakened by the unques-
tioning obedience to the unified state which military defense
requires, but a nation whose zeal for democracy has been
sharpened and made effective by crisis after crisis of individual
responsibility.

Plight of the Enemy Government

Meanwhile the prestige of conquest has turned to international ridicule as our people remain unsubdued and the invading forces encounter no perils upon which their heroism can feed. At the first indication that neither raw materials nor investment fields are to be gained, the business interests upon which the foreign government depends will criticize sharply the policy which has dislocated commerce by putting a former customer out of the running. As month after month conscript armies and wealth continue to be poured into the invaded territory the taxpayers become restive; self-interest, suppressed for a time under the passions of fear and hate, becomes once more articulate; and solid citizens lose their enthusiasm for financing the devastation of a country whose good faith in non-aggression has now been demonstrated. Within a few days, or weeks at the most, the invading soldiers themselves, bored with inaction and undermined by propaganda, will unfailingly sicken of orders to kill and destroy and will lose their morale in the steady absence of opportunities to show courage and achieve distinction. Calls for new recruits bring response from few but the criminal classes, and unwilling conscripts cannot be depended upon to maintain the policy of ruthlessness.

Meanwhile, such countries as remain neutral at first, not sufficiently idealistic to protest at the threatened invasion, will soon be pressed by their own business interests to demand that ports be reopened and commerce with our people again made possible.

The invading government finds prestige and finances decreasing day by day, while the popular will to war, upon which military power depends for existence, has withered and died for lack of that upon which to feed. At home and abroad the expedition becomes the butt of ridicule. The opposition party, which openly or underground has long awaited the moment of weakness, stands ready to strike for control as soon as the bulletins of unsuccessful terrorism have had their effect upon workers and taxpayers. If some face-saving pretext is not speedily found to bring the recall of the mutinous forces, the military government will go down to defeat, carrying with it the hollow fabric of dictatorship in that country.

The Chances of Victory

But can this complete and speedy victory be guaranteed? It cannot. Pacifists are not endowed with omniscience, merely with common-sense, and non-violence cannot claim immunity from those chances of war which have brought so many campaigns to naught.

The outcome indicated is inescapable, however, granted the two points of our hypothesis: first, that the invaded population is united in unarmed resistance, and second, that the enemy nation, though ruthless and unscrupulous under an artificial standard of ethics, is not a community of pathological fools. Non-violent resistance is the only type of defense which, from beginning to end, yields to the enemy not even a prospect of any of the usual rewards of invasion: prestige, glory, indemnity, subject people, trade or military advantages, available territory, triumph of ideals. The pleasure of wanton destruction is the only satisfaction to be derived, and it is true that this impulse is to be reckoned with in dealing with children, with imbeciles, with intoxicated or desperate men. By no stretch of imagination, however, can the mere lust of killing strangers motivate the sane business men of an industrial nation to keep on financing armies indefinitely for unprofitable idleness overseas.

All victory consists in breaking down the will to war of the enemy people. Military defense tries to do this through fear, which frequently produces the opposite effect. Non-violent defense works through self-interest, slower to arouse but more reliable in the long run.

It will be noted that the foregoing plans take absolutely no account of appeals to the compassion or ethics of the enemy. We have done this, not from a belief in the existence of nations or human beings completely callous to such an appeal, but in the desire to make our hypothesis as difficult as can be conceived. It would be unscientific, however, to shut our eyes to the existence of religion, humanity, and love of justice as elements in individual and group psychology . . .

*   *   *   *   *

Under the old system, religion and ethics in the foreign country could usually be harnessed through fear to the military machine. Unarmed defense, however, prevents all clouding of the ethical issues, and cannot fail to enlist on the side of the invaded people all men of good will, wherever found.

*   *   *   *   *

Cecil E. Hinshaw: NON-VIOLENT RESISTANCE:
A NATION'S WAY TO PEACE

THE IRONY OF WAR

It will indeed be ironical if the elimination of military strength as a valid concept of defense should be the result of military developments. Yet that appears to be the prospect.

There are very few responsible leaders today, and their number decreases steadily, who believe that successful military defense, in the event of total atomic war, is possible. It should be even more clear that the coming development of guided missiles reduces such prospects even more. Without trying to prove the case absolutely, for we live in a world where we decide our choices largely on the basis of probabilities, let it suffice to state that a rational person who attempts to support the probability of successful defense in the event of total atomic war is assuming a terrifying burden of proof.

But many other people have not yet accepted what seems so evident. The reasons are two. Any change with such vast repercussions in thought and action can only come slowly in society, gradually penetrating into the consciousness of people as it is accepted emotionally as well as intellectually. The second factor in our present immobility of thought is that people cannot live in a vacuum and will continue to rationalize an old error until a positive and hopeful alternative can be found.

This pamphlet therefore proceeds on the assumption that there is no longer any necessity among thoughtful people of proving that national defense of a military nature in the event of total atomic war is an illusion.[3]

BALANCE OF TERROR

The only real hope left to most people today is the gamble that the threat of terror through "massive retaliation" will prevent the coming of total war again. If our enemies know that, though we cannot defend ourselves, we can and will retaliate with weapons which they are equally powerless to resist, surely neither they nor we will ever start a war. So, this reasoning goes, an uneasy peace can be preserved by this balance of terror itself and we can live in the hope that changes in Communist countries will sometime reduce the tension and allow the building of genuine peace.

This argument is much more logical than the belief in defense and it deserves a careful answer. . . .

Those who defend this thesis ought to realize, however, the gamble that is involved and should be aware that atomic war may come even though neither side intends for it to happen.

[3] Herman Kahn, author of the recent *On Thermonuclear War* (Princeton University Press, 1960), speaks of possibly 40,000,000 American deaths.—Ed.

Rather than a sudden outburst of atomic attacks, probably the greater danger is that we would slide gradually into real war from the starting point of a "little" war.

But now, having recognized the very real danger that a game of lethal bluffing may all too easily end in disaster, let us assume that such will not be the case, that we can avoid atomic war. Even on the basis of this optimistic analysis, we still face formidable problems.

One of those problems, too little faced as yet, is simply the matter of the experimentation for the making and use of atomic and hydrogen weapons. . . . The most casual reader today can hardly avoid being aware of the statements by responsible scientists warning that atomic experiments may exact a terrible price from the world, perhaps even from unborn generations through the genetic effects that may be multiplied in our posterity.

*   *   *   *   *

THE LIMITATION OF LIMITED WARFARE

Some of those who maintain that we shall probably never fight a total atomic war argue that "little wars"—a kind of limited warfare like that in Korea—will be the pattern of the future. If this is true, we must ask more exactly what the nature of such wars will likely be.

If the wars of the future are to be similar to the Korean war, and if they can be so sharply limited, America faces a strategic problem of immense proportions. Conventional warfare requires tremendous manpower, especially when it is fought on the semi-guerrilla pattern to which much of the world is so well adapted. For America to engage in other such wars, especially in Asia, is to pit our limited manpower against the tremendous superiority of manpower of the Communist countries. The geography of Korea limited the possible use of large numbers of troops but no such limits would be imposed in most other places.

There should be no illusion as to help from America's so-called allies in such contests. Very little manpower is available to us from South America, Africa, and Asia and not even very much from Europe. For all practical purposes America will have to fight such wars alone if they are fought in the future.

Further, the rapidly developing peoples of other lands are going to equal or nearly equal us in conventional warfare technology soon so that we cannot continue to count on enormous fire-power superiority.

*   *   *   *   *

The logical consequence of trying to fight such wars with conventional weapons thousands of miles from home, handicapped by the problems of logistics across vast distances, is to bleed the United States of its strength, to court military and psychological disaster, and to align ourselves with questionable reactionary forces in far lands in order to try to strengthen a desperate military position.

It is at this point that we can most easily understand why military officials in the United States do not wish to fight a war on the plan just described and expect, instead, to use limited atomic weapons in such a war. The nature of those weapons that might be used can only be surmised but presumably atomic artillery shells and quite small atomic bombs would be included. Recent tests, however, indicate that these "small" atomic explosions approach the category of unlimited destruction in the area in which the struggle occurs.

If the enemy did not counter with similar weapons, we might secure military victory, though even that prospect can be considerably dimmed by guerrilla warfare and wide dispersion of the enemy. But there seems no particular reason why the enemy could not, if he should choose, use such weapons in return. If so, we might well be at a considerable disadvantage because of the need of concentrating troops more heavily at some points and because of reliance on ocean transport, which would likely be dangerously vulnerable, especially to atomic-powered submarines and to atomic bombs dropped from planes.

Few Americans have faced the extent of the psychological defeat we shall suffer in Asia if we initiate the use of any kind of atomic weapons. . . .

Actually an announcement by the enemy in such an event proclaiming refusal to use barbaric atomic weapons on the grounds of humanitarian considerations could place America in such an extremely disadvantageous position as to make most improbable any support of significance from Asian and perhaps European sources. Further, it would produce an embarrassing position in which we might find ourselves unable to continue the use of atomic weapons, both because of world-wide disapproval and also because of internal dissension in our own country on the matter. For we have not really considered the moral position we would be in if we should use atomic weapons only to find that a presumably immoral enemy capable of using them refused on moral grounds to retaliate in like manner.

Perhaps the greatest danger of all in this concept of limited warfare is the terrible risk of the enlargement of the conflict. The temptation to the losing side will be very strong to use ever more destructive weapons. For we may be reasonably sure that such weapons will be available even to small countries in the future. Thus there is created the slippery slide down which the whole world may involuntarily go as the momentum of angers, fears, hatreds, and suspicions plunges leaders no longer rational into the abyss.

* * * * *

Underlying all of these problems is the haunting specter of the condemnation of our own consciences as well as the moral judgment of the world if we dare to begin an atomic conflict, even though it be limited. And, if the enemy precipitates atomic and hydrogen warfare, we still are faced with the terrible fact that our retaliation will surely involve us in the slaughter of millions of innocent people, young and old, who have not at all consented to the action of their government. The shadows of Hiroshima and Nagasaki are long across the soul of America. Is the destruction of the enemy in retaliation, knowing that our own brutality can in no way defend us, justified by any standard of morals and principles we have valued and taught? If death is our lot in any case, would the meager satisfaction of knowing the enemy dies with us make our torture more bearable? . . .

LOSING FRIENDS AND ALIENATING PEOPLE

To the degree that Communists become confident that atomic war is unlikely or impossible, we can expect them to devote increasing time, attention, and resources to the battle to influence the undecided portions of the world. There are two methods open to them for accomplishing this purpose. And they have demonstrated both willingness to use and ability to execute these means.

The inflammation of old sores scarcely healed over from the wounds of imperialism will be reopened, stirring strife and quarrels between factions and nations. Such intrigues slow the constructive work in underdeveloped countries and also keep the United States in the minds of millions of people as the successor to the imperialism they learned to hate in the days of white men's domination. Nor will the Communists be reluctant to use such opportunities to wrest from us the control of natural resources, especially oil in the Middle East and, perhaps later, uranium in Africa.

On a rather more constructive basis, the second weapon the Communists will use in the psychological conflict for the loyalty of newly independent people will be the promise of practical aid in the vast projects and plans to which so many governments now look for relief from the crushing burdens of poverty, illiteracy, and hunger. Russia and China have a considerable psychological advantage here that is seldom recognized in America. Both of them are industrializing rather successfully without any considerable outside help, and the new countries in fierce pride want to do everything for themselves they possibly can. . . . Further, both Russia and China are now engaged in the gigantic task of industrializing masses and they therefore seem much closer to the problems of Asia and Africa, the more so because the problems of village peoples in old cultures and overpopulated lands are so different from America's problems in the industrialization of a new country.

But the really dangerous advantage Communism has is its eager alliance everywhere with the forces of revolution against feudalism and intrenched wealth. And the very nature of the struggle means that the opponents of change—the landlords, the large industrialists, the wealthy native rulers—turn to us for help and support. So, against our own traditions and, often, our desires, we are cast in the dangerous and unenviable role of defending the very forces and people we ought to be opposing. Our need for alliances with elements of military, political, and economic strength in order to oppose Communism is such that we join hands with dictators. . . .

Americans find it hard to understand why our beneficence expressed in technical aid and distribution of surplus food is often so little appreciated and seems to have rather small effect. The answer is in what has just been said. So our motives are deeply questioned. And even the good results—increased agricultural production and industrial development—too often simply result in making the wealthy wealthier. This accentuates the gap between the poor and the rich and becomes grist for the Communist propaganda mill.

* * * * *

Wise and understanding aid, given primarily through the United Nations to help people help themselves, coupled with far more willingness on our part to trade freely, is both essential and promising. And, if it were freed of the unfortunate results that flow from unholy alliances with corrupt military and political elements, it would benefit the countries many times more than is the case now. Then we would be free, too, to act in accordance with our own traditions. . . .

POSITIONS OF STRENGTH

In the building of a concept and practice of defense that will not fall into the errors we have observed in present practice and generally accepted theories, we need to begin by a survey of the resources at our command. Even as a general whose forces have been shattered must take stock of what is still available as he plans for a new campaign, so recognizing the bankruptcy of present military defense, we must marshall all the elements of strength available and must find, if possible, new technics and resources.

The Power of Freedom

In spite of the painful fact that our practice of the principles of freedom still falls too far short of our theory, the measure of success we have achieved and the ideal we accept as our guide still stand as beacon lights to our world, the promise of a better future. The criticisms rightly made of our failures are actually a testimonial to the expectations that others have of us. . . .

That man is made for freedom is an article of our faith. While we perhaps can not prove it in scientific fashion, we can marshall considerable evidence that the nature of man is more responsive to freedom than to tyranny. And the evidence from history is irrefutable that he longs for freedom and will under some circumstances struggle desperately to obtain it. The upsurge of nationalism in much of the world today, even a great deal of the violence in our times, is striking evidence of man's thirst for liberty.

Our own traditions and principles are in harmony with this fundamental drive in man's nature. Our practice has not always been so attractive, however. But we have already observed that a prime reason for part of our failure in practice, especially in our relations with Asia and Africa, is the handicap and blight that the requirements of military defense produce. If we could be free of military entanglements, we would indeed have a major opportunity to help vast numbers of people express their natural desires and tendencies to move toward lives of freedom rather than to submit to tyranny.

*   *   *   *   *

Religion

Nothing is easier than to point out the inconsistencies and failures of organized religion. The truly amazing fact, though, is the ability through the centuries of this weak human instrument, in the face of the greatest difficulties and in spite of human shortcomings, to produce the persistent rebirths of spiritual power and life that give men faith and hope, inspiring loyalty and devotion, and motivating deeds of mercy and love.

This is not to suggest that religious institutions are not subject to failure and misuse, both in Communist and non-Communist countries. There is nothing magical about religious enterprises to insure their continuance or their success. And especially must we penitently recognize our present lack of spiritual depth and vitality, understanding that full churches and multiplied worship services cannot at all be equated with religious health and may even be a sign of sickness.

Religion answers to a deeply felt need in man, a need that can never be erased by any tyranny or materialism, else churches would not have survived and even flourished under the circumstances that have obtained in some parts of the world. And there is growing evidence that Communist governments, even while they still maintain many restrictions on the practice of religion, have been forced to recognize this elemental fact in man's nature.

* * * * *

Productive Capacity and Technical Knowledge

No one can travel through the vast areas of human need that characterize most of our world without being aware of the inescapable and indubitable necessity of providing some reasonable answer to man's material distress. To do this efficiently and rapidly, and to do it in a manner that means respect for the cultures and contributions of the people who are being assisted, is to create one of the most powerful weapons that can be forged in the struggle with tyranny.

For it is dangerously true that one of Communism's chief attractions is the promise it holds out, not altogether false, that the organizational efficiency of a dictatorship can rapidly industrialize a country and remold the habits and attitudes that presently constitute tremendous barriers to successful industrialization. The fact that Communism has not yet found an answer to declining agricultural production among the peasants and the fact that Communism's material progress is at great human cost do not mean that people in Asia and Africa will necessarily be deterred from choosing Communism. For they are willing to pay a very great price for industrial development, believing, whether rightly or wrongly, that they can sufficiently modify Communism later on to preserve the freedom they cherish.

Yet it should be abundantly clear that a system of more freedom and liberty can build a firmer foundation for material progress and human well-being. And there surely can be no doubt that we presently have in our hands the immense technological achievements and material resources needed to help under-developed countries realize their possibilities. . . .

The Limitations of Tyranny

One of the worst mistakes in American thought has been the easy assumption that totalitarian governments are as powerful as they claim to be. So it is common in the West to hear the Communist boast echoed—the assertion that dictatorships can completely mold and determine the life and thought of the people of a country. The falsity of this claim should be apparent to any thoughtful person by now. It simply is not true that now or in 1984 or ever in the future a government can or will be able to dehumanize men completely, transforming them into automatons.

To say this is not to minimize the very real dangers that dictatorship brings. Even a relatively mild attack of the disease can cause real damage to a country, as we should now know. Without doubt a dictatorship can use fear, brutality, psychology, propaganda, promises, threats, and bribes to achieve in measure some of its ends. In fact, it is because of this danger that we must steadfastly oppose the advance of totalitarianism in any form in our world.

The error has been to believe that a dictator could have steady and continuing success in *all* his nefarious plans. There is no evidence to indicate that tyrants can thus become gods, transforming men into robots or puppets. On the contrary, man, made in God's image, has a point beyond which he does not go in accepting slavery, even though the cost of rebellion is life itself.

* * * * *

Any law enforcement agent can verify the simple truth that is here involved. There is a limit beyond which no government, no matter what its nature, can go in enforcing laws that are contrary to the will of the people.

The Power of Passive Resistance

What has been noted above becomes explicit and politically significant when we consider the meaning of mass, organized refusal of a people to obey a government. There is no power that can force the obedience of masses of people to laws and authority they have decided to resist simply by passive resistance.

Gandhi's contribution at this point to our problem is monumental. He demonstrated that jails and concentration camps can never be used to imprison enough people to break such a program of non-violent resistance. Nor can the use of violence and terrorism thwart the intentions of a people determined and prepared to resist a dictator.

There will be those who will say that India is not a fair example, that the circumstances were so different as to make Gandhi's experience not applicable to us. . . . But the differences in this case are by no means so great as most people suppose.

In response to those who say that India acted only from weakness, that she had no other choice than passive resistance, two observations should be made. First we approach a period where the utter failure of armaments, as we have heretofore observed, makes us so vulnerable that we are presumptuous if we suppose we can move from strength because of military power; that we are, in fact, relatively any stronger militarily than India was in relation to England. Secondly, the assumption that India could have won her freedom in no other way is wrong. Events since then should amply vindicate the thesis that India could have won her independence by violence (as Subha Chandra Bose and others in India said in opposition to Gandhi) even more quickly than did Indonesia. . . .

Other critics will say that the British really yielded before they were forced to and that a more ruthless and less idealistic opponent could and would have maintained the hold upon India in spite of the non-violence campaign of resistance. This view magnifies the goodness of England beyond what the facts warrant and minimizes the evil in the English rule. Such people forget the Amritsar massacre when 1500 unarmed Indians were shot down in cold blood. And a host of other brutal acts by the British forces should remind us that even good men can become cruel despots when they are caught up in a tyrannical system as in Nazi Germany or British rule in India. Further, the goodness in the British that resulted in yielding so generously may be attributed in part to the validity of the Gandhian method, aimed as it was precisely at this point— winning the British *consent* rather than simply forcing their removal.

But there is a deeper issue here and that is whether Communists from a country like Russia are so different by nature and training from the British that these methods would be destined to fail if used against them. So we must investigate what we can learn of the probable Communist response to such methods of resistance.

As to the "Russian nature," if there is such, it is not very profitable to speculate. There is evidence that Russians can be terribly brutal. And there is proof that good church people in America could and did display a now almost unbelievable brutality toward slaves and toward American Indians. Then there is evidence that Russians, both in historical incidents and in literature such as that of Tolstoy and Dostoyevsky could be gentle, merciful, and kind—even to a fault, if such be possible. And the same is true of Americans, as of English, and as of people everywhere.

But some will say that Communist rule over a long time so changes men that, regardless of how they personally feel, they will obey any order, no matter how revolting and cruel.

But if this is the case, how does one explain the refusal of seventeen Russian officers and soldiers in the East German revolt of 1953 to obey the orders of their superiors, a refusal that they must have known would end in court-martial and death, as it actually did end? It is inconceivable that the Russian occupation army called in to quell that non-violent uprising would not have been composed of the most trusted, best disciplined, and most thoroughly indoctrinated Communists available. Why, then, did they pay with their lives rather than to obey the orders of their superiors?

Some critics will reply that, even so, this can happen with only a very few and we must not generalize on such a small basis. After all, most of the Russians *did* obey. And this must be admitted. Generalization here is impossible. But, by the same logic, no generalization is possible on the other side. For apparently genuine and trusted Communists *have* refused to obey orders, even at the cost of their lives.

Obviously the real question is whether there is reasonable prospect that such repudiation of Communism, if we used passive resistance on a large and organized scale, could develop into a powerful enough movement to defeat the attempted tyranny. No proof can be expected on either side. Here we arrive at what may properly be termed a "calculated risk."

Perhaps the most reasonable conclusion is that the result would probably depend on the extent to which the passive resisters were able to persist, regardless of enemy persecution, in maintaining a united stand in a spirit free of hatred and largely imbued with friendship and love. That this is the proper way to state the case becomes most evident when we ask whether a nation composed entirely of Gandhis could succeed in such a program. Almost every one will agree that passive resistance would in that case defeat the tyranny. But it is right to point out that no nation will ever be composed of Gandhis. So the real question is neither whether the enemy is completely devilish or whether we are completely saintly. Rather, it is whether a free people—*ordinary* free people—can, with proper leadership, develop, organize, and carry on a concerted, persistent, and effective program of passive resistance against tyranny. If there is reasonable hope that they can do so, we have at hand a weapon of resistance to evil that can replace the now antiquated, useless, and dangerous atomic warfare upon which we still rely for defense.

THE MORAL EQUIVALENT OF WAR

A half century ago, William James wrote an essay, pregnant with prophetic insights into the future, in which he called for a moral equivalent of warfare. For James recognized that men could never be expected to abandon warfare, however futile and vicious it became, until the moral equivalent of war could be evolved. And today we can add that our need is desperate for a practical equivalent of military warfare.

We have now to investigate whether the five "positions of strength" we have just reviewed can be welded together to form a workable and promising equivalent of war, able to replace the military program which no longer serves its proper purpose. The best manner of making such an investigation is to develop an hypothesis or proposed plan for a national defense program based on these principles. For it is in the attempt to make a specific, though theoretical, application of them that we can best determine the possible validity of these principles.

This approach requires the assumption that a country would decide to follow the course here to be outlined. Whether any country, and specifically our own, would ever make such a decision is obviously a valid question. But it should also be obvious that it is properly asked *after* the theoretical considerations are finished, after the plan has been presented and explained. For no one can act or vote intelligently on something of which he is in ignorance.

* * * * *

. . . Let no one suppose the answer here proposed is without risk. No such answers are open to us in any case. What we have to do is to weigh the risks and chances of success of the national defense plan here proposed against the prospects offered by any alternate plan. Precisely because there is so little hope in any other plan that can be offered we have a right to assume that our plan will not be ruled out of consideration just because risks are involved.

NEW WEAPONS FOR OLD

We begin now the difficult, dangerous, and tentative work of putting together our building blocks for defense, our positions of strength—*The power of freedom, Religion, Productive capacity and technical knowledge, The limitation of tyranny,* and *The power of passive resistance*—into a pattern of national defense, a pattern that will rigidly exclude the element of military power we have previously seen to be the chief and immediate cause of our present dilemma, the block in the log jam that prevents us from releasing the flood tides of constructive energy in our world.

Having recognized that no immediate action of this kind is in prospect, we begin with our theoretical proposition at that time in the future when our nation would accept the necessity of changing its foreign policy and its program of defense. . . . And in order to consider this theory we must presume the victory (probably after initial defeats) of such a political force at the polls.

The first act of such a duly elected government would be to issue a proclamation in accordance with the promises it would have made in the election campaign, stating to the whole world that this country recognized the bankruptcy of military defense. Accordingly it would ask all nations to join in total disarmament down to police forces. But, the proclamation would continue, this government would proceed to take such action unilaterally if necessary. Further, all countries, without any exceptions, would be urged to send official representatives to observe the disarmament process here in order that there might be no doubt as to the sincerity and the execution of our proposal to disarm so far as our military defenses were concerned.

The proclamation would further state, again in harmony with the political campaign promises made, that our government would immediately develop a program of passive resistance to be used if any attempt were ever made to invade us. This would begin with the building of a new department of defense in the government, charged with the responsibility for the research, planning, and organization necessary for implementing the decision.

Finally, the proclamation would announce that our government, as rapidly as savings in manpower and resources were effected by the new plan, would make technical assistance and capital available on a very large scale to under-developed countries through the United Nations, the specialized agencies, and private agencies. It should be clear that such aid would be available to all countries without any political restrictions and that it would be the responsibility of other agencies than this government to administer the aid. For the effectiveness of capital for grants and loans and of technical assistance is greatly increased when it is administered through a third party or a multilateral arrangement. Further, the announcement should state that projects for exchanges of students and visitors of many kinds would be encouraged in an effort to build international good-will and understanding.

What would be the effect of this three-fold program of unilateral disarmament, the adoption of passive resistance as a policy of national defense, and of generosity in technical assistance, capital grants, and loans on an unprecedented scale? Certainly it would produce tremendous reaction throughout the world. For its boldness could not be ignored anywhere. The probable effects need to be considered in three separate areas: the effect on the non-Communist countries besides ourselves, the effect on the Communist countries, and the results in our own country of such a policy.

ON WINNING FRIENDS AND INFLUENCING PEOPLE

While there are more limitations than some idealists realize on the good that aid programs can do, nonetheless it should be apparent to almost everyone that one of the most powerful weapons any nation can possess in winning the vast uncommitted areas of the world to its side is the wise and judicious use of capital and technical assistance. . . .

* * * * *

To those who pessimistically reply that our aid programs thus far have produced little evidence of increased friendship, I would point out several essential facts to consider. First and foremost, our aid programs have been so closely tied to a bankrupt military policy, as I have previously observed, that it is quite unrealistic to judge a completely non-military aid program by our past and present experience. Next, we have insufficiently realized the very great obstacles to success in any bilateral aid program such as most of our present technical assistance aid projects are. Yet this relationship followed necessarily from the attempt to make the aid programs serve military aims also. In spite of these limitations, our aid programs have made significant contributions toward helping to save a number of political situations in our world because the welfare of people has been genuinely advanced by the help we have given.

The possibilities in a truly great technical assistance program—perhaps ten or more billion dollars a year offered to the United Nations to be used as grants and as a gigantic loan fund for development purposes, plus the offer of technical advisers, and supplemented by other programs through specialized and private agencies—are almost unlimited in the results that could be achieved in Asia, the Middle East, Africa, parts of Europe, and South America. It is hopeless to expect we can feed and support the world and any technical assistance program that attempts mere charity is doomed to failure. But a plan aimed at releasing the vast potential human and material resources yet unrealized, a plan that aims at helping people to help themselves by providing the particular assistance without which the resources of these nations can not be mobilized, can produce almost immediate gains and the promise of vastly greater improvements in the future.

To those who believe that the elimination of American military might would mean the overrunning of these countries by the Communists before and even in spite of the accomplishments we visualize, I suggest these considerations. First, a people who have hope and faith in their future do not provide the internal chaos and disorder that Communism needs in order to take over a country without paying a heavy price. Next, there would be no military excuse that Communists could use, as they did in Czechoslovakia, that we sought to use these countries as military allies against Communist countries. And, most important of all, the example we would have set of reliance on passive resistance would greatly strengthen the forces in such countries desirous of following a Gandhian pattern. So the result would probably be the development of a united program of many nations, linked together in a passive resistance defense program, undergirded by a new optimism that democracy could effectively solve the problems of industrialization and land reform.

Without doubt we must admit that we still run risks that some of these countries might be absorbed by Communism. But it should be sufficient to point out that no military policy has yet been devised to stop the onward march of Communism when internal conditions in a country make possible the civil war which Communists can use to seize power. . . .

* * * * *

MORAL JUJITSU

When we turn to the probable effect on the Communist countries of this passive resistance foreign policy, we see that it can be a kind of moral jujitsu, using the strength of the opponent to accomplish in him the desired changes. For such a course as we are describing is so completely contrary to Communist dogma that our action would catch the Communist world quite off balance. And the attempt, if it were made, to anticipate the results of our actions, and to counter them would necessarily mean giving up the rigid Communist doctrines about the nature of capitalism and democracy. In fact, it is difficult to see how Communism could adjust to the revolutionary situation we would pose without making basic changes in its own structure, changes that would be in the right direction.

The possibility of a united world Communism would surely be lessened by our action. Already there is considerable evidence that Communism is faced with the hard fact that nationalism and the inevitable pressures within a country tend to separate one Communist country from another. Not even the attraction of a common bond of economic and political program is sufficient always to overcome these nationalistic tendencies, the centrifugal force perhaps ultimately fatally destructive of any plans for united world Communism.

With the possibility removed that the non-Communist world constituted a military threat, the naturally divisive forces that exist between Communist countries would assert themselves more strongly than they do at present, rivalries would tend to develop, and the military strength of the Communist countries, if retained, would tend to be divided into opposing camps.

This same kind of effect would also surely develop within the ruling dictatorship of a Communist government. It is already clear that a dictatorship is a naturally unstable political element. And that instability is due in considerable measure to the suspicions and jealousies that develop in the ruling group. As long as they fear an outside military power, these fears tend to be subordinated. But when there is no longer foreign military strength to fear, these internal dissensions are much more likely to develop. There can be little doubt that Hitler's hold on his people was strengthened by military opposition to Germany. For many Germans were driven, howbeit reluctantly, to support Hitler as the only alternative to what they believed, although wrongly, would be much worse—the military defeat of their country.

Still another problem for the Communists would be created by our policy of unilateral disarmament, passive resistance, and technical assistance. The effect on the citizens of the Communist countries would be considerable. The news certainly could not be kept from the people there, though it would likely be misinterpreted. But in any form the information that we had disarmed would result in tremendous pressures for more consumer goods in the Communist countries. Justification of a military policy would be much more difficult and consequently the trend toward more consumer goods would be extremely hard to resist. And the chain of events that would follow from such a development surely leads more toward peace than war.

By the same logic any imperialistic venture of a Communist government into a country not armed militarily would be most difficult to explain to the people of the Communist nations, even with all the power of a great propaganda machine available.

All these considerations indicate that our proposed policy would tend to create confusion in Communist ranks, to keep them busy with their own internal problems, and probably would move them gradually, or even rapidly, away from some of the worst evils of totalitarianism. And certainly our policy would relax, even remove, the fears that presently help them to justify their military program. For this reason we would appear to have little to fear from an attempted Communist invasion of our (or any other) militarily disarmed country. On the contrary, it might well be true that the result of our policy would be that Communist governments in order to compete effectively with us in technical assistance programs and in order to deal with pressures at home, would accept our proposal for universal disarmament and would move, though slowly, in a direction that would mean more assurance of peace in our world.

That such Communist cooperation in universal disarmament would then be possible, perhaps even probable, becomes evident when we consider the psychological position in which failure thus to cooperate would place the Communists. In the eyes of their own people and in the view of the rest of the world all their preceding peace talk would be proven to be hollow and hypocritical. The United States would become the protagonist of peace, the moral leader of the world. And this would lose for the Communist countries one of the most powerful attractions they now have for the masses of people in Europe and Asia. For Russia and China to remain armed when we disarmed (and probably most other non-Communist countries with us) would cost the Communists very heavily in the esteem of the world. Would they be willing to pay that price? Or might they rather conclude that they should join in universal disarmament in order to compete more favorably with us for the support and loyalty of the rest of the world?

*   *   *   *   *

THE STRATEGY OF PASSIVE RESISTANCE

To think and plan politically in a responsible manner does not allow us, however, to assume without questions, that our projected policy would yield such admirable results so easily. . . . We must therefore now deal realistically with the effect on our own country if it adopted and developed this policy, and if an attempt were to be made to take advantage of our disarmed state. The fact that such an invasion appears unlikely to develop does not at all free us from the responsibility for preparation to meet it.

Also, the prospect of having to face such an aggression would be very much lessened by adequate preparation to deal with it if it were to happen. . . .

To know what action we should take, we must first consider the kinds of aggression in which an enemy country might engage, keeping in mind that the answers we provide for our own country can reasonably be expected to apply to other countries that might face the same kind of assault.

One fear that some people may have can be disposed of quickly. That is the possibility that an enemy would, if we refused to accept an ultimatum to yield control of our country, respond by bombing and destroying our undefended cities.

Such destruction would be meaningless in view of the obvious fact that there would be no physical barriers to the occupation of the country anyway, which presumably would be the goal of the enemy. If we credit the invasion forces with the degree of intelligence assuredly necessary for a projected occupation of another country, then it should be transparently clear to them that such wanton destruction would only increase the actual problems of occupation—problems of physical rebuilding and of psychological victory in the occupied country. Further, the horrified reaction of the whole world would create a gigantic problem in foreign policy and foreign relations for the government that was responsible for such an act. The obvious consequence of our policy of unilateral disarmament and generous aid would have been to remove utterly any idea that we were threatening another nation and thus the complete absence of any justification for the crime would mean an instantaneous and continued condemnation of and resentment against those responsible. It is scarcely conceivable that any reasonably sane people would thus involve themselves in such enormous problems with so little prospect of gain from the deed.

Far more realistic is the assumption that we would be invaded by an occupation army in much the same way that a militarily defeated country is occupied by a military force to secure control of the country. It is therefore against this kind of aggressive action that our policy of defense must be directed. And in order to describe this policy we need now to go back in point of time to the initiation and preparation of the policy of passive resistance that would be used in the event of having to meet such aggression.

As previously suggested, the governmental decision to abandon military defense would come at the same time as a policy of passive resistance would be publicly announced.

*   *   *   *   *

Those of us who see clearly the futility of continued reliance on military defense must, in addition to the endeavor to win the consent of other people to our view, also assume two other responsibilities—the theoretical planning of a passive resistance defense policy in its general outlines, and the organizational beginnings of such a force.

This pamphlet purports to be no more than an initial and modest beginning so far as theoretical planning is concerned. Obviously an adequate answer can only be given as a number of able people from different fields of training and experience correlate their knowledge into a unified plan. Even then it will necessarily evolve gradually as do all human enterprises.

*   *   *   *   *

The second responsibility immediately resting upon us is the organization of those who share these convictions into a working and effective group. Both the winning of the nation to this policy and the successful operation of the program thereafter requires such organizational effectiveness. In fact, we would have no right to ask our country to follow such a policy were we not able at the same time to point to a corps of able, dedicated, disciplined people operating in a proven organizational structure.

It is at this point that we can learn much from Gandhi's experience in India. As many as 400,000 people were there organized into such a group as I have described. The continuing effect in India today of that organization is quite considerable. Certainly the success of India's passive resistance movement could not have been achieved without such an organization. But Gandhi came to see that he had not built a strong enough group. We ought, therefore, to think in terms of a larger organization in order that the influence on the country would be greater. As a rough estimate let us suggest a goal of one million people organized in such a group.

The functions of this organization would be: 1) the teaching and persuasion of the American people, winning them to an acceptance of a passive resistance policy, 2) the application of these principles to our own American problems, such as racial discrimination, 3) the development of a specific plan of operation for the nation when passive resistance is adopted, 4) the formation of a skeletal organization to serve as a pilot model of people willing to act as volunteers in a passive resistance defense corps, and 5) the continued purification and spiritual growth of the members.

*   *   *   *   *

WEAPONS OF LOVE

At this point we now stand ready to answer the question previously posed—How would we meet an occupation army?

Our defense would rest on two principal "weapons of love" —civil disobedience, and the persuasive power of words and non-violent actions aimed at changing the minds of enough people in the occupation force to render it impotent in the attempt to rule our nation.

The civil disobedience program would have as its purpose preventing the occupation army from gaining effective control of the nation. No tyrant can rule if the great mass of the people refuse to obey. Prisons can not be large enough to hold them. Mass refusal to pay taxes can imperil the financial basis of the occupation army. . . .

The civil disobedience program would also be expressed through strikes of various kinds—short total strikes, slow down strikes, and work stoppages in key places and industries to paralyze any attempt to rob the nation of its resources. Such a program can be particularly effective in a highly industrialized nation where the laborers have already learned how to act in concert together, using the strike as a lever to gain higher wages and improved working conditions.

The effectiveness of this type of campaign depends upon a number of factors—the wisdom of the original plans, the preparation of the people, the quality of the leadership, and the persistence of the people.

As to the original plans, these would have been made by the department of defense. There properly would be, as in a military campaign, many different plans, geared to differing circumstances and conditions. As much as possible, difficulties should have been foreseen and planned for, thus mitigating the problems and lessening the chance of failure.

We have already considered the preparation of the nation, but now we see more clearly the importance of such preparation and the form of the educational program previously needed. . . . This would include provisions for a long chain through which leadership could be passed in the event that leaders were imprisoned or killed. We can learn much here from Gandhi's experience in India and from the underground resistance forces in Europe during the Nazi occupation. And we can have faith that such leadership will keep replenishing itself in a time of crisis, as it did in India and in Europe, by the continual accession to the cause of capable leaders who are inspired and challenged by the example of those imprisoned or killed.

The persistence of the nation in the civil disobedience campaign would be essential. All the other points just mentioned would help strengthen this will to persist. But finally it must arise from the power and strength of the people themselves. And this can only be the product of a nation that is culturally and religiously strong. For this reason we must understand clearly that this is not merely a technic of defense—it is fundamentally a way of life. Such a defense would go ill, for example, with a practice of racial segregation such as is now all too common in our country.

* * * * *

No greater mistake could be made than to suppose that such a campaign as this could be carried out without loss of life and property. To be realistic at all, we must recognize that such an invading army as we have posited would have instructions to use cruelty and even barbarity on a considerable scale if necessary and if it appeared to offer any hope of breaking the resistance.

But before we consider this human and material cost in greater detail, let us remind ourselves that no kind of defense possible to us today can promise safety to the occupants of a nation, or even the hope of safety, without the acceptance of great risk and heavy costs.

* * * * *

The real question is the calculated judgment as to which method of defense will cost least and be most likely to succeed in defending and preserving those values that we cherish more than life itself.

Even so, the price tag for passive resistance still can not be easily dismissed. Any occupation army would certainly arrest the leaders of a passive resistance policy, or those leaders they would know about and be able to locate. It would be expected that government officials, industrial and labor leaders, communications officials, and religious leaders would thus be imprisoned. Some attempt might be made to imprison ordinary people, particularly in limited areas, but this could not be carried very far simply because of the immense problem of handling masses of people who persist in refusing to obey, even at the point of a gun.

Admittedly some of these hostages would be tortured and killed. How many, it is impossible to predict, but at the worst, it would not approach the loss in atomic warfare. For the tyrant, the chief value in such killing, as the public whipping in dealing with a wayward child in a schoolroom, is the expectation that others will obey more readily thereafter. If the brutality does not accomplish this intended result, the danger of its indefinite continuance is not as great as it first appears.

If we would deal with the irrational fears of some that this policy would simply mean the obliteration of the occupied nation—the merciless killing of millions—we need to consider several factors. First, this policy of passive resistance is not parallel to what was done by those killed in Nazi Germany or in the kulak rebellion in Russia. For the people killed in those cases—and there *were* millions killed—were not organized at all in the kind of program we are considering. Rather, we should look at Denmark and Norway under the Nazis, and East Germany in June of 1953 under the Communists, for the nearest parallels (even in those countries it was a very imperfect, incomplete, and unorganized program) to what we are describing. And it is remarkable in those instances how *little* killing did take place. These cases tend to show that human nature cannot become so depraved and mechanized that it is completely impervious to the appeal made by passive resistance.

And this requires much more consideration of how passive resistance reacts upon an aggressor. But in order to understand this power, let us start with the most normal human reactions to suffering.

The first step in understanding this power of passive resistance is the recognition of the natural aversion of men to suffering. All normal men dislike to witness suffering. Even the mass fascination that makes men stare at the injured in an accident does not remove the distaste for pain, whether in ourselves or in others. Our attitude toward suffering animals also demonstrates this basic quality of our nature. The cruelty we sometimes show toward animals, as when we pass by an injured dog on the highway without stopping to aid is probably due to our subconscious wish not to have to observe the animal's misery. And it may well be true also that the unusual person who seems sadistic is ultimately to be explained by the inner civil war that drives him to extremes in an effort to drown his conscience.

The second step in the logic of passive resistance is the understanding that our natural repugnance to suffering is accentuated when we are the cause of that pain.

*   *   *   *   *

The third step grows out of the second. If the pain we have caused in others is the result of evil in us, if we are the aggressors, the innocence of our victim contrasts with our own brutality and then our need becomes desperate to have some psychological justification for our action. Normally that justification is available either in the resentment and physical resistance of the enemy or in his cowardice. Thus when our evil action is met by violence or cowardice, or when we know that our enemy waits only the opportunity to use violence, when we know that he hates us in proportion to the suffering he has incurred, we use his responses to convince ourselves he is the kind of person who would have harmed us if he had had an opportunity. Somehow his hatred of us and his use of violence help us to achieve some measure of self-respect even though we have been aggressively evil.

The final phase in understanding the power of passive resistance is reached when the evildoer is met by forgiving, suffering love. Add this to the natural aversion to suffering, the horror at having been the cause of it, and the revulsion that comes from finding in the non-violence of the opponent no basis for self-justification, and the aggressor is left shaken and psychologically defenseless. To continue a physical attack upon one who chooses from courage to be physically defenseless, to be faced by firm refusal to yield to evil, yet to be met by steadfast love—this is simply more than human nature is

354   NON-VIOLENT POWER WITH EXPRESS PRINCIPLE

prepared psychologically to face. No defense has yet been prepared, or can be prepared, for this kind of warfare. The manhood and character hitherto submerged in the aggressor rises to the surface and he is bewildered and confused—puzzled by the unfamiliar reactions in himself and by conduct in his enemy he cannot understand. Self-respect is no longer his, even the possibility of achieving it through his present conduct has been stripped from him.

If he carries his wrongdoing to the point of causing the death of his innocent, physically defenseless, yet spiritually unconquered opponent, he has posed for himself an unanswerable psychological problem—the same problem that has never been successfully met by those who have caused the deaths of martyrs. Actually the aggressor despises himself. Almost beside himself, perhaps temporarily insane, he may resolutely refuse to yield to the psychological pressure upon him. Even the death of Gandhi may not win the unrepentant heart of the evildoer. But neither can he ever escape from the civil war that rages within him, the kind of inner conflict graphically portrayed by Francis Thompson in *Hound of Heaven*.

Part of the strength of passive resistance as a national policy lies in the fact that success in dealing with an aggressor nation, as distinguished from opposition to a single individual, does not require that we convert all the members of that nation. Victory with even a small minority greatly weakens the morale and power of an enemy by creating internal division in his ranks. The greater the excesses of brutality by some, the more probability there is that some of the enemy forces will revolt.

*   *   *   *   *

At this point we are ready to make our transition to the second "weapon of love" that we would use against an aggressor. Actually we have already been considering it in part as we have dealt with the psychological impact of passive resistance upon the evildoer. For this second weapon is the power of all the means of persuasion at our command in leading the individual members of an occupation army to see both the futility and the evil of their policy. We seek to secure their own refusal to continue to obey unjust orders.

That such a goal is not at all impossible should become apparent when we remember the case previously mentioned of the refusal of the seventeen Russian officers and soldiers in East Germany in the June, 1953, uprisings to obey the orders of their superiors. And we call to mind the thousands of cases of defection and desertion from Communist armies.

Apart from all other considerations, a dictatorship would make one of the most daring gambles in history if it were to send a conscript army to a country like our own. The revelation of what life could be like, both in material abundance and in political freedom, coupled with the opportunity among friendly people to escape, would be a powerful motivation to desertion.

When one adds to this the psychological impact made upon an occupation army by a policy of passive resistance, even of acceptance of martyrdom, the reasonable conclusion would seem to be that few men could withstand such pressure.

But there is still to be added the result that would flow from a program—planned and organized before the invasion—of goodwill, friendliness, and appeals to reason and conscience directed by the people toward the occupation army in the inevitable daily contacts. We have hardly begun to understand what propaganda could mean on our side in such a case.

To those who doubt that our people could sustain such a policy, subduing the natural tendency to hate and fear, I would suggest the immense advantage we would gain by thoroughly instilling in the public the simple truth that the soldier of the occupation army, even when he acts brutally, is a human being, made in God's image, and that his conduct is the natural, almost inevitable result of the environment in which he has lived, the training he has had, and the pressures of the dictatorship upon him. In considerable measure this knowledge of the enemy would undergird a nation-wide therapy directed toward the invaders that would be rather like the therapy we now use in mental hospitals. And once a person sees himself as the doctor in the doctor-patient relationship, it is far easier to practice self-control and to follow the Golden Rule.

At this point we can scarcely more than glimpse the possibilities. Only a few individuals have broken through the hate and fear barrier that causes so much mental and psychological illness, but those few pioneers who have done so are making it increasingly clear that love and goodwill can actually work miracles, that no man is ever totally depraved.

* * * * *

What, then, would be the result of the use of these "weapons of love"?

At the worst, it would be a long and costly struggle over a generation or two, hurting the economy of the country badly (for strikes and civil disobedience are two-edged swords and we should have to be prepared to suffer ourselves, even though we would rightly expect the civil disobedience campaign to cost the enemy much more heavily), and resulting perhaps in the liquidation of thousands of our best people. But the continuance of a passive resistance policy offers real hope that the enemy would ultimately be conquered. For no tyranny is ever free from the immutable laws of change that operate throughout history, upsetting all attempts to perpetuate a static system, destroying the grand designs of all tyrants.

At the best, the policy of passive resistance, if we were to be invaded, would result in making a farce of the army of occupation, ruining its morale and resulting in it becoming a symbol of failure and disgrace to the world, as the members of it deserted and as the enemy government found the virus of civil disobedience and love of liberty spreading through its own troops, reaching the people at home and ultimately destroying the dictatorship there.

But even at the worst, who can believe that atomic war would be better?

*　*　*　*　*

CONCLUDING REFLECTIONS

CONCLUDING REFLECTIONS: THE RELEVANCE OF NON-VIOLENCE IN OUR DAY

It would be difficult if not impossible to summarize within a few pages readings as diverse as those presented in this volume. However, it may be fruitful to examine, by way of concluding reflections, a few of the questions which have either emerged explicitly or which may be regarded as extensions of the symposium. Here we note briefly the ideal conception of a non-violent society; the relation of non-violence to democratic doctrines; the relevance of non-violent resistance in totalitarian situations; the uses of non-violence for war and invasion; and a few comments on the crisis in contemporary civilization.

The Nature of the Ideal Non-violent Society. In a thoughtful pamphlet written originally near the beginning of World War II, the Indian scholar K. G. Mashruwala suggests that while all of us apprehend fairly well the meaning of violence—it is associated, as he suggests, with "malevolence, hatred, revenge, enmity, murder, injury, war, cruelty, barbarity, torture, deception, rape, loot, exploitation, and so on"—the term non-violence is still very much weighted with ambiguity.[1] On the whole, Mashruwala is right, as the readings in Part I frequently emphasize.

Perhaps we can grasp the meaning of non-violence more fully if we first sketch out the general lines of a society based on ideals of non-violence and then turn to the problem of how it can be achieved. In the process, the role and place of non-violent resistance may become clearer.

The ideal of a non-violent society, while never spelled out very fully, would appear to imply one in which social and political organizations are not used to manipulate men for the glory and gain of other men; in which the employment of physical force is always discriminate and never deliberately injurious—or disappears altogether; and in which conflict, assuming

[1] K. G. Mashruwala, *Practical Non-Violence* (*And Ideology of Non-Violence*) (Ahmedabad: Navajivan Publishing House, 1946), p. 3.

its inevitability in the life of man, takes place without resort to violence and increasingly at the level of ideas.

A non-violent society would clearly recognize the necessity for ample social and political freedom for the person. Similarly, it would see associations and groups as entitled to a certain autonomy or right to self-government. "Nations" would be among these groups.

But the war-making, sovereign nation-State of modern times could have no place within a non-violent society. And because so much of our life today turns on the demands of the war-making nation-State, its destruction would constitute a revolution in man's thought and institutional life. One's imaginative powers are inadequate to describe a world without military bureaucracies, conscription, bemedaled generals, twenty-one gun salutes, budgets dominated by the call to mass violence, and the centralization of power engendered in considerable measure by the war-State. At the very least, the nature of the historical "State" would be radically transformed as one of its major functions ceased to be preparation for war.

In a non-violent society, gross disproportions of power and wealth would not exist and, where they threatened, would be corrected by disciplined withdrawal from co-operation of disadvantaged groups. This withdrawal would help restore a kind of balance and would make easier a restatement of the framework within which groups co-operate for the common good. Even were a world "State" to arise, the necessity for non-violent resistance would not be eliminated; for "power" relations of some kind would still exist and with them the possibility of dangerous imbalances in power.

A non-violent society, too, would elaborate the machinery necessary for resolution of intergroup conflict and would facilitate an understanding of conditions that might, if uncorrected, lead to violence. A hallmark of such a social order would be the continuous, positive effort to root out the social and psychological bases of violence through the development of education, mental health services, a non-violent police system whose work would be primarily preventive, and conditions encouraging a measure of stability in family life. A non-violent ethic would have far-reaching ramifications for the treatment of criminals, as our readings suggest, and equally for the care of the mentally ill. It would not tolerate capital punishment, prisons, or treatment of mental patients that is merely custodial.

In a non-violent society, moreover, a very high proportion of all persons would be acutely conscious of the fact that violence and tyranny arise as much out of the inner attitudes of ordinary men as they do from acts of the ruler. An individual without self-respect is much more likely to become an instrument of a tyrant than one who, for whatever reason, has come to value himself. But tyranny and violence are both the root and the fruit of a lack of self-respect: the very exercise of tryanny and violence against the person threatens to reduce him to a mere thing; while at the same time his tendency to live at the level of the vegetable so much of the time will encourage tyranny and violence.

Respect for human personality would be one of its central characteristics. This would be reflected in a non-authoritarian educational system and in social guarantees of a basic minimum of material well-being. There would also be a large measure of political, economic, and administrative decentralization in order that decision-making and implementation might be as close as possible to those who would be expected to conform to the decisions. And insofar as possible, an effort would be made to arrive at decisions by consensus.

Certain over-all decisions, of course—such as those involving allocation of resources—would have to be made centrally. There would necessarily be some central planning, for violence is as likely to arise because of too little central planning as because of too much.

Democracy and Non-violence. If some such vision (granted that it is blurred at the edges) seems to characterize the non-violent society, what are the means for its attainment? How can it be implemented at the political level? How can it be brought about by individual action?

It is at this point, as many of our readings have suggested, that the advocate of non-violence and non-violent resistance seems to be speaking somewhat differently from those who might share his ideal of a non-violent society. That is to say, the democrat, for example, would probably applaud the goal of a non-violent community, as would the socialist; but for the most part, democrats and socialists will defend the use of violence as means, under certain circumstances, even though with some reluctance. The exponent of non-violence and non-violent resistance, however, maintains that some means are utterly excluded from consideration. War is such a means, and so is every other method that departs in spirit from the ends which are to be sought. If we search for a society in which human life is to be respected and enhanced, we cannot expect to advance its cause now by institutions like war, that show little regard for human life, whatever their short-run outcomes may be: even though a given nation is "preserved" through war, the attainment of a non-violent society is always retarded. If we hope to achieve a social order in which gross disproportions of power (whether economic, social, or political) do not exist, we cannot employ means which in themselves greatly encourage thoughtless obedience and autocratic structures of governance. If we desire a society whose institutions and habit patterns are non-violent, the means used must themselves not press for the reverse. As the New Testament points out, one cannot expect to gather figs from a thistle tree.

This organic relationship between means and ends, stressed by such modern writers as John Dewey, Aldous Huxley, and Jacques Maritain, would appear to be almost obvious. But so accustomed are we to responding to aggressive conduct by counteraggression and to violence by counterviolence that we lose sight of the general principle in practice. This is true not only when we resort to such overt violence as war and the threat of war but also when we employ tactics of deception, misrepresentation, and evasion in political discussion. The central value of non-violence is respect for truth, as Gandhi, Thoreau, Tolstoy, and many others have pointed out; and to the degree in which truth is esteemed lightly in our political conduct, overt violence lurks near.

It is as an exemplification of truth that non-violent resistance is to be partly understood. The objectives of those who utilize non-violent resistance as a method are open and public; the opponent is notified of those objectives and of the means to be used for their implementation; and the connotations of "conspiracy" (as that term is usually understood) are absent. In the strategy and tactics of non-violent resistance is implied a strong confidence in Godwin's abstract truth as an ultimate victor and also a hardheaded awareness of the realities of power in politics and social relations. Truth itself is coercive but often its full impact cannot be felt without utilizing at the same time the kind of "power" implied when one group withdraws its co-operation from another or challenges in action the habit patterns and laws of a violent society. In the strategy of non-violent resistance, we have an effort to combine the harmlessness of the dove with the "wisdom" attributed by the Bible to the serpent. And this combination, precisely because it recognizes that discussion must take place within a context of power relations—albeit non-violent power relations—gives to non-violent resistance its great effectiveness when used in the right spirit and with proper organization.

Non-violent resistance as means—all the way from public protest to civil disobedience—would seem, moreover, to be consistent with what we usually think of as "democracy." The spirit of democracy, surely, is utterly antagonistic to violence; yet it is equally hostile to acts which would stifle free development of personalities and groups. Non-violent resistance offers a means whereby both of these values can be maintained.

Critics of non-violent resistance, like Reinhold Niebuhr,[2] sometimes assert that the ethics and politics of non-violence are "utopian" in that they seek to impose a pure "love" ethic on a realm where at best only "justice" can be attained. But most of the readings in this volume are fully cognizant of the world of "power" and of claim versus counterclaim. All that the advocates of non-violent resistance as means would maintain is that it is far more compatible with the achievement of a truly non-violent society than the means of violence; and that it is, moreover, also far more efficacious. As Mashruwala again notes,[3] the issue is not one of pure love or "benevolence" versus violence. Rather it is one "between just and proper selfishness on the one hand, and malevolence with pseudo-just or unjust selfishness on the other." And he adds that it is possible to be "selfish"—that is, to seek to have one's just claims recognized—"without violence or malevolent intentions."

The advocate of non-violent resistance as means will, of course, fully admit that many non-violent patterns are already established in modern society, far removed as it may still be from an ideally non-violent community. Thus wherever channels of discussion remain open; parliamentary bodies genuinely deliberate; courts adjudicate under specified rules of law; citizens are consulted about the formation of public policy; the police use physical force, if at all, only in a discriminating and non-injurious way; and problems of social justice occupy

[2] Note particularly *Moral Man and Immoral Society* (New York: Scribner, 1932); *Children of Light and Children of Darkness* (New York: Scribner, 1944); *Christianity and Power Politics* (New York: Scribner, 1940); and *Faith and History* (New York: Scribner, 1949).

[3] Op. cit., p. 6.

a central place in political discussion—wherever conditions of
this kind obtain, fundamentals of non-violence, both as means
and as ends, already exist. Naturally, the exponent of non-
violence will seek to sustain and expand all such patterns. Indeed, characteristics of this kind may be said to be common
to both "democracy" and non-violence.

It is sometimes suggested, however, that if parliamentary
and generally "democratic" procedures are available it is illegitimate to resort to many forms of non-violent resistance
and particularly to those which involve any measure of civil
disobedience. The minority, so it may be argued, must submit
to the majority and not challenge its decision. If it wishes to
become the majority, let it hasten to go through regular political channels and not resort to the various forms of non-
violent "direct action." The critic points out, as we have admitted, that the means of ordinary discussion, debate, and
legislative activity are excellent exemplifications of "non-violent" resolution of conflict. To critics taking this position, the
utilization of non-violent power in the form of non-violent resistance is somehow a species of "violence" in that it violates
the presumed canons of democracy. When submarines are
boarded by direct action groups, as in Reading 21, or restaurants embarrassed by Sit-Ins, as in Reading 20, it may be
maintained that other means of non-violent action have not
been utilized and that such actions violate the principle that
minorities should submit to the majority will until the latter
can be changed.

Aside from the fact, however, that democratic procedures
may not have been fully available (thus, Negroes were excluded from the vote and from full participation in forming
the "majority" will), such an objection ignores the notion
that no majority decision, any more than a decree issued by
a dictator, can be absolutely binding in a moral sense, whatever status it may possess politically and legally. No majority
can be assumed to be "right" in all its decisions and will
sometimes violate what appear to be legitimate aspirations or
"rights" of particular groups. Under such circumstances, the
group involved—or its leaders—will have to decide whether
the violation is an attack on its basic claim to existence under
minimum conditions or merely an undermining of secondary
or non-essential claims. In the former instance, the group may
wish to consider offering some form of non-violent resistance
in order to preserve its basic integrity as a group. But if the

violation is of secondary claims only, it may decide that greater harm to the society as a whole would result from resistance than would ensue from obedience. As conceived here, in other words, majority rule is only one value of a democratic society; and sometimes it may appear to be in conflict with other equally precious values. Whether non-violent resistance can be justified in any given instance depends in part, of course, on the particular circumstances involved; but it cannot be ruled out in all conditions and, indeed, must be seen as a possible positive contribution to democratic means and ends.

Under actual circumstances, of course, there has never been a society in which democratic ideals have even been approached in most respects. Electorates are sluggish, information is withheld, income distribution is almost always highly distorted in favor of the upper 10 per cent of the population, and military-industrial complexes have an enormous advantage over ordinary citizens in manipulating opinion-making agencies. Under conditions of this kind, non-violent resistance —whether in its mild form of peaceful public protest or in its extreme form of disciplined and deliberate civil disobedience— can perform an indispensable role in arousing opinion, redressing distorted power balances, and re-establishing active consent as the basis for governance. The openness, appeal to truth, willingness to undergo voluntary suffering, and non-retaliatory ethic characteristic of the theory and practice of non-violence constitute built-in limitations on any tendency to use the means for autocratic or tyrannical ends. When thousands of Quakers, Baptists, and other sectarians suffered in seventeenth-century English jails for their convictions about religious toleration and just legal procedure they exemplified the spirit and possibilities of non-violent resistance. And a similar observation might be made, for example, about the thousands of Roman Catholics who, in Communist Poland, have dared to continue their religious practices in the face of anti-Catholic State dogma and often persecution: they have done much to force a liberalization of the political regime, when resort to violence could have resulted in even greater repression.

Non-violence and the Rise of Totalitarianism. As has been suggested at many points in this volume, a central political question arising out of readings such as those presented is the relevance today of non-violence and non-violent resistance for the growth and possible overthrow of totalitarian systems.

This general issue, in turn, gives rise to two specific queries. First, can the principles of non-violence help prevent the rise of totalitarianism? Secondly, assuming that totalitarianism has already been established, can it be undermined by non-violent techniques of various kinds? Adequate answers to questions of this kind cannot be given within the space of a few paragraphs but we might attempt here to summarize what the readings and the political history of the twentieth century suggest.

Two questions

Let us use the rise of National Socialism in Germany as the basis for answering both questions. Many factors were responsible for its development: the stock-market crash of 1929 and the subsequent world-wide depression; dissatisfaction with the Peace of 1919; effects of the great postwar inflation; authoritarian traditions within German culture; failure of the Allies to carry out their disarmament pledges; bureaucratization of the labor and socialist movements; Hitler's understanding of "mass" culture; and others. But two over-all though interrelated phenomena appear to have been decisive: first, the worsening of economic conditions after 1929, with the atmosphere of hopelessness which this engendered; and second, the collapse of the will to resist within Germany itself.

National Socialism made very little headway politically until the effects of the stock-market crash began to make themselves felt in the German economy after 1930. Only after the early part of 1932 did the accession of Hitler to power appear, in some sense, to be "inevitable." Had world statesmen, including, above all, American leaders, possessed enough understanding to prevent the long economic slump or even to shorten its duration, it is very doubtful whether Hitler's appeal to the German people would have had much effect. As gross economic difficulties continued, however, he found his support growing; and this enhanced popularity was abetted by the "authoritarian" tradition in German political culture. Desperate men turn to desperate remedies, particularly where there is no firmly embedded heritage of constitutional government.

But only the dark economic picture of 1929 to 1933 could have provided the opening. In considerable measure, the non-German world was responsible for Hitler's increase in popularity and for the near fanaticism with which he was supported by many. By non-violent actions involving economic reform the world outside Germany might have averted the conditions that made Hitler's appeals decisive. But such changes would have required an alteration in basic outlook on the part of Americans and others—a greater willingness to experiment with "planned" forms of economic order, an accentuated sensitivity to the interdependence of mankind, and an understanding of the necessity for positive action to prevent the development of authoritarian schemes. Instead, Americans, together with the British and French, tended to hold that National Socialism was a conspiracy of wicked men for which outsiders bore no major responsibility.

After the rise of National Socialism, Western thought usually tended to think in terms of violent solutions rather than of non-violent devices. Thus, the Western nations could have offered asylum to all the Jews of Germany and Eastern Europe before 1939 and even after the opening of the war. But they were unwilling and unprepared to accept more than relatively small numbers.

Insofar, therefore, as National Socialism was the result of acts of omission by other nations, its rise might have been averted by many forms of non-violent, non-military policy. In fact, it is difficult to see how violence could have helped at all.

But we cannot in justice condemn merely the non-German world. There was, no doubt, a decline in the will to resist on the part of millions of Germans. Tens of thousands who could not support Hitler lacked the will and the organization to resist him. The studies of Bruno Bettelheim have shown to what a small degree this will to resist existed even within concentration camps.[4] Explanations of this rather startling phenomenon will, of course, vary. But we cannot doubt the fact itself. By contrast, a largely non-violent strike shortly after World War I (see Reading 12) had prevented a military takeover.

It seems probable that, given proper leadership and specific training in non-violent resistance, the rise of Hitler could have been prevented. But the masses of organized Social Democracy and the trade unions seemed paralyzed for action: for some reason, they hesitated to use the weapon which they had successfully employed against Wolfgang Kapp and his soldiers. The labor movement as a whole was imprisoned by narrow

[4] See, on the general problem of autonomy in human personality, Bruno Bettelheim, *The Informed Heart: Autonomy in a Mass Age* (New York: Free Press of Glencoe, 1960).

conceptions of propriety and legality: it apparently did not see how the law was being manipulated for the ends of autocracy and hence hesitated to turn to such techniques as non-violent political strikes and civil disobedience. Much of it continued to oppose Hitler, to be sure, through formal parliamentary channels; but it appeared not to understand that this was not enough.

There tended to be an erosion of the will to resist in what seemed to be little things; and this, of course, made it still easier to acquiesce when the Hitlerian dictatorship did appear. Again and again, Germans accepted what they thought were slight inroads into their liberties—as in the use of the emergency powers of the Weimar Constitution—and did not see that submission in small things would facilitate acceptance of larger encroachments. Because the will to resist did not develop in relatively small matters before 1933, it became increasingly difficult to encourage it—with many exceptions, of course—when National Socialist acts began to destroy republicanism after 1933.

Often where the will to resist did seem to exist, it took a military or violent form. Thus there was a paramilitary "republican" protective group to counteract the pre-1933 military organization of the Nazis. But military means were inappropriate to defend the ideals which Social Democrats and other republicans ostensibly espoused: the Nazis could always best them at such methods. Only non-violent resistance in some form could have been an appropriate weapon for the opponents of National Socialism. With it and the will to use it, the Hitlerians would not have gained office. Without it, Social Democratic and other anti-Nazi resistance did not have an effective outlet.

Once the National Socialists attained power, the opportunity to resist non-violently progressively declined, with the adoption of sharp restrictions on freedom of association and other similar measures. Hence the answer to our second question—Could non-violent resistance have defeated the Nazi regime once it attained power?—must be a highly qualified one. No method and no technique of social conflict can perform miracles. After 1933, political repression made it increasingly unlikely that men could get together for effective non-violent resistance. To be sure, opportunity is never completely eliminated, as was shown by the underground movements which did develop in Germany. But without a philosophy and practical experience of non-violence to guide it, the underground was relatively ineffective politically.[5] Even so, it is heartening and surprising that it existed at all, considering the rigorous suppression of the State.

But our readings have suggested that even under "totalitarian" conditions and with little previous discipline in non-violence, non-violent resistance can make a serious impression on totalitarian rulers. Thus the Norwegian resistance, although never complete and certainly not animated by an express doctrine of non-violence, helped make Nazi rule in Norway very difficult. And the spontaneous, largely non-violent strike at Vorkuta, while it achieved only minor concessions, demonstrated the potentialities of non-violence even under adverse conditions. Both Norway and Vorkuta, moreover, underscore the observation stressed throughout this volume that we cannot expect to undermine totalitarian patterns overnight, particularly when we are largely unversed in the theory and practice of non-violent power. Even so, there were instances of Russian soldiers refusing to fire at unarmed demonstrators during the great wave of "direct action" protests in Eastern Europe in 1953.

When considering the relevance of non-violent resistance to totalitarian situations, we should never forget that the Indian and South African struggles were and have been carried on under conditions not highly favorable to the resisters. Although the British Government in India was not, it is true, "totalitarian," it is an understatement to say that it was not always benevolent. Its officers carried out massacres of unarmed men, women, and children, as at Amritsar (1919); its regulations provided for imprisonment without trial; its backing in British opinion was for many years very strong (although the support admittedly declined later on); and its military might sought to overawe an impoverished and unarmed populace. Despite all this, non-violent resistance developed and was a very important factor in the ultimate destruction of British rule.

In South Africa, the non-benevolence of the government and of "white" opinion has been even more apparent; and although non-violent resistance is still in its beginning stages,

[5] For some aspects of the German underground, see J. James Donohoe, *Hitler's Conservative Opponents in Bavaria* (Leiden: E. J. Brill, 1961) and Franz Schneider, "The Silent Revolt," *America,* September 6, 1958.

there is some evidence that if it continues to develop under adequate leadership it, too, will play a vital role in changing power relationships. Readings 5 and 19 told us something of the problems which resisters in South Africa faced and continue to confront; and despite the growing repression of the South African Government,[6] there is reason to believe that the self-consciousness and understanding of Native and Colored populations are also growing. It is almost certain that resort to violence by Native and Colored people would set back the cause of equality immensely; for it would tend to eliminate potential divisions and self-doubts within the South African ruling classes and help them rationalize an even more extreme use of government violence.

But what, it may be asked, of Hungary—the bloody suppression of the Hungarian revolt of 1956 by Soviet troops? It is astonishing, in some respects, that this question arises so frequently in connection with discussions of non-violent resistance. First of all, the Hungarians were never committed to non-violence, had little training in its disciplines, and fairly early began to resort to violence themselves. Secondly, insofar as they did employ essentially non-violent methods—before and in the early part of the revolt—they appeared to be far more successful than in their resort to violence.[7] To be sure, the repression was a brutal affair and obviously no advocate of non-violence could or would defend it. But neither would he support the Hungarians' turning to violence: in so doing, he would contend, they made both a moral and a political error, understandable though it might be in the given circumstances. Had the Hungarians utilized non-violent resistance only, there would still have been no guarantee of their immediate success; as we have repeatedly pointed out, all forms of conflict are hazardous.

Our conclusion about the relevance of non-violence and non-violent resistance to totalitarian situations must be that while there is no open sesame and no one formula to which one can turn, non-violence explicitly embraced and informed

[6] One of the latest instruments of repression is a rule forbidding newspapers even to quote from speeches and writings of certain selected (and presumably dangerous) persons. Among those on the list is Albert Luthuli (see Reading 19).

[7] For a detailed report on the genesis and development of the Hungarian revolt, the reader should consult the United Nations Report published in 1957.

by knowledge can indeed play an important role in the prevention of tyranny. And while prevention is always better than cure, it would seem that non-violent resistance can also, under certain circumstances, help speed the internal disintegration to which all tyrannies are subject.

But we should also reiterate, as we have throughout this volume, that the effective use of non-violent resistance depends not only on adequate training and commitment, but also on the "objective" situation: external conditions must be ripe for effective campaigns, and if they are not, it is the part both of wisdom and of morality not to resort to non-violent resistance. Campaigns in the face of unsuitable objective conditions might actually set back the achievement of justice. Commitment to non-violence does not mean that we can dispense with political wisdom. Indeed, it accentuates the need for those practical insights which we associate with the office of politician at its best.

Non-violence, War, and Invasion. What light do the readings cast on the problem of war prevention and resistance of invasion? Actually, most of the observations made in connection with the rise of totalitarianism are applicable. In the end, as readings in Part I suggested, a nation is subdued by an external invader only with its own consent. If, through lack of proper organization beforehand, absence of training in non-violent disciplines, and a low-level will to resist, it succumbs, its loss of autonomy is in great degree self-inflicted. The arguments of Godwin, Gandhi, Gregg, and Case and the experiences of Norwegian, Hungarian, Indian, and certain general strike resistances are impressive on this point. The fact that no major nation has yet tried the way of non-violence means, of course, that we have no direct experience upon which we can rely. But if it were tried, within a context like that outlined in Reading 22, the indirect experience we have already had would seem to point to a success at least as great as that of military violence—and without the latter's enormous toll in physical, social, psychical, and moral damage.

At any rate, it is difficult to see how anyone with a concern for morality can possibly defend modern war and policies based on its threat. From the viewpoint of the morality of the means—and accepting the fact that there are important distinctions between their economic and political systems—there would seem to be little difference between Communism and Western Democracy in practice: both of them resort to threats of mass annihilation and both seem to be willing to shatter the whole structure of civilized society in the name of some abstraction which neither can define with precision. Each claims it is "defending" itself when it resorts to the most horrible preparations for mass slaughter. How any civilized human being can support either side, in view of these considerations, is difficult to understand. If the world does somehow survive, men in a future generation will look back to our time with both amazement and loathing: amazement that so many millions, East and West, tamely submitted themselves to be slaughtered and to slaughter; loathing at the rank hypocrisy involved in the whole process, with each side proclaiming its devotion to the highest civilized values. Just as we inquire today how millions of Germans could have submitted their fates to the commands of an immoral dictatorship, so will our descendants ask how millions of human beings professing "Christian" moral ideals could with scarcely a murmur build up stock piles of bacteria, H-bombs, and missiles to kill their fellow men and women.

A frequent answer is that while war would indeed be destructive, the possession of military might deters others from making war or invading "free" territory. This is doubtful, however; for despite existence of military alliances, Communist systems continue to expand, notably in Asia. But even if we grant that military power has provided a limited deterrence in the past, can we continue an arms race indefinitely without bringing world war measurably closer? Many students of the problem have persuasively maintained that the more the arms race (with its emotional context) is accelerated, the greater is the probability that "deterrence" of war will be utterly frustrated. Our descendants, if any, will ask how we could have been so completely foolish as well as immoral.

Descendants would quite legitimately put many queries of this kind. But the reply today is usually another question: What else can we do? It is at this point that the advocate of non-violent power has most to say. For he is asserting, essentially, that the development of an organized movement against both war and invasion, together with widespread commitment to completely unarmed defense, would be most likely to accomplish such widely proclaimed objectives as the frustration of invasion and defense of basic freedoms.

Before turning to the implications of non-violence for war and invasion, it might be well to point out that the fear of in-

vasion is in some measure a groundless one, particularly insofar as it refers to the possibility of the Soviet Union or China
occupying the United States or the United States invading the
Soviet Union or China. For the Soviet Union to "control" the
vast territory of the United States would be a very difficult
task, even without military or formally organized non-violent
resistance. The center of control would be remote from those
to be controlled. Even today the Soviet Union has difficulties
with its Eastern European satellites who are relatively close to
it and who, moreover, resemble it in many ways. Any attempted invasion of the United States with the purpose of
control would magnify these difficulties enormously. As Ambassador Kennan puts it, Americans seem not to recognize
how hard it is to operate "far-flung lines of power" or to see
that there are definite "limits to the effective radius of political
power from any center in the world."[8]

Despite this undoubted fact, however, the advocate of non-
violence must deal with the possibility of invasion, since it
conceivably could occur. He must, moreover, suggest what a
thoroughgoing policy of unilateral disarmament might imply
for domestic and international policy in general.

A turn toward non-violence by any major nation would, as
several of the readings and introductory notes stress, necessitate a fundamental change in outlook, not only with respect
to defense, but also in reference to the economic and international orders. Unilateral disarmament, to be effective in any
sense, would entail such measures as the deliberate construction of a system of non-violent resistance, with as much energy devoted to it as we devote today, for example, to space
exploration; a considerable measure of public economic planning to make far better use of human and material resources
than we do today; surrender of nationally administered international services (like the Panama Canal) to international administration; full acceptance of the rule of law in international
affairs, including jurisdiction and possible extension of jurisdiction of the International Court of Justice; and commitment of a very substantial proportion of the national income
(possibly 10 per cent or more—and in addition to sums now
utilized) for an indefinite period to the economic, social, and

[8] See George F. Kennan, *Russia and the West under Lenin and
Stalin* (Boston: Little, 1961). A similar thesis is suggested in his
earlier work, *Russia, the Atom, and the West* (New York: Harper,
1958).

educational development of the world, not excluding the United States. Within a context of this kind, we could far better defend the freedom of Americans than through the threat of military violence—no matter what the character of the "other side." We could revolutionize the whole pattern of international politics and help transform the power struggle into a non-violent one. This would happen because the "other side" would feel compelled to respond in kind—both because of internal pressures and because it would find that its own interests could best be preserved by such measures. Non-violent acts on a large scale could be expected to provoke "retaliation" of a non-violent character, just as violent measures call forth violent responses.

Nor is this expectation utopian. What does seem to be "utopian" (in the unfavorable sense of that term) is our present expectation that we can somehow get peace through arms build-ups; that wholesale preparations to kill will, as if by magic, be transmuted into world order; that indefinite reliance on military violence can be combined with preservation of "the American way of life"; and that we can expect to promote conciliation through such measures as threats to destroy enemy cities, refusal to recognize diplomatically the government of a fifth of mankind, and research into better and more efficient ways of killing. Expectations of this kind run counter both to common sense and to the insights of most ethical systems.

If we reject as immoral and impractical policies based on violent intimidation, what other alternative do we have save the doctrine and practice of non-violence? Between the gross immorality of threatening to incinerate millions of men, women, and children, on the one hand, and the injustice of tame acquiescence in possible tyranny, on the other, there is the way of non-violent resistance. Undeveloped as it is— whether in theory or in experience—it would seem to offer the only means for helping to redress wrong and to preserve the legitimate autonomy both of individuals and of groups (including national groups). Cognizant of the dilemmas of morality involved in such issues as resistance to invasion, it nevertheless accepts fully the inevitability of power and power relations. But it argues that, particularly under modern conditions, the most effective form of power is non-violent power.

Yet the full development of a doctrine and practice of non-violent power depends on the willingness of groups to experiment with it, even short of a fully worked-out set of principles. Herein lies one element of significance in such movements as the Sit-Ins and "Freedom Rides" and in forms of non-violent direct action like those exemplified in the Polaris protests (Reading 21). Whether successful or not, experiments of this kind can prove enormously valuable as we grope for the basis upon which to build non-violent resistance to invasion.

We should never forget, of course, that a policy of non-violent resistance to invasion would entail a price. Not only would there have to be rigorous training and discipline beforehand but there would and could be no guarantee of success or of immunity from suffering. At a minimum, the scheme would involve: a table of alternative leadership, so that leaders hanged or imprisoned would automatically be succeeded by their understudies; thousands of hard-core Satyagrahis who would be in the forefront of non-co-operation and civil disobedience campaigns; thorough preparation for psychological resistance, so that the general population would respect the persons of the invaders while refusing, in concert, to co-operate with their acts; and careful planning for food supplies. Unarmed resistance, as a matter of fact, requires at least as much planning as military defense.

Whatever the practical advantages of non-violent over violent opposition—and the readings, particularly in Part I, have suggested many—the moral superiority of non-violence consists in the fact that while under it we might have to suffer injustice (disruption of ordinary ways of life, physical injury, torture, or even death), we do not commit it (we do not deliberately kill, we confine coercion to that which does not seriously injure, and we constantly seek avenues for negotiation). And in the last analysis the advocate of non-violent resistance believes, with Socrates, that it is always better to suffer injustice than to commit it.

The critic may sometimes concede the practical and moral advantages of non-violent resistance to invasion but then assert that "Americans would never accept it." Apparently there is something about the American psychological and cultural make-up which insists on violence. Unlike such Indian groups as the Pathans, who though reared in a military tradition became some of Gandhi's most trustworthy Satyagrahis, Americans are seemingly wedded forever to violent methods of conflict. Or so this version of the American character would have us believe.

But there is reason to doubt this interpretation. To be sure, American history has been a violent one in many respects, with its Indian battles, its Civil War, and the covert and overt violence of its industrial life. Yet there is another side. Voluntary associations have played an enormous role in the American scene and they certainly exemplify non-violent conduct at its best. Americans share the religious tradition of the West which, whatever its practice, has within it a very strong ethic of non-violence. Moreover, studies of the American soldier in World War II reveal the startling fact that on two out of every three occasions when he should have pulled the trigger against the enemy, he was unable to do so. The explanation, according to General S. L. A. Marshall, a leading student of the problem, is that the soldier's home training against violence controlled his wartime actions—despite his army discipline. Medical Corps psychiatrists, moreover, found that fear of killing, rather than fear of being killed was the leading cause of battle failure.[9]

Utilization of non-violent resistance would eliminate this split in the American character and would enable Americans to oppose invaders without the subconscious doubts and anxieties that afflicted them in World War II. They would be integrated around the pole of non-violence. Like the Americans who engage in Sit-Ins and "Freedom Rides" for racial justice, they would find that non-violent resistance is not only more practical but that it also leads to a new sense of self-respect and self-confidence. If thousands of Americans can be attracted to non-violent direct action in the cause of race equality, what reason is there to suppose that they cannot become equally devoted to unarmed defense against invasion?

The Crisis in Civilization. It has often been asserted that there is a severe crisis in modern civilization. The nature of the crisis is variously described. Many profess to see it primarily in the struggle between East and West. Some talk as if it centered in the conflict between the imperatives of technology and the means of controlling it for desirable ends. Yet others speak of the spontaneous life of society and the natural

[9] For a general's discussion of combat soldiers' failure to shoot in World War II, see S. L. A. Marshall, *Men Against Fire* (New York: Morrow, 1947).

community as against the planned, bureaucratized, and rationalized political segment.

Without denying a certain validity in each of these diagnoses, it would seem appropriate here to suggest in conclusion that the major crisis may have to do with the question of whether civilization, which produced the ideals of non-violence, can in fact discard the means of violence before those means destroy it. Will the methods of large-scale violence, also the product of civilized ingenuity, tend so completely to dominate—indeed, fascinate—their creators that the ideals of non-violence, enshrined in both religious and secular thought, will be largely forgotten?

It is not certain that civilization will not use its violent instruments to destroy its non-violent achievements and frustrate its aspirations. In the name of protecting the values of non-violent ends, elaborate and sensitive social organization and technology may be employed to defeat those ends through the use of violence as means. If this is not to be the outcome of our contemporary madness, it will be because men discover in time that they can neither attain nor defend the ends of non-violence and democracy by the methods of violent power: any apparent success is more than counterbalanced by the evil ends set up by the means.

Once they make this discovery, human beings will turn to the doctrine of non-violence and to the discipline and practice of non-violent resistance. Without regarding non-violent resistance as the only key to an ideal society, they will see in it, nevertheless, a form of power somewhat compatible with the goals they profess.[10] Their means will have been brought measurably into harmony with their ends; and they will find that in repudiating the immorality of killing they will also have discovered a far more useful method than violence for the attainment of justice.

[10] The ramifications and implications of power, both violent and non-violent, are complex and far-reaching. See, for example, Bertrand Russell, *Power: A New Social Analysis* (New York: Norton, 1938), . . . and Bertrand de Jouvenel, *Power—The Natural History of Its Growth* (London: Hutchinson, 1948) and *Sovereignty; An Inquiry into the Political Good* (University of Chicago Press, 1957).

FOR FURTHER READING

Excluded are books and articles from which readings have been taken or to which reference is made in footnotes or elsewhere. The list is suggestive, not exhaustive.

PRINCIPLES

Allen, Devere (editor). *Pacifism in the Modern World.* New York: Harper, 1929.

———. *The Fight for Peace.* New York: Macmillan, 1930.

Andrews, C. F. *Mahatma Gandhi's Ideas.* New York: Macmillan, 1930.

Burns, C. Delisle. *The Principles of Revolution: A Study in Ideals.* Oxford University Press, 1920.

Diwakar, R. R. *Satyagraha: The Power of Truth.* Chicago: Regnery, 1948.

Frank, Jerome D. "Breaking the Thought Barrier: Psychological Challenges of the Nuclear Age," *Psychiatry,* Vol. 23, No. 3, August 1960.

Gandhi, Mohandas K. *Autobiography: The Story of My Experiments with Truth.* Washington: Public Affairs Press, 1948 and 1954.

Huxley, Aldous. *Ends and Means: An Inquiry into the Nature of Ideals and into the Methods Employed for their Realization.* New York: Harper, 1937.

Lanz, H. "The Doctrine of Nonresistance and Its Antithesis," *International Journal of Ethics,* Vol. 37, 1926, pp. 53–66.

Lewis, John. *The Case against Pacifism.* New York: Norton, 1941.

Muste, A. J. *Non-Violence in an Aggressive World.* New York: Harper, 1940.

Paullin, Theodore. *Introduction to Non-Violence.* Ithaca, New York: Pacifist Research Bureau, 1944.

Ramsey, Paul. *War and the Christian Conscience.* Duke University Press, 1961.

Sharp, Gene. "The Meanings of Non-Violence: A Typology," *Journal of Conflict Resolution,* Vol. III, March 1959.

Sibley, Mulford Q. *The Political Theories of Modern Pacifism.* Ithaca, New York: Pacifist Research Bureau, 1944.

Sorokin, Pitirim A. *The Ways and Power of Love.* Boston: Beacon Press, 1954.

Tolstoy, Leo. *The Law of Love and the Law of Violence,* tr. by Mary Tolstoy. New York: Rudolph Field, 1948.

POLICY, PRACTICE, CASES

American Friends Service Committee. *Speak Truth to Power.* Philadelphia: American Friends Service Committee, 1954.

Andrews, Charles F. (editor). *Mahatma Gandhi at Work.* New York: Macmillan, 1931.

Backlund, Sven. "The General Strike in Sweden in 1909," *Labour Magazine,* August 1926.

Brandt, Richard. *Hopi Ethics, A Theoretical Analysis.* University of Chicago Press, 1954.

Brant, Stefan. *The East German Rising, 17th June 1953,* tr. by Charles Wheeler. London: Thames & Hudson, 1955.

Byrd, Robert O. *Quaker Ways in Foreign Policy.* University of Toronto Press, 1960.

Cook, Fred J. *The Warfare State.* New York: Macmillan, 1962.

Destree, Jules. "La grève générale en Belgique," *Revue Socialiste,* June 1913.

Eliot, Thomas D. "A Criminological Approach to the Social Control of International Aggressions," *American Journal of Sociology,* Vol. LVIII, March 1953.

Fernsworth, Lawrence A. *Spain's Struggle for Freedom.* Boston: Beacon Press, 1957.

Freeman, Ruth. *Quakers and Peace.* Ithaca, New York: Pacifist Research Bureau, 1947.

Gibney, Frank. *The Frozen Revolution: Poland.* New York: Farrar, Straus, 1959.

Hiller, Ernest T. *The Strike: A Study in Collective Action.* University of Chicago Press, 1928.

Houser, George M. *Nonviolent Revolution in South Africa.* New York: Fellowship Publications, 1953.

King, Martin Luther. *Stride toward Freedom: The Montgomery Story.* New York: Harper, 1958.

Lapp, Ralph E. *Kill and Overkill: The Strategy of Annihilation.* New York: Basic Books, 1962.

Lewin, Jules. "The Rise of Congress in South Africa," *Political Quarterly,* July 1953.

Nott, Katherine. "Danili Dolci: Nonviolence in Italy," *Commentary,* February 1961.

Outze, Børge (editor). *Denmark during the German Occupation.* Copenhagen: Scandinavian Publishing Company, 1946.

Riesman, David. "Some Observations on the Limits of Totalitarian Power," *Individualism Reconsidered.* Chicago: Free Press, 1954.

Rothfels, Hans. *German Opposition to Hitler.* Chicago: Regnery, 1948.

Schwartz, Ernst. *Paths to Freedom Through Non-Violence.* Vienna: Sensen Verlag, 1959.

Solberg, Richard W. *God and Caesar in East Germany.* New York: Macmillan, 1961.

Tabata, I. B. *The Boycott as Weapon of Struggle.* Cape Town: All African Convention Committee, 1952.

Walker, Charles. *Organizing for Nonviolent Direct Action.* Cheyney, Pennsylvania: Charles Walker, 1962.

Willen, Paul. "Communist Hungary: The Locusts and the Briefcases," *The Reporter,* October 21, 1954.

Zahn, Gordon C. *German Catholics and Hitler's Wars.* New York: Sheed & Ward, 1962.

Zinn, Howard. "Finishing School for Pickets," *The Nation,* August 6, 1960.

INDEX

African National Congress, 260

Ager, Trygve M., cited, 156

Agrippa, at Rome, 114–15

Ahimsa, 89, 237

Allard, Paul, cited, 57

Allen, Devere, 379

All-India Non-violent Non-co-operation Movement, 239

All-India Trade Union Congress, 246

Alvarado, Pedro de, 232, 234–35

American Friends Service Committee, 380

American government, Thoreau's attitude to, 28–29

Amos, 11

Amritsar Massacre, 243, 341, 369

Anarchism, and non-violent resistance, 25

Anarchists, The, novel, 97

Andrews, C. F., 379, 380

Apartheid, 256, 277

Aristobulus, 113

Atlanta University, student protests, 292

Ausgleich, Austria-Hungary, 138

Austria-Hungary, costs of World War I, 318

Austro-Prussian War, 153–54

Backlund, Sven, 380

Baptists, non-violent power, 365

Barbastro, Luis de, 234

Barclay, Robert, 218

Belgian Federation of Labor, 126

Belgium, armed defense (World War II), 319; costs of World War I, 318; general strike (1913), 117, 118–25; strike against military service, 127–28

Bellegarrigue, Anselm, quoted, 96

Benares, non-violent resistance, 90

Benbow, William, and origins of general strike, 116

Bengal, non-violent resistance, 91

Bennette, Fred C., 296

Berk, Robert, 311

Berolzheimer, Fritz, cited, 68

Berth, Edouard, 106

Bettelheim, Bruno, cited, 367

Beust, Baron, 154

Bhagavad-Gita, 11

Bigelow, Albert, quoted, 306

"Black Act," South Africa, 30, 32–34

Bok, Curtis, cited, 73

Bombay, non-violent resistance, 93

Bondurant, Joan V., cited, 238

Bose, S. C., 341

Bourne, Randolph, cited, 69

Boycott, as weapon of struggle, 94

Brahmans, non-violent resistance against, 92–93

Brammer, Karl, cited, 129, 131

Brandt, Richard, 380

Brant, Stefan, 380

Brockway, Fenner, 103

Burgess, E. W., cited, 57

Burns, C. Delisle, 379

United States (*cont'd*)
289, 290; sit-ins, 289, 290, 291–99; unarmed defense, 2, 316–56

Universal military service, general strike, Belgium, 127–28

Upanishads, 11

Valerius, Manius, dictator, 110

Vandervelde, Emile, 119, 121–22

Van Overbergh, Cyrille, cited, 120, 121, 122

Violence, and coercion, 46, 47–51, 52–54; and general strike, 116–17; and military defense, 1; and physical force, 7–8, 46; conflict between ideals and practice, 1, 2; limitations of, in treating crime, 73–76; problem of definition, 8

Vitellius, president of Syria, 112

Vorkuta, and non-violent resistance, 86, 187–204

Walker, Charles, 381

Walker, Roy, cited, 156

"Walking Purchase," 216–17

Walser, A. A., cited, 78

War, analogies with non-violent resistance, 77–81; and non-violent resistance, 371–76; appeals of, 76–77; as an institution, 70–71; defensive and aggressive, 2; irony of, 332–33; moral equivalent of, 342–43; more costly than non-violent resistance, 81–82

War Resisters League, 305

Ward, Barbara, cited, 136

Western culture, and non-violent resistance, 80–81

Whiston, William, 111

Willen, Paul, 381

Willmer, Harry A., cited, 68

Windus, Margaret, Polaris Action, 311

World community, and non-violent resistance, 72

Wright, Richard, cited, 136

Xuma, A. B., African National Congress, 268

Yahweh, 11

Yengwa, M. B. Natal, 263

Zahn, Gordon, 381

Zechariah, 11, 12, 14

Zerubbabel, 14

Zimmerwald movement, and Henrietta Holst, 104

Zinn, Howard, 381

Zulu war, 32

DATE DUE